NAPOLEON

NAPOLEON

THE END OF GLORY

MUNRO PRICE

OXFORD
UNIVERSITY PRESS

OXFORD
UNIVERSITY PRESS

Oxford University Press is a department of the
University of Oxford. It furthers the University's objective
of excellence in research, scholarship, and education
by publishing worldwide.

Oxford   New York
Auckland   Cape Town   Dar es Salaam   Hong Kong   Karachi
Kuala Lumpur   Madrid   Melbourne   Mexico City   Nairobi
New Delhi   Shanghai   Taipei   Toronto

With offices in
Argentina   Austria   Brazil   Chile   Czech Republic   France   Greece
Guatemala   Hungary   Italy   Japan   Poland   Portugal   Singapore
South Korea   Switzerland   Thailand   Turkey   Ukraine   Vietnam

Oxford is a registered trade mark of Oxford University Press
in the UK and certain other countries.

Published in the United States of America by
Oxford University Press
198 Madison Avenue, New York, NY 10016

Library of Congress Cataloging-in-Publication Data
Price, Munro.
Napoleon : the end of glory / Munro Price.
pages   cm
Includes bibliographical references and index.
ISBN 978-0-19-993467-6
1. Napoleon I, Emperor of the French, 1769–1821.   2. France—History—1789–1815.
3. France—Politics and government—1789–1815.   I. Title.
DC203.P755   2014
940.2'7–dc23   2014001693

9 8 7 6 5 4 3 2 1
Printed in the United States of America
on acid-free paper

For Terry and Martine Morris

Acknowledgements

Researching and writing this book would have been impossible without a Leverhulme Research Fellowship for 2011–12, and I am very grateful to the Leverhulme Trust for this. Research in Paris was greatly helped by the kindness of my old history master Terry Morris and his wife Martine, a French historian, who lent me their flat there for several months that year. I am also grateful to them for over thirty years of friendship.

In Austria, Carl Philip Clam-Martinic generously allowed me to consult the remarkable papers of Carl Clam-Martinic, who played a significant role in the events of 1813 and 1814. He also kindly permitted me to use pictures of family artefacts connected with his ancestor in the book. Simon Cox, aided by the wonders of a digital camera, was a great help in photographing the papers. In Vienna, Bill Godsey and Christopher Wentworth-Stanley gave valuable archival advice.

In the Czech Republic, Magister Jan Kahuda of the National Archives in Prague showed kindness and efficiency in enabling me to consult Metternich's papers there, the Acta Clementina. Magister Jakub Kaisersat and Magister Veronika Svehlova, of the State Regional Archives at Trebon, were very friendly and helpful through my time working there on the Schwarzenberg family papers.

In France, I am grateful to the descendants of Armand de Caulaincourt, duke of Vicenza, for permission to consult his microfilmed papers held at the Archives Nationales in Paris, and to Prince Jérôme Murat for helpful insights into the actions of his ancestor Joachim Murat, King of Naples, in 1813. I am also grateful to Steven Clay for his advice on the fascinating holdings of the Archives Nationales concerning Napoleonic public opinion. M Frédéric Fourgeaud, of the Bibliothèque Municipale de Bordeaux, kindly helped me to track down and consult the Lainé papers deposited there.

In England, the staff of the British Library, and especially the London Library, were unfailingly pleasant and efficient.

Among historians I am indebted for help and advice to Tim Blanning, William Doyle, Michael Broers, Antonia Fraser, Philip Mansel, Adam Zamoyski, Rafe Blaufarb, Tom Munch-Petersen, and Ambrogio Caiani.

At Bradford, my colleagues Gabor Batonyi and Christopher Guyver were a source of ideas and encouragement, and very decently shouldered the extra work inevitable in a small group when one member is on leave.

At OUP, my editor Luciana O'Flaherty and the assistant editor, Matthew Cotton, have given much encouragement and good advice throughout the publishing process, and the copyediting and production team of Tom Chandler, Emma Slaughter, and Deborah Protheroe have combined friend-liness with great efficiency.

I am also grateful to my agent, Georgina Capel, for all her help and enthusiasm. Judy and Stanley Price made helpful suggestions, and Clive Blackwood and Dan Paterson lent useful comments and some important books.

Contents

List of Illustrations

List of Plates

List of Maps

Dramatis Personae

*George Gordon, earl of **Aberdeen*** (1784–1860). British diplomat and statesman. Ambassador to Vienna in 1813; later prime minister from 1852 to 1855.

*Amable-Guillaume-Prosper Bruguière, baron de **Barante*** (1782–1866). French historian, writer and politician; prefect of the Loire-Inférieure between 1813 and 1815.

*Michael Andreas **Barclay de Tolly*** (1761–1818). Field-marshal, one of the architects of Napoleon's defeat in 1812, and commander of the Russian army from the summer of 1813 to 1815.

*Paul **Barras*** (1755–1829). The leading member of France's governing Directory from 1795 to 1799. Displaced by Napoleon, and henceforth one of his bitterest enemies.

*Eugène de **Beauharnais**, viceroy of Italy* (1781–1824). Napoleon's stepson, the son of his first wife Joséphine.

*Jean-Baptiste **Bernadotte**, marshal of France, from 1818 king Charles XIV John of Sweden* (1763–1844). A mediocre general but a very able politician, elected crown prince of Sweden in 1810.

*Louis-Alexandre **Berthier**, marshal of France, prince of Neuchâtel, prince of Wagram* (1753–1815). Napoleon's chief of staff, and his closest military collaborator.

*Jérôme **Bonaparte**, king of Westphalia* (1784–1860). Napoleon's youngest brother.

*Joseph **Bonaparte**, king of Naples from 1806 to 1808, then of Spain from 1808 to 1813* (1768–1844). Napoleon's older brother; commanded the defence of Paris in 1814.

*Pauline **Bonaparte**, princess Borghese* (1780–1825). Napoleon's beautiful and dissolute youngest sister, and the most loyal of his siblings.

*Ferdinand, count **Bubna** von Littitz* (1768–1825). Austrian soldier and diplomat.

*Friedrich Wilhelm, count **Bülow** von Dennewitz* (1755–1816). Distinguished Prussian general, who played a leading role in the struggle against France between 1813 and 1815.

*Jean-Jacques Régis de **Cambacérès**, duke of Parma* (1753–1824). Arch-chancellor of the empire, in effect Napoleon's prime minister.

*Lazare **Carnot*** (1753–1823). The greatest military organizer of the French Revolution; a republican opponent of Napoleon, but rallied to him on the allied invasion of France in 1814.

*Pierre-Joseph **Cambon*** (1754–1820). Important revolutionary politician, specializing in finance, and afterwards a republican opponent of Napoleon.

*William, earl **Cathcart*** (1755–1843). British soldier and diplomat. Ambassador to Russia from 1812 to 1820.

*Armand de **Caulaincourt**, duke of Vicenza* (1773–1827). Napoleon's grand equerry, and from November 1813 his foreign minister.

*Count Carl **Clam-Martinic*** (1792–1840). Austrian soldier and statesman; Schwarzenberg's aide-de-camp between 1812 and 1815.

*Emmerich Joseph, duke of **Dalberg*** (1773–1833). Franco-German diplomat and statesman, and a confidant of Talleyrand.

*Géraud **Duroc**, duke of Friuli* (1772–1813). Grand marshal of the palace to Napoleon, and his closest friend.

*Agathon Jean François, baron **Fain*** (1778–1837). Napoleon's secretary.

*Joseph **Fouché**, duke of Otranto* (1759–1820). Leading revolutionary politician, later Napoleon's minister of police from 1804 to 1810, and again in 1815.

*Dominique-Joseph **Garat*** (1749–1833). Leading revolutionary politician, later a republican opponent of Napoleon.

*Friedrich **Gentz*** (1764–1832). Writer and publicist, and Metternich's closest adviser between 1812 and 1815.

*Laurent, comte Gouvion **Saint-Cyr**, marshal of France* (1764–1830). An able soldier, later a reforming minister of war under the restored Bourbons.

*Henri **Grégoire*** (1750–1831). Prominent revolutionary politician, champion of black and Jewish emancipation, later a republican opponent of Napoleon.

*Karl August, prince von **Hardenberg*** (1750–1822). Reforming Prussian statesman; chancellor from 1810.

*Wilhelm von **Humboldt*** (1767–1835). Prussian philosopher, linguist and statesman. Minister of education, 1809–10, then ambassador to Vienna, and Prussian representative at the Congress of Châtillon.

Jacques-Etienne **Macdonald**, *marshal of France, duke of Tarentum* (1765–1840). Of Scots Jacobite extraction; a mediocre commander, but widely respected for his honesty and outspokenness.

Auguste-Frédéric Viesse de **Marmont**, *marshal of France, duke of Ragusa* (1774–1852). The youngest of Napoleon's marshals, and particularly trusted by him.

Jean-Pierre Bachasson, comte de **Montalivet** (1766–1823). Napoleon's interior minister from 1809 to 1814.

Jean-Victor **Moreau** (1763–1813). Successful French revolutionary general. Exiled to the United States in 1804 for conspiring against Napoleon; returned to Europe in July 1813.

Joachim **Murat**, *marshal of France, king of Naples* (1767–1815). Napoleon's best cavalry commander, and his brother-in-law.

Louis, comte de **Narbonne-Lara** (1755–1813). French soldier and diplomat; made ambassador to Vienna in March 1813.

Count Karl von **Nesselrode** (1780–1862). Russian diplomat, and Czar Alexander I's chief foreign policy adviser between 1813 and 1815.

Michel **Ney**, *marshal of France, duke of Elchingen, prince of the Moskowa* (1769–1815). Famous for his courage, but an erratic commander.

Nicolas-Charles **Oudinot**, *marshal of France, duke of Reggio* (1767–1847). An extremely brave soldier, but of limited ability as a commander.

Etienne-Denis, baron **Pasquier** (1767–1862). French statesman; prefect of police of Paris from 1810 to 1814. Later made a duke, and the last chancellor of France.

Joseph, count **Radetzky** *von Radetz* (1766–1858). Chief of staff of the allied armies in 1813–14; later a field-marshal and the most successful Austrian commander of the nineteenth century.

Prince Andrei **Razumovsky** (1752–1836). Russian diplomat, ambassador to Vienna from 1792, and patron of Beethoven. Russian representative at the Congress of Châtillon.

Wilhelmina, duchess of **Sagan** (1781–1839). A wealthy and beautiful eastern European noblewoman, fascinated by politics, and Metternich's mistress between 1813 and 1815.

Auguste, baron de **Saint-Aignan** (1770–1858). French soldier and diplomat; captured by Cossacks at Weimar in October 1813.

Anne René **Savary**, *duke of Rovigo* (1774–1833). Napoleon's minister of police from 1810 to 1814.

Emmanuel-Joseph **Sieyès** (1748–1836). Prominent revolutionary politician, later a republican opponent of Napoleon.

Johann Philipp, count von **Stadion** (1763–1824). Austrian diplomat, Metternich's predecessor as foreign minister, and Austrian representative at the Congress of Châtillon.

Sir Charles **Stewart**, *later marquess of Londonderry* (1778–1854). British soldier and diplomat, suicidally brave and highly eccentric. Castlereagh's half-brother, in April 1813 appointed British minister to Berlin.

Karl Wilhelm von **Toll** (1777–1842). Quartermaster-general of the Russian army, and a close military adviser to Czar Alexander I.

Sir Robert **Wilson** (1777–1849). British general and later Radical politician; British liaison officer with the Russian and then the Austrian army between 1812 and 1814.

Ludwig Peter, prince **Wittgenstein** (1769–1843). Field-marshal, commander of the Russian army in the spring of 1813.

Johann David, count **Yorck** *von Wartenburg* (1759–1830). Veteran Prussian general who in 1812 played a decisive role in his country's move from alliance to war with Napoleon.

Introduction

Do not lament my fate; if I have decided to go on living, it is to serve your glory. I wish to write the history of the great things we have done together![1]

With these emotional words, Napoleon said farewell to the veterans of his Imperial Guard at Fontainebleau on 20 April 1814, and took the road into exile on Elba. He kept the promise he made that day. He devoted the last five years of his life to composing his memoirs, and laying the foundations of the Napoleonic legend. Where Napoleon led, innumerable writers and historians have followed. Not all of them have 'served his glory'; many have criticized him fiercely. Yet he remains today one of the most intensely studied figures in world history. Well over 200,000 books have been written about him since his death.[2]

The emphasis in these works has changed with the passage of time. Initially, it was Napoleon's extraordinary personality and career that fascinated historians. There have been great biographies of him, such as those of Lefebvre, Tulard, Holland Rose, and Fournier, and many more no doubt will be written.[3] His military exploits, such a central part of his legend, have always generated an industry of their own. Yet increasingly the focus of research has widened to include the major changes his rule brought both to France and to his empire beyond her borders. In 1982, Jean Tulard published a pioneering study of Napoleon's empire, and this has been followed within the last decade by Thierry Lentz's four-volume *Nouvelle histoire du premier empire*. Jacques-Olivier Boudon has assessed the impact of Napoleonic religious policy across Europe and Alan Forrest the burden of conscription, while Michael Broers has analysed Napoleon's cultural imperialism and Charles Esdaile has placed his wars in an exceptionally broad international perspective.[4]

Yet despite all that has been written, certain crucial aspects of Napoleon's story are still neglected—especially his fall. Much of this is a question of perspective. Napoleon's final defeat in 1815 at Waterloo was so dramatic that to the public it has become the crucial moment of his destruction. In Britain, the fact that he was beaten by a British general, Wellington, has given it a special importance. Victory over Napoleon has become a staple of patriotic history and an important element of national pride.

In fact, this perspective is false. Napoleon at Waterloo was not a recognized head of state, but an adventurer condemned as an outlaw by the other European powers. He had already been forced to abdicate once. It was this first overthrow, the previous year, that was decisive, and deprived him both of his throne and his legitimacy. His return to France in 1815 was a last desperate attempt to reverse this verdict, and its failure was inevitable.

The events that led to Napoleon's first abdication remain far less familiar to British readers than Waterloo, no doubt because Wellington and his army played only a secondary role. In the great battles of 1813 and 1814— Bautzen, Dresden, Leipzig, Laon, and the capture of Paris, Napoleon was opposed instead by Russians, Austrians, and Prussians. Although British subsidies were essential to her continental allies, no British troops fought in these battles, except for one rocket battery at Leipzig. It was here that Napoleon's fate was decided, but with the exception of Dominic Lieven's excellent book on the Russian war effort, there are few significant works in English on the subject.[5]

As well as offering an unfamiliar story, the conflict of 1813–14 also raises a central question. At several moments during these years, Napoleon's opponents offered him compromise peace terms, yet he consistently failed to explore them. Was this because they were patently insincere, and not worth pursuing? Or were they in fact genuine, and Napoleon's rejection of them merely arrogance and obstinacy? Whatever answer is given has major implications for one's view of the Napoleonic wars. If Napoleon's enemies had no intention of making peace with him, then the conflict was an irreconcilable clash, which could end only with complete victory for one side and utter defeat for the other. If, however, the offers were honestly meant, then a settlement between France and her adversaries was possible, and the ultimate responsibility for their failure rests on a single man.

This book seeks to resolve this question. It does so with the help of important new archival sources. Ironically, several of these remain untapped precisely because so much has been published about Napoleon. In the century after his death, the memoirs and many other papers of those who had known him appeared in print, leading to the assumption that the archives they were taken from contained nothing more of interest. This is emphatically not the case. The two best examples here are the papers of Caulaincourt, Napoleon's foreign minister in 1813–14, and Metternich, his Austrian counterpart and the leading diplomat of the coalition formed against France. Caulaincourt's memoirs were published in 1933, but these did not include a mass of autobiographical notes, including an entire section of several hundred pages on the 1813 campaign, and some important correspondence, now in the Archives Nationales in Paris. Eight volumes of Metternich's papers appeared in the 1880s, but this was only a small selection from his vast archive now in the Czech National Archives in Prague, the Acta Clementina, which has only recently been properly catalogued. Some of the most significant new material in this book comes from these two sources.

The Caulaincourt and Metternich papers are both in public archives. Some sources—it is impossible to estimate how many—remain in private hands. I have been fortunate enough to gain access to one of these, the papers of Count Carl Clam-Martinic, aide-de-camp of Field-Marshal Schwarzenberg, allied commander-in-chief in 1813 and 1814, and later Austrian war minister. These contain important, and controversial, observations about the 1813 campaign, and a remarkable description of Napoleon himself, whom Clam accompanied on his journey to Elba.

Military and diplomatic events played the key role in Napoleon's fall, but I have also tried to reflect the hopes and fears of the ordinary people he ruled. Like many other highly authoritarian leaders, Napoleon was obsessed by public opinion. 'Nothing could be more changeable', he once remarked of it, 'but it never lies.'[6] Testimony to this conviction is the remarkable series of monthly reports on 'public morale' he ordered from the prefects of every French department from October 1812. These are also now in the Archives Nationales, and have not yet been systematically studied. Even allowing for self-censorship and the desire to please the Emperor, they paint an extremely revealing picture of what French people at the grass roots thought about the war whose burden they bore. They also shed light on an important political and psychological question. Napoleon always claimed that the French would overthrow him themselves if he concluded a less than glorious peace, and consistently used this argument to refuse a compromise settlement. Through these monthly reports, I have tried to establish whether Napoleon's perception was based on reality, or was instead the product of delusion.

Attempting to understand a personality as complex and brilliant as Napoleon's has occupied many historians throughout their working lives. Often they have done so through biography, whereas this book covers only a short period of Napoleon's life. Yet the moment of a great man's fall offers a special insight into his character, his motives, and the reasons for his failure. That is what drew me to these three years.

I

Napoleon and his Empire, December 1812

At 2 p.m. on Saturday 5 December 1812, Napoleon's carriage entered the small town of Smorgoni, on the border of Lithuania and White Russia. For miles behind it stretched the debris of the greatest army he had ever assembled: 450,000 French and allied troops had invaded Russia the previous June. Of the 100,000 who had reached Moscow, only 10,000 fighting soldiers now remained after six weeks of retreating the way they had come, beset by freezing temperatures and bands of marauding Cossacks. Though the world did not yet know the extent of the disaster, it was clear that a major blow had been struck at Napoleon's domination of Europe.[1]

Smorgoni was little more than a village, built mostly of wood, and with just a few thousand inhabitants, the vast majority Jewish, as was the case with most of the urban centres in the region.[2] This remote settlement, however, did have one peculiar claim to fame. In the seventeenth century the local landowners, the powerful Radziwill family, had established there a training academy for dancing bears which had acquired a European reputation. This fact was known to Napoleon's soldiers, and momentarily distracted them from their miseries as they approached the town. In the words of Baron Lejeune, the general and painter of battle scenes, in his memoirs:

> Smorgoni, the name piqued our curiosity. We knew that the inhabitants of this village, situated in the middle of an immense region of forests, made their living from hunting bears and selling their fur, and from the gymnastic education of the young bears, whom they would take performing throughout Europe. Everybody had fled before us; they had taken to their heels with their merchandise and their pupils.[3]

Figure 1. Freezing French soldiers near Smorgoni, 3 December 1812. An eyewitness sketch by Major Faber du Faur.

In this incongruous setting, Napoleon reached a momentous decision. Setting up his headquarters in a manor house in the village, he summoned his senior officers, and told them that the time had come for him to leave the army and return to France. If the Russian advance were to be stemmed, a new army would have to be raised, and this could only be done from Paris. 'I am leaving you', he declaimed, 'but it is to go and raise 300,000 more soldiers.' Napoleon barely acknowledged the disaster that had befallen his existing army, still less his own responsibility for it. Instead, he presented to his marshals and generals a picture of a brilliantly organized campaign frustrated by unforeseeable accidents of fate, above all the burning of Moscow and the freakishly early drop in temperature:

> The unheard-of audacity of arsonists, an exceptionally extreme winter, cowardly intrigues, foolish ambitions, some errors, perhaps even treason, and shameful mysteries that will no doubt one day be uncovered, all this has brought us back to where we started! Were ever such favourable prospects ruined by such unpredictable vexations![4]

The Emperor then announced who would accompany him to Paris and who would remain with the army. Caulaincourt, his Grand Equerry, would travel with him in his carriage and organize the relays of horses needed at each stage of the journey. His secretary, Baron Fain, his valet Constant, Duroc, the Grand Marshal of the Palace and General Mouton would follow in two other carriages. Napoleon's brother-in-law Joachim Murat, the king of Naples, was given command of the army, with orders to concentrate what was left of it at Vilna—which, as it turned out, he signally failed to do. Marshal Berthier, the veteran Chief of Staff, who was completely exhausted by the privations of the retreat, burst into tears at being left behind and received a blast of Napoleon's famously foul temper: 'You can't come too; you have to stay with the King of Naples. I know you're useless, but nobody else does, and your name will have some effect on the army.'[5]

With these arrangements made, there was no longer any reason for delay. At 10 p.m. Napoleon took his leave of Murat and the marshals, climbed into his carriage, and rolled off into the night.

Figure 2. Napoleon leaving the Grand Army at Smorgoni, 5 December 1812. European school, nineteenth century.

The portly, balding 43-year-old who spent the journey back to Paris alternately sleeping and delivering long monologues about war, politics, and his own life story to his companion Caulaincourt (who dutifully noted them each day and later published them in his memoirs)[6] was already regarded as one of the great men of history. First and foremost, he was a military genius, though his real talent lay in the application of new strategy and tactics rather than their creation. Just as remarkable were his administrative gifts, which had steered France away from post-revolutionary chaos and imposed a structure of government, much of which remains in place today.[7]

In contrast to his extraordinary mental powers, Napoleon's physical appearance was unremarkable. Contrary to myth, he was not especially short; he was probably 5 foot 6 inches, which was slightly taller than average for his time. He had good features—a wide forehead, aquiline nose and piercing grey eyes—but these were offset by his pallor, and in his youth at least, by his general untidiness. Until he reached his 30s he wore his hair long, hanging down each side of his face, as one contemporary put it, 'like a spaniel's ears'.[8] Thereafter it began to thin, and he wore it short and brushed forward in the Roman style.

Napoleon's intellectual brilliance was combined with a mesmerizing personality. He had remarkable charisma and willpower, and throughout his life remained undaunted by obstacles others would have regarded as insuperable. Allied to this was a furious temper, generally displayed when he was thwarted, which made even his toughest subordinates quail. These qualities made him a natural leader of men and ensured that his marshals and generals, whose courage and ferocity had become famous throughout Europe, regarded him with awe not unmixed with fear. As the notably hard-bitten Marshal Augereau put it after meeting Napoleon for the first time: 'That little bugger scares me.'[9]

The core of Napoleon's personality was a driving need for domination. This was essential to his rise as a brilliant young general applying the new style of mobile offensive warfare pioneered by the French Revolution. Yet it did not adapt so well to the civilian functions he assumed when he became head of state. In particular, it stored up problems for his diplomacy. It was perfectly well suited to dictating peace terms to a defeated enemy after a crushing military victory, as with Austria in 1805 and Prussia in 1807. But it had no place in negotiations between equal partners seeking peace through rational compromise.[10] As Napoleon's supremacy waned after 1812, this was the only path open if he wished to save his empire by more than military means, and here his imperious, authoritarian style placed him at a significant disadvantage.

Moreover, by 1812 Napoleon was beginning to show signs of both physical and mental deterioration. In his youth he had been painfully thin, but from 1805 he gained weight dramatically, becoming increasingly obese. The familiar image of Napoleon, with his full face, short, thinning hair, and plump body, only dates from the last fifteen years of his life. He also became prone to painful complaints. The principal ones were dysuria, in which urination becomes difficult, haemorrhoids, and unexplained stomach cramps. Strikingly, Napoleon was partly incapacitated during each one of his last three major battles: by dysuria at Borodino, anxiety-induced stomach pain at Leipzig, and, most famously, haemorrhoids at Waterloo. A sense emerges that by this time even his tough constitution was beginning to buckle under the strain of twenty years' campaigning and battles on a greater scale than any he had fought before. As he himself muttered at Leipzig: 'My mind resists, but my body gives in.'[11]

Behind these temporary ailments may have been a more serious condition. The changes in Napoleon's physical shape by 1810 were accompanied by changes in his character, which many contemporaries noticed. His powers of concentration and decision were no longer what they had been, his extraordinary energy was no longer constant but came in fits and starts, and it alternated with periods of sluggishness and somnolence. At least some of Napoleon's mistakes during his later campaigns can be ascribed to these factors. In 1913, they led the British physician Leonard Guthrie to launch the theory that around the age of 40 his pituitary gland, which controls the hormones in the body, began to fail.[12] In 1959, the surgeon James Kemble took this argument to a wider public with his book *Napoleon Immortal*. Eleven years later, a variation on this theme was suggested by the French doctor Pierre Hillemand, who argued that Napoleon was suffering from a tumour in the pituitary region.[13]

Pituitary dysfunction certainly fits many of the symptoms Napoleon began to display from around the age of 40. Physically, it would account for the obesity, particularly round the hips, and the genital shrinkage noticed at his autopsy on St Helena.[14] Mentally, it could also have caused the increasing sluggishness and indecision that so disconcerted his subordinates. Two pieces of evidence in particular point to this conclusion. Napoleon generally ate quickly and in moderation, and took regular exercise, normally through riding. These habits did not change significantly after he reached 40, implying that his weight gain in particular must have had an endogenous cause. It is also quite common for sufferers from pituitary deficiency to enjoy enhanced mental abilities and energy in youth before decline later sets in, which exactly fits Napoleon's case.[15] It is notoriously difficult to make retrospective diagnoses of the health of historical figures, given the enormous discrepancy between the medical knowledge of their time and that of today, and the consequent difficulty of interpreting the available evidence. Nonetheless, it does seem that as he entered middle age something more was at work in Napoleon than the natural process of ageing, and in the absence of any more convincing hypothesis a pituitary condition seems plausible.

Yet even a Napoleon in decline was a formidable adversary, and his enemies were well aware of the fact. He remained the greatest—and most feared—military commander of the age; as the Duke of Wellington put it: 'His hat on the battlefield is worth 40,000 men.'[16] The Russian catastrophe had badly dented, but by no means destroyed, the spell cast by his previous victories, and it is noticeable that few of the commanders who fought the French after 1812 cared to face him in person. Yet if defeating Napoleon by force of arms looked an uncertain prospect, the only alternative was to come to terms with him. In this case, all parties would be entering uncharted waters. At no previous point in his career had Napoleon ever negotiated from a position of weakness, or even of equality; since 1797 he had been accustomed to setting his own terms at the conclusion of a victorious war, often in his defeated opponent's capital. It was very unclear whether he would willing, or able, to make peace any other way.

From Smorgoni Napoleon headed west to Vilna and Kovno. Shortly after-wards, at the relay-station of Gragow, he switched from his carriage to a sledge for easier travel over the snow and ice. After crossing the Russian border he entered the Duchy of Warsaw, a satellite state he had set up as part of the Treaty of Tilsit in 1807. This was loyal territory. The Poles had seen the duchy as a first step towards the restoration of an independent Poland and had proved themselves staunch allies; many had enlisted in the French armies.[17]

Further west, between Posen and Glogau, Napoleon had to cross briefly into Prussia. He was reluctant to do this, but it was unavoidable. Prussia was nominally his ally, and had even contributed 20,000 troops to the Russian campaign who were currently besieging Riga. It had only done so through sheer necessity, to save itself from being wiped off the map after he had comprehensively crushed Prussia's armies in 1806.[18] Napoleon feared that if the Prussians learned he was travelling with virtually no escort across their territory, they might decide to take revenge on him, and speculated half-jokingly what form this might take. It was possible, he thought, that they could capture him and his party and hand them over to the English. 'How do you think you'd look in a iron cage in London?' he asked Caulaincourt, and then burst out laughing. More seriously, he commented that a highway murder or ambush would be easy to arrange, and carefully checked that the pistols he was carrying were primed.[19]

With some relief, the travellers crossed into Saxony in the afternoon of 13 December. Saxony was a client state of Napoleon's, and a leading member of the Confederation of the Rhine, an association of thirty-five kingdoms and principalities he had created in 1806 to keep western and central Germany under French control. The king of Saxony, Frederick Augustus I, a cautious, honourable 62-year old, was one of the few fellow-monarchs Napoleon regarded as a personal friend. As a result, he had been made ruler of the Duchy of Warsaw on its creation. Woken in his palace at Dresden in the small hours of the 14 December by the news of the Emperor's arrival, he lost no time in demonstrating his loyalty. He immediately got up, found a sedan chair for hire outside the palace, and had himself carried at 3 a.m. to the French ambassador's house, where Napoleon was staying. There, he had a long interview with him, and made all the necessary arrangements for his onward journey.[20]

It remained to be seen whether the other German states would prove so faithful in adversity. Apart from Saxony, the most powerful of these were Bavaria, Baden, and Württemberg. These states had followed a pro-French path for over a decade. They had done so essentially through fear of French military power, and it was unclear if they would stick to it once the disaster in Russia became known. Westphalia, a substantial new state formed in 1808 in northern and central Germany and given by Napoleon to his youngest brother Jérôme as its king, still needed time to establish itself. The other members of the Confederation of the Rhine ranged from medium-sized territories like the Duchy of Nassau, to tiny principalities like Schwarzburg-Rudolstadt, which covered only a few hundred square miles. Their loyalty would depend on that of the larger states.[21]

Whether ruled by their native dynasties or by Bonaparte parvenus, the states of the Confederation formed a central part, but only a part, of

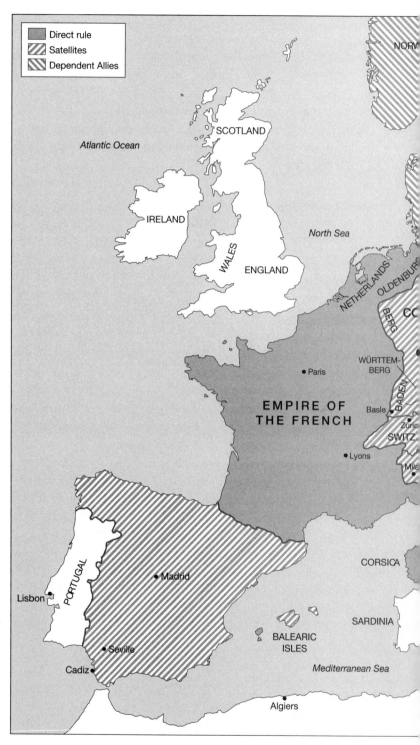

Map 1. Napoleon's empire in 1812.

Napoleon's dominions. To the south lay Italy, which was almost entirely under French control. Its traditional rulers, expelled from the mainland, clung on in Sardinia and Sicily only thanks to the protection of the Royal Navy. The peninsula itself had been carved up into three parts: the north-west directly annexed to France, the north-east and centre formed into a satellite kingdom of Italy ruled by Napoleon's stepson Eugène de Beauharnais as his viceroy, and in the south the kingdom of Naples, with Napoleon's brother-in-law, the flamboyant Marshal Joachim Murat, as its king.[22]

Northern Italy and the Confederation of the Rhine formed the inner core of Napoleon's empire outside France, which had up until now been quiescent under his rule. Beyond this was an outer empire, made up of territories more recently brought under French hegemony, and significantly more resistant to the invader. The driving force here had been Napoleon's determination after 1806 to enforce the continental blockade, his trade embargo with Britain designed to force her to peace by destroying her economy. This required control of the continental coastline to prevent smuggling and ensure obedience to Paris. As a result, Spain had been invaded in 1808 and Napoleon's elder brother Joseph installed as its king, but the new order had struggled from the start against a popular uprising aided by a British expeditionary force led by Lord Wellington. Two years later, the north German coast around Hamburg and Lübeck had been directly annexed to France. Although there was no open revolt as in Spain, the destruction of trade through enforcement of the blockade created widespread hostility to French rule. The only part of this outer empire where the new arrangements were popular was the Duchy of Warsaw, since the Poles saw Napoleon as an ally against their traditional enemy, Russia.[23]

Spurred on by their new masters, all the territories of the empire had to a greater or lesser extent adopted the reforms pioneered in France by the Revolution and consolidated by Napoleon. The basic inspiration was the Civil Code, the *Code Napoléon*. This was the codification of French law published by Napoleon in 1804, proclaiming the principles of equality before the law, the freedom of labour, religious toleration, and the career open to talents. Almost as influential was the Concordat, the agreement Napoleon had signed in 1801 with the Pope that confirmed much of the ecclesiastical policy of the Revolution and subordinated the Catholic church to the state. The result had been a wave of dramatic social change across Europe, particularly the dissolution of monasteries and the abolition of feudal privilege. This was far more effective, however, in the inner than the outer empire: in Spain there was furious popular opposition to religious reform, while in the Grand Duchy of Warsaw the abolition of serfdom, though promulgated on paper, remained a dead letter in practice.[24]

Napoleon's civil and religious legislation was to have a profound and durable effect on Europe. Yet it had other motives, at once more immediate and more cynical. A rationalized and streamlined administration in the empire was essential to providing the two commodities the Emperor needed most—money and manpower. To a remarkable degree, this was achieved. The exploitation of the empire ensured that, until the last stages of the Napoleonic wars, France was spared much of this burden. In the decade after 1804, fully half of their cost was met from the territories beyond France, and in France itself there were no increases either in taxation or public loans until 1809.[25] The conquered lands also provided fiefs and pensions distributed to Napoleon's senior officers to reward military success—and to ensure their continuing loyalty. In 1807 alone, twenty-seven marshals and generals between them received 20 million francs' worth of revenue from Poland.[26] As to manpower, Napoleon's ruthless demands on the non-French parts of his empire, allies, and satellite states had added roughly a million men to his armies between 1804 and 1815. Of the huge army of 600,000 men he mustered for the Russian campaign, probably just under half were French.[27]

Napoleon now had to defend this threatened empire, in the first instance by getting back to Paris without delay. Just an hour after meeting the king of Saxony, he left Dresden, this time in a rather more comfortable sledge, switching to a carriage at Erfurt. Crossing the partially frozen Rhine at Mainz, he sped on to Verdun and Meaux, reaching Paris in the night of 18 December. Arriving at the Tuileries palace at 11.45 p.m., he and Caulaincourt were at first refused admittance by the porter, who failed to recognize them beneath their stubble and voluminous wrappings.[28]

France itself had always been the nerve-centre of Napoleon's rule. It was not, however, the France of today, but one swollen by the substantial territories directly annexed to her over twenty years of successful warfare. These comprised Belgium, Holland, the north German coast up to Hamburg, the left bank of the Rhine, much of north-west Italy, and even, on the other side of the Adriatic, the so-called 'Illyrian provinces' of modern Slovenia and Croatia. With the exception of the Illyrian provinces, which were ruled by a governor-general, all these new acquisitions were administered like the rest of metropolitan France, with a prefect implementing the orders of Paris, and with representatives in the legislature in the capital. However, the difference between this 'greater France' and satellite states like Westphalia or the kingdom of Italy, which on paper seemed clear, was more apparent than real. For example, both the foreign minister and the secretary of state of the kingdom of Italy resided not in its nominal capital Milan, but in Paris.[29]

Napoleon had come to office as a man of order, capable of restoring stability and good government to France after a decade of revolutionary upheaval. To most contemporaries, this entailed curbing the turbulent legislatures that had dominated that period, and strongly reinforcing the executive. By 1812, Napoleon had promulgated three constitutions, each reflecting an increase in executive power. The head of state alone had the power to initiate legislation, to declare war and make peace.[30] At first, Napoleon exercised this authority within a republican context, as First Consul. Then, in 1804, concluding that political stability could only be guaranteed by a hereditary system, he made himself Emperor of the French. The logic of this decision required an heir, yet Napoleon and his wife Joséphine had never had children. Six years later he remedied the situation by divorcing Joséphine and marrying the daughter of the Emperor of Austria, the Archduchess Maria Louisa, who now became Marie-Louise, Empress of the French. In March 1811 Marie-Louise gave Napoleon his longed-for son, grandiloquently entitled 'King of Rome', and the Bonaparte dynasty had its heir.

If the constitutions of the empire limited Napoleon's power in theory, they rarely did so in practice. There was a parliament with an upper house, the Senate, and a lower house, the Legislative Body, but it occupied a subservient position. The Legislative Body was given the essential attribute of a representative assembly, the right of consent to taxation, but this was more theoretical than real. The annual budget presented to it was always sketchy in the extreme, and it had no control over the ever-increasing extraordinary expenses made necessary by continual war. The powers of both houses were further circumscribed by their very small electoral base. Their members were chosen, in a complicated indirect process, by electoral colleges composed of the six hundred most heavily taxed citizens in each French department. This gave an electorate of approximately only 70,000 for a population of 30 million, though more citizens did participate

indirectly through choosing the members of the electoral colleges. Elabor-
ate means were employed to ensure the docility of both bodies; the Senate
chose the deputies of the Legislative Body from a list drawn up by the
electoral colleges, but a third of its own members were nominated by
Napoleon himself. The legitimacy of the two houses was further compromised by the submission to plebiscites of major political decisions, such as the
establishment of the empire in 1804. Although these were carefully orchestrated, they gave Napoleon an authority as representative of the French
people that powerfully challenged that of his parliaments.[31]

Napoleon's ministers fared no better. They were responsible only to him,
and he treated them as little more than his clerks. When he was angry, he
would sometimes hit them, once knocking the minister of justice backwards
onto a sofa.[32] Far more powerful was a non-ministerial dignitary, Jean-
Jacques de Cambacérès, arch-chancellor of the empire. A tall, corpulent
man with heavy black eyebrows and an old-fashioned powdered wig,
Cambacérès was in many ways Napoleon's prime minister, a fact which
has only recently been recognized.[33] An eminent lawyer and former revolutionary politician, he played a crucial role in drafting the civil code, and
Napoleon relied heavily on his advice both on major issues and day-to-day
adminstration. In Napoleon's absence, it was Cambacérès who took over
the reins of government, presiding both the Council of Ministers and the
advisory Council of State. Throughout the Russian campaign, he was
Napoleon's deputy in Paris, and sent him detailed reports by courier via
Warsaw.[34]

Even in this highly centralized regime, some opposition did survive. Its
best-organized and most dangerous element was royalism. This had the
great advantage of a clear aim—the restoration of the younger brother of the
executed Louis XVI, whose supporters recognized him as King Louis
XVIII, to the French throne. Much of western France, especially the
Vendée, had risen in support of the monarchy and the Catholic church
during the Revolution, and in this region a degree of lawlessness and
banditry, often with royalist overtones, remained.[35] Royalism had also
been given a boost by Napoleon's recent breach with the papacy. In
1809, as a protest against the French occupation of Rome, Pope Pius VII
had excommunicated Napoleon, who had promptly had him arrested.
For over twenty years, the causes of church and king had been linked,
since the Revolution's attack on them both. The Pope's imprisonment
added many new recruits, particularly young Catholic nobles, to the

partisans of the exiled Bourbons. The most concrete result was the formation in 1810 of the *Chevaliers de la Foi*, an elaborately organized secret society
aiming at the restoration of the monarchy. For the moment it remained
underground, but in 1814, when France was invaded, it was to play a critical
role in Napoleon's fall.[36]

The republicans threatened the regime in different ways. They had fewer
foot-soldiers than the royalists, since their popular armed wing, the *sans-
culottes* of central and eastern Paris, had been crushed in 1795. However,
several of their leaders had survived the bloodletting of the Revolution, and
could serve as potential rallying-points for the left-wing opposition. Probably the most capable was Lazare Carnot, a former member of the revolutionary Committee of Public Safety and 'organizer of victory', who had
created the mass conscript armies that had saved France from invasion and
turned her towards European conquest. A rather forbidding man who
prided himself on his integrity, Carnot had publicly opposed the foundation
of the empire in 1804 and retired into private life the following year. He
seemed to have renounced all political activity, but Napoleon still kept a wary
eye on his actions.[37] Another eminent survivor was Emmanuel-Joseph Sieyès,
a former *abbé* and one of the most important theorists and politicians of the
first years of the Revolution. Wizened, austere, and a compulsive intriguer, he
had collaborated with Napoleon in the coup d'état of Brumaire, but had then
swiftly been sidelined. Outwardly he remained loyal to the regime, and sat in
the Senate, but Napoleon took his hostility for granted.[38]

Another symbol of the left in the Senate was the venerable Abbé Grégoire. Campaigner for the abolition of slavery and for Jewish emancipation,
and a prominent member of the revolutionary assemblies, he had voted in
the Senate against the proclamation of the empire.[39] The authorities,
however, did not take him seriously as a conspirator. One reason for this
was his domestic arrangements, which, for a man of the cloth, were
unconventional. As a police report for 1814 put it:

> [The Abbé Grégoire] lives with one Mme Dubois, a former singer at the
> Opera, whose husband, a man called La Tour, was a dancer and died two years
> ago. This woman is so old that any scandalous commerce between her and the
> Abbé Grégoire is inconceivable, but he is under her thumb, and she runs the
> whole household. He calls her *the saintly lady*. Everybody in the house is
> usually in bed by 8p.m.[40]

If the Abbé Grégoire's routine precluded late-night plotting, Napoleon's
parliaments did contain more active members of the opposition. These

formed a loose alliance of moderate, constitutional republicans known as the Ideologues. They had the advantage of numbering some of the most distinguished minds in France, such as the historian Pierre Daunou and (although he did not share all their ideas) the brilliant philosopher and writer Benjamin Constant. In the Senate, they also had links with Sieyès and another leading figure of the Revolution, the former republican minister Dominique-Joseph Garat. However, Napoleon had purged many of them in 1802 for attacking the Civil Code, and this had broken the group's spirit. It was to take the Russian disaster and the prospect of invasion for the senators and deputies to challenge Napoleon once more.[41]

Opponents like the Ideologues were prepared to operate within the system. The same could not be said for one of Napoleon's longest-standing and most dangerous rivals, Paul Barras. As the leading member of the Directory, the last government of the Republic, Barras had originally been Napoleon's patron. In 1796, he had given him his first independent command, of the Army of Italy, paving the way for his first great series of victories. He had also patronized him in a more personal way, passing on to him his own cast-off mistress, Joséphine de Beauharnais, whom Napoleon promptly fell in love with and married.

A handsome, imposing, and notably debauched man, Barras had dominated the Directory for five years, a feat that had required both skill and toughness. Yet the Directory had struggled to maintain its authority at home, and presided over a worsening military situation abroad. Barras was the principal victim of Brumaire, but whereas five years previously he would have gone straight to the guillotine, he was instead merely sent into retirement and allowed to keep the substantial fortune he had made in office. In 1801, however, he had been exiled from Paris, sent to Brussels for four years, then escorted by a hundred policemen to a country house near Marseilles in his native south of France. There, he was kept under close surveillance, with his activities the subject of minutely detailed police reports.[42] Another prominent revolutionary figure, Pierre-Joseph Cambon, de facto finance minister during the Reign of Terror, also lived in retirement nearby, just outside Montpellier.[43]

When Barras had been forced from power, two of his leading colleagues had stayed on to serve Napoleon at the highest levels of the state. Now, however, they too had fallen into semi-disgrace. They were Talleyrand and Fouché. Charles-Maurice de Talleyrand, Prince of Benevento, was formidable both as a diplomat and as a politician. An elegant man, apart from a club foot, his impassive features were framed by a mane of carefully arranged white hair. He had been an extremely successful foreign minister for seven years after Brumaire but, alarmed by Napoleon's growing appetite for conquest, he had resigned in 1807 and then taken the extraordinary—and treasonable—step of betraying the Emperor's policy secrets to Austria and Russia to help them check his ambitions. Despite famously rounding on him in January 1809 and calling him 'a shit in a silk stocking', Napoleon never realized the full extent of Talleyrand's betrayal.[44] Talleyrand remained Vice-Grand Elector of the empire, firmly embedded in the hierarchy of power, and bided his time.

Joseph Fouché was just as wily as Talleyrand and far more sinister. Thin and angular, with hooded eyes set in a long yellow face, he had blood on his hands as the organizer of the brutal repression of Lyons during the Reign of Terror. However, for a mixture of personal and political reasons he had played a key part in ending the Terror, and re-emerged in the last months of the Directory as minister of police. The job suited him perfectly, and soon made him one of the most feared men in France; he was a superb organizer, with excellent political antennae and an unrivalled nose for conspiracies and intrigue. However, like Talleyrand, he had become concerned by Napoleon's expansionism. In 1810, he had made secret peace overtures to England, and Napoleon had found out about these and sacked him. Now he was living in retirement at his country house outside Paris, but his distance from Napoleon was obvious, as was his continuing appetite for power.[45]

Against this range of opposition, Napoleon could deploy some powerful weapons, the most effective, ironically, fashioned by Fouché himself. This was the police, probably the best-organized and most efficient of its day. At its head was the ministry of police on the Quai Voltaire in Paris, grouped in six sections. Under its direction, France was divided into four police *arrondissements*, three of which were controlled by a councillor of state and a fourth, that of Paris, with its own prefect. Napoleon kept a close watch on all its functions, receiving daily bulletins from both the minister and the prefect of police of Paris. The system had some flaws; the fact that the prefect of police of Paris had direct access to the Emperor created an institutional rivalry with the minister of police, and the policemen themselves, the 20,000 militarized gendarmes, were commanded not by the minister but by a regular soldier, Marshal Moncey. Still, although reliable statistics are sparse, it seems that the police did achieve a significant lowering of the crime rate under the empire.[46]

By its nature the effectiveness of the secret police is more difficult to assess, but it was certainly a powerful instrument of surveillance, particularly in Paris. Each section of the ministry of police had its own network of spies and informers operating at all levels of society. Napoleon even had agents of his own who reported to him directly, underlining his suspicion of those who served him, especially Fouché. For those unfortunate enough to be deemed threats to the safety of the state indefinite detention in a special category prison could be prescribed, though each case had to be reviewed annually. By the end of the empire these prisoners numbered 2,500.[47]

Napoleon was convinced that the unbridled licence of the press had played a major part in the turbulence of the Revolution, and he was determined to rectify this. As early as January 1800, he closed down sixty of the seventy-three newspapers then operating in Paris. By the end of his reign this figure had sunk to just four. In 1810, the provincial press was reduced to one newspaper per department, placed under the supervision of the local prefect. For those papers that survived this drastic winnowing, a rigorous censorship was imposed. Napoleon himself corrected the proofs of the regime's official organ, *Le Moniteur*, and wrote many of the articles. Each of the leading Parisian newspapers had its own censor. The result, as intended, was that the press became simply a conduit for government propaganda and practical information; all debate and criticism vanished from its pages.[48]

Overall, Napoleon's empire was a highly authoritarian state, in which the executive and the army wielded immense power. The legislature, though not abolished, was almost totally subservient to the Emperor, and there was little room for free expression in either the public or private spheres. Yet the edifice, though imposing, did have its weak spots. There was opposition, which if tamed was by no means eradicated. Above all, the continuing war created permanent uncertainty. If Napoleon were killed in battle, this would pose a major, perhaps fatal, challenge to his regime. Even the rumour of his death could have unpredictable consequences.

This is what happened on the morning of 23 October 1812. A small band of republican conspirators, armed with a forged announcement of Napoleon's death, briefly took control of several key strategic points in Paris. The alarming news reached the Emperor a fortnight later. The sooner he returned to France, he realized, the better. He could not immediately do so, since the pursuing Russians still had to be beaten off. With this achieved, however, he delayed no longer, left his dying army at Smorgoni, and sped westwards to his capital.

2

Plots and Alarms, 1812–1813

The conspiracy that brought Napoleon back from Russia was dangerous largely because it was so unexpected. Its author and prime mover was a 58-year-old general named Claude-François Malet. A staunch republican, whose military career had stalled after Napoleon's seizure of power, he had been arrested for plotting against Napoleon in 1808. Since 1810, he had been detained in a private sanatorium on the outskirts of eastern Paris, the early-nineteenth-century equivalent of an open prison. Its lax security enabled him to devise a detailed and extremely audacious plan for a coup d'état, whose key instrument was a forged decree of the Senate, a *senatus-consultum*. This proclaimed that Napoleon had been killed just outside Moscow—a not implausible hypothesis—and set up a provisional government, whose members it named.[1]

Armed with this document, Malet and the small band of allies he had recruited aimed to take control of units of the Paris National Guard and seize the capital. Malet, who seems to have been very well informed about the Paris garrison, searched for a suitably credulous National Guard commander to whom to present his credentials, and found one in Commandant Soulier of the 10th cohort, stationed not far from the sanatorium, at the Popincourt barracks.

Malet also brought to this scheme a technique which he applied 'with diabolical cleverness'.[2] This was to compromise, in writing or by word of mouth, as many potential allies as possible, so that when the crisis came they would feel they had no option but to join him. Thus the *senatus-consultum* he forged named as members of the provisional government several prominent figures known to be sympathetic to republicanism, from Sieyès to Carnot to Garat, even though he had never met them. Malet hoped that if he managed to take control of Paris they would spontaneously join him; if they hesitated, he calculated that being implicated in his plot, however fraudulently, would make them sufficiently scared of Napoleon's vengeance to achieve the same end.

At 10 p.m. on the night of 22 October 1812, Malet put his plan into action. He climbed the wall of the sanatorium, met his confederates, and with them made his way to the Popincourt barracks. Commandant Soulier was completely taken in by the forged orders and *senatus-consultum*, and tamely handed over his troops. Now with several hundred soldiers at his back, Malet marched to the prison of La Force. He had decided some time before that to take over the key ministries he needed allies of senior military experience, and he knew that La Force contained two republican generals who had also fallen out with Napoleon, Lahorie, and Guidal. Lahorie was an elegant man of noble background but radical convictions. Guidal was a very different character; coarse, energetic, and a heavy drinker. At La Force, Malet's orders were obeyed as meekly as they had been at Popincourt, and Lahorie and Guidal were swiftly delivered up to him. He repeated to them the news that Napoleon was dead, and they enthusiastically set off to arrest the minister of police, René Savary, Duke of Rovigo, and the prefect of police, Baron Pasquier.[3]

At 7 a.m. on 23 October, Savary was asleep in his bed. Contrary to his usual practice, he had stayed up working all night in his apartment at the ministry on the Quai Voltaire, and had decided to sleep in for a few hours. Suddenly he was woken by a loud hammering on the door of his study, which he always locked at night. He turned over and tried to ignore the noise, but then heard a crash as the door panels were smashed in. His first thought was that the building was on fire and that his staff were trying to rescue him, so he stumbled into the study in his nightshirt and opened what was left of the door himself. He was confronted by a mass of soldiers under arms, headed by Lahorie, with whom he had served in the army. Lahorie told him excitedly: 'You're under arrest. Count yourself lucky you're in my hands; at least this way you won't be harmed.'[4]

A tough, resourceful man, whose good looks and relative youth contrasted with the fear he inspired as police minister, Savary was rarely caught by surprise. He was unable, however, to make any sense of what Lahorie now told him: 'The Emperor was killed under the walls of Moscow on 8th October.' Savary was flabbergasted. 'You're talking nonsense', he replied, 'the Emperor wrote to me that day; I can show you the letter.' Lahorie refused to believe him, and when Savary tried to convince the soldiers that Lahorie himself was an escaped prisoner, and should be arrested, he had no more success. At this point another officer, an older man 'with an atrocious face', rushed into the room with a drawn sword, and, according to Savary, might have run him through had he not tripped over a piece of furniture. He pointed the sword at Savary's chest. 'Do you know who I am?' he demanded. 'I am General Guidal, whom you had arrested in Marseilles and brought to Paris.' Savary knew the name well; he had had Guidal arrested nine months before.[5]

Under an escort commanded by Guidal, Savary was frogmarched into a waiting hackney carriage, his destination the prison of La Force. As the carriage passed down the Quai des Lunettes, he saw an opportunity to escape. Still in his nightshirt, he jumped out and began running down the quai towards the Palais de Justice. However, Guidal and the soldiers caught up with him and dragged him on foot the rest of the way to La Force. There, he joined Pasquier and another senior police official, Desmarets, under lock and key.[6]

For his part, Lahorie proceeded east and occupied the Hôtel de Ville. This success had major symbolic as well as practical importance; the over-throw of the monarchy on 10 August 1792 had been planned at the Hôtel de Ville, which was thus indelibly associated with the establishment of the Republic. Meanwhile, Malet and a company of the 10th cohort headed towards their next objective, the headquarters of the military governor of Paris in the Place Vendôme. Here the coup d'état began to go wrong. The governor, General Hulin, was a giant who had led the storming of the Bastille in 1789 and was known to be devoted to Napoleon. When informed by Malet of Napoleon's death and his own arrest, he demanded to see the orders. Malet promptly drew a pistol and shot him in the face. Hulin collapsed on the floor, and Malet assumed that he was dead. In fact Hulin survived, though it proved impossible to extract the bullet from his skull, and he lived to the age of 82.[7]

Malet's luck had now run out. Although he did not realize his chief had been shot, Hulin's deputy Colonel Doucet found the orders handed to him suspicious, and refused to accept them. Malet again reached for his pistol, but was overpowered and tied to a chair. Squads of the Imperial Guard were quickly despatched around Paris to restore order. Lahorie was arrested at the ministry of police, Savary and Pasquier were liberated from prison, and the 10th cohort of the National Guard was sent back to barracks at Popincourt. As for Guidal, in the course of the morning he had lost confidence in the conspiracy's prospects, and had gone to ground.[8] A few hours later, however, he too was arrested.

Cambacérès, the acting head of government in Napoleon's absence, was only informed of Malet's coup as it was coming to an end. He swiftly ordered a temporary closure of the Senate, and put Paris in a state of siege. Later that morning he summoned the Council of Ministers to organize the further necessary measures. A circular was drawn up to be sent to the prefects relating what had happened, and an announcement drafted for the official newspaper, the *Moniteur*. As for the captured conspirators, Cambacérès insisted they be tried by a closed military commission, to give as little publicity as possible to their cause.

The sequel was grim but inevitable. Five days later Malet faced his judges along with twenty-three others, whose only crime for the most part was to have taken his orders at face value. He bravely took responsibility for the whole plot himself, and asked that his co-defendants be acquitted. Nonetheless, fourteen death sentences were handed down, including Malet himself, Lahorie, Guidal, and—*pour encourager les autres*—the credulous Soulier. The condemned men were shot by firing-squad on the afternoon of 29 October on the plain of Grenelle, at a spot which was then open country

Figure 3. The execution of General Malet and his fellow-conspirators, 29 October 1812, by Jean Duplessis-Bertaux. General Guidal, in the foreground, is still standing after the second volley.

and is now occupied by the Dupleix metro station. The execution was botched; Guidal, the last to die, was only finished off by the third volley.[9]

Malet's failure, coupled with the erroneous impression that he had been confined in a sanatorium because he was actually insane, has often led to his conspiracy being dismissed as the work of a single, possibly unhinged adventurer.[10] The scheme certainly had major flaws. It was entirely based on the assumption that a reservoir of republicanism existed in France, just waiting to surge up the moment a breach was made in the regime's defences. Whether such a reservoir actually existed or not is unprovable, but without it the plotters would have been isolated even if they had managed to take control of Paris.

Another weakness was the assumption that once a new regime was installed in Paris, the army and its commanders would meekly abandon Napoleon and transfer their loyalties to the new authorities. Napoleon himself underlined this to Caulaincourt when told of the coup in Russia: 'Malet was mad. He must have been to think that neutralizing the police and deceiving a few corps commanders . . . for three hours could overturn the government, with an army of 200,000 men still intact outside the country.'[11] It is striking that no marshal figured in the provisional government. Perhaps Malet was relying on measures not men; he had drafted a proclamation to the army announcing a general peace and the abolition of conscription. To soldiers recovering from the bloodbath at Borodino or retreating from Wellington in Spain, these promises could have been tempting.

If Malet's plot only ever had an outside chance of success, it did expose dangerous cracks in the structure of Napoleon's rule. The most obvious one was pointed out once again to Caulaincourt by the Emperor: 'Not one of those soldiers and officials to whom my death was announced thought of my son.'[12] It was an alarming sign of how personal Napoleon's power remained, and of how far his efforts to establish his dynasty still had to go, that the news of his demise was immediately taken as the cue for an entirely new political system. Another significant flaw concerned the Senate. Investing himself with its authority was Malet's most original and effective idea, and was responsible for what success he had. Although the tactic failed on this occasion, experienced observers noted the danger it had momentarily posed to the regime, and the potential it might hold for the future.

The most astute of these observers was Talleyrand. He was an old friend and patron of Caulaincourt, and during the Russian campaign sent him regular letters about the situation in France. Several of these were about the Malet coup, the first written the day after the conspirators were arrested. Significantly, Talleyrand did not dismiss the plot as doomed to failure from the outset. 'For a moment', he concluded, 'there was a real danger.' Two days later, he had recovered his poise, but underlined the lessons to be drawn from the experience:

> The only impression left on the public by the affair is astonishment at the ease with which soldiers can be deceived by a senatus-consultum. That has led to some concerns about the Senate, whose nullity, apart from in elections to the Legislative Body and the Appeal Court, should be better known . . . That is what [the government] needs to know. Those, between ourselves, are my conclusions.[13]

With his customary perspicacity, Talleyrand had gone to the heart of the matter. Concerned to give his dictatorship a veneer of respectability, Napoleon had carefully fostered the lie that the Senate actually counted for something. This had been so effective that, at the announcement of the Emperor's death, many people who should have known better were prepared to concede authority to it rather than immediately proclaim Napoleon II. Talleyrand's solution was logical, if cynical: 'It is important that the limits of the Senate's authority be made plain, and all the efforts of the Emperor's servants should be directed to propagating this.'[14]

The full irony of these words would only become apparent eighteen months later. In the spring of 1814, having turned against Napoleon, Talleyrand would employ the precise tactic he was here denouncing, and depose Napoleon by senatorial decree. Given how carefully he had noted it in October 1812, it is probable that Malet's manipulation of the Senate gave him the idea. The only difference was that this time the decree was genuine.

Whatever its legacy for the future, with the execution of its leaders the Malet plot appeared to be over. To contemporaries like Talleyrand, it was a Parisian affair, conceived and defeated in Paris, and that has been the received opinion ever since. In fact Malet's conspiracy had wider ramifications, extending to other parts of France. Although these were not straightforward, Napoleon was well aware of them, and this helps explain his continuing preoccupation with a republican menace at the expense of others that posed a greater threat. The link leads back to the last man left standing before the firing squad at Grenelle, General Guidal.

According to Napoleon, Maximilien-Joseph Guidal was 'the worst villain in existence'.[15] Tall, imposing, and frighteningly ugly, he was a veteran soldier and a radical republican. Born in Grasse in 1764, he had joined the pre-revolutionary army and after 1789 had been promoted rapidly on active service in Italy and the Vendée, becoming general of brigade in 1799. This was the highest military rank he achieved. After a series of political disagreements with his superiors he was sent back in disgrace to Grasse and then, in 1809, placed on the retired list. That same year, he obtained permission to move from Grasse to Marseilles.

What the authorities did not know, or had forgotten, was that Guidal had dangerous connections in the city. It was the place of exile of Paul Barras, the leading figure of the Directory overthrown by Napoleon in 1799. A Provençal like Guidal, Barras had been living since 1805 at his property of Les Aygalades just outside the city. As a prominent oppositional figure, he was kept under careful police surveillance, and all his visitors noted. Guidal made his way to Les Aygalades almost immediately on arriving in Marseilles; Barras had helped his career during the Revolution, and was godfather to his son. The first thing he sought was financial help, since he was in straitened circumstances, and Barras agreed to pay for his son's education at the Lycée de Montpellier.[16]

Figure 4. Paul Barras.

Inevitably with two such irreconcilable enemies of the regime, conspiracy against Napoleon was high on the agenda. It is difficult to establish the full extent of this, but the two men did organize one solid project, the escape and return to Spain of its former king, Charles IV, who had been deposed by Napoleon in 1808 and was now also in exile in Marseilles. This scheme introduced a further element, the support of England. The Royal Navy controlled the Mediterranean, and could strike at virtually any point it chose. It kept the French fleet blockaded at Toulon, and mounted regular raids on the surrounding coast. In November 1809, Barras and Guidal made contact with it and offered to smuggle the ex-king onto one of its ships, but the English government eventually decided that Charles would be too difficult a client.[17]

Despite this check, the conspirators remained in close touch with the English fleet, and assigned it a pivotal role in a much wider scheme they now hatched. This was to support the seizure of Marseilles and Toulon as part of a general rising in the south of France. As a police report later put it, 'Their object was to convince the English of the supposed discontent of the people of the Midi, to portray them as ready to mount a revolution, and to obtain money, arms and troops to take Marseilles and Toulon by surprise in league with the rebels of the interior.'[18]

This was treason on the grand scale, and Guidal was its prime mover. By 1812 he had built up a substantial network of conspirators, first in Grasse and then in and around Marseilles. How far Barras was involved in this second conspiracy is unclear. The likeliest scenario is that he knew something of what was afoot, but kept himself carefully in the background. As one of the plotters later put it when interrogated about Barras's role: 'I'm sure that once things were well under way, he'd have shown himself.'[19] A major figure like Barras had too much to lose by compromising himself too early, and he could afford to wait.

For any contemporary who had lived through the Revolution, a plan to seize Toulon and Marseilles and open them to the English fleet had profound resonance. This was exactly what the royalists in Toulon had done at the height of the Terror, in August 1793. Remarkably, both Napoleon and Barras had played crucial parts in the siege and recapture of the town that winter by the Republic. Napoleon had commanded the artillery that had forced the English fleet to withdraw, and laid the foundations of his military reputation. Less gloriously, Barras had helped organize the brutal repression that had followed Toulon's fall, in which up to 2,000 people had been executed. A second revolt of Toulon, this time with the republicans welcoming in the English, would not only pose a major danger to Napoleon's regime but also have great symbolic significance.

By this time, rumours of Guidal's activities had reached Napoleon himself. On 17 January 1812 he wrote to Savary: 'I have learned that General Guidal is on the coast of Provence and involved in various plots... If he really is in Provence, have him arrested immediately and seize his papers.'[20] As usual, the Emperor was promptly obeyed. Just over a week later Guidal was tracked down in Marseilles and some of his networks dismantled. He was taken to Paris and imprisoned in La Force. Over the next nine months, however, he gave his captors very little information. He may have been very cunning, or his captors may not have tried very hard to make him talk.[21] It is possible that he was simply forgotten amid the feverish preparations for the Russian campaign. As a result, he was still at La Force the following October, when Malet liberated him, incorporated him into his plans, and sealed his fate.

Guidal's silence up to that moment ensured that his last, and potentially most dangerous, conspiracy, remained intact—the plan to seize Toulon and Marseilles. By the beginning of March 1813 the remaining plotters felt ready to act. They aimed first to take possession of Toulon by seizing the strategically placed Fort Lamalgue, garrisoned by reluctant and discontented conscripts they were confident would join them, and then to signal the English fleet to enter the harbour. They also drew up a proclamation strikingly similar to Malet's of the previous October, announcing an immediate peace, the abolition of conscription, and the calling of a congress to give France a new constitution.[22]

On the night of 30–31 March 1813 the plot's leaders, reinforced by fifty to sixty peasants from the surrounding area, prepared to march on Toulon from the nearby town of Le Beausset. However, a last-minute disagreement broke out over whether to galvanize support by killing unpopular local officials, and this delay gave the authorities time to act. A battalion of regular troops broke up the gathering, and the conspirators either fled or were arrested. Undaunted, the remainder decided to persevere, but to switch their focus to Marseilles. Once again, they planned to seize a crucial fort and the arsenal, call out the port workers, and bring in the English fleet. At the last minute, however, one of their number got cold feet and went to the police. On the night of 30 April, his unsuspecting colleagues were intercepted on their way to a meeting by two squads of gendarmes and fired on;

two were wounded and captured, and the rest dispersed. With this fusillade, the conspiracies of Toulon and Marseilles were effectively over.[23]

Unlike General Malet, the plotters of the Midi had not benefited from Napoleon's absence. By the time they took up arms, the Emperor had been back from Russia for three months, and his response was swift. Revealingly, his first move was against Barras, whose links with Guidal and Charles IV were now clear. On 8 April, Barras was ordered to move immediately to Rome, and threatened with imprisonment in the Chateau d'If off Marseilles if he delayed. Wisely, he did not test Napoleon's patience; by 13 April, he was on the road.[24]

As more details reached Paris of the attempt on Toulon, Napoleon's reaction was the same as Cambacérès' to the Malet affair. However it was dealt with, it should be denied publicity, so it could not spawn imitators. On 15 April, on Napoleon's instructions, Savary wrote to the Marseilles authorities: 'I notice . . . that too much importance, and above all too much publicity, is being given to the discoveries made. This could make people believe that there are still factions strong enough to challenge the government. It encourages the criminal projects of the malevolent, and excites the agitators instead of crushing them.'[25] Six months after the Malet conspiracy, a similar republican plot had been uncovered, and Savary's words reveal the government's unease.

The same priorities marked the judicial phase of repression. Although seventy-three conspirators were arrested, only thirteen, those who had contacted the English fleet, were actually tried. They appeared before a military commission rather than a civil court, and were charged simply with espionage, excluding any hint of their plans for a wider rising. As Maurice Agulhon observes: 'It seems Napoleon feared the effect a major trial would have.' After three months of proceedings, the commission handed down six death sentences. On 20 December 1813, in an epilogue to the previous year's scene on the Plaine de Grenelle, the condemned men were shot in an olive grove on the outskirts of Toulon.[26]

Just how much of a threat the Toulon and Marseilles conspiracies posed to Napoleon remains unclear. Yet Pelet de la Lozère, the councillor of state sent from Paris to oversee the investigations, certainly took them seriously. 'These projects', he wrote, 'were extremely criminal, and with time could have become very dangerous.' Their wide geographical extent and the numbers mobilized suggest that more Frenchmen than historians have generally thought were prepared to take up arms against the empire in its last years. The police reports speak of the plotters having confederates in Nîmes, the Bas-Languedoc, and Alais and Anduze in the Cévennes.[27]

For Napoleon, the movements had another disquieting aspect, and this concerned leadership rather than the grass-roots. Barras was swiftly exiled, but he was not the only republican of national stature connected to the plotters. Several of the interrogation reports mentioned the name of Cambon, former leading member of the Committee of Public Safety responsible for its financial policy, and currently living in retirement near Montpellier. Some conspirators claimed he had links with them, and that he would preside over the constitutional congress scheduled to meet once the coup had succeeded. According to Pelet de la Lozère, Cambon went to the Montpellier police in September 1812 and 'half-admitted' that some form of rising was being planned in the Midi.[28] One can only speculate about his motives; perhaps he was trying to cover himself in case the attempt went wrong. Whatever the truth, it seems there was more than one republican elder statesman waiting in the wings, who could plausibly be called on once an insurrection had succeeded.

Given their similarity, and the overlap of personnel in the form of General Guidal, could the Malet affair and those of Toulon and Marseilles actually have formed one larger conspiracy? In that case, they would have had a significantly greater chance of damaging the regime. Here, however, the evidence is contradictory. One official report claimed that the principal conspirator at Anduze had had prior knowledge of the Malet coup. For this to be the case, Malet and Guidal would have to have been working together before October 1812, and no proof of this exists. Yet even if they did spring from the same source, the two plots were so similar in aims and makeup that the effect was almost the same. As soon as the news of the Malet coup reached Marseilles, on 3 November 1812, four hundred conspirators gathered in the early morning to seize strategic points in the city. The attack was only called off when news was received that Malet had failed.[29]

The Malet, Toulon, and Marseilles affairs thus gave Napoleon much material for concern. However, he drew the wrong conclusion from them, focusing his attention on the republican threat. When, before leaving Paris for his next campaign, he ordered increased police surveillance of the opposition, Savary naturally assumed this meant the republicans. Hence he instructed his subordinates to concentrate their efforts on those who had been 'notorious as firebrands during the Revolution, promoters of unrest or tribunes of the people'.[30]

In fact the real danger lay elsewhere. The Malet affair gave the Bourbon cause an infusion of hope, and also showed it had strengths the republicans did not possess. In Louis XVIII it had an undisputed head who, unlike Barras or Cambon, was not at the mercy of Napoleon's police. Its secret networks, above all the Chevaliers de la Foi, were better structured than their rivals', and received an influx of new members after October 1812.[31] Finally, there were many former royalists who had taken service in Napoleon's court and administration over the past decade, who might be tempted at the right moment to return to their old allegiance. The republicans could create sensations, but the royalists had longer-term advantages to which Napoleon paid too little attention.

For any coup against Napoleon to succeed, it would need not just a core of militants, but the support or at least acquiescence of the wider French population. Yet to judge by the Malet affair at least, there was little prospect of this. On 23 October, the same day the coup was crushed, the minister of the interior Montalivet sent a circular to all 123 prefects of the empire, demanding details of the public's response as it emerged. The results were reassuring. 'The prefects' correspondence', he informed Napoleon, 'assures me that throughout the whole of the empire this event has inspired no other sentiments than indignation and scorn towards the plot's authors.'[32] However, the false announcement of Napoleon's death did strike a chord; fifteen prefects reported rumours and alarms about the Emperor's health over the following month.[33] Significantly, Montalivet's circular of 23 October enclosed another ordering the prefects to submit in future monthly reports on the state of public opinion in their departments.

Anxiety rather than sedition was the overwhelming response of the French public to the successive shocks of late 1812. This reached a peak when, on 16 December, the 29th bulletin of the Grande Armée, detailing for the first time the extent of the Russian disaster, was published. All the sources agree that this caused consternation across France. Writing to Napoleon on 23rd January 1813, Montalivet put it as tactfully as he could. 'The 29th bulletin', he wrote, 'has produced a painful sensation in the majority of departments.' In fact, of ninety-eight prefects' reports from December to January, forty-two mentioned the horror caused by the bulletin, but its effect may well have spread wider. The only discordant note was struck by the department of Bouches-du-Weser in north Germany, only recently annexed to the empire, whose inhabitants showed 'lively satisfaction' at the bad news.[34]

For Napoleon, the litmus test of loyalty was willingness to fight for him, and it was soon clear that this had not been eroded. The Emperor's first priority on returning to Paris was to replace the army he had lost in Russia in time for the next campaigning season. To achieve this, the mechanism of conscription, central to all French victories and conquests over the past twenty years, had to be set to work and brought to maximum efficiency. One factor, however, always remained unpredictable, and caused the authorities concern. This was the extent of desertion and draft evasion which, though less exact than the prefects' reports, was something of a barometer of public opinion.

Conscription was a complicated process, defined by the Jourdan Law of 1798. By its terms, all unmarried or childless Frenchmen between 20 and 25 were eligible for unlimited service in wartime and divided into five classes according to age. The overall total of each levy was fixed by the Senate, which in collaboration with the prefects decided how many men from each class in each department were needed. At the most basic level, that of the commune, each contingent was selected by drawing lots. Since 1800, however, those chosen were allowed to pay a replacement to serve for them if they had the money. Considering that this was the first time mass armies had ever been put into the field through systematic conscription, the results were impressive: between 1799 and 1813 just over two million Frenchmen were put into uniform, and in the process changed modern warfare for ever.[35]

In early 1813, the Senate was particularly inclined to do Napoleon's bidding over conscription. Although there were rumours that Malet had had some links with it, Napoleon had refused to follow them up, and the senators were grateful. On 11 January 1813 they voted a new levy of 350,000 men to make good the disasters of Russia. Of these, 100,000 came from the National Guard, another 100,000 from ransacking the lists of those not chosen in previous years, and a further 150,000 by anticipating the draft of 1814.[36]

Remarkably, the call-up was greeted with equanimity, even enthusiasm. Overall, the percentage of deserters and draft evaders was relatively low, at 10 per cent. This was higher than in 1810 or 1811, but these had been exceptionally good years, when resistance to conscription had been virtually eliminated. Between 1806 and 1810 it had reached an average of 13 per cent, and between 1800 and 1804 had risen as high as 27 per cent.[37] The vast majority of prefects reported that the levies were proceeding without difficulty, and continued to do so until May 1813. The prefect of the Charente wrote that the people had been expecting a fresh burst of conscription after the Russian disaster, so 'had not been particularly astonished' when it was announced. Elsewhere, there were signs of a patriotic reaction to defeat; in Strasbourg one citizen offered 10,000 francs and two of his horses to aid the war effort.[38]

The smooth execution of the levy of 350,000 men revived Napoleon considerably. It convinced him that he had the support of France in recovering his international position in the way he understood best, through warfare. Domestically, the general repudiation of the Malet plot had been reassuring, and only the republicans needed to be carefully watched. But appearances were deceptive. In the coming months, it would become increasingly clear that most French people were becoming weary of the prospect of indefinite war. It was no coincidence that the plotters of Paris, Marseilles, and Toulon had called for a general peace and an end to conscription; they had known this would strike an echo. Yet Napoleon chose to ignore this warning.

Partly this was because he had more immediate problems. He had managed to raise a new army with remarkable speed, but the victorious Russians were poised to invade eastern Europe. In the face of this advance, the loyalty of France's reluctant ally Prussia could not be guaranteed. Worse, the disasters of the winter might make Austria question the wisdom of her own French alliance. Finally, for both Austria and Prussia the prospect of important subsidies from France's most inveterate enemy, England, might act as a powerful inducement for changing sides. As Napoleon assembled a new army for the coming campaign, all these questions were imponderable. Their resolution would depend as much on his opponents' decisions as on his own.

3

Russia, Austria, and Napoleon, 1812–1813

C zar Alexander I of Russia entered Vilna on 23 December 1812, a fortnight after its evacuation by the fleeing French. He was greeted as a conquering hero; his carriage was surrounded by cheering soldiers, who unharnessed its horses and dragged it to his residence themselves. The next day the army's veteran commander-in-chief, Field-Marshal Kutuzov, gave a great ball during which captured French flags were laid at the Czar's feet, a scene immortalized by Tolstoy in *War and Peace*. Outside, semi-naked French stragglers still wandered through the freezing streets, and the hospitals were piled high with the dead. As many as 30,000 corpses lay in and around the city.[1]

The victory of 1812 was the defining moment of Alexander I's life and reign. Before it, his record of achievement was at best mixed; after it, his status was transformed as the man who had first turned the tide against Napoleon. Born in 1777, the son of Czar Paul I and the Czarina Marie Feodorovna, Alexander certainly looked the part of a monarch; he was tall, charming and handsome, though by his 30s his fair hair was receding considerably. His personality, however, was deeply enigmatic, shaped by the bitter conflict between his unstable father Paul, and his formidable grandmother Catherine the Great. Despite the fact that Paul was her son, Catherine had detested him and virtually adopted Alexander as a replacement. Steering a course through these treacherous waters forced Alexander to conceal his true feelings from an early age, and to develop a remarkable capacity for dissimulation. Moreover, his education, devised by Catherine herself, had been based on some of the most liberal doctrines of the Enlightenment. This would later make him, as Czar, that strange contradiction, an autocratic ruler who professed liberal, even republican, principles.[2]

Alexander was also profoundly marked by the circumstances of his own accession to the throne, the result of Paul's murder, after five years of increasingly erratic rule, in a palace revolution in 1801. Although Alexander had been privy to the coup, he had insisted that his father's life be spared, though whether he tacitly accepted that this might not be possible has proved controversial ever since. In the event, Paul's death filled Alexander with guilt and remorse that never left him.

The paradoxes of Alexander's nature baffled his contemporaries, and caused many to dismiss him as weak and changeable. This impression was reinforced by the first years of the new Czar's reign. Domestically, Alexander introduced some liberal reforms, but failed to persevere with them. In 1805, in conjunction with Austria, he went to war against Napoleon, but was disastrously defeated at Austerlitz and then again, only slightly less disastrously, at Friedland. He then changed policy completely, and not only made peace with Napoleon at Tilsit, but signed an alliance with him. Although this change of course was largely justified by necessity, it was extremely unpopular in court circles, and taken as further proof of Alexander's lack of backbone. Yet the Czar's critics underestimated him. A far shrewder assessment came from Caulaincourt, who got to know him well as French ambassador to Russia from 1807 to 1811:

> People believe him to be weak but they are wrong... his amenable personality has its limits, and he will not go beyond them; these limits are as strong as iron, and will not be abandoned. His personality is by nature well-meaning, sincere and loyal, and his sentiments and principles are elevated, but beneath all this there exists an acquired royal dissimulation and a dogged persistence which nothing will overcome.[3]

1812 proved just how right Caulaincourt was. Alexander was not overawed by the French invasion, and even when Napoleon occupied Moscow refused to listen to his peace overtures. Indeed, he declared that rather than negotiate he would live on potatoes and grow a beard to his chest like a peasant.[4] As a result, Napoleon stayed far too long in Moscow waiting for an answer that never came, while the Russian army was reinforced and winter approached, and then retreated too late with terrible consequences. Alexander's steady nerve not only saved Russia, but changed the history of Europe.

Much of the Czar's 'dogged persistence' during these crucial weeks stemmed from a factor that had previously played little part in his life. As he anxiously waited in St Petersburg for news from the front, he increasingly turned to religion. Partly he was influenced by his devout friend Prince Alexander Golitsyn, and partly by his own reading of the Bible, which now became his constant companion. In particular, he took comfort from the words of the 91st Psalm: 'I shall say of the Lord, "He is my refuge and my fortress, my God in whom I trust."' When Napoleon was forced to retreat, and his withdrawal turned into catastrophe, Alexander saw this as a clear mark of God's favour and as a sign that henceforth he should faithfully do His will. As he confided to the Lutheran bishop Eylert: 'The flames of Moscow lit up my soul and the judgement of the Lord which manifested itself on our frozen plains filled my heart with an ardent faith I had never felt before.'[5]

In this exalted state of mind, Alexander made a crucial decision, which he announced to his assembled generals at Vilna on Christmas Eve 1812, which was also his birthday. The war would not stop at Russia's borders, but would be carried beyond them into Poland and Germany, with the liberation of Europe as its aim.[6] This new strategy had immense consequences. Had Alexander followed Kutuzov's advice and advanced no further, Napoleon would have retained much of his power. The continental system would probably have collapsed, but his empire would have remained largely intact. Instead, the Russian drive westwards set in motion a train of events, both military and political, that eventually brought him down.

For Alexander, the conflict was in many ways a personal duel between himself and Napoleon. 'Napoleon or me, I or him,' he had declared in September 1812, 'we cannot both rule at the same time.' Once the French retreat had started, he added that the only secure peace would be one signed in Paris, reflecting his visceral desire to avenge the burning of Moscow.[7] However, the demands of *Realpolitik* meant that over the next two years it would not always be possible for the Czar to fulfil all his desires. In particular, as Russia took the offensive she acquired new allies, some of whom were less committed to Napoleon's overthrow than Alexander, and their views had to be accommodated. As a result, even the Czar's determination not just to defeat but to topple his rival sometimes wavered.

Alexander's boldness was balanced by the caution of his chief diplomatic adviser, Karl von Nesselrode. From a German family with roots in the Rhineland, Nesselrode had joined the Russian foreign service and served in the embassies at The Hague, Berlin, and, with great success, Paris. A dark, bespectacled, scholarly-looking man of 32, Nesselrode was shrewd, discreet, and highly pragmatic.[8] In the new year of 1813, he submitted to the Czar a memorandum setting out, in his view, the best peace Russia could realistically hope to achieve. Significantly, it said nothing about invading France or dethroning Napoleon. Instead, it argued, the most sensible policy would simply be to reduce French power to manageable proportions. The best way to achieve this, Nesselrode argued, would be to 'force France back within her *natural limits*, so that all lands not contained between the Rhine and the Scheldt, the Pyrenees and the Alps should cease to be part of the French Empire, or even dependent upon it'.[9] This was an important statement; the concept of France's 'natural limits' would play a crucial role in the diplomacy of the next two years.

Even this goal, Nesselrode warned, could not be achieved without the help of Austria and Prussia. Austria, of course, was still closely tied to Napoleon by marriage as well as by alliance. By the time Nesselrode wrote his memorandum, however, there were clear signs that Prussia was shifting her allegiance from France to Russia. The process had begun in the last days of 1812. At the end of December the Prussian contingent attached to the retreating French army, and acting as a rearguard, was intercepted by the Russians at the village of Tauroggen on the road to Königsberg. Its commander General Yorck, like most of his compatriots, hated the French and deeply disliked being under their command. He entered into negotiation with the Russians, and made a remarkably bold decision. On 30 December, at a windmill near his headquarters, he signed an agreement removing his corps from French control and adopting neutral status.[10]

The Convention of Tauroggen, as it came to be known, changed the nature of the war, but in the short term placed King Frederick William III of Prussia in an extremely delicate position. He received the news of Yorck's unilateral action on 2 January 1813 while walking in his gardens at Potsdam, and immediately saw that it placed him in a cleft stick. If he disavowed Yorck, he risked a rising by his own people, who loathed French domination and were chafing to throw it off. If he did not, he would incur the still formidable wrath of Napoleon, and might even be arrested by the substantial French garrison in Berlin. In these circumstances, his first concern was his own safety. On 22 January, after careful secret preparations, he left Potsdam with his family and Guards regiments for Breslau, the provincial capital of Silesia. Shortly afterwards his senior ministers joined him there, making the city to all intents and purposes the seat of government.[11]

Frederick William had regained his freedom of action, but still hesitated over the course he should take. The continuing popular clamour against the French, and the real possibility that if he did not turn against Napoleon his own generals might turn against him, forced him to decide. By January 1813, two-thirds of the Prussian army was beyond his control, and this situation could not be allowed to continue.[12] On 28 February, Frederick William signed an alliance, the Treaty of Kalicz, with the Russians. This promised full Prussian military support to the war against Napoleon, with the aim of breaking his power in North Germany. In exchange, Prussia would regain all the territories and resources she had lost since 1806, or receive equivalent compensation if this did not prove possible. A fortnight later, on 16 March, Prussia declared war on France.

The adhesion of Prussia significantly boosted Russia's strength, but it remained unclear whether their combined armies could match the reserves and new forces Napoleon was frenetically marshalling for the spring campaigning season. If, however, Austria could be induced to change sides, this might decisively tip the balance; indeed, one of the articles of the Treaty of Kalicz was an invitation to her to do so as soon as possible. But Austria's policymakers had different ideas, and had already been developing them for some time.

Alongside Napoleon himself and Alexander, Francis I of Austria and his foreign minister Metternich were the central players in the drama of 1812–14. Forty-four in 1812, Francis I had already reigned for twenty years. Thin, cadaverous, and taciturn, he had once been dismissed by Napoleon as 'that skeleton . . . who owes his throne only to the merit of his ancestors'. This was far from accurate. Francis was not intellectually outstanding, but he was certainly not stupid. Homely and unpretentious, he was a devoted family man, and these virtues made him generally popular with his subjects, particularly the Viennese, whose dialect he enjoyed speaking. His capacity for work was remarkable, though his obsession with detail often exasperating.[13]

Francis' greatest quality was his resilience. Over the past decade he had lost two major wars to Napoleon, and been forced to accept French hegemony over the continent. He had been sustained in these trials by unswerving devotion to the Habsburg dynasty and its survival. With France now on the defensive, he was not about to make a hasty decision. Deeply cautious and conservative, he had no desire to risk the upheavals of war for either Napoleon or Alexander. Brokering peace between them was much more to his taste, especially as this would restore to him much-needed prestige. This was why, on hearing of the retreat from Moscow, Francis exclaimed: 'Now I can show the Emperor of the French who I am!'[14]

Francis' views coincided exactly with those of Metternich, his foreign minister and principal collaborator. Klemens Wenzel Lothar, Count Metternich, was about to enter the decisive phase of his career.[15] Although he had served Austria all his working life, he was not by birth an Austrian but, like Nesselrode, a Rhinelander. As a student at Strasbourg University in July 1789 he had watched a revolutionary crowd sack the city hall, and five years later he and his family had been forced to flee to Vienna from the advancing French armies.[16] His hatred and fear of the French Revolution were not in doubt, but he was no unthinking reactionary. Although his political ideal was traditional absolute monarchy, he was not opposed to all reform.[17] From this standpoint he had some sympathy for Napoleon, who had at least put the genie of mob rule back in its bottle. In their loathing of revolutionary radicalism, Metternich and the Emperor shared the same viewpoint.

In fact, by December 1812, Metternich had been collaborating with Napoleon for three years. In 1809 Austria had gambled on a war with France, had been defeated, and needed to chart a new course. Appointed foreign minister in the wake of this disaster, Metternich saw that French predominance in Europe was now an established fact, and felt that instead of challenging it, Austria should adapt to it, creating a partnership that would moderate its excesses. The symbol of this policy was the marriage of Marie-Louise to Napoleon, which Metternich personally negotiated. When Marie-Louise duly produced a son, immediately entitled 'King of Rome', in March 1811, not only was the Franco-Austrian alliance reinforced, but the Habsburgs acquired a family interest in the Bonaparte dynasty.

In 1812, Metternich was 39, elegant, polished, and extremely plausible. Stendhal once remarked: 'His blue-eyed, benevolent gaze would fool God himself.' For Henry Kissinger, who wrote what is still a fundamental work on Metternich's foreign policy, he was 'a Rococo figure, finely carved, all surface'.[18] Metternich was also remarkably vain, not only physically but also intellectually. His memoirs and letters reveal an immense self-satisfaction that rarely faltered. Yet as a statesman he was humane, rational, pragmatic, and highly effective. In 1795, he had married Eleonore, the granddaughter of Kaunitz, the great Austrian chancellor and foreign minister. A plain, highly intelligent woman, Eleonore was Metternich's principal confidant and tolerated his numerous affairs. Since he wrote more frankly to her than to anyone else, their correspondence is an important, and neglected, source for his actions and motivation between 1812 and 1814.[19]

The marriage link between France and Austria was reinforced in March 1812 by a formal military alliance. By virtue of this, three months later an Austrian contingent of 30,000 men entered Russia alongside Napoleon's army. As a gesture of French goodwill, this operated independently, and was commanded by an Austrian, Prince Karl Philipp Schwarzenberg, an experienced soldier and diplomat who had been Austrian ambassador to France for the previous two years.[20] During the Russian campaign Schwarzenberg was placed on Napoleon's most southerly flank, and cannily avoided almost any fighting. As a result, his corps remained more or less intact, awaiting further orders from Vienna.

Metternich's diplomatic response to the retreat from Moscow was a bold, but carefully crafted new strategy—Austrian mediation between France and Russia, with a compromise peace as its goal. This had several attractions. It would maximize Austria's bargaining power as a major continental state whose resources remained largely intact. It would also exploit her pivotal geographic position just south of the new theatre of war in central Europe, able to menace the flank of whichever side refused her overtures. Above all, it offered a way out of the French alliance, which, since the treaty of March 1812, had become far too close for Metternich's liking. For the mediation to be acceptable to Alexander I, Austria could not formally be linked to France, which meant her release from the alliance treaty of March 1812. By the same token, since Austria obviously could not be fighting on Napoleon's side while acting as mediator, Schwarzenberg's contingent would have to be withdrawn, as diplomatically as possible, from the French orbit.[21]

Metternich's 'armed' mediation, backed by an independent military force, was controversial at the time, and has remained so ever since. Almost all French historians of the period have held that his real aim from the moment of the Russian disaster was to destroy Napoleon. The mediation, they claim, was simply a ruse that enabled Austria to change sides in stages while avoiding the impression of betraying her ally too flagrantly. Equally, the compromise peace at which it ostensibly aimed was not a serious proposition, but a trap for Napoleon. It was designed to fail, so that he could be blamed for its failure, portrayed as an incorrigible warmonger and separated from moderate opinion within France.[22] This interpretation received its classic form in the early twentieth century, in Albert Sorel's

L'Europe et la Révolution Française. The most important recent French history of Napoleon's empire, published by Thierry Lentz in 2010, echoes Sorel's verdict on Metternich's policy: 'a cynical diplomacy, but how very clever'.[23]

Paradoxically, Metternich himself supplied material for this unflattering portrait. In his memoirs of the period, which he wrote in 1820, he was happy to present himself as Napoleon's inveterate enemy, only proposing peace terms that he knew the Emperor would refuse, thus undermining his domestic support. The only reason Austria did not turn on France immediately, he alleged, was her need to build up her army, limited after her defeat in 1809 to 150,000 men. Pretending to broker a peace settlement would thus buy time for her to bring decisive weight to bear on Russia's side. As he claimed to have told Francis I at this juncture: 'the path to war lies through armed mediation.'[24]

These assertions, however, do not accord either with Metternich's more general political philosophy, nor with his words and actions at the time. The distinguished schools of diplomacy Metternich had attended at Strasbourg, and later at the University of Mainz, stressed as its principal goal the preservation of equilibrium between states, and he remained faithful to this all his life.[25] In the context of late 1812, equilibrium would not be served by the humiliation of France and a change in her regime. This would simply increase Russia's power to a dangerous degree, and substitute the Czar's hegemony for Napoleon's. This concern was particularly acute for Austria. As a central European power, she was potentially threatened by Russia to the east, Prussia to the north, and France to the west, and could only preserve herself by keeping them in a state of mutual balance. A France that remained powerful but returned to acceptable limits, with a half-Habsburg heir to the throne, would be an important counterweight to the Czar's ambitions.[26]

If mediation was meant to lead to war with Napoleon rather than a general settlement, it is unlikely that Metternich would seriously have considered the terms of such a peace. Yet in fact there is evidence he did so from an early stage. In December 1812, he confided to his friend Count Hardenberg, the Hanoverian representative in Vienna, his 'political dream'. Significantly, at its heart lay the same proposal his fellow-Rhinelander Nesselrode would make two months later to Alexander I: France should retreat behind her 'natural limits' of the Rhine, the Alps, and the Pyrenees. Metternich added that the German states should regain their independence under the protection of Austria and a reconstituted Prussia, Italy should be divided into two substantial states, and Russia should return to her pre-1807 frontier.[27]

This vision is striking, but it is based on a second-hand source, a report by Hardenberg rather than from Metternich himself. Far more direct proof of Metternich's sincerity in seeking a compromise peace comes in his correspondence with Schwarzenberg. Portly and bewhiskered, Schwarzenberg had an air of stolidity that belied his keen intelligence and shrewdness. He was also honest, trustworthy, and generally well-liked. Having gained Napoleon's confidence as Austrian ambassador to France, Schwarzenberg was predisposed to dialogue with him, and his considerable experience both of diplomacy and warfare made him irrepleaceable to Metternich. The letters between both men from the winter of 1812 to the spring of 1814, which have only partially been published, are an essential source for the history of the period.[28]

The frankness of these exchanges is striking, but not surprising. It would have been counterproductive for Metternich to lie to someone as crucial to his plans as Schwarzenberg. He may have been devious in other contexts, but these letters reveal what he was genuinely thinking, and show that for him peace was an end in itself, not merely a ruse to outwit Napoleon. As early as 3 October 1812, just after the fall of Moscow, Metternich expressed to Schwarzenberg the hope that a French victory in Russia would be balanced by defeats in Spain, giving an opportunity to negotiate a moderate European settlement. 'The end is very close on the other side of the Pyrenees,' he commented. 'If only the result were a general peace!'[29]

The news that Napoleon's offensive had stalled in Moscow, and that he had made peace overtures to the Czar, gave Metternich his opportunity. On 9 December, he addressed formal instructions to Engelbert von Floret, Schwarzenberg's temporary replacement as Austria's ambassador to France, who had accompanied Napoleon into Russia. Floret was to propose to the duc de Bassano, the French foreign minister, who was also with the army, that Austria sound out Russia and England about the possibility of peace talks. A phrase Metternich used two days later to Schwarzenberg offers further evidence that his peace initiative aimed to help rather than to harm Napoleon. 'All Europe is in a state of tension difficult to describe,' he wrote, 'what is happening is unprecedented, and I have good reason to suppose that Napoleon should be extremely grateful to us, and to me in particular.

Austria at this moment is giving him proof of great loyalty and of sentiments that few other powers would display.'[30]

Metternich's strongest statement of his genuine commitment to peace came in a letter of 16 January 1813. It came in the form of a comment on similar sentiments expressed by Napoleon's own chief of staff. Marshal Berthier, Prince of Neuchâtel, had been the Emperor's closest military collaborator for the past sixteen years. Now 59—fifteen years older than Napoleon—he had been shattered by the retreat from Moscow and his dearest wish was to return to Grosbois, his palatial estate outside Paris. On 24 December 1812, he had written to Schwarzenberg, a good friend, a letter graphically depicting the horrors of the retreat. He made clear what he hoped the outcome would be: 'Peace, our Wednesdays at Grosbois returning from the hunt, wives, children and friends, good health; that is what I wish for both you and myself in the new year.' Schwarzenberg sent a copy of this to Metternich, who replied heartily and concisely endorsing Berthier's words: 'I want only rest; I cry like Neuchâtel, *peace, peace* and have no other desire.'[31]

As to the nature of this peace, for Metternich the distinction between a 'general' settlement between all the combatants, and a 'separate' one between only some of them, was crucial. In the twenty years since the French wars had begun, there had been many separate peace treaties between France and her enemies, but only fourteen months in which hostilities on all sides had entirely ceased. Metternich felt, with some justification, that the issues at stake were too complex and wide-ranging to be resolved by one, or even several, bilateral treaties between individual belligerents. Yet a general peace conference also had its drawbacks. The main one was that the most intractable issues would dominate the proceedings at the expense of areas where agreement was easier to reach. Of these potential stumbling-blocks, the most obvious one was Franco–British rivalry.

Peace between England and France was the greatest prize at which Metternich aimed, but it was also the most difficult to achieve. Both countries were locked in a conflict that was not simply continental, but the latest phase in a century-old struggle for global dominance. By 1812, this struggle had reached a stalemate. With the exception of Spain and Portugal, Napoleon dominated the continent, but England had conquered all of France's colonial possessions and achieved unchallenged maritime supremacy. For the continental concessions implied in Metternich's peace plan, the most obvious compensations for Napoleon to demand were return of the captured French colonies and the dismantling of wartime British restrictions on maritime trade. He also had a powerful card to play of his own: his control of Holland and Belgium and the port of Antwerp in particular, whose suitability as an invasion base posed an existential threat to England. It was unclear whether either side would give up its trump cards—naval and colonial power for England, the Low Countries for France—in the interests of a general settlement.[32]

What Metternich did not know when he sent Floret his instructions in Russia was that Napoleon had already abandoned the army and was en route to France. Left behind in Lithuania, Floret was of no further use; his mission would have to be accomplished in Paris, and for this a new envoy was needed. Metternich's choice fell on Count Ferdinand Bubna. Stout and jovial, though afflicted by gout, Bubna, like Schwarzenberg, was an experienced soldier and diplomat. He also knew Napoleon, having met him during the peace negotiations of 1809. His task now was to obtain Napoleon's consent to Austrian mediation, and to gauge what his next moves might be. Ostensibly, Bubna was simply delivering a letter from Francis I, and his instructions forbade him to enter into formal negotiations.

Bubna arrived in Paris on 30 December 1812, and was received at the Tuileries the following evening. Napoleon kept Bubna on his feet for two and a half hours as he talked and paced up and down his study, which must have been agonizing for Bubna, since his gout had flared up during his journey. It was clear that Napoleon was mostly thinking of the coming campaign; early in the meeting he demanded that Austria double the size of Schwarzenberg's auxiliary corps, which Bubna did his best to convince him was impossible. Austrian mediation, Bubna's central object, he agreed to with little argument, and even sketched out his peace terms. Considering the scale of the Russian disaster, these were uncompromising; his armies would withdraw from Portugal and Spain, but his brother Joseph must retain the Spanish throne, his brother-in-law Murat must remain king of Naples, and he would cede 'not one village' of the Duchy of Warsaw. Yet Metternich, when he received these conditions, was not discouraged, seeing them simply as the opening gambit in a negotiation.[33]

The next stage of the mediation could now begin. At the beginning of February 1813, Metternich despatched two envoys, Baron Ludwig von Lebzeltern and Freiherr Johann von Wessenberg, to seek Russian and British acceptance of Austria's good offices. Lebzeltern arrived on 5 March at the Russian headquarters at Kalisz and was greeted effusively by the Czar, whom he knew well from a previous posting in St Petersburg. Concerned not to alienate Austria, whom he hoped might eventually change sides, Alexander agreed to accept her mediation provided England and Prussia did so too. Things did not go so smoothly for Wessenberg in London. Arriving there on 29 March after an exhausting journey, he found the English press and public opinion, buoyed up by Napoleon's defeat in Russia and Wellington's victories in Spain, deeply hostile to a compromise that might squander the fruits of victory. The Prince Regent, effectively head of state since the final madness of his father George III, received Wessenberg cordially but unofficially on 9 April, and on the same day his government formally declined Austrian mediation.[34]

This refusal was a grave blow to Metternich's plans. From now on the general peace he wanted so much would have to be a two-stage process; first a continental peace between France, Russia, and Prussia, and then a final negotiation with England. A continental settlement would help considerably in this, since England would then risk isolation if she did not come to the conference table. But the task of reaching a continental settlement was itself greatly complicated by England's absence. In particular, and with some justification, Napoleon could refuse to make critical concessions on the mainland without knowing what England might demand of him afterwards. Though still not impossible, Metternich's task had become significantly harder.

The final power that Metternich had to draw into his negotiations was Prussia. To achieve this, he gave assurances that French historians have again seen as evidence of his intention to betray Napoleon. In January 1813, while Prussia and Austria were still both nominally allies of France, the Prussian government asked Metternich if its friendly relations with Austria would be jeopardized if it broke with France. He replied that they would not, which were surprising words from an ally of Napoleon. Yet this response cannot be so neatly pigeonholed, since Metternich was engaged in a delicate balancing act. Even after the Russian disaster he still thought that the major obstacle to a compromise peace would be Napoleon's obstinacy, and that Prussia's defection might force him to see reason. Metternich calculated that Russia's reinforcement by Prussia 'significantly tips the scales in favour of peace, by diminishing France's resources'. He did not, however, see this as a first step towards Napoleon's actual overthrow.[35]

The same is true of Austria's military planning at this time. As the Russian armies advanced, Schwarzenberg's auxiliary corps fell back before them and then, without consulting Napoleon, agreed to an armistice at Zeyes on 30 January 1813. At the same time, the corps was withdrawn from French

overall command. Under the pretext of defence against Russia, a further
70,000 Austrian troops were mobilized. Albert Sorel and his disciples assert
that these measures too were really directed against France. It is much more
likely that they simply aimed at recovering Austria's independence from all
sides, rather than preparing an offensive alliance against Napoleon. Metternich did not hesitate to threaten Napoleon's enemies with force as well, if
necessary. If Russia and England brought exaggerated claims to the conference table, he warned, this, and only this, would drive Austria to 'increase
the limited support stipulated in her treaty with France.'[36]

Although they had accepted Austria's mediation, in the meantime Napoleon
and Alexander had no intention of halting the war. Alexander had just won a
great victory, and his declared aim was still the liberation of Europe from
French domination. For his part, after the Russian catastrophe Napoleon felt
an urgent need to reassert himself on the battlefield, and to prove to friends
and enemies alike that he was still the military genius they feared. Throughout
the spring of 1813, he made his preparations. The *senatus-consultum* of 11
January had levied 350,000 conscripts for the army, and 137,000 raised the
previous autumn were already in the last stages of basic training. On 20 March
the Legislative Body passed the 1813 budget, which increased revenue by
confiscating municipal property in return for government bonds.[37]

On 30 March, to bind Austria further to him, or at least to make it even
more embarrassing for her to desert him, Napoleon announced that Marie-
Louise would become regent when he left for the front. The decision was
also motivated by domestic politics, making the order of succession absolutely clear in the event of any repetition of Malet's coup d'état. There was a
long tradition of female regencies in France, most notably that of Marie de
Medici during the minority of Louis XIII, and Anne of Austria during that
of Louis XIV. Following Napoleon's patriarchal instincts, however, the
constitution forbade a woman to exercise the regency, so the Senate had
to amend it. Marie-Louise was assisted by a council consisting of the princes
of the blood and the grand dignitaries of the empire. In theory this included
Napoleon's brothers Joseph and Louis, and his stepson Eugène de Beauharnais, but none of these were currently in France. As Arch-Chancellor,
Cambacérès was 'first councillor of the regency' and Marie-Louise's principal adviser. As Vice-Grand-Elector, Talleyrand also had a seat.[38]

On 9 April, at the palace of Saint-Cloud, Napoleon received Schwarzenberg, who had left the command of the auxiliary corps and was returning to
Paris as Austrian ambassador. Schwarzenberg's report to Metternich of the
interview, which lasted almost four hours, is the most penetrating account
that we possess of Napoleon's motivation at this juncture.[39] Schwarzenberg's impression was that he had changed; he was 'mild, confiding... but
more thoughtful and preoccupied than he had ever seemed before'. His self-
confidence had clearly been shaken by the retreat from Moscow. As
Schwarzenberg tellingly observed: 'he seemed like a man who fears being
stripped of the prestige he has previously enjoyed; his expression seemed to
ask me if I still thought he was the same man.'[40]

As the interview wore on, it became clear that Napoleon had two basic
concerns. The first was that, following Prussia's example, Austria would
now desert him. 'He fears nothing so much as a break with Austria,'
Schwarzenberg wrote. 'He knows the inevitable result would be a war
whose outcome would be difficult to predict.' Napoleon therefore emphasized his willingness to make peace, claiming that the obstacles to this would
come not from him but from England. He also offered Austria a crude
territorial bribe to stay loyal. 'Speaking fast and between his teeth', he
outlined a plan to punish Prussia for her treachery by wiping her from the
map, with her province of Silesia going to Austria. Schwarzenberg replied
virtuously that his Emperor's goal was not to destroy existing states, but to
create 'a just equilibrium between the powers'.[41]

Napoleon's second concern was even more profound. This was about the
consequences at home if he made too many concessions. His words on this
subject were extremely revealing:

> You are wrong to think that I do not sincerely wish for peace, but my position
> is difficult; if I made a dishonourable peace, I would be lost; an old-established
> government, where the links between ruler and people have been forged over
> centuries can, if circumstances demand, accept a harsh peace. I am a new man,
> I need to be more careful of public opinion, because I need it on my side. If
> I signed a peace of this sort, it is true that at first one would hear only cries of joy,
> but within a short time the government would be bitterly attacked, I would lose
> the esteem and also the confidence of my people, because the Frenchman has a
> vivid imagination, he loves glory, exaltation, he is hard-bitten.[42]

These words offered a remarkable insight into what Napoleon thought of
his countrymen. They also reflected the turbulent legacy of the French
Revolution. In Napoleon's view, military glory was essential for a new

regime like his, in a country like France with its ingrained martial instincts, and it was his Bourbon predecessors' neglect of this that had led to their overthrow. 'Do you know the original cause of the fall of the Bourbons?' he asked Schwarzenberg rhetorically. 'It dates from Rossbach.'[43] The battle of Rossbach of 1757 was France's first great defeat of the Seven Years' War, which had permanently damaged the monarchy's prestige.

If his regime did succumb, Napoleon was in no doubt as to who would benefit. 'With a sort of emotion', he went on: 'Ah, if I was unlucky, anything could happen; anything could happen to my dynasty; the Bourbons don't worry me, it's the Jacobins who would seize hold of France, and then who knows where the combustion would end.'[44] The Jacobins had been the leading radical grouping in the Revolution, and their most extreme wing had been responsible both for the Reign of Terror at home and the first revolutionary conquests abroad. If he himself were tarnished by an inglorious peace, Napoleon argued, the standard of French nationalism would pass back into these bloody hands. Their military reputation in tatters since Rossbach, the Bourbons would seem a poor alternative.

This argument may simply have been a form of blackmail, disguising Napoleon's unwillingness to make peace on any terms other than his own. Yet invoking the horrors of the Revolution was more than just a cynical ruse. The Malet conspiracy, and those of Toulon and Marseilles, had shown that there were still groups of republicans prepared to mount a rising. For Napoleon, this revived older dangers. He had traumatic memories of the 1790s, and appears to have been genuinely alarmed that an inglorious peace would revive their savagery and strife. As a young lieutenant, he had witnessed the overthrow of the monarchy by the Paris crowd on 10 August 1792, and the subsequent massacre of Louis XVI's Swiss Guard. It was the first time he had ever seen fighting.[45] As he later recalled: 'None of the battlefields I have seen since have ever seemed piled with so many corpses as those heaps of Swiss, whether because they appeared to be more in such a small space, or because it was the first scene of this sort I had witnessed.' He had also been disgusted by the atrocities he saw committed, adding: 'I saw well-dressed women performing the most unspeakable indecencies on the bodies of the dead Swiss.'[46]

Napoleon's biographers have often underlined the profound impression made on him by 10 August 1792, and ascribed to it the abiding fear of angry crowds that contrasted so strikingly with his courage on the battlefield.[47] As a soldier, Napoleon regarded falling in battle as inherently glorious, and a risk to be faced with equanimity. In contrast, he recoiled from the sort of death he had seen inflicted by an enraged civilian mob. The brutalities of 10 August also held a political lesson. Louis XVI had been overthrown in the middle of a revolutionary war. His distaste for the conflict had been obvious, his patriotism had become suspect, and deposition and death had been the consequences. As Napoleon saw it, the warning was clear. He had inherited that war, and if he failed to pursue it at all costs and to total victory, he risked sharing Louis XVI's fate. In this light, his assertions to Schwarzenberg were not a negotiating ploy, but expressed a genuine fear.

Schwarzenberg had tried to argue that peace could be achieved without the need to 'risk the chances of a campaign', but Napoleon had already made his decision. Just six days later, he left for the front. Before his departure, on Sunday 11 April, he held a grand military review in the courtyard of the Tuileries for what turned out to be the last time. Twenty years later, Balzac recaptured the scene with loving precision in *La Femme de Trente Ans*: 'The greater part of the vast gravelled space was as empty as an arena, ready for the evolutions of those silent masses disposed with the symmetry of military art. The sunlight blazed back from ten thousand bayonets in points of flame; the breeze ruffled the men's helmet plumes till they swayed like the crests of forest trees before a gale.'[48]

So soon after the Russian disaster, the scene evokes that patriotic reaction within France on which Napoleon counted so heavily, and whose appropriation by others he so much feared: 'Most of the gazers in the crowd had bidden farewell—perhaps forever—to the men who made up the rank and file of the battalions; but even those most hostile to the Emperor, in their hearts, put up fervent prayers to heaven for the glory of France.' Yet Balzac also struck another note, of fragility and unease, beneath the frenzied enthusiasm that greeted Napoleon's appearance: 'There was something preternatural about it—it was magic at work . . . or rather it was a fugitive image of a reign itself so fugitive.'[49]

4

War and Diplomacy, Spring 1813

On 17 April 1813, after a virtually non-stop journey of forty hours from Paris, Napoleon arrived at Mainz, where half his forces were concentrating. He stayed there for a week, attempting to create order out of the confusion of the first stages of a campaign. Through his own extraordinary efforts over the previous three months, he was well on the way to replacing the army destroyed in Russia. Now, however, the theatre of war had shifted several hundred miles east, to the centre of Germany. Lands entirely dominated by France just a year before were now on the front line.

The catalyst for this was the defection of Prussia, which had given a tremendous impetus to the Russian advance west. By the terms of the Treaty of Kalicz, she agreed to put 80,000 troops in the field, while Russia promised 150,000 of her own.[1] This was achieved by a mobilization of remarkable speed and efficiency, whose foundations had been laid over the previous five years. After her shattering defeat by Napoleon in 1806, Prussia had undergone a thoroughgoing process of reform. In the military sphere, this had involved adapting the new French model of the meritocratic, citizen army. Three-quarters of the officers of the old army were dismissed or retired, commissioned ranks were thrown open to non-nobles, and a new Ministry of War was set up. Infantry tactics became more flexible, and the more brutal punishments such as running the gauntlet were abolished. The army was also expanded, albeit surreptitiously. After 1806, Napoleon had insisted that it be limited to 42,000 men, but under the so-called *Krumpersystem* devised by the military reformer General von Scharnhorst, each year a proportion of these were retired and replaced by new recruits who thus received training. By February 1813, this scheme had turned out 36,500 extra reservists ready to join the colours.[2]

It took the moment of decision after the Russian disaster to force through the most important military reform of all. On 9 February 1813, a royal decree created a *Landwehr*, or militia, of 110,000 men, a significant step towards the formation of a citizen army. There was a rush of volunteers, though with variations according to region and social class. Artisans constituted 2 per cent of the population, but 12 per cent of Landwehr volunteers. Even more strikingly, the educated comprised 7 per cent of the population, but 41 per cent of volunteers. In contrast peasants, who formed 75 per cent of the Prussian population, provided only 18 per cent of volunteers. By this token, Prussian patriotism in 1813 was a strongly urban phenomenon. Whatever its roots, it yielded impressive results. By mid-March 1813 almost 70,000 men had been put into the field, and over the next months these numbers increased again sharply.[3]

In several areas of Prussia, as well as other areas of Germany, this mobilization was reinforced by a popular anti-French rising. In East Prussia, stragglers from the army retreating out of Russia were set upon by armed bands of peasants. In the following months, revolts broke out in the North German port cities of Hamburg and Lübeck, and as far west as the Grand Duchy of Berg on the Rhine. Traditionally, this upsurge has been seen as the beginning of modern German nationalism, anticipating Germany's subsequent unification. 1813 certainly did see an outpouring of nationalist literature, from the propaganda of Father Jahn to the poetry of Arndt and Körner. The philosopher Fichte had already published his influential *Addresses to the German Nation* in 1808, but he cancelled his lectures at the University of Berlin so his students could join the Prussian army.[4] On 17 March Frederick William III issued a proclamation, *An Mein Volk*, in which he exhorted his people to expel the French. A week later, he and Alexander I published a joint declaration, again calling for a popular insurrection and holding out the prospect of a unified Germany. More practically, an administrative council was set up to govern the newly liberated German territories on a centralized basis, headed by the former Prussian prime minister, and German nationalist, Baron vom Stein.[5]

Despite these stirrings, whether the majority of Germany's people or her rulers were really motivated by a desire for national unity remains debatable. Frederick William's enthusiasm for the cause quickly cooled once Napoleon had been pushed back to the Rhine, and German unification had to wait for a further fifty-eight years. Frederick William addressed his proclamation *An mein Volk* not just to German Prussians, but also to the

Map 2. The Confederation of the Rhine in 1812.

significant numbers of Silesians, Pomeranians, and Lithuanians who happened to live within Prussia's borders. Dynastic loyalty, rather than new ideas of ethnic or even linguistic identity, formed the basis of the appeal. The same is true of the popular response the proclamation generated. There is strong evidence that this focused on the person of the king and on Prussian patriotism, rather than any pan-German nationalism. Elsewhere in Germany, the pattern was similar; in the kingdom of Westphalia, the people rose up not to achieve national unity, but to restore the previous ruler deposed by Napoleon, the Elector of Hesse-Kassel.[6]

Perhaps the most potent recruiting-sergeant of all was simple hatred of the French, born of years of brutal exactions. It is no coincidence that Prussia had suffered more from French domination than any other German state. After her defeat in 1806, she had lost half of her territory and population, and been forced to pay an indemnity and the costs of a two-year occupation that came to a staggering 217 million thalers, almost bankrupting the state. The consequences of these demands for the ordinary inhabitants were predictably dire. Massing in East Prussia in the summer of 1812 for the invasion of Russia, the French troops took almost all the harvest, plundered farms, and if horses were not available for requisitioning used peasants as beasts of burden. In this context, the fact that most Prussian volunteers and recruits in 1813 came from regions occupied at some point by Napoleon's armies is hardly surprising. Neither is the anti-French ferocity they displayed in the battles of the next two years.[7]

There had been rebellions in Germany against Napoleon before; what made this one different was the presence of a victorious Russian army on her eastern border. Unaided, patriotic risings against the French had been doomed to failure. Now, with Russian support, success seemed possible. Unrest was further stoked by the speed at which news of Napoleon's defeat spread, aided by the crumbling of censorship in the wake of the disaster. For their part, the Russian generals were not slow to exploit the situation. They had a great superiority in cavalry, particularly in light horsemen such as Cossacks, over the French, who had lost huge numbers of horses in the 1812 campaign. In the early spring of 1813, they used this to launch three flying columns over the river Oder to raid into North Germany. These units had spectacular success, capturing Hamburg and Berlin itself, and contributing substantially to Frederick William III's decision to break with Napoleon. These daring attacks also seriously alarmed the French commanders, who fell back west behind the line of the river Elbe.[8] Thus by March 1813 a combination of Russian shrewdness and upheaval in Germany had forced the French out of Prussia and Poland almost without a fight. This ensured that the following campaign would be fought in the heart of central Europe, further undermining Napoleon's position and his authority.

With their way cleared by the Cossacks, the Russian and Prussian forces advanced on the Elbe. They were divided into three armies. To the north, 30,000 Prussians under generals Yorck and Bülow linked up with 19,000 Russians led by General Wittgenstein. To the south, 27,000 Prussians and 14,000 Russians commanded by General Blücher marched on Dresden, followed by the main Russian force of 30,000 men under their commander-in-chief, Kutuzov.[9] Overall, the soldiers were of variable quality. Many of the hastily raised Prussian *Landwehr* units had poor firing skills and were very badly equipped, sometimes lacking coats and shoes. Those from Silesia, in particular, proved unable to face enemy fire. Yet others, such as those fighting under Yorck on the northern flank, proved very effective. The morale of the Prussian troops was also improved by the more humane discipline recently introduced, while the standard of the officers had been raised by the opening up of commissions to non-nobles.[10]

The Prussians were especially fortunate in their leaders. Yorck and Bülow were both tough, experienced soldiers, who added substantially to their reputations in the fighting of 1813 and 1814.[11] But the outstanding Prussian general of the coming campaign proved to be their colleague Blücher. The 71-year old Gebhard Leberecht von Blücher was a jovial, hard-drinking, fiercely patriotic, cavalry veteran, though his abilities were sometimes compromised by uncertain mental health. In 1808, he had had a serious breakdown, whose most alarming symptom was the conviction that he was pregnant with an elephant. Francophobic even in his delusions, he believed it had been fathered on him by a French soldier. By 1813, however, he had recovered. Despite occasional relapses, over the next two years he emerged as the only allied commander whose attacking energy matched Napoleon's.[12]

In contrast, the allied command structure posed problems. Strategy was decided in unwieldy councils of war, which gave particular authority to the two monarchs, Alexander and Frederick William, who were both with their armies in the field. In practice, since Frederick William was very much the junior partner, Alexander assumed an increasingly central role in military affairs. This was partly a response to dissensions among his own generals. Kutuzov, who had cleared the French from Russian soil, fell ill at Bunzlau in Silesia and died there in April 1813. A few days later, General

Wittgenstein was appointed as commander-in-chief of both the Russian and Prussian armies, but he failed to impose himself on his colleagues, and as a result relied heavily on Alexander. The Czar shouldered this burden out of inclination as well as duty. He had always had a taste for military glory, and for personally leading his armies. Unfortunately, while his strategic decisions were often sound, he was a poor battlefield commander, as he had proved, with disastrous effect, at Austerlitz in 1805. His interventions in the battles of 1813 and 1814 were rarely helpful, and complicated, rather than eased, the problems his generals faced.[13]

With so many of Napoleon's veterans lost in the 1812 campaign, the Russian army, not the French, was now the most experienced and effective in Europe. Observers were almost unanimous in praising the dogged courage and resilience of the Russian infantry, its ferocity in attack and steadiness in retreat. Recruited by conscription from the serf population, the soldiers served a twenty-five-year term that was in effect for life, under ferocious discipline. Even officers could be beaten by their superiors. A series of military reforms from 1808 had introduced more flexible infantry formations and improved the artillery, which was both excellent and plentiful. However, in the spring of 1813 the army faced serious logistical problems. It was exhausted by the fighting of the previous year; of Kutuzov's main army, which had numbered 97,000 in September 1812, only 42,000 men were fit for duty, while fully 48,000 were in hospital. Substantial reinforcements were on their way, but a march of over 1,000 miles lay between them and the theatre of war. Until they arrived, the existing troops would have to hold the line.[14]

For the moment at least, this gave Napoleon the advantage. Although the army that had invaded Russia had been destroyed, it had left behind on its march enough reserves at the depots to begin the process of rebuilding the shattered regiments. To these could be added four regiments of the Imperial Guard withdrawn from service in Spain, four further guard battalions stationed in France and Germany, and 12,000 gunners from the French naval artillery. These veterans stiffened the first wave of 75,000 conscripts now arriving. Remarkably, four months after the retreat from Moscow, Napoleon had managed to recreate an army that outnumbered the Russians and Prussians by 200,000 to 110,000. Its quality, however, was uneven. Although the new recruits proved steady on the battlefield, they were not prepared for the extensive foraging and exhausting marches so crucial to

Napoleon's style of mobile warfare, and sickness and straggling became an increasing problem.[15]

The major problem Napoleon faced was a shortage of cavalry—175,000 horses had died in Russia, and the gap left could not be filled. The crisis was compounded by the loss of Poland and north-eastern Germany, which contained many important stud-farms. France was ransacked for horses, but they took time to train, and were often of poor quality. The same was true of the conscript cavalrymen; many went into the field unable even to saddle their horses properly. In the spring of 1813, Napoleon thus lacked sufficient cavalry to fulfil two crucial functions: firstly to act as a screen for his army and gather intelligence about the enemy's movements, and secondly to pursue a defeated enemy after a battle and turn their retreat into rout. Had the French cavalry been able to perform these tasks as in the past, the outcome of the campaign could have been very different.[16]

The strategy Napoleon formed in 1813 was typically bold. At its heart was an offensive through north-east Germany to the Polish border, to outflank the Russians and threaten their communications. In Napoleon's view, this plan offered other important advantages. If Berlin were recaptured along the way, Prussia could be knocked out of the war, or at least her mobilization severely disrupted. In addition, a series of French garrisons, left stranded in fortresses along the rivers Oder and Vistula by the Russian advance, could be relieved. In total these numbered 50,000 troops, including 8,000 in Stettin, 4,000 in Torun, and 27,000 in Danzig—a significant potential reinforcement for the French army. As it turned out, this plan could not be fully implemented, since the strength of the Russo-Prussian advance in the southern sector, towards Dresden and the river Elbe, made it necessary for Napoleon to concentrate the bulk of his forces there. Yet he kept returning to it in the course of the campaign, twice despatching significant forces northward to take the Prussian capital.[17]

Even had it been possible to execute it fully, this strategy was probably flawed. The military value of relieving the garrisons on the Oder and the Vistula remains dubious, since a significant number of the men stationed there were sick, wounded, or invalid survivors of the retreat from Moscow. In fact, they may have been performing a better service by staying where they were, forcing appreciable numbers of the enemy to besiege them, than by rejoining the main army. In his study of the war of 1813 in Germany, Michael Leggiere has further argued that Napoleon miscalculated the importance of Berlin to Prussia's war effort, and that even if he had captured

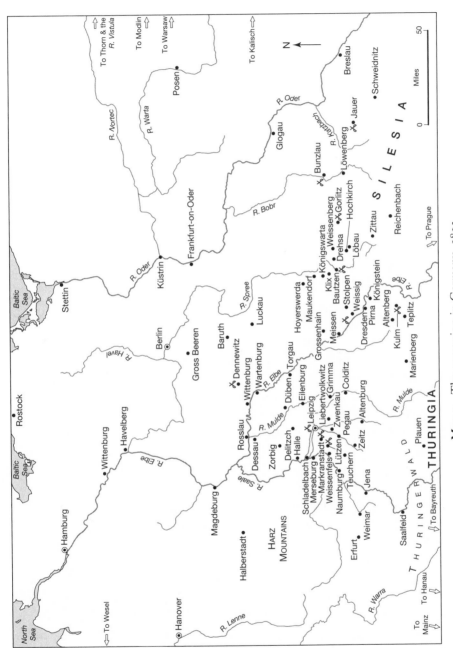

Map 3. The campaign in Germany, 1813.

it Prussia's mobilization, which centred on East Prussia and Silesia, would not seriously have been affected. Napoleon also overestimated the effect of capturing Berlin on Prussian morale; the Austrians had abandoned Vienna and kept on fighting in both 1805 and 1809, and the Russians had evacuated and burned their historic capital Moscow just six months before without slackening their war effort. By twice attempting to take Berlin with detached forces, Napoleon violated his own cardinal principle of keeping his troops concentrated to deliver a knockout blow to the enemy. This was all the more dangerous given how short a time his superiority of numbers would last. The Russians and Prussians had far greater reserves of reinforcements, which would soon arrive on the scene.[18]

On 24 April, Napoleon left Mainz and headed east for the river Saale between Merseburg and Naumburg, the area of concentration for all his troops. He knew that the main Russo-Prussian army had crossed the Elbe and was massing between Leipzig and Altenburg. For the moment, it had to be dealt with, and the attack on Berlin postponed. Napoleon decided to attack the enemy's right flank and push on to the Elbe at Dresden, at a stroke cutting his enemies' lines of communication east and their link with Berlin to the north. This achieved, he would then revert to his original plan and march on Berlin. On 1 May, his forces crossed the Saale, heading for Leipzig and then Dresden. Almost immediately, a misfortune struck. The veteran Marshal Bessières, commanding the Imperial Guard, rode into the line of fire of an enemy cannon and was killed outright. He was a personal friend of Napoleon, who was shaken by his death.[19]

Though Napoleon did not know it, his line of march meant that the right flank of his army was exposed to attack by the Russians and Prussians under Wittgenstein, who were now to the south of him. This flank consisted of the 3rd corps under Marshal Ney, the hero of the retreat from Moscow. On the morning of 2 May, it was bivouacked in a scattered formation in and around the town of Lützen, while Napoleon in the centre pressed on towards Leipzig.[20] Despite Napoleon's instructions, Ney failed to make a proper reconnaissance of the surrounding area. Seeing his opportunity, Wittgenstein ordered an attack just before midday. Ney was caught by surprise, but was saved by the fact that his men around Lützen were stationed in a series of easily defensible villages, and that Marshal Marmont's nearby 6th corps came swiftly to his aid. There was furious fighting around the villages, which changed hands several times, but the French line was not broken.

Further along the road to Leipzig, Napoleon could now hear the gunfire, and realized that a full-scale battle was under way to his right. He immediately turned back, and was on the field by 2.30 p.m. He arrived in the nick of time, since Ney's and Marmont's line was beginning to give way. Seeing how critical the situation was, and determined to retrieve his reputation after his defeat in Russia, he himself led his troops to the assault. 'This was probably the day, of his whole career, on which Napoleon incurred the greatest personal danger on the field of battle,' Marmont later recalled.[21] By 5.30 p.m. the front had stabilized, and reinforcements were in place for a counterattack on the enemy's centre and left flank. At 6, after a massed artillery barrage at point-blank range, the Imperial Guard went forward, broke the opposing lines, and forced the Russians and Prussians into a retreat. The battle of Lützen was thus a French victory. It was not, however, the decisive one that Napoleon so badly needed, and there were other warning signs. Crucially, the lack of cavalry prevented a pursuit of the enemy that could have turned their retreat into a rout. The fact that the Imperial Guard, normally kept in reserve, had to go into action also showed that Napoleon no longer had the resources he had once enjoyed.[22]

Nonetheless, Lützen provided the necessary answer to those who thought that Napoleon was a spent military force, and the sense of relief in the French camp was palpable. This is clearly reflected in a letter sent two days later from the battlefield itself by Caulaincourt, who was accompanying the army, to the comte de Narbonne, the newly-appointed French ambassador to Vienna. 'The Emperor directed all the operations himself,' Caulaincourt wrote. 'His Majesty was once again the general-in-chief he had been in Italy and Egypt.' This information was not meant for Narbonne alone. Schwarzenberg and Bubna, the Austrian diplomats who had most recently seen Napoleon, were now back in Vienna, and Caulaincourt instructed Narbonne to pass on to them his account of the battle, so that they could 'make good use of these details at their court'.[23] The news of Lützen, suitably presented, might persuade them to use their influence to keep Austria on France's side.

Napoleon's next moves marked a reversion to his original strategy. Marshal Ney was sent north with 45,000 men—later reinforced to 84,000—to relieve the besieged French garrisons at Torgau and Wittenberg, and then march on Berlin.[24] Meanwhile, Napoleon himself would push on eastwards in pursuit of the enemy's main body. The plan was meant to be flexible—if the Russians and Austrians decided to make a stand, Ney could be recalled to give the French forces a decisive superiority. However, sending off a commander on a specific mission while reserving the option to call him back risked creating confusion—which is what in fact happened.

On 3 May, Napoleon resumed his advance. On the 8th he reached Dresden, the capital of Saxony, which would be his headquarters for the rest of the campaign. The king of Saxony, Frederick Augustus I, was Napoleon's most important German ally, but the recent upheavals had made him waver in his allegiance. An ultimatum threatening him with the loss of his throne and being treated 'like a felon' ensured his return to the French side.[25] Over the next week Napoleon remained in Dresden awaiting reinforcements and reorganizing his army. On 16 May he received word from Marshal Macdonald, commanding a reconnaissance in force of the surrounding area, that the Russo-Prussian army had stopped retreating, and was fortifying a strong position around the town of Bautzen, on the road to the east. This gave Napoleon a chance for the decisive victory that would complete the work begun at Lützen, yet he did not immediately take it. Three weeks after the start of the campaign, diplomacy was returning to the fore.

While Napoleon was fighting with his armies, Metternich had not been idle. The first stage of Austria's mediation had been completed, and Lebzeltern, Wessenberg, and Schwarzenberg had sounded out the initial dispositions of Russia, England, and France. Now that the campaign had begun, the focus had shifted to the military headquarters of the warring sides, in central Germany, where Napoleon, Alexander, Frederick William, and their key advisers were now based. For this second stage, Metternich decided to employ new envoys. Schwarzenberg, who had now returned from France, was needed in Vienna, so Bubna was recalled to serve as Austria's representative to Napoleon. For liaison with the Russians and Prussians, Lebzeltern was replaced by a more senior figure, Metternich's predecessor as Austrian foreign minister, Johann Philipp von Stadion. On 8 May, Stadion set off for Alexander's and Frederick William's headquarters, now at Gorlitz, and three days later Bubna left for Dresden to meet Napoleon.[26]

Before they departed, Metternich gave both men instructions which set out for the first time possible terms for a compromise peace. Those to Stadion were the most detailed, and also the most complicated. The main reason for this was the uncertainty inseparable from war. Metternich acknowledged that 'the result of the first battle will greatly influence the decisions of the Powers', and indeed he completed Stadion's instructions just hours before the news of Lützen reached Vienna. If the Russians and Prussians won a major victory, he wrote, they could make extensive demands, amounting to the dismantling of Napoleon's empire beyond the Rhine. These 'maximum' terms would include the destruction of the Duchy of Warsaw and a return to the previous situation in Poland, the restoration of all Prussia's territorial losses in North Germany, the end of French domination in Germany and the return of all French conquests beyond the Rhine.[27]

The maximum terms also stretched beyond Germany. They stipulated Dutch independence from France, the restitution of all the French provinces in Italy and the restoration of the Papal States. The satellite kingdom of Italy, ruled from Milan, was to become independent from France. This meant that Napoleon himself would have to abdicate its crown, which he had worn since 1805, but left open the possibility of a member of his family, such as his stepson Eugène de Beauharnais, the kingdom's current viceroy, to succeed. Austria also had specific demands for herself: a return to her frontier of 1801 in Northern Italy, and the recovery of Illyria and Dalmatia.[28]

Clearly Napoleon would never agree to such demands unless he had been comprehensively defeated, so Metternich accompanied them by 'minimum' terms in case the Russians and Prussians failed to achieve this, or were themselves beaten. To these he added the minimum that Austria herself would expect for her good offices as mediator. For Russia and Prussia, he set this minimum as the return to Prussia of 'southern Prussia' (essentially those lands lost to the Duchy of Warsaw) and France's renunciation both of her German conquests beyond the Rhine and of her protectorate over the Rhine Confederation. For Austria, he defined it as the dissolution of the Duchy of Warsaw; the restitution of Illyria and Dalmatia; and a new border with Bavaria.[29]

The terms Bubna brought to Napoleon were more straightforward. Essentially, they were the Austrian minimum, with just two differences. They explicitly demanded the destruction of the Duchy of Warsaw, and for Austria herself stressed the need for 'a good frontier in Italy'. Two of the points in the minimum terms, however, Metternich instructed Bubna only to raise in conversation. The first was the desirability, for all the Powers, of

an end to France's protectorate over the Rhine Confederation. The second
was the redrawing of Austria's border with Bavaria.[30]

The fact that the terms set out in Bubna's instructions differed significantly from those to Stadion has caused much controversy among historians.
For Metternich's detractors, they furnish further material for the charge that
his pursuit of peace was a sham. In their view, the moderate terms brought
by Bubna were intended simply to tempt Napoleon into negotiations; the
further Russian and Prussian demands would then be brought forward,
provoking him into breaking off the talks and appearing before European
public opinion as the chief obstacle to peace. 'Everything was calculated to
lure Napoleon into the trap,' concludes Albert Sorel, 'attractive proposals
from Austria to induce him to accept mediation and a peace congress, [then]
increasing demands at the congress to infuriate him and make him retract all
his concessions.' Underlining how influential this argument remains today,
this passage of Sorel's is cited approvingly in Thierry Lentz's major study of
the end of the French empire, written in 2004.[31]

This approach, however, fails to take into account the extremely fluid
circumstances in which Metternich was operating, and the need for flexibility these imposed. Given this, his proposals were inevitably complicated,
but they were entirely coherent, and far from merely a device designed to
cast Napoleon as a warmonger. No doubt Metternich's preference was for
the maximum terms, but he knew these would be very difficult to achieve,
particularly if Napoleon gained another victory. In May 1813, Metternich
thought that Russia, Prussia—and Austria as mediator—would have to settle
for far less, which is why he also set out minimum terms for Stadion to
convey. In fact, these minimum terms almost exactly mirror the proposals
Bubna brought to Napoleon in Dresden. Comparing Bubna's proposals
instead to Stadion's maximum, as Sorel does, distorts Metternich's aims and
ignores their basic consistency.

The school hostile to Metternich also underestimates the fact that he was
dealing with two extremely difficult men who also happened to be the most
powerful rulers in the world—Alexander and Napoleon. Emerging from a
life-and-death struggle on his native soil with Napoleon, the Czar remained
sceptical about the prospect of any meaningful negotiation with him. He
was especially determined that any mediation should not rob Russia of the
fruits of her victory. Alexander was also deeply suspicious of Metternich, the
author of an alliance with Napoleon that had led to Austrian troops invading
Russia alongside the French army just ten months previously. For his part,

Napoleon was accustomed to dictating rather than negotiating peace, and was temperamentally unsuited to compromise. Menaces would not extract concessions from him, but neither would complaisance. As Metternich shrewdly warned Bubna, he 'should not give Napoleon the idea of hood-winking us by delays and evasions'.[32] Knowing Czar and Emperor as he did, Metternich could have had no illusions about the difficulty of his task.

The first challenge was not long in coming. On 13 May, Stadion arrived in Gorlitz, immediately went into conference with Nesselrode and the Prussian chancellor Hardenberg, and communicated Austria's maximum and minimum terms. The next day he met both Alexander and Frederick William, who were staying nearby at Wurschen. The Czar was at his most charming, but questioned Stadion at length about the exact circumstances in which Austria would break with Napoleon. On 16 May, Nesselrode pre-sented Russia's conditions for making peace with Napoleon. They repre-sented a significant toughening of the Austrian maximum. In place of Metternich's vaguer formulation, Austria and Prussia were to be restored to their pre-1805 and pre-1806 territorial status respectively. Italy was 'to be free everywhere from the government and influence of France'—a sweep-ing statement that nonetheless gave much space for interpretation. A final condition that had not figured in the Austrian demands was added—the restoration of the Bourbon dynasty in Spain.[33]

On the same day that this 'Wurschen programme' was drawn up, Bubna met Napoleon in Dresden. The interview began at 8 p.m. and ended five and a half hours later, at 1.30 a.m. Napoleon began in affable mood, but as soon as serious discussion began worked himself up into a fury. 'His Majesty the Emperor,' Bubna reported, 'spoke . . . with a red-hot vehemence that is difficult to describe, since no words could do it justice.' He accused Austria of arming to make war on him, and of trying to turn the other German states against him. He was no longer interested, he declared, in Metternich's peace initiative: 'I don't want your armed mediation—you're simply muddying the waters.' He had accepted it, he went on, while Austria was still his ally, but now that she had withdrawn her contingent from his army, this was no longer the case.[34]

In the face of this onslaught, Bubna did manage to set out the three preconditions in his instructions. 'So as not to provoke another explosion', however, he omitted the two further issues Metternich had directed him to raise in conversation if possible—the end of France's protectorate over the Confederation of the Rhine, and a new Austro-Bavarian border. Even the

three original points were too much for Napoleon. He insisted instead on a
guarantee of all the French departments that had been created in Italy and
Germany, which was clearly incompatible with Austria's stipulation that he
withdraw behind the Rhine. He was willing to accept the dissolution of the
Duchy of Warsaw—'it doesn't matter to me, it's a long way away'—but
since the only French troops there were a few besieged garrisons he had in
reality little prospect of salvaging it. He then gave vent to an extraordinary
outburst that Bubna took care to record:

> I won't hesitate to sacrifice my life . . . I will perhaps perish, and my dynasty
> with me. It's all the same to me. You want to tear Italy and Germany away
> from me, you want to dishonour me. Monsieur! honour above all, then wife,
> then child, then dynasty. We shall overturn the world and its established
> order. The existence of monarchies will be called into question. The best of
> women [Marie-Louise] will be the victim, her fate will be wretched. France
> will be turned over to the Jacobins. What will become of her child, in whose
> veins Austrian blood flows? . . . I don't want to make Austrian blood hateful to
> France.[35]

It is difficult to disentangle all the themes in this furious invective. One was
clearly Napoleon's mystical, fatalistic concept of his own destiny. For him,
as long as his career was glorious and wholly exceptional, it did not matter
how it ended. Bubna analysed this belief in some penetrating lines: 'He
trusts in his star and wants—above all considerations of policy—to leave his
biographers material so that in days to come they can say that Napoleon
achieved more than any other mortal. To leave his name to history is his
determined will; whether this harms his empire, or even his dynasty, if he is
unlucky, is for him a secondary consideration.'[36]

Yet Napoleon's words may have been more rhetoric than reality. Later in
his harangue he admitted: 'The closest thing to my heart is the fate of the
King of Rome.'[37] He was clearly convinced that the principal threat to his
son's prospects remained the Jacobins, and that the most powerful weapon
they could have would be a dishonourable peace that the French people
would reject. Behind these dire predictions, once again, loomed the shadow
of the French Revolution. In 1792, France and Austria had gone to war, and
Louis XVI and his Austrian wife Marie Antoinette had been accused of
complicity with the enemy. The outcome, which Napoleon himself had
witnessed, had been their destruction. If Austria turned against him now, he
was warning, he himself could suffer the fate of Louis XVI, Marie-Louise
that of Marie Antoinette, and the king of Rome that of their son the hapless

dauphin. Napoleon was returning to the theme he had first broached with Schwarzenberg the previous month. It had an element of emotional black-mail; he knew that Marie-Louise was Francis I's favourite daughter, and that Francis would certainly read Bubna's report. Yet even if Napoleon exaggerated for effect, his 'red-hot vehemence' carried the imprint of conviction.

The exhausted Bubna cannot have left Napoleon with much hope for the success of his mission. At 7 a.m., however, he was visited by Caulaincourt. It was clear that Napoleon, regretting his anger and unable to sleep, had called for Caulaincourt and sent him to smooth things over. This was an encour-aging sign, and when Bubna was called to a second audience at 2 p.m., he found Napoleon in a much calmer mood. The Emperor refused to discuss any of the Austrian preconditions apart from the dissolution of the Duchy of Warsaw, but did agree to an armistice followed by a peace conference. For his part, Bubna went to the heart of the matter and challenged Napoleon's obsession that only military glory could guarantee his rule. 'I then spoke about the habits His Majesty had acquired as an army general,' he wrote, 'and which he had continued on the throne, and finally said openly, that everybody wished that . . . Napoleon would finally become [a peacetime] Emperor, and set aside his love, so clear to all, of being *Imperator in Castris*. His Majesty laughed heartily, and replied: "How could I not show myself at the head of my armies?"'[38]

A few hours later Bubna returned to Vienna on the next stage of his shuttle diplomacy. On arrival he immediately reported to Metternich, who was delighted that Napoleon had accepted the armistice and peace congress. Metternich's optimism at this stage is revealed in a letter to Schwarzenberg, undated but clearly sent that day. The letter also contains the most unequivo-cal evidence of Metternich's sincere wish for a settlement. 'In a word', he wrote, 'we have the matter in hand just as I wanted it, and we only need good sense, calm and a major military buildup to come into port without firing a shot.'[39]

Yet Metternich was rejoicing too soon. Napoleon's agreement to nego-tiate had not been as straightforward as Bubna thought. Although he had conceded an armistice and a peace conference, Napoleon had not with-drawn his rejection of Austrian mediation; in the second meeting it had simply not been mentioned. Napoleon remained furious that Austria was edging away from her alliance with France and as the price of this betrayal, as he saw it, was asking for Illyria. From this moment dates Napoleon's increasing obsession with this remote territory, which Austria wanted back and he, at least on the terms offered, was not prepared to return. In contrast, he felt, Russia had fought him openly and honourably, and if sacrifices had to be made to end the war, he preferred to make them to the Czar. He therefore decided to make a direct overture to Alexander, and chose Caulaincourt as his emissary.

Armand Augustin de Caulaincourt was one of the Emperor's most trusted servants. He came from an aristocratic family in Northern France that had accepted the Revolution, and had himself joined the army in 1792. Since then, he had had a distinguished career both as a soldier and as a diplomat. In particular he had served as French ambassador to Russia and counted Alexander I as a personal friend, which suited him ideally for his present mission. Intelligent and honest, he was not afraid to speak his mind even when inconvenient. These qualities had impressed Napoleon, who in 1804 had made him Grand Equerry, and in 1808 Duke of Vicenza.[40]

On two specific counts, however, Caulaincourt had less cause to be grateful to Napoleon. In 1804, after an attempted assassination by royalists, Napoleon had assigned him a role in the kidnap on neutral German soil of a Bourbon prince, the duc d'Enghien, thought to be the author of the conspiracy. Although in fact innocent, d'Enghien was brought to Paris, tried by court-martial that night, and shot three hours later, in an act that horrified Europe. Caulaincourt had not known this was Napoleon's intention and was shocked when he learned what had happened, but his reputation never recovered from his association with this brutality. More recently, Napoleon had disapproved of Caulaincourt's long-term relationship with his mistress Mme de Canisy because she was already married, and opposed all her efforts to free herself from her husband because he did not want divorced women at court. Caulaincourt was an honourable man, but Napoleon's actions, so damaging to his public standing and private happiness, cannot have failed to arouse some resentment.[41]

Napoleon had left his foreign minister the duc de Bassano in Paris, and until the duke rejoined him in mid-May made Caulaincourt his acting replacement on campaign. During this time Caulaincourt received and replied to all ambassadorial despatches. This did not please the foreign minister. Hugues Maret, duc de Bassano, was a veteran diplomat whose career dated back to the first years of the Revolution. From 1799 he had been secretary of state, co-ordinating all correspondence between ministers and organizing the daily business of government, before moving to the foreign ministry in 1811. He was perhaps Napoleon's most loyal subordinate. To be superseded by a younger colleague, if only for a month, was hardly reassuring. Furthermore, Caulaincourt was a friend and protégé of Talleyrand, himself a notably long-serving foreign minister until his resignation in 1807. Talleyrand and Bassano were not only rivals but personal enemies. 'There's only one person stupider than M Maret', Talleyrand once remarked, 'and that's the duc de Bassano.' Surviving Napoleon, Caulaincourt, and most of their contemporaries, the two men were to carry on their feud well into the 1830s.[42]

One major issue of principle, apart from those of personality, divided Talleyrand and Caulaincourt from Bassano. Both men were convinced that Napoleon should cease his wars and conclude a durable peace, even at the price of considerable territorial sacrifices. Talleyrand broadly favoured a French withdrawal to the 'natural limits' of the Rhine, the Alps, and the Pyrenees. The similarity with Metternich's and Nesselrode's views was striking, and may not have been coincidental; since 1808 Talleyrand had been secretly advising them on how best to frustrate Napoleon's policy of expansion, and receiving substantial payment for his services. For his part, Caulaincourt had vocally opposed the invasion of Russia, and in an interview with Napoleon in June 1811 had tried desperately to warn him of the consequences. Remarkably, his favour had not suffered as a result.[43]

Bassano, by contrast, had a reputation as a warmonger, even though on occasion he did support some arguments for peace. He was, however, dazzled by Napoleon's talents and charisma, and even when he did argue with him always ended by capitulating. As Metternich put it: 'His only point of reference was Napoleon's genius.' Bassano's ambitious wife, who loathed Talleyrand and Caulaincourt as her husband's rivals, ensured that his feud with them became permanent: just before the Russian campaign, she staged a puppet-show in her Paris salon satirizing their supposed pacifism. In the principal scene, Talleyrand, as 'the lame magician', taught an automaton resembling Caulaincourt to answer to all his questions: 'Peace brings happiness to mankind.'[44]

On 18 May 1813, from Dresden, Napoleon dictated instructions for Caulaincourt's mission to the Czar. 'Wishing to avoid the battle that, from the position the enemy has taken, appears imminent, and to spare humanity a useless effusion of blood', he ordered Caulaincourt to present himself at the Russian lines and, if Alexander was willing to receive him, propose an armistice and a peace conference. Napoleon also set out his ideas for a directly negotiated settlement with Russia and Prussia, bypassing Austrian mediation, at this conference. His central aim was to buy off Russia and Prussia by dismantling the Duchy of Warsaw, and 'destroy[ing] Poland forever'. Russia's troublesome western neighbour, the forward base for the invasion of 1812, would be removed permanently. By now the duchy was probably beyond salvation, but Napoleon's abandonment of a state he had created only six years previously was a cynical betrayal of the thousands of Poles currently fighting in his armies.[45]

Prussia would benefit from Napoleon's plan in even more concrete terms. She would gain the lion's share of the duchy's territory, from Danzig in the north through Warsaw down to the Austrian border. There was, however, a sting in the tail. In exchange, the French-dominated Confederation of the Rhine would be extended east to the river Oder, absorbing a slice of western Prussia including Berlin. As Caulaincourt put it, the new Prussia would in fact be 'a semi-Polish kingdom of Prussia', with her capital moved east to Warsaw, Danzig, or Königsberg. It was very doubtful whether Frederick William III would accept this bargain. Caulaincourt was dubious about its prospects from the start, and warned that it would lead nowhere. The scheme is important less for its chances of success than for its demonstration of how little of the core of his empire Napoleon was willing to sacrifice at this stage.[46]

Even while he was formulating proposals for Alexander and Frederick William, the Emperor was planning for the possibility that they might be refused. If they were, fighting would certainly resume, and this time he was determined to score a decisive victory. Although the Russians and Prussians had fortified the rising ground beyond Bautzen and were now in a strong position with the river Spree to their front, they were still numerically inferior to the French. If Napoleon concentrated his forces, he would outnumber his opponents by two to one. On 16 May, he ordered Ney, marching north towards Berlin with 84,000 men, to turn back and rejoin the main army. By the 18th, Ney had changed direction and was heading south-east. On the same day, Napoleon advanced out of Dresden with the Imperial Guard towards the enemy position.[47]

On 19 May, Caulaincourt received a reply from the Russian headquarters to his request for a meeting with the Czar. It stated simply that Alexander was currently inspecting his troops in the field, and was unable to make any arrangements for an interview.[48] The rejection of Napoleon's overture was unmistakeable. It was clear that the next day would see a battle.

5

Napoleon and Metternich

The battle of Bautzen began around 1 p.m. on 20 May 1813, when Marshal Oudinot's troops, forming the right flank of Napoleon's line, crossed the river Spree and began attacking the Russians drawn up beyond. They pushed forward for a good distance before being halted by cavalry. Meanwhile, Marshal Macdonald had constructed two trestle bridges over the river upstream under heavy enemy bombardment, and by 6 p.m. had taken Bautzen itself by storm.[1]

Napoleon's battle-plan offered a very real chance of destroying the Russian and Prussian armies for good. He aimed to fix them in their existing position by a series of pinning attacks by Oudinot on their left, and Macdonald and Marmont on their centre, distracting them from the approach of Ney's corps from the north towards their right. In case his advance was detected, Ney was to make it appear that he was simply joining the attacks on the enemy's centre. Then, when all was in place, he would swing back to the right and outflank them. This would force them to extend their line to counter the threat, enabling Soult's and Bertrand's corps to punch through their right centre. Their line broken, the Russians and Prussians would then be rolled up from the right, pursued southward, trapped against the Austrian frontier and compelled to surrender.

Underlining its importance to him, of all Napoleon's battles Bautzen was probably the one he prepared in most detail beforehand. Naturally, the one thing he could not foresee was the enemy's plans, but in fact these played into his hands. Given Wittgenstein's lack of authority, the *de facto* commander of the Russo-Prussian forces was Alexander I himself, and he proved no better a general at Bautzen than he had previously. In particular, he made the mistake of letting political considerations dictate his strategy. He was obsessed with the need to keep his lines of communication with Austria open, and was convinced that Napoleon would try to break these by attacking his left flank, driving his army northwards away from the Austrian border. This of course was exactly what Napoleon wanted him to think. As the battle began, the Czar's attention was entirely focused on the threat to his left, away from his right centre and right, where Napoleon planned his knockout blow.[2]

The success of this blow depended on Marshal Ney's outflanking manoeuvre. Ney was not, however, the best choice to execute such an operation. The 'bravest of the brave' was a superb fighting soldier, but had difficulties commanding any formation larger than a corps, and at Bautzen he was leading an almost separate army of 84,000 men. He was also extremely obstinate and hot-tempered. Ney was sufficiently aware of his deficiencies to employ the noted military theorist Antoine-Henri Jomini as his chief of staff, but did not always take his advice.[3] This time his task was complicated by a series of uncharacteristically vague orders from Napoleon about the route he should take to approach the battlefield.

By 10 a.m. on 21 May, Ney was in position, facing the village of Preititz which anchored the Russo-Prussian right flank. At this point it was only lightly held, and if Ney had attacked immediately, as Jomini urged him to do, it would have been taken easily. A message from Napoleon now arrived, ordering that the assault take place at 11. It was clearly out of date, but Ney had a rare moment of hesitation, and refused to budge before the appointed time. 'One may perhaps modify an order of the Emperor at a distance if one knows something he doesn't, but doing so on the battlefield would be unpardonable,' he told Jomini. As a result, the Russians and Prussians in front of him were given time to reinforce, and instead of walking into Preititz, Ney only took it at 3 p.m. after a series of costly frontal attacks. When Jomini begged him instead to bypass the village and swing into the enemy's rear, he lost his temper. 'I don't know the first thing about your bloody strategy,' he shouted, 'all I know is to how to march to the sound of the guns!' Alarmed staff-officers thought the two men would come to blows.[4]

Meanwhile, with the battle stationary in the French centre Napoleon had taken the chance to catch up on some rest. In an extraordinary demonstration of his ability to command sleep at will, he lay down on the ground in a square of the Imperial Guard and dozed off for two hours, despite enemy shells bursting close by. Then, at 2 p.m., he launched the critical assault of Soult's and Bertrand's corps on the enemy's right centre. Aided by heavy fire from an advanced battery of sixty guns, they forced their way onto the heights in front of them, defended by Blücher, and pushed him back to the village of Kreckwitz. There, Blücher managed to hold on, largely because Ney's failure to outflank him properly meant he did not have to overextend his line. Now it was the French who in turn came under a storm of artillery fire. Unable to break the opposing masses, they were forced to a halt.

It was only now that the Czar realized where the real danger lay, and began to send troops across the battlefield to support his right. Simultaneously the Russians and Prussians also began a limited withdrawal on their left, but Oudinot's corps was too exhausted to exploit this. Napoleon at once brought up all his available guns and began to pound the enemy in that sector. Then, sensing that the moment of decision had come, he sent forward the Imperial Guard in a renewed attack on Kreckwitz. The veterans marched up in perfect parade order, then charged home with the bayonet, and Blücher finally began to retreat.[5] Ney's failure to cut off his rear enabled him to escape encirclement with just fifteen minutes to spare. By the time Ney's corps finally arrived on the heights around Kreckwitz, the thousands of enemy troops Napoleon had hoped to trap there had melted away.

From 4 p.m. on the Russians and Prussians began a general withdrawal eastwards. Napoleon had certainly won the battle of Bautzen, but it was not the crushing victory he so desperately needed. The enemy was not routed, but retired in good order. Worse, the French losses in killed, wounded, and missing were severe: over 20,000, double those of their opponents. Napoleon had hoped to repeat Austerlitz, but the result was more like Borodino. Most historians lay the main blame for this on Ney, yet Napoleon was also responsible. He knew Ney's limitations, but assigned him a crucial role in an ambitious manoeuvre that he himself had never attempted before— bringing all his forces together not before, but during a battle. Overall, the most judicious conclusion on both Ney's and Napoleon's mistakes at Bautzen is that of the early twentieth-century historian F. L. Petre: 'Napoleon, for the first time in his career, deliberately aimed at concentrating on and not short of the battlefield, and the event showed that the instruments at his disposal were not sufficiently good for his purpose.'[6]

The next day was no better for Napoleon. He was determined to harry the enemy forces and break up their retreat, but this proved impossible. The Russian rearguard covering the withdrawal fell back in textbook fashion, its artillery halting regularly in strong positions along the road to delay the French advance. This infuriated Napoleon, who rode to the head of his troops to hurry along the pursuit. That afternoon, just outside the village of Markersdorf, a Russian round shot narrowly missed him, ricocheted off a tree, and plunged into his staff, cutting General Kirgener in half, disembowelling Duroc, Grand Marshal of the Palace, and stopping just short of Caulaincourt and Marshal Mortier.[7] Duroc was carried to a nearby farmhouse where he died a few hours later and Napoleon, distraught, broke off the action, something he had never previously done. Duroc was his closest friend, and had known him since 1793. Napoleon was paying a personal price for this campaign he had never had to pay before.

While the Russian and Prussian troops remained in good order, the same could not be said of their commanders. A week after Bautzen, Alexander relieved Wittgenstein of command of the Russian army and replaced him by Mikhail Barclay de Tolly, a cool, cautious general of Scots extraction, and a veteran of the 1812 campaign.[8] Barclay was immediately faced by a clash between military and political priorities. Two lost battles, added to Wittgenstein's poor administration, had left the army in considerable confusion. Logistically its most obvious option, which Barclay favoured, was to retire along its line of communications into Poland and reorganize. Yet retreating in this direction, away from Austria, would considerably lessen the prospect of help from that quarter. As Dominic Lieven puts it: 'It would probably have doomed Austrian intervention, certainly in the short run and perhaps for ever.'[9] Further, this withdrawal would have left Berlin exposed to a second French thrust. At a military conference on 2 June, when a Russian retreat across the Oder into Poland seemed imminent, Blücher and Yorck threatened to march their troops north to protect their capital. The Russo-Prussian alliance seemed on the point of disintegrating.

At this crucial moment Alexander redeemed his poor generalship at Bautzen with an impressive display of statesmanship. Back on political ground, his touch was much surer and his best qualities—resilience, clear-sightedness, and calm in a crisis—came to the fore. As he told Stadion, with whom he had several long conversations during these days, all his hopes were fixed on Austria, and he would do nothing that might jeopardize its support. In this mood, he firmly resisted Barclay's proposal to withdraw into Poland.[10] Nonetheless, he and his allies remained in a very difficult situation. The surrounding countryside was too poor to provide adequate supplies, and the only defensive positions from which a stand against Napoleon could be made needed considerable strengthening. What rescued them from this dilemma was not a military, but a diplomatic breakthrough.

In the days after Bautzen, Napoleon had picked up the threads of his negotiations with Bubna a fortnight previously. He had gambled on a decisive victory that would make Austrian mediation unnecessary, but this had not materialized. If he were not to alienate Austria conclusively, he had to show he was serious about an armistice and a peace conference. Like the Russians and Prussians, he also had pressing military reasons for desiring a suspension of hostilities. His army was exhausted and had sustained heavy losses over the past month. Above all, he desperately needed to build up his cavalry, whose weakness had allowed the enemy to escape in good order after both Lützen and Bautzen. Caulaincourt may have exaggerated when he claimed that this was Napoleon's 'real and only motive' for seeking an armistice, but it was certainly an acute concern.[11] Thus on 25 May he proposed a truce, and four days later discussions began in and around the small town of Pleiswitz, with Caulaincourt representing France, and Generals Shuvalov and Kleist Russia and Prussia respectively.

At this point Caulaincourt's papers become a crucial source for the history of 1813, all the more so for being largely unexploited. His published memoirs, one of the most important surviving testimonies of Napoleon's reign and which cover the period 1807 to 1815 in three thick volumes, contain a mysterious gap from the opening of the 1813 campaign to February 1814. Yet in fact Caulaincourt did leave manuscript memoirs of at least some of these months, from Napoleon's return from Russia to early June 1813, which have never appeared, and remain in his family archives.[12] It is unclear why the editor of the published memoirs, the distinguished historian Jean Hanoteau, chose to omit them. He may simply have thought they were too technical for the general reader. Certainly, they recount the battles and diplomacy of the campaign in sometimes numbing detail. Yet one suspects that Hanoteau, as a patriotic Frenchman, may also have suppressed them because their judgement of Napoleon is too unflattering; throughout he is portrayed as arrogant, inflexible, and unwilling to make genuine concessions for peace. A good example of this is Caulaincourt's account of the armistice talks, which includes a telling criticism of the Emperor's inability to negotiate:

> The abuse of his gifts was natural to him, as the abuse of his strength is to a gladiator. The habit of being his own master at home and abroad had made him despise subtlety. Thus he was neither adroit nor nimble in this negotiation, the first he had ever had to conduct as equal to equal.[13]

After Alexander I's rejection of Napoleon's direct overture just before Bautzen, it was clear that Austrian mediation could not be avoided. The

armistice during which this would take place, however, was a purely
military affair, to be agreed by the belligerents, France, Russia, and Prussia.
According to Caulaincourt, his own task in securing this was made virtually
impossible by Napoleon's inflexibility and constant demands. Some of this
stemmed, once again, from domestic insecurity. Napoleon was determined
that two months should be allowed for the armistice and peace conference,
rather than one, as the Russians and Prussians wished, since in France,
'where everyone argues',[14] the shorter period would make it seem that his
opponents were dictating terms to him. Other stipulations, however, were
entirely strategic, such as his refusal to evacuate Breslau, which his forces
had just captured. Napoleon's obstinacy on these points brought the negotiations within an ace of collapse.

In this unenviable position, one of the few people Caulaincourt could
turn to was Marshal Berthier, Napoleon's chief of staff, who had written so
feelingly to Schwarzenberg of the need for peace a few months before.
Berthier wanted peace partly as a good in itself, but also because of the toll
war was taking on him; he was just a few months short of 60, and the rigours
of the retreat from Moscow had made him dangerously ill. He was one of
the few people who still dared to argue with the Emperor, and Caulaincourt
paid tribute to this quality in his memoirs:

> The greatest mark of [Berthier's] devotion was his courage in telling the
> Emperor the truth, in daring to contradict and even resist him, if he thought
> he was being too severe or unjust. The anger and impatience with which [the
> Emperor] reacted did not deter [Berthier] from raising these matters again if
> necessary, and he only gave way when the resulting irritation made it clear he
> would be ordered to stop: only then did he obey. One could say that he never
> feared getting what was termed at the palace a *pummelling*.[15]

At every moment between 1812 and 1814 when peace seemed a real
possibility, Berthier intervened to support it. However, his clearly declining
health after the Russian campaign limited his effectiveness as an advocate,
and Caulaincourt recognized this: 'Sleepless nights, excessive fatigue, and
simple age had been undermining [his] faculties for two years.'[16] This is
reflected in the tone of Berthier's letters at this time, which reveal a man on
the edge of physical and mental breakdown. The consequences of this
would ultimately be tragic.

During the armistice negotiations Caulaincourt received orders from
Napoleon directly, but also via Berthier as chief of staff, and he used the

marshal as a safety-valve to relieve his growing exasperation at the Emperor's obstinacy. The crisis came on 3 June, when a credible report was received that a French force had violated the ceasefire by seizing a convoy of Prussian ammunition boats. Feeling that his integrity was at stake, Caulaincourt sent Berthier a furious letter demanding his recall:

> I beg Your Highness to find a replacement for me in negotiating the armistice...I am no longer useful in these talks in which I can no longer inspire confidence. Placed as I am in such a disagreeable position while expending so much zeal and sacrifice to serve His Majesty, my self-esteem dictates that I no longer participate in matters which are compromising the honour I inherited from my father and which I wish to preserve intact.[17]

As it turned out, Caulaincourt did not have to carry out his threat, because the next day the Russians and Prussians backed down, accepted Napoleon's offer of a six-week armistice, and conceded French possession of Breslau. They shrewdly calculated that they needed the truce more than Napoleon. If fighting resumed now their alliance could fall apart, whereas within two months they would be bolstered by substantial reinforcements. They were also deeply conscious of the need to win Austria to their side. By yielding to Napoleon's peremptory demands they could draw a contrast between his intransigence and their moderation and favourably impress Francis I and Metternich. On both counts these tactics had the desired effect, making the armistice a short-term victory for Napoleon, but ultimately a defeat.[18]

Caulaincourt's letter of resignation is eloquent testimony to his disagreements with his master, but there is evidence he may have taken these a step further. On 31 May, the Russian envoy Shuvalov reported to the Czar that Caulaincourt had taken him aside and revealed that several corps of the French army were currently in a weak position. Apparently he wished the Russians to attack and defeat them, since, in his own words, 'the moment we gain a victory, we stop listening to reason'. For 'we', one should clearly read 'Napoleon'. According to Shuvalov, Caulaincourt returned to this theme several times over the next few days, each time revealing further military details about his own side. Shuvalov was baffled, since Caulaincourt, if he was being sincere, was committing treason. 'In a word', he told Alexander, 'to hear him one would say he wants the French army to have a sharp reverse so peace can be concluded as quickly as possible.'[19]

When Shuvalov's letters were first published in 1900, they caused considerable controversy, with several historians branding Caulaincourt a

traitor. Others disagreed, pointing out evidence that both Shuvalov and
the Czar suspected Caulaincourt might actually have been acting on
Napoleon's orders, using false information to lure his enemies into a
trap.[20] On balance, however, this seems far-fetched. For whatever reason
Caulaincourt was compromising his honour, which, as his resignation letter
to Berthier shows, mattered a great deal to him. He may have felt that
advancing the cause of peace justified this, but is unlikely to have thought
the same about a dubious trick whose only effect would have been to
reinforce Napoleon's intransigence. It seems safest to conclude that Caulaincourt's overtures to Shuvalov should be taken at face value, and that he
was indeed trying to engineer a French defeat as a way of encouraging
serious negotiations. The similarity with the actions of his mentor Talleyr-
and in 1808 is striking, though unlike Talleyrand he never wished for, nor
received, any financial reward. It is a comment on the extremes to which
Napoleon pushed two of his most intelligent servants that both decided the
best way to serve their country was to betray their master.

On 5 June, the armistice of Pleiswitz, imposing a ceasefire until 20 July,
was formally signed. Although the document dealt only with military
matters, it was understood that Austria would use this time to call the
belligerents to a peace conference. Across the warring states, hopes began
to rise that perhaps the years of conflict might finally come to an end. In
France, from the provinces to the Paris salons, the clamour for peace
became so pronounced that Napoleon heard of it in Germany. In Prague
it was echoed by Schwarzenberg, busily rebuilding the Austrian army but
hoping that it would never be called on to intervene. On 9 June, he wrote
to Metternich: 'We are rearming as actively as possible . . . but for pity's sake
make our zeal unnecessary; end with your pen what [we military men] can
only complicate further.'[21]

The diplomacy of the three crucial months from June to August 1813 was
played out in a small area of central Europe stretching along the border of
present-day Germany, Poland, and the Czech Republic from Dresden to
Breslau. Throughout this time Napoleon was based at Dresden, apart from a
ten-day visit to Mainz to see Marie-Louise. The Russian and Prussian
headquarters were at Reichenbach, some way to the east near Breslau. On
31 May, Francis I, deciding he could only mediate effectively if he was close
to the scene, left Vienna with Metternich for the small town of Gitschin,

midway between the opposing forces.[22] Rather ominously, he took up residence in a palace on the main square built by the ruthless seventeenth-century warlord Wallenstein. At Gitschin, Reichenbach and two nearby country houses, Ratiborschitz and Opotschna, Francis, Alexander, Frederick William, and their ministers, gathered to decide whether, and on what terms, peace with Napoleon was possible.

Negotiating in this way and in this place suited Metternich particularly well. At such a decisive moment, it was essential for him to ensure that he had the full agreement and confidence of Francis I in everything he did. He knew that his master was deeply averse to joining the war against France, out of both concern for his daughter Marie-Louise and fear of a repetition of the defeats of 1805 and 1809. If a break with Napoleon did become necessary, it would be much easier to persuade Francis of this in the seclusion of Gitschin than amid the intrigues of the court at Vienna. Metternich also had personal reasons for welcoming a stay in this neighbourhood. Ratiborschitz belonged to one of the great *femmes fatales* of the period, Wilhelmina, Duchess of Sagan, and she was currently in residence. Beautiful, statuesque, and addicted to intrigue both sexual and political, she had known Metternich since 1801, but the relationship had always been platonic. In June 1813, however, the two began an affair that was to last two years, to the end of the Congress of Vienna.[23]

Between 7 and 10 June, in a series of often stormy meetings at Reichenbach, Stadion, Nesselrode and the Prussian chancellor Hardenberg thrashed out a basis for peace. Their task was to reconcile the moderate terms Bubna had presented to Napoleon with the much harsher ones of the Russians' and Prussians' 'Wurschen programme'. To do so, Stadion introduced an important new feature. This was a set of what he termed *sine qua non* conditions. If Napoleon rejected these and Alexander and Frederick William accepted them, Austria would join the war on the Russian and Prussian side. Stadion did not set out as precisely what Austria would do if Napoleon accepted the conditions but the Russians and Prussians still demanded more. However, he made it quite clear to Nesselrode and Hardenberg that in that case they could not count on Austria's military support. He also promised them that under no circumstances would Austria take up arms for Napoleon. The obvious conclusion was that Austria would remain neutral.[24]

The *sine qua non* conditions themselves reflected Austria's original minimum terms, but were in several respects somewhat milder. The dissolution of the Duchy of Warsaw and the return of Illyria to Austria still figured, as did the expansion of Prussia. However, instead of restoring all her German conquests beyond the Rhine, France was now required to sacrifice only Hamburg and Lübeck; the return of the rest would be linked to a future general peace which would include England. These were the demands for which Austria was prepared to fight. To these Stadion added two more, which Austria would support by all means short of war at a peace conference. The first was French renunciation of the protectorate of the Confederation of the Rhine, and dissolution of the Confederation itself. The second was the restoration to Prussia of all the territories it had lost since 1805.[25]

By stating the terms on which Austria would go to war against Napoleon, Metternich and Stadion were taking a calculated gamble. They hoped that the threat of having to resume the struggle against Napoleon without Austrian help would force Russia and Prussia to accept them and bring about peace. Yet if war did resume, could Austria realistically expect to remain neutral as her neighbours fought to the death, knowing that whoever won would certainly punish her for sitting on the fence? This was the most agonizing question Metternich faced.

The situation developed further in mid-June, when Russia and Prussia gained crucial new financial resources. On 14 June, at Reichenbach, Prussia signed a subsidy treaty with England, as did Russia the following day. In exchange for £2,000,000, to be divided between them in proportion to their efforts, Russia would maintain an army of 160,000 men in the field, and Prussia one of 80,000. In addition, though the details were not finally settled until September, they received on the same basis £2,500,000 worth of credit, administered through an issue of 'federative paper'. This breathed new life into the Russo-Prussian war effort, which had been seriously threatened by lack of funds. By the same token, it weakened Austria's bargaining position.[26]

It was immediately clear how distasteful the *sine qua non* terms were to Russia and Prussia. Hardenberg was particularly angry, claiming that they would lead only to 'an unsatisfactory truce'. He and Nesselrode insisted that they be treated simply as 'preliminary points' paving the way for a general peace in which England would be included. Metternich and Stadion had no option but to agree. This formula was convenient but merely postponed Austria's final decision. Napoleon had consistently stated that he was prepared to make far more sacrifices for a general peace that included England than for a continental one, and Metternich clearly hoped that these would be enough to ensure a final settlement. But if they were not and the conference broke up, Austria would again be faced with the agonizing choice of staying neutral or joining Napoleon's enemies.

The most powerful opposition to the *sine qua non* proposals came from Czar Alexander himself. He saw them as further proof that Metternich was trying to appease Napoleon, and to deny the Russians and Prussians the Austrian reinforcements they so desperately needed. The only way to pacify the Czar, Metternich realized, was to reassure him personally. On 17 June, the two men met at the grand Renaissance country house of Opotschna, mid-way between Gitschin and Reichenbach. Metternich exerted all his charm and powers of persuasion to convince Alexander that his real sympathies lay with Russia and Prussia. How exactly he did so remains unclear. In his memoirs he claimed to have told the Czar he was only advancing the *sine qua non* terms because he knew Napoleon would refuse them, enabling Austria to break with him. It is unlikely, however, that this was the truth. The balance of evidence is that Metternich genuinely hoped Napoleon would accept his terms, and only told the Czar the opposite to gain his consent to the negotiations.[27]

These complicated manoeuvrings gained Metternich little respite. The next day he went on to Ratiborschitz for a tense conference with Hardenberg, his colleague Wilhelm von Humboldt, and Nesselrode. The day after this he received a pressing note from Nesselrode stating that the Czar was still very unhappy with the *sine qua non*, and felt that Prussia and Austria needed to be strengthened far more to contain Napoleon in future. Meanwhile, Nesselrode and Humboldt were working feverishly on a new draft of the terms tough enough to satisfy Alexander.[28]

The two ministers were aided in their work by a remarkable and increasingly influential figure: Friedrich Gentz, the writer and publicist. Gentz was originally a Prussian state official, but had moved to Vienna in 1802. A brilliant stylist, he had become Austria's foremost propagandist in the press, in pamphlets and in official proclamations. In the longer term, as a political thinker (and not least as the German translator of Edmund Burke's *Reflections on the French Revolution*) he was one of the founders of modern European conservatism. He was an old friend of Nesselrode, had been Metternich's closest adviser since 1812, and his correspondence with them forms one of the most important sources for the period. For over a decade he had consistently attacked Napoleon's domination of Europe in print, and now at Ratiborschitz he was helping bring it to an end.[29]

The fruit of this activity was a draft convention that Nesselrode personally brought to Metternich at Gitschin on 23 June. It strengthened the *sine qua non* with two more stipulations: that France would be allowed no say in how the Duchy of Warsaw was partitioned, and that all French garrisons there and in Prussia should immediately be removed. Beyond this, if Napoleon rejected these terms, it committed Austria to fight for the full 'Wurschen programme' of expelling France from Italy, Holland, and Spain. Harsh as these conditions were, they allowed Austrian mediation to proceed. They also ensured that if this failed, Austria would have allies instead of being isolated. Metternich agreed to the terms, and on 27 June the convention was signed on his behalf by Stadion at Reichenbach, alongside Nesselrode and Hardenberg.[30]

The meetings at Opotschna and Ratiborschitz had one further consequence. Napoleon was alarmed by the news that Metternich had spoken with the Czar, and decided on a riposte. Via his foreign minister Bassano, he sent him an invitation to Dresden. Metternich knew this was the next essential step in his mediation, yet he dreaded it. 'My unlucky star is leading me to Dresden,' he wrote to Stadion.[31] He needed to know, face to face, whether Napoleon would accept the *sine qua non* terms. If he did, this could create enough diplomatic momentum to make Alexander and Frederick William swallow their doubts and end the war. But time was short. With the Russians and Prussians on the defensive, Austria's weight in the balance was decisive. Yet the longer the armistice went on, enabling their reinforcements to arrive, the less critical this weight became. If Napoleon did not swiftly endorse the terms, the chances of peace would be seriously diminished. Small wonder even Metternich was daunted.

Metternich arrived in Dresden on 25 June, and the next morning presented himself at the Marcolini palace, in the suburbs of the city, where Napoleon was staying. 'It would be difficult to describe', he later recalled, 'the impression of painful anxiety on the faces of the glittering crowd of Napoleon's henchmen gathered there.' Berthier sidled up to him and whispered: 'Don't forget that Europe needs peace, especially France, which only wants the war to end.' At 11 a.m. Metternich was ushered into Napoleon's study. He would be kept there for nine and a half hours.[32]

What was actually said during the meeting will always remain controversial, since only Napoleon and Metternich were in the room; there was nobody present taking minutes. From Napoleon's side, the standard account is the one published in 1824 by his secretary Baron Fain, who had it from Bassano. Some further comments were dictated by the Emperor on St Helena. For his part, Metternich wrote a short report as well as a 'summary précis' of the conversation immediately afterwards for Francis I. Seven years later, he returned to the subject at much greater length in his memoirs, but distortions of hindsight make this the least reliable source. However, two further accounts exist. The most important is by Caulaincourt, which is far more detailed than the others and based on a long discussion with Napoleon just a few hours after the event. It appeared in the *Revue d'Histoire Diplomatique* in 1933, but has been almost completely neglected since. The other, only just discovered, is a letter Metternich wrote two days later to his wife Eleonore, which adds interesting details on Napoleon's state of mind and on Metternich's own motivation.[33]

Crucially, Caulaincourt's recollections dispel one of the commonest misapprehensions about the meeting. Neither Fain's nor Metternich's accounts mentioned the *sine qua non* terms, leading the two most influential historians of 1813, Sorel and Oncken, to state categorically that Metternich did not put them to Napoleon.[34] For Sorel in particular, this was further proof that Metternich's peace initiative was not sincere, but a means of betraying Napoleon and joining his enemies. Yet Caulaincourt makes it clear that Metternich did in fact set out the conditions, speaking of the dissolution of the Duchy of Warsaw, the enlargement of Prussia, French withdrawal from Hamburg and the return of Illyria to Austria. He even 'vaguely' mentioned one of the two extra Russo-Prussian demands, the end of France's protectorate over the Confederation of the Rhine. All this reinforces the evidence that Metternich's peace initiative was genuinely meant, and an attempt not to trap Napoleon, but to save him.[35]

Napoleon's response was a passionate tirade. 'So you're proposing that the end result of our alliance . . . should be to weaken me more than four lost battles? . . . You even want me to give in to the Prussians . . . You want to humiliate France, undermine me, paralyse my strength.' Metternich famously recalled in his memoirs that Napoleon threw his bicorne hat in fury into a corner. Writing to his wife two days later, however, he claimed the Emperor did so four times, 'swearing like the Devil'. As could have been predicted, Napoleon then argued that making major sacrifices now would deprive him of his bargaining power when he eventually came to negotiate with England: 'Is this the way to bring England to the conference table? . . .

I won't impress [her] by pulling back my legions with their tails between their legs.' Austria's only reason for mediating, he asserted, was to escape from her alliance with France, and make territorial gains herself. At no stage did Napoleon come close to making the concessions essential to Metternich's peace plan.[36]

What Napoleon was prepared to concede, and all that he thought necessary to satisfy Austria, was the return of Illyria. 'Do you want Illyria?' was his riposte to Metternich, 'I'll give it to you.' In fact, this was an obsession with him. Discussing the meeting afterwards with Caulaincourt, he constantly returned to the subject: 'Austria's real aim in all this, I'm quite sure, is to get back Illyria . . . At the bottom of all this is Illyria . . . Metternich wants Illyria, and he thinks this is the right moment to get it.'[37] Underlying Napoleon's words was a conviction that Austria could be kept neutral, and that the only thing needed to ensure this was the return of the province. This was a tremendous miscalculation, based on an inability to accept that Austria might really be prepared to turn against him. As Caulaincourt put it, for Napoleon 'this was a defection that he refused to believe could ultimately happen.' It may be, as Sorel has argued, that he could not believe his father-in-law Francis I would abandon him.[38] Yet he was too experienced a statesman not to know that even family ties are not sacrosanct in politics. It is more likely he balked at the truth that Austrian neutrality demanded the sacrifice of his empire.

Napoleon's fixation on Illyria raised wider questions than the return of one former Austrian domain. It emphasized his deeply cynical and material view of international relations. He genuinely seems to have thought that territorial gain—or in this case regain—was all that Austria cared about. In fact, Francis I and Metternich broke with him because they felt that the equilibrium of the whole of Europe was at stake. They felt that in future this should be backed by a new treaty system guaranteeing the rights of all European states, and Metternich put this forward at Dresden. Yet Napoleon simply replied: 'Those are vague words.'[39] This response is highly revealing. Within two years Metternich was to justify his words, attempting at the Congress of Vienna to put at least some of these ideas into practice. For Napoleon, in contrast, the only foundations of diplomacy were power and force; the concept of independent states negotiating freely with one another within a framework of international law had little meaning for him.[40]

If Napoleon thought Austria had its price, he also thought that Metternich had his. This led him to make his greatest blunder of the Dresden interview. All the French accounts claim that, in a moment of anger towards the end of the meeting, he accused Metternich of having accepted a bribe from England to turn Austria against France. According to Caulaincourt, this was a variation on his theme that he was being asked to make disproportionate sacrifices before England had even agreed to negotiate. Napoleon knew that Russia and Prussia had just signed subsidy treaties with England at Reichenbach, and suspected Austria might be about to follow suit. As a result, he lost his temper:

> You're ignoring everything England's gained, but [you're saying] she'll need even more, and that that will have to come from me . . . She's just signed two treaties at Reichenbach with Russia and Prussia; has she also drafted a third? . . . You should know something about that, M de Metternich; how much has she paid you for that?[41]

Metternich never mentioned this outburst, but given that all three French sources do, it seems likely that it did in fact occur. It is not surprising that Metternich omitted it, since if he had not, he would have had to explain why, as a man of honour, he had not left the room immediately. Presumably, the stakes at the meeting were so high that he was prepared to swallow even this shocking accusation. As a result, Napoleon had difficulty judging his reaction. Discussing the incident afterwards with Caulaincourt, the Emperor was uncomfortably aware that he had offered Metternich an unpardonable insult, but tried to convince himself that it had not been taken as such:

> *Whether I had gone too far*, or whether M de Metternich found himself unmasked, or was simply too shocked to reply, he remained silent. I stared him down. He remained impassive . . . *Since money had stuck to M de Metternich's fingers before, [my] reproach probably didn't shock him.*[42]

Only years later, just six weeks before his death on St Helena, was Napoleon finally able to admit that his angry jibe had permanently damaged his relationship with Metternich. He claimed then, with considerable dramatic licence, that by the end of the meeting he had actually persuaded him to drop the rest of the *sine qua non* in exchange for Illyria and some further unspecified territorial concessions to Austria. This smacks too much of wish-fulfilment to be taken seriously, and contradicts not only all the other accounts but also Metternich's diplomatic consistency both before and after Dresden. Then, Napoleon went on, his ill-judged words about the

English bribe had ruined everything. 'I thought I'd won him back to my side', he recalled, 'and forgot myself enough to say: "I've already given you 20 million, do you want 20 million more? You can have it. But how much has England offered you?" Lightning couldn't have had a swifter effect. M de Metternich's mortal pallor showed me the enormity of my mistake. I had just made myself an irreconcilable enemy.'[43]

Napoleon probably exaggerated the effect of his words. There is, in fact, no evidence that he himself had previously bribed Metternich, so most likely he was simply embroidering his story here. All the accounts agree that the two men parted on civil terms. Metternich claimed to his wife that at the end Napoleon declared 'that I was one of the people he liked best in the world, and that even if we went to war tomorrow he wouldn't esteem me any the less'.[44] For his part, Metternich had performed the remarkable feat of keeping calm in the face of a barrage of verbal attacks, and avoiding any reply that could lead to an open breach.

Yet the crucial fact was that apart from Illyria, Napoleon had accepted none of the *sine qua non* terms. Though this did not make Metternich give up his peace diplomacy, it must seriously have undermined his faith in it. He had met for nine hours with the man on whom more than anyone else his mission depended, and had found him obdurate. If a settlement were to be reached, dramatic developments would be needed, and quickly. Metternich wrote in his memoirs that on leaving the study he turned to Napoleon and burst out: 'Sire, you are lost!' No other source mentions this, but if he did utter these words one can see why.[45]

Metternich stayed several more days in Dresden, both for discussions with Bassano, and in the hope that Napoleon might have a change of heart. His main business with Bassano was an extension of the armistice. He wanted this for two reasons. With three weeks already gone, the first was to give more time to reach a settlement if Napoleon did decide to negotiate. The second was to give Austria longer to rearm. On the night of 27 June he wrote to Schwarzenberg: 'Would prolonging the armistice help us? What would be the last possible deadline?' Two days later Schwarzenberg's reply arrived: 'In twenty days my army will be reinforced 75,000 men; this extra time would be a great help, but one day beyond that would cause problems.'[46] Achieving this goal, however, was a very delicate matter. Even if Napoleon decided extending the armistice would be to his military advantage, the Russians and Prussians, desperate for Austrian aid as soon as possible, were bound to be opposed. Unperturbed, Metternich risked their fury to give both Napoleon and Schwarzenberg more time—for the one to reconsider the peace terms, and for the other to build up Austria's independent deterrent.

The rest of his time Metternich spent rediscovering the baroque splendours and polished culture of Dresden, which had been his first diplomatic posting twelve years before. On 28 June, he wrote a letter to his wife Eleonore describing his experiences of the past few days and giving a revealing glimpse of his state of mind. Despite his bruising encounter with Napoleon, he was buoyed up by a quasi-religious belief in his mission, coupled with his usual egotism:

> It's difficult to believe the scenes I've been through, but the good God who endowed me with unshakeable calm has given me the victory throughout and will protect me to the end of my great enterprise. I'm beginning to believe a bit in my star like Napoleon. When I see that I'm making all Europe turn around a point I alone fixed months ago at a time when everyone I talked to about my ideas dismissed them as complete madness or worthless illusions!

> You can have no idea of the effect my presence has had on the people of Dresden. There's a continual crowd of people under my windows wanting to see what I look like. Complete strangers accost me in the street to find out at first-hand if I think there's a chance of peace.[47]

In describing to Eleonore his walks around Dresden in these days, Metternich displayed more appealing qualities than vanity. These were a basic humanity, and a view of war and its effects very different from Napoleon's. 'You can't imagine the misery and horror that reign here,' he wrote. 'The last battles have cost the French more than 80,000 dead and wounded. All the houses that can be have been converted into hospitals; at present there are 25,000 sick and wounded in Dresden and its suburbs.' The contrast between Dresden's surviving beauty and the terrible suffering it was now witnessing reinforced Metternich's distaste for Napoleonic imperialism. He made the point almost poetically to Eleonore: 'All the avenues . . . are bristling with gun batteries; meanwhile the Japanese Garden is filled with the most beautiful roses. I went in there for a moment and could easily have wept over these continual upheavals that are called the history of empires.'[48]

The next day there was still no word from Napoleon, and Metternich decided there was no point waiting any longer. That evening, he told Bassano he was leaving Dresden the next morning. The announcement had its effect. During the night Napoleon finally came to a decision. At 7 a.m. on 30 June, just as he was stepping into his carriage to begin his journey,

Metternich received a note summoning him to the Marcolini Palace at 8. On his arrival he found Napoleon taking a walk in the garden. The Emperor took Metternich into his study, rang for Bassano who swiftly appeared with pen and paper, and the three men sat down at a small table. Formally accepting Austrian mediation for the first time, Napoleon turned to Metternich and simply said: 'Dictate the articles as you wish.' Metternich did so and Bassano, acting as secretary, took them down. They set an opening date of 10 July for a peace conference in Prague, and a negotiating deadline of 10 August. The armistice would be extended until then, and Metternich undertook to get Alexander's and Frederick William's agreement to this. An hour later, he was on the road back to Gitschin.[49]

The reasons for Napoleon's sudden capitulation are not absolutely clear, but several factors must have played a part. Some were obviously military. Extending the armistice would benefit him at least as much as his enemies, and above all allow him further to strengthen his cavalry. He also wanted to wait for the harvest, to ensure his troops were properly fed when they took the field again. The political choices were much more difficult, and his delay in making them is evidence that he found them agonizing. He still found it difficult to conceive that Austria would actually turn against him. However, there was no point in provoking her by turning her mediation down flat, and at the least negotiations, like the armistice, would gain time. If the conference at Prague broke down, he would have committed himself to nothing; after all, in accepting Austrian mediation he had said not a word about the *sine qua non*.

But in one area Napoleon's decision, and the manner in which he took it, had far-reaching consequences. They gave Metternich a glimmer of hope that, despite his tremendous obstinacy, the Emperor might just possibly be coaxed into concessions for peace. Napoleon's actions on 30 June offered an indication of how this might happen: unexpectedly, unilaterally, and at the very last minute. Metternich noted this sign carefully, and it informed all his future dealings with the Emperor. Henceforward he relied less on slow-moving traditional diplomacy, and saved his energies for the eleventh hour. The first test of his approach would come at Prague.

6

The Congress of Prague

The news that a peace congress was to meet at Prague echoed far beyond the conference rooms and army camps of Saxony and Bohemia. The diplomatic chess-game that had started there would now be played before a much wider audience, that of European public opinion. Although freedom of expression was tightly controlled in all of the belligerent states, their rulers could not afford to ignore whether their people would welcome peace, or accept further war. For Napoleon in particular, this question was fundamental.

The growth of public opinion was one of the most important developments of the period, and in recent years has been one of the most studied.[1] The essential factor was the growth of literacy, which had risen rapidly in the course of the eighteenth century: by 1789, 47 per cent of French men and 27 per cent of French women could read and write. In Paris, the figures were significantly higher, with 90 per cent of men and 80 per cent of women able to sign their wills.[2] The result, particularly in France, was an explosion of books, newspapers, and pamphlets. For the first time in modern history, this created an informed public that wished to follow, and even participate in, public affairs, and discussed them not only at home but in cafés, reading rooms, provincial academies, and town squares. Though its extent is unclear, this appetite also extended to the non-literate, who gathered to hear newspapers read in public or scanned the caricatures in print-shop windows.

The French Revolution had transformed public opinion into a major political force, with the establishment of representative institutions through which it could directly influence government, and the abolition—for a time—of censorship. Napoleon was determined to return the genie to its bottle, reducing his parliaments to rubber stamps, drastically curbing the press, and devoting substantial resources to official propaganda. Yet he continued to regard it with an almost superstitious awe. 'Public opinion', he once remarked, 'is an invisible, mysterious power that nothing can resist; nothing could be more changeable . . . but it never lies.'[3] As a result, while ensuring it never regained its former power, he monitored it obsessively, and whenever it differed from his own policy, he took careful note. Opinion may have been forced from centre stage, but it remained a menacing presence in the wings.

Napoleon's concern for public opinion has left an extremely valuable legacy for historians, yet one which remains oddly neglected. One of the main functions of his prefects in the departments was to keep watch on the public mood, and to report to Paris on any noteworthy developments. In the autumn of 1810, the minister of the interior, the comte de Montalivet, sent a circular formalizing this, and requiring the prefects to send him monthly reports on the *esprit public*, best translated as public morale, in their jurisdictions. Shortly afterwards these instructions were allowed to lapse but, revealingly, they were renewed in the wake of the Malet conspiracy.[4] Thereafter, the reports arrived monthly on the minister's desk until the fall of the empire. They survive in the Archives Nationales and give a fascinating insight into the elements that made up French public opinion of the day.[5] Some of the prefect's material came from conversation with his own social and professional circle in the department's chief town, and more from the reports he received regularly from the sub-prefects in the smaller centres. The prefect himself also frequently toured different parts of the department, picking up news and comment at first hand from all classes of citizens. A further source was police surveillance of public places and private gatherings, noting, as one report put it, 'what is said in the law courts, the theatres, cafés, restaurants and social circles'.[6]

These were not the only barometers of public opinion. Two others, involving actions rather than words, were evasion of conscription and, more extreme, anti-conscription rioting. These always caused deep alarm, since the prefect's primary task was to ensure the smooth flow of local recruits to the Emperor's armies. Another more intangible but extremely powerful indicator, was rumour. This gave a good idea of the sort of information— and speculation—circulating in town and countryside. In a society where freedom of expression was strictly curtailed, it was also a revealing guide to the public mood. As the statesman and historian Prosper de Barante, then prefect of the Loire-Inférieure, wrote perceptively to Montalivet in June

1813: 'Even false rumours are a fairly sure indication of the state of opinion. They are a way of judging peoples' hopes and fears.'[7]

From the end of 1812 the prefects' reports give the most detailed picture recorded of the French people's attitude to war and peace over the next eighteen months. They are thus an esssential means of testing Napoleon's repeated assertion that if he made a dishonourable peace they would return to their revolutionary ways, rise up and overthrow him. The material presented here, from a representative sample of sixteen departments up to the Rhine frontier, which includes France's main cities, strongly contradicts this assumption.[8] In fact, it points to the reverse conclusion, that the French in 1813 and 1814 were desperate for peace, honourable or dishonourable, and that the main reason they turned against Napoleon was because he failed to conclude it. In continuing to the end to believe otherwise, the Emperor was flying in the face of an overwhelming body of evidence. It was an extreme, and tragic, example of self-delusion.

Inevitably French public opinion in this period reacted to circumstances, but it followed a clear direction. The 29th bulletin of the Grand Army announcing the Russian disaster caused amazement and disbelief. There was 'consternation' in Calvados, and in the department of Forêts, formerly Luxembourg, through which many survivors of the debacle passed on their way home, the prefect noted that 'even the malcontents were dumb-founded by the immensity of the reverse.'[9] Yet despite the shock, in general there was solidarity with the Emperor, and support for continuing the struggle. In the Doubs, the Gironde, and the Charente, for example, the reports for early 1813 presented the *esprit public* as generally good, with conscription proceeding smoothly. Many departments also equipped cav-alrymen at their own expense to replace those lost in Russia—124 in the case of the Charente.[10]

Over the following months, however, a note of unease crept into the prefects' reports, along with the first signs of a longing for peace. This was amplified by rumour, operating as an indicator of opinion in the way Barante described. 'It is thought that peace proposals have been made', wrote the prefect of the Indre on 18 February 1813, 'and as people greatly desire this, they have seized on the news with avidity.' A similar rumour, this time that a peace conference was about to open in Vienna, was recorded in the Yonne on 2 March, and another, in the Loire-Inférieure three days later, that Talleyrand and the senior diplomat the Comte Otto had begun negotiating in London.[11] Barely disguising his sympathy with these hopes

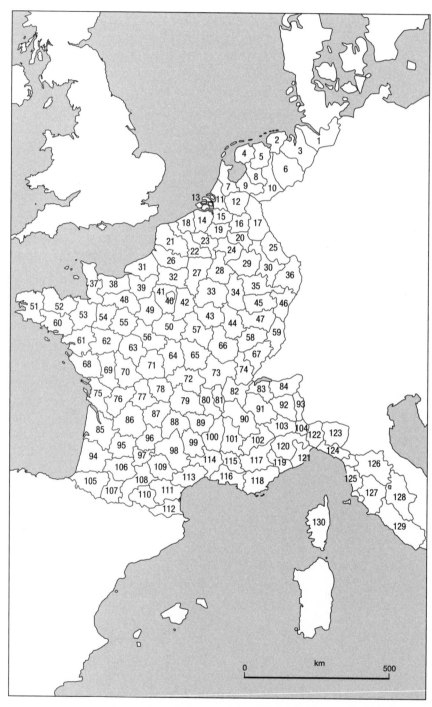

Map 4. The departments of France in 1812.

1 Bouches-de-l'Elbe
2 Ems-Or.
3 Bouches-du-Weser
4 Frise
5 Ems-Occid.
6 Ems-Sup.
7 Zuiderzee
8 Bouches-de-l'Yssel
9 Yssel-Sup.
10 Lippe
11 Bouches-de-la-Meuse
12 Bouches-du-Rhin
13 Bouches-de-l'Escaut
14 Escaut
15 Deux-Nethes
16 Meuse-Inf.
17 Roer
18 Lys
19 Dyle
20 Ourthe
21 Pas-de-Calais
22 Nord
23 Jemmapes
24 Sambre-et-Meuse
25 Rhin-et-Moselle
26 Somme
27 Aisne
28 Ardennes
29 Forêts
30 Sarre
31 Seine-Inférieure
32 Oise
33 Marne
34 Meuse
35 Moselle
36 Mont-Tonnerre
37 Manche
38 Calvados
39 Eure
40 Seine
41 Seine-et-Oise
42 Seine-et-Marne
43 Aube
44 Haute-Marne

45 Meurthe
46 Bas-Rhin
47 Vosges
48 Orne
49 Eure-et-Loire
50 Loiret
51 Finistère
52 Côtes-du-Nord
53 Ille-et-Vilaine
54 Mayenne
55 Sarthe
56 Loir-et-Cher
57 Yonne
58 Haute-Saône
59 Haut-Rhin
60 Morbihan
61 Loire-Inférieure
62 Maine-et-Loire
63 Indre-et-Loire
64 Cher
65 Nièvre
66 Côte-d'Or
67 Doubs
68 Vendée
69 Deux-Sèvres
70 Vienne
71 Indre
72 Allier
73 Saône-et-Loire
74 Jura
75 Charente-Inférieure
76 Charente
77 Haute-Vienne
78 Creuse
79 Puy-de-Dôme
80 Loire
81 Rhône
82 Ain
83 Léman
84 Simplon
85 Gironde
86 Dordogne
87 Corrèze
88 Cantal

89 Haute-Loire
90 Isère
91 Mont-Blanc
92 Doire
93 Ses
94 Landes
95 Lot-et-Garonne
96 Lot
97 Tarn-et-Garonne
98 Aveyron
99 Lozère
100 Ardèche
101 Drôme
102 Hautes-Alpes
103 Pô
104 Margo
105 Basses-Pyrénées
106 Gers
107 Hautes-Pyrénées
108 Haute-Garonne
109 Tarn
110 Ariège
111 Aude
112 Pyrénées-Orientales
113 Hérault
114 Gard
115 Vaucluse
116 Bouches-du-Rhône
117 Basses-Alpes
118 Var
119 Alpes-Maritimes
120 Stura
121 Montenotte
122 Gênes
123 Taro
124 Apennins
125 Méditerranée
126 Arno
127 Ombrone
128 Trasimène
129 Tibre
130 Corse

for peace, the prefect of the Hautes-Alpes made a telling point on 19 March. Montalivet's speech to the Legislative Body on the situation of the empire, he told the minister, had made the people of his own department 'feel more acutely than ever before the need for peace; everyone is saying to themselves while admiring this immense survey: how would it look if the sovereign was not distracted by war?'[12]

With the announcement of the armistice, the trickle of these sentiments became a flood. In half of the departments studied here, the prefects reported public joy at the news, and others may well have done so had they not been afraid of seeming to endorse pacifism in a time of war. Significantly, the departments that welcomed the armistice were spread evenly across the country, from the Bouches-du-Rhône around Marseilles to the Nord around Lille, and from Calvados and Loire-Inférieure in the west to Indre and Rhône in the centre and east. 'All hopes are centred on peace', wrote the prefect of the Charente, 'and the people have reacted with thankfulness to their sovereign's generous initiative in proposing the Congress of Prague.'[13] This was rather overstating Napoleon's role, but the message was clear. In the Nord, commented another report, 'everybody is awaiting with confidence the outcome of the armistice just concluded.'[14] The most revealing words, however, came from Barante in the Loire-Inférieure. These rejected, in the clearest possible terms, Napoleon's contention that a less than victorious peace would cause his overthrow. On the contrary, Barante concluded, 'the desire for peace becomes daily more intense, and if this hope appeared to have solid grounds, public jubilation and gratitude towards the Emperor would burst forth everywhere.'[15]

Barante's comment underscored the fact that the real menace to Napoleon's position came not from peace, but war. By announcing the armistice, he had unleashed hopes it would be dangerous to disappoint. The 'universal joy' his prefects reported showed how eagerly great numbers of French people greeted the prospect of an end to twenty-one years of war. If this failed to materialize, there was a grave risk that domestic morale could collapse. Serious discontent, even further plots or risings, might follow. If the momentum created by the truce was not to backfire, concluding peace, even at the cost of painful sacrifices, was urgently necessary. Yet there is little evidence that Napoleon realized this.

Back in Bohemia, Metternich now had the unenviable task of telling his Russian and Prussian colleagues of the extension of the armistice. He met them on 4 July at Ratiborschitz, and the result, as Nesselrode later recalled, was 'one of the stormiest conferences I have ever attended'.[16] Metternich claimed that the current armistice deadline of 20 July did not give Austria sufficient time to rearm adequately, exposing her to a devastating attack by Napoleon. He even raised the possibility of Vienna being besieged. This may not entirely have been bluff. Napoleon had spent much time at Dresden impressing upon him how substantially the French army was being reinforced, and this may genuinely have alarmed him. The reaction of Nesselrode and Hardenberg shows just what reluctant partners they were in Austria's peace initiative, and the difficulties they threw up at every stage of the process. They accused Metternich of breaking his word, and complained that they would not be able to keep their troops supplied for the extra three weeks. Eventually they agreed to refer the decision back to their respective monarchs, and on 11 July received the agreement of Alexander and Frederick William to the prolongation.[17]

Extending the armistice, however, did not prevent Russia and Prussia planning for a resumption of the war. On 9 July, Alexander and Frederick William met for a further country-house conference, this time at Trachenberg just north of Breslau. They were joined by the heir to another throne, but one whose background was far humbler than theirs. Jean-Baptiste Bernadotte was the son of a provincial lawyer from Pau in the Pyrenees who had joined the army, risen rapidly through the ranks to become a marshal of France, married into the fringes of the Bonaparte family, and in 1810 been adopted by the childless king of Sweden as his successor. A mediocre general, but an able and unscrupulous politician, Bernadotte had quickly come to the conclusion that Sweden's strategic and economic interests were better served by siding with Russia and England than the overbearing Napoleon. In April 1812, he had signed a secret alliance with Alexander, promising to attack the French in northern Germany. In exchange, Russia would support Sweden's conquest of Norway, currently ruled by France's ally Denmark. Bernadotte arrived at Trachenberg to advance these plans, and to coordinate the movements of his 40,000 troops with those of his allies.[18]

On 11 July, Bernadotte held a council of war with two of his own generals, Frederick William's military adviser Knesebeck, General Volkonsky, the Russian army's chief of staff, and General von Toll, its quartermaster-general. The result, which they drew up the next day, has become known as the 'Trachenberg plan'. Its basic assumption was that Austria would declare war on France, thus enabling an aggressive strategy. The allied forces would be divided into four parts. The largest would be the army of Bohemia under Schwarzenberg numbering 230,000 men, followed by that of the North under Bernadotte with 11,000, that of Silesia under Blucher with 95,000, and a reserve of 60,000 under the Russian general Bennigsen. It was assumed that Napoleon would advance on Schwarzenberg,

in which case Bernadotte would attack him in the rear. If instead he repeated
his previous strategy and moved north towards Berlin, Schwarzenberg and
Blücher would march to aid Bernadotte. The plan concluded with a flourish:
'All the allied armies will take the offensive; their meeting-place will be the
enemy camp.'[19]

Since Austria was not yet a member of the coalition, it was not represented at the Trachenberg conference. When he heard of it, Francis
I immediately asked Schwarzenberg to make his own contribution to the
strategic plan, which he swiftly did. This was mostly the work of Schwarzenberg's brilliant chief of staff, Karl von Radetzky, in whose honour Strauss
later composed the famous March.[20] However, Schwarzenberg added some
important considerations of his own:

> In his position, Napoleon must wish to fight a major battle as soon as
> possible . . . We . . . must not allow this battle to take place until all conditions
> point to the fact that we will win it.

> In order to create this opportunity, the French army must be weakened by
> marches and minor actions . . . This can be achieved by assembling our armies
> in three masses . . . but it will only succeed if we adhere to the iron law that the
> army which is attacked by Napoleon withdraws, and the other two armies
> quickly assault him in flank and rear and thus draw him away from the first . . .

> When . . . losses have sufficiently weakened the enemy, we will be able to push
> him back from the Elbe and against the Saale and here, possibly in the area of
> Leipzig, we can offer him battle with our united forces, and fate will take care
> of the rest.[21]

Schwarzenberg has often been criticized as a lacklustre commander, but these
words show considerable military acumen. Avoiding engaging Napoleon
himself except in overwhelming force, while attacking and defeating his
subordinates in detail, was to prove central to allied success in the coming
campaign. Schwarzenberg's speculation that the decisive battle might be
fought around Leipzig was also uncannily prescient. On 19 July, the Austrian
plans were forwarded to Alexander. They were then combined with the one
drawn up at Trachenberg to form the plan of operations if hostilities resumed.

On 12 July, the Austrian, Prussian, and Russian envoys arrived in Prague
for the congress. Metternich represented Austria, Humboldt Prussia, and
the State Councillor Johann Protasius von Anstett Russia. Humboldt,
though personally prickly, was a distinguished figure: a former minster,
and currently Prussian ambassador to Vienna. Anstett, however, was a very
different proposition. Born in Strasbourg, he had emigrated to Russia in

1789. Napoleon, however, had previously declared that he would not negotiate with Frenchmen serving other Powers. Politically, Anstett was no friend of his native country, and his manners were generally regarded as uncouth. Napoleon could only have seen Alexander's appointment of Anstett as a calculated insult—which it was—and this did nothing to ease his suspicions of the congress. It was small consolation that Metternich was almost as shocked by the nomination as he was.[22]

With negotiations about to open, Metternich had one last preparation to make. While he still hoped for peace, Napoleon's intransigence at Dresden had convinced him that the chances for this were slim. But if war between Austria and France was the likeliest outcome of the Prague congress, it was essential that he had the full support of Francis I. This was all the more important given Francis' deep reluctance to resort to arms and his concern for his daughter Marie-Louise. On the day he left for Prague, Metternich sent Francis a memorandum asking for his firm backing in each of the three possible eventualities he foresaw for the congress. These were: agreement of all parties to the Austrian minimum, Napoleon's rejection of the terms, or Napoleon's acceptance and Russia's and Prussia's rejection. Obviously the first outcome would pose no problems. It was the second, which he also saw as the most likely, that most concerned Metternich, and the essential purpose of his memorandum was to gain the assurance that 'if France does not accept the peace terms, Your Majesty will remain true to his word and seek his salvation in the closest cooperation with the allies.'[23]

Metternich also considered the third possible outcome, and in terms that raise the possibility that by this point he no longer desired peace. He edged away from his previous position that if Napoleon accepted the minimum terms and Russia and Prussia refused them, Austria should stay neutral. Now he argued that the question could only be decided at the last minute, and that he would address it in a further memorandum when the moment arose. He added, however, that Austria's decision 'could only be in favour of the allies'.[24] These words seem to support Sorel's contention that Metternich's peace diplomacy was merely a 'fantasmagorical game',[25] and that he always intended to join Russia and Prussia whether Napoleon agreed to his conditions or not. This view underestimates the tremendous pressure on Metternich—and Austria—at that moment. Metternich's preferred solution was peace, and he worked tirelessly for it, but if war resumed and Austria stayed neutral, she risked all the Powers turning on her. In that case, she ran a very real risk of destruction. Ultimately, Metternich was not prepared to risk Austria's existence for an ally as unreliable as Napoleon.

Even if Metternich thought that Austrian neutrality was no longer feasible, it was by no means certain that his master felt the same way. Francis' deepest wish, as he put it in his reply, was 'peace, lasting peace'. To achieve this he was prepared, as was Metternich, to postpone the return of Illyria to the next stage of negotiations, for a general peace including England. This is further proof of how much both men were prepared to sacrifice to reach a settlement. Francis was even willing to waive a further demand in the Austrian minimum, the liberation of the Hanseatic ports, if this would aid agreement. To achieve these aims, he wrote, Metternich could count on his full support. Yet although Francis acknowledged the possibility that Napoleon might accept the terms and his opponents refuse them, he studiously avoided endorsing Metternich's assertion that in that case Austria would have to join Russia and Prussia. Given his determination to spare the 'loyal subjects and . . . beautiful lands, to which I cleave with body and soul' from the horrors of war, it is quite possible that Francis might have rejected this advice.[26]

For his part, Napoleon showed little enthusiasm for the negotiations to begin. In particular, he was slow to send his own envoys to Prague. Partly this was a reaction to the nomination of Anstett. He even ordered Savary to publicize in the French newspapers the fact that Anstett was of humble birth and originally from France, 'which proves how little Russia must want peace, if she makes such a singular choice'. He also used the 'frivolous pretext', in Oncken's words, of a delay in agreeing the military details of the armistice extension to justify dragging his heels, even though Alexander and Frederick William had already agreed the new deadline.[27] Finally, he was occupied with organizing a ten-day journey to Mainz. He would meet Marie-Louise there, who would travel from Paris, and planned to return only a few days before the armistice expired. His purpose, he told Caulaincourt, 'was to give the Empress another child'.[28] Behind the coarse jocularity lay a serious point: a second male heir would have strengthened his diplomatic position. Napoleon's real aim was at once to assert his independence from the negotiations, and to pile the pressure on the other Powers for last-minute concessions. In this he was acting exactly as Metternich had predicted.

Napoleon's strategy was particularly risky in the light of news he had received on 30 June, just after Metternich had left Dresden. Nine days before, in Spain, Wellington had won a crushing victory over a French army at Vitoria. Napoleon's own brother, Joseph, king of Spain, was almost captured, and lost 143 guns and all his baggage. After five years of savage war, French power in Spain was at an end. Marshal Soult was immediately despatched to shore up the collapsing front, but within a month Wellington had reached the Pyrenees. As Napoleon played his game of bluff in Germany, France herself was faced with invasion.

On 22 July, just three days before his departure for Mainz, Napoleon finally sent for Caulaincourt and told him he would represent France at Prague, with Narbonne as his second. Caulaincourt replied tartly that since Napoleon's attitude in their last conversation 'had shown that peace was impossible', he had no desire to be his 'straw man', and that unless real sacrifices were being considered Bassano had better be sent instead.[29] The terms Metternich had brought to Dresden the previous month, he argued, were perfectly reasonable. The return of Illyria and the north German conquests was unavoidable, and French influence in Germany as a whole depended less on the protectorate of the Rhine Confederation than friendship with Bavaria and Saxony. Caulaincourt also echoed Metternich's conviction that there was little time left to conclude a settlement—'the moment is upon us'. At this Napoleon burst out: 'You want me to pull down my trousers to get a whipping', and stormed out of the room, slamming the door behind him.[30]

This was just the first round. On each of the following two nights Napoleon, who was clearly having difficulty sleeping, summoned Berthier and ordered him to persuade Caulaincourt to change his mind. Berthier visited Caulaincourt three times, the last at 5 a.m. on the morning of 24 July, to press the Emperor's case. He brought assurances that Napoleon had now reflected and was prepared to make 'the greatest sacrifices', but the only specific one he mentioned was the return of Illyria. Caulaincourt also saw Bassano, who told him 'to have confidence, and that His Majesty's genius would find a way of reconciling and arranging everything when the moment arrived'.[31] This was one more example of Bassano's blind faith in Napoleon that Caulaincourt found so irritating. More important, it underlines how those who knew Napoleon best shared Metternich's view that if he did decide to make concessions, it would be at the very last minute.

At 3 p.m. on 24 July, just a few hours before leaving Dresden, Napoleon saw Caulaincourt once more. He confirmed he was ready to return Illyria, but in answer to Caulaincourt's repeated questions about Germany and Prussia, he simply replied that he would show flexibility during the negotiations. He added that Caulaincourt would be given all the necessary latitude to conclude peace. Although still dissatisfied, Caulaincourt felt he had no option but to accept the mission. Turning on all his charm, Napoleon complimented him, assuring him of his esteem, and told him to collect his written instructions from Bassano. Rather ominously, he also quoted a couplet, 'Du destin qui fait tout / Tel est la loi supreme' (Destiny decides all / That is the supreme law).[32] He was to repeat it often in the course of the next months.

That night, Napoleon departed for Mainz. On the afternoon of 26 July Bassano handed to Caulaincourt Napoleon's completed instructions. Reading them, Caulaincourt was horrified. As he put it bluntly in his manuscript memoirs, 'The Emperor had broken his word.'[33] Caulaincourt was simply to propose a return to the status quo before the invasion of Russia. This was justified by pretending that the Russian disaster had not actually taken place. 'You will never admit that we were beaten,' Caulaincourt was told, 'on the contrary you will assert that we were always victorious. If we sustained some losses through the inclement weather just as the enemy did, these losses have been made good.'[34] There was a hint that Russia and Prussia could make territorial gains, since Napoleon recognized that their advances since 1812 had already destroyed the Duchy of Warsaw. Yet there was no reference to concessions in Germany: the return of Hamburg and Lübeck were not mentioned, and neither was renunciation of the protectorate of the Rhine Confederation. Finally, Caulaincourt and Narbonne were given none of the latitude in negotiating that Napoleon had promised. They could only forward the Russian and Prussian proposals, to which he would respond on his return to Dresden.

Beneath Napoleon's intransigence lay a twofold aim: to revive the overtures made before Bautzen and settle directly with Russia, and to punish Austria for her treachery in moving from alliance with France to independence. Napoleon was explicit about this in the instructions. His goal, they stated, was 'to negotiate with Russia a peace glorious for her, to make Austria pay for her bad faith and her political mistake in breaking the 1812 alliance through the loss of her influence in Europe, and in this way reconcile France and Russia'. Even Illyria was to be denied Austria, through a single barbed sentence: 'Mediators, whose role is essentially disinterested and impartial, can ask nothing for themselves.'[35]

Napoleon's instructions put Caulaincourt in an impossible position. He was being sent to Prague with proposals which could not possibly bring

peace, and with which he himself disagreed. In fact, Napoleon had broken
faith with him not once, but twice. He had lied to him about his willingness
to make concessions, and left Dresden before he could find this out. Now
Caulaincourt could not refuse his mission without formally disobeying his
master. He had a further reason for persevering which does him credit: if he
did not go to Prague, the slim chance of a settlement that Napoleon could
endorse on his return from Mainz would be completely lost. As he himself
put it: 'Any delay or difficulty on my part would have made it seem that our
government was refusing to negotiate, since the congress was already well
behind schedule. Therefore I sacrificed myself.'[36] He arrived in Prague,
where Narbonne was waiting for him, on 28 July.

The Congress of Prague is usually described as a farce.[37] On the surface,
this seems accurate. Formal negotiations never took place, since there was
deadlock on procedural matters. The French wanted face-to-face talks, the
Russians and Prussians communication in writing, and the matter could not
be resolved. However, dismissing the congress in this way ignores the fact
that the meaningful negotiations took place behind closed doors, with
Metternich acting as broker. Caulaincourt immediately realized that, with
the restrictions placed on him by Napoleon, this would be the only way to
achieve progress, and he and Metternich exchanged the initial visits proto-
col demanded the very day he arrived in Prague. According to Metternich,
as soon as they were alone Caulaincourt came straight to the point. He
asked whether Austria was determined to fight Napoleon if he rejected her
terms, or whether she might still consider a neutrality sweetened by territorial bribes. When Metternich replied that Austria would fight, Caulaincourt exclaimed: 'Then perhaps we will have peace!', and urged him to put
tough conditions to Napoleon. That, he explained, was the only way to
convince him that Austria would go to war if necessary, and persuade him to
compromise. He then made a remarkable appeal:

> I am not here to represent the Emperor's whims, but his real interests and
> those of France. I am just as European on the questions before us as you are.
> Send us back to France by making either peace or war, and you will be blessed
> by thirty million Frenchmen and all the Emperor's right-thinking friends and
> servants.[38]

The scene is so extraordinary that one could suspect Metternich of inventing it. After all, he was later to embroider the truth in parts of his memoirs.
Yet he wrote this account of the meeting on the day it happened, and in a

report to Francis I, whom it would have been dangerous to deceive. There is also the independent evidence that Caulaincourt had acted in this way just two months before, during the armistice negotiations, when he told his Russian counterparts that a French defeat was the only way to secure a speedy peace. Caulaincourt must also have been furious with Napoleon for tricking him over the content of his instructions for Prague, and it may have been simple anger that prompted him to approach Metternich. It is thus likely that he did make the overture, willing to trust the minister of a foreign country more than his own master.

Armed with Metternich's assurance that Austria would fight if she had to, Caulaincourt set out to impress this on Napoleon. On 30 July, he wrote bluntly to him: 'The moment is critical. Your Majesty will find yourself at war with the world if peace is not concluded in *ten days*.'[39] Yet with their hands tied by their instructions and the issue of negotiating verbally or in writing deadlocked, he and Narbonne found their position increasingly uncomfortable. Narbonne had been in Prague, condemned to inactivity, since 10 July, and had already made his feelings on the matter clear to Bassano. On 21 July, he had written: 'The pretexts and even valid reasons for delaying the opening of the congress diminish every day the chances of success.'[40] When Caulaincourt joined him, the two men began sending increasingly aggrieved joint letters to Dresden. On 4 August, they warned: 'We fear that our prolonged silence will give our adversaries an excuse, which will seem justified, to throw all the blame for the delay onto us.' Two days later they protested they were working as hard as they could in the circumstances: 'We are doing all that we can given our embarrassing position.'[41]

Significantly, Narbonne's letters to Bassano show that his attitude towards Metternich had changed considerably. As ambassador to Vienna since March 1813, he had strongly suspected him of duplicity, but was now convinced he genuinely desired peace. Reporting on 17 July on Metternich's frustration at the delay to the congress, Narbonne commented that his words 'gave an impression of honesty that cannot be doubted. M de Metternich... appeared deeply embarrassed and sincerely distressed'. On the 21st he repeated that nothing in Metternich's behaviour 'presented anything... that resembles bad faith... I am certain that he thinks the time for trickery is over'.[42] Caulaincourt, of course, shared this view. Metternich, he later recalled, 'appeared to us sincerely hopeful that a settlement could be achieved on the conditions he had made only too clear to the Emperor'.[43] This is further confirmation that, far from keeping the peace terms vague to make agreement impossible, Metternich had indeed presented them honestly to Napoleon at Dresden, and that their essential points were known to all parties.

As everybody had foreseen, the impasse was only broken on 5 August, when Napoleon returned to Dresden. That day, cutting through the formalities of the congress, he wrote to Caulaincourt telling him to find out from Metternich, in the strictest secrecy, 'the terms on which Austria thinks peace can be made and whether, if the Emperor Napoleon accepts them, she will side with us or remain neutral'. Caulaincourt received the proposal the next day, and that evening put it to Metternich. Unsurprisingly, Metternich replied that he would have to consult Francis I, who had now moved from Gitschin to the castle at Brandeis, on the outskirts of Prague. He returned on the evening of 7 August with what Francis termed his 'ultimatum'. If Napoleon had not accepted this by the time the armistice expired, on the 10th, Austria would declare war on France.[44]

Metternich then read out the conditions, which Caulaincourt took down himself. They were a slightly reinforced version of the original Austrian minimum. The Duchy of Warsaw would be dissolved and divided between Russia, Austria, and Prussia, with Prussia receiving Danzig. Hamburg and Lübeck would become independent cities once again, and the rest of France's north German conquests would be returned at the conclusion of a general peace including England. France would renounce the protectorate of the Rhine Confederation, Prussia would be enlarged with a defensible frontier on the Elbe, Austria would regain Illyria, and all the European states, large and small, would sign a guarantee of mutual security.[45]

If there was ever a moment when Napoleon could have made peace after the retreat from Moscow, it was now. Even the toughening of the minimum was calculated to achieve this end. It reflected Caulaincourt's advice to Metternich that a watered-down version would make Napoleon think Austria was not prepared to back it with force if necessary. Crucially, Metternich was also determined that the conditions should not differ in any material way from those he had agreed with Nesselrode and Hardenberg at Ratiborschitz. This was to give Russia and Prussia no possible excuse to reject them and expose Austria to the situation he dreaded most, Napoleon accepting while they refused. Although Metternich thought it was highly unlikely Napoleon would accept, he wanted to ensure that if he did, his opponents did too and a settlement was reached. He made this clear on 8 August to Stadion, enclosing a copy of the ultimatum to be presented to Alexander and Frederick William:

> It can do nothing but entirely satisfy [the allied sovereigns] since it sets out, as conditions for peace, the six articles which Their Majesties have agreed as their terms. In the very improbable case that Napoleon accepts them, it has the advantage of speeding up and concluding the negotiations, for which there would no longer be time if we stuck to the present forms; in the opposite case, which we regard as almost certain, we are happy to give the allied courts further proof of our firmness, and of a loyalty which should unite them more closely to us, and gain us their unwavering attachment under all circumstances.[46]

Caulaincourt too knew the crisis had come. On the same day he forwarded the conditions to Napoleon, with an accompanying letter carefully designed to make the maximum impression on him. He shrewdly argued that acceptance would in no way be dishonourable, and coupled this with a heartfelt plea to his master to swallow his pride for the sake of his people:

> No doubt Your Majesty will feel this ultimatum requires some sacrifice of *amour-propre*, but none of this will really affect France, and your true glory will in no way be diminished. For pity's sake, Sire, weigh peace against the risks of war, recognize . . . France's weariness, her noble devotion, her sacrifices after the Russian disasters, hear the prayers of this noble France for peace, and those of your faithful servants, proud Frenchmen, who tell you as I do that you must calm the fever in Europe, break up the [enemy] coalition through peace, and whatever your projects may be, postpone for the future what the greatest successes will not bring you today.[47]

Napoleon received Caulaincourt's despatch at 3 p.m. on 9 August. There is no record of his immediate reaction, but proof of how seriously he took the situation comes from one fact—the steady stream of letters and orders he usually sent out stopped abruptly during that morning, and only resumed on the 11th. Within two hours he and Bassano had drafted a counter-proposal. This accepted the destruction of the Duchy of Warsaw, and returned the Illyrian provinces, apart from Istria and Trieste, to Austria. However, Danzig was to become a free city rather than be given to Prussia, and the king of Saxony was to be compensated for the loss of the Duchy of Warsaw by the award of new German territories. Behind this clause lay Napoleon's own project of extending Saxony to the river Oder and pushing Prussia eastwards. There was still no mention of Hamburg, Lübeck, or renouncing the protectorate of the Rhine Confederation.[48]

These were important concessions, but they fell significantly short of the Austrian demands. Had Napoleon sent them straight off to Prague before the deadline expired, Metternich might just conceivably have accepted them as a basis for negotiation. However, instead of doing so Napoleon opted for a bizarrely indirect course. He loathed being issued with an ultimatum, and sought the dignity of a few days' leeway. Since the armistice allowed for an extra week after 10 August for the armies to prepare to resume fighting, he calculated that Metternich would be prepared to consider this as within the deadline. At 5.30 p.m. he sent for Bubna, who had been in Dresden as Austrian representative since late May, trying vainly to see him. In a two-hour meeting, Napoleon spelt out to him verbally his counter-proposal. Bubna would immediately set this out in a report to reach Prague the next day just before the deadline expired. Then, having ostentatiously slept on his decision, Napoleon would send his confirmation to arrive on the 11th.[49]

This was an extraordinary risk to take for the sake of saving face. Yet Bubna seized on the concessions with enthusiasm. That day and the subsequent week, he consciously took on the role, in Bassano's words, of 'apostle of peace'.[50] For him, Napoleon's response, though leaving something to be desired, was a major advance towards a settlement, and he strongly urged Metternich not to reject it. 'Your Excellency now holds', he wrote, 'the first proof of a happy success produced by Austria's efforts, a great step forward towards the goal, for which I heartily congratulate His Majesty and Your Excellency as its authors.' Although Bubna advised that nothing could be done about Hamburg and Lübeck until England had been brought into the negotiations, he expressed the hope that Napoleon could be brought to give up all of Illyria.[51]

Bubna might stress that Napoleon 'would not unsheathe the sword for Poland and Illyria',[52] yet this underestimated the major issues that remained. Above all, the Emperor was clearly determined to preserve his hold on Germany intact, whatever he may have been prepared to concede elsewhere. His proposals preserved his allies Saxony and Westphalia, as well as the Rhine Confederation with himself as its protector. Metternich may privately have inclined to this, but Russia and Prussia would have accepted nothing less than the full six conditions of the ultimatum. Had Metternich entertained the French counter-proposals, they would have turned on Austria and forced her into the position he feared most, isolation. Thus when Bubna's report arrived, he simply kept it to himself. Throughout the

Map 5. Metternich's peace proposals at the Congress of Prague, 7 August 1813.

day of 10 August Anstett and Humboldt waited, watches in hand, for Napoleon's formal reply. By midnight nothing had come and, visibly relieved, they told Metternich that the armistice had expired. Metternich ordered the lighting of a line of beacons, specially prepared between Prague and the Austrian frontier, to signal to the Russian and Prussian armies beyond that Austria was entering the war on their side.[53]

When Napoleon's reply arrived the next day, Caulaincourt tried desperately to keep the negotiations alive. Metternich agreed to continue talking, but told him that now the armistice was over, he would have to address any proposals to Austria, Russia, and Prussia together rather than just Austria. In reply to Napoleon's counter-offer, Metternich stipulated that Hamburg must become independent and Austria regain Trieste; he also pointed out that if Saxony were extended to the Oder, Prussia would lose Berlin. At midnight Caulaincourt wrote back to Bassano, recommending concession over Hamburg and Saxony and begging for authority to hold discussion with all three Powers. If granted the latitude withheld from him so far, he argued, he still had some chance of achieving a result.[54]

The last act unfolded on the morning of 14 August, when Bubna himself arrived from Dresden bringing Caulaincourt a reply. Bubna's jorney was well beyond the call of duty; his gout was so painful that he had been virtually unable to stand when meeting Napoleon on the 9th. Now, at the thirteenth hour, Napoleon abandoned his north German conquests—but still would not give up Hamburg and Lübeck. He was also determined to keep Trieste, and insisted on compensation for Saxony 'as a matter of honour'.[55] Despite this, when Caulaincourt went to see him Metternich commented that had these proposals arrived on the 10th they might have brought about peace.[56] This may just have been diplomatic talk, but it is quite possible that had Metternich put them to him, which he was bound to do, Francis I would have accepted them. After all, on 12 July, Francis had instructed Metternich to defer the return of Illyria and the liberation of Hamburg and Lübeck if necessary. Yet now that Austria's trump card—the threat of staying neutral—had disappeared, the chances of her persuading Russia and Prussia to settle for these terms were slim indeed.

The next day Alexander arrived in Prague and Caulaincourt, not wishing to stay in the same city as the leader of an enemy power, moved just outside, to the castle of Königsaal, which Francis put at his disposal. In the meantime, Bubna had taken Napoleon's new offer to Francis, who promised to put it to Alexander. Still hopeful, though extremely ill, Bubna added that if

this bore fruit, he would bring the news back to Dresden 'dead or alive'.[57]
He may not have been exaggerating; Caulaincourt remarked that since his
arrival in Prague Bubna 'had only got up to go and see the Emperor
[Francis], and had gone straight back to bed on his return'.[58] In the event,
Bubna's services were not needed. When Francis set out Napoleon's proposals to Alexander, the Czar flatly turned them down. He had what he
wanted, Austria as an ally rather than a mediator, and no longer needed to
make concessions. Caulaincourt left immediately for Dresden, and the
negotiations came to an end.

Had Napoleon shown any diplomatic skill in the summer of 1813, he
could probably have kept Austria neutral, or at the very least put her in an
exceptionally uncomfortable position. That he failed to do so may indicate a
general decline in his powers, which the rigours of the Russian campaign
cannot have helped. Most likely he was never more than half-committed to
a peaceful solution during these months, ultimately preferring the simpler, if
riskier, path of war. On 13 August, as the sands of negotiation were running
out, Bassano noted 'the secret joy His Majesty feels at finding himself in a
difficult situation, but one worthy of his genius and experience of war'.[59]
That shrewd observer Bubna had also sensed this during his interview of 9
August: 'He gave the impression of a successful general determined to play a
great role in history, about to take on the combined might of all his
enemies.'[60] More prosaic, but equally true, was Caulaincourt's verdict:
'Because concessions were made too late, everything was bungled and the
game was lost.'[61]

Nowhere in Europe had the Prague negotiations been followed more
anxiously than in France. If, as Barante had written, rumours acted as an
index of public hopes, it was clear there was a general longing for peace. In
one striking example, copies of what purported to be the agreed peace terms
began circulating throughout the country, first appearing in Marseilles. The
supposed clauses in the Marseilles version related mostly to maritime and
Mediterranean affairs, and were probably tailored to suit local interests.
Thus Spain, Malta, and Sicily, it was claimed, would return to their former
rulers, the kingdom of Italy would go to 'a foreign prince', the English and
French navies would remain at their current strengths, France's overseas
colonies would either be given back or exchanged for Egypt, and the rest of
the French empire would survive intact.[62]

Significantly, the circulation of these handbills reached its height in early August, just as the moment of decision arrived at Prague. On 7 August, the prefect of the Gironde reported that a very detailed version had appeared in Bordeaux, having apparently been sent from Paris. Some of its clauses mirrored those seen at Marseilles, such as the return of Spain to the Bourbons and of Malta to the Grand Master. Others were fanciful, to say the least: Ferdinand IV to give up Naples and Sicily for the throne of Macedonia, or the return not only of Rome but also Avignon to the Pope. Yet the rest, including the restoration of Prussia and the preservation of the Rhine Confederation, were not implausible.[63] On the same day the prefect of the Charente noted that the same handbill was going round Angoulême. On 11 August, the prefect of the Gironde wrote again to the interior minister to say that letters from Rennes had just brought more of these 'apocryphal peace articles'. 'I inform Your Excellency of this', he continued, 'to alert him that there seems to be a plan to distribute them throughout France.'[64]

Whether there really was an organized campaign around these handbills and for what purpose, or whether, as more likely, they spread by being copied and passed on at local level, they were revealing evidence of the public mood and its desire for peace. In contrast, when the news that the congress had failed reached France, the reaction was shock and depression. In Marseilles, where the rumours that peace had been signed had made the citizens 'drunk with joy', the resumption of hostilities left them 'stunned'.[65] In the Charente, hope for a settlement gave way to 'anxiety', while in Bordeaux it persisted even after the announcement that negotiations had failed.[66] At the other end of the country, the prefect of the Nord warned Montalivet: 'I cannot hide from Your Excellency that among all classes there is an emphatic wish for the peace that the extension of the armistice had led us to expect.'[67]

These were straws in the wind, but ominous ones nonetheless. Yet Napoleon chose to ignore them and to persist in the illusion that France still wanted glory more than peace. The armistice and the Prague congress had raised high hopes of a settlement. Now they were dashed, and the erosion of Napoleon's domestic support had begun.

7

From Dresden to Leipzig

The flaming beacons that announced the end of the armistice signalled a turning-point in the campaign of 1813. By 10 August, Austria was ready to throw 130,000 men into the balance against Napoleon. This gave an essential infusion of strength to the battered Russian and Prussian armies. In exchange, Francis I made one condition. This was the appointment of Schwarzenberg, already heading the Austrian contingent, as commander-in-chief of all the allied forces. The stipulation made sense, both from Austria's point of view and that of the coalition. With his close links to Metternich, Schwarzenberg could ensure that as far as possible the allies' military strategy matched Austria's diplomatic goals. After the chaos caused by a confused chain of command and the resulting defeats at Lützen and Bautzen, a supreme commander was also badly needed. The task was immense, and Schwarzenberg accepted it with high-minded stoicism. As he wrote to his wife on 16 August: 'All my being, as well as my life, I dedicate to this high and holy purpose. I have neither wished nor intrigued for this dangerous and honourable position; whether my unlucky star or wise Providence . . . has placed me there, only the future can tell.'[1]

As commander-in-chief, leading hundreds of thousands of men and negotiating daily with foreign generals and crowned heads, Schwarzenberg had huge responsibilities and very few people on whom he could genuinely rely. One was his trusted adjutant, Count Carl Clam-Martinic, then in the first stages of a distinguished career that would make him Metternich's confidant and ultimately Austrian war minister.[2] Just 21 in 1813, Clam had joined the army four years previously and served in the Austrian auxiliary corps in Russia, where he had first come to Schwarzenberg's notice. Personable and highly intelligent, he was soon selected by his chief for important missions. Throughout the campaigns of 1813 and 1814, as well as showing great courage on the battlefield, he was a keen observer of

Figure 5. The pipe smoked by Schwarzenberg during the 1813 campaign.

the often turbulent politics of headquarters. Clam's papers survive, unused so far by historians, and shed significant new light on allied military and political decision-making in this crucial period. His manuscript 'Recollections' of 1813, which he wrote in later life, are strongly favourable to Schwarzenberg, to whom he was fiercely loyal, but he always tried to relate his experiences with detachment and objectivity.[3]

Clam had accompanied Schwarzenberg on his journey to Paris to see Napoleon in March and April 1813. It was then that he got to know Schwarzenberg well, and formed an impression of his character and abilities. In particular, he recognized the quality that, far more than his military talent, was to make Schwarzenberg an effective commander-in-chief—his skill as a negotiator and conciliator. 'From this time,' Clam wrote, 'dates my view of Schwarzenberg, which has since been strengthened and confirmed . . . that, although through birth, upbringing, education and on first impression he was a soldier, he was by intellectual and moral inclination much better fitted to be a diplomat'.[4] Proof of this came on Schwarzenberg's return from Paris, when Francis I not only gave him command of the army being collected in Bohemia, but made him a field-marshal as well. Clam was struck by the subtle way in which Schwarzenberg used his modesty to disarm the jealousy of his colleagues. The promotion, Clam recalled,

> was an event which was bound to inflame against him all the envy, resentment and pride in the hearts of Austria's senior generals. It is doubtful whether his rise from being the youngest cavalry general to field-marshal, and now the most important man in the Monarchy, gained him more admirers or enemies, but he triumphed by using his great tact, treating his success simply as a stroke of fortune.[5]

From the army's headquarters in Bohemia, Clam followed the Congress of Prague with growing scepticism, and when it broke up had no doubt about where the blame lay. 'Napoleon did not want peace', he wrote, 'yet he could have achieved it by making sacrifices which would have been far outweighed by the advantage of breaking up an alliance, which after a year of one-sided and fruitless negotiations was finally becoming formidable, but whose unity could still have been destroyed by immediate concessions.'[6] This was an exact reflection, from the Austrian side, of the conclusions of Caulaincourt and Narbonne. Yet whatever the causes of the congress's collapse, its consequences were clear. An effective Austrian army had to be put into the field, and this was now Schwarzenberg's overriding priority.

Opinions remain divided about the quality of the troops Austria led into the coalition in August 1813. Given the circumstances, it was hardly surprising that this should have been variable. After her defeat in 1809, the Austrian army overall had been reduced to 150,000 men, but in practice Austria's disastrous postwar situation ensured that it was much smaller than that. It was only with difficulty that the auxiliary corps had been scraped together in 1812 for the Russian campaign. From this starting-point, to have an army of 130,000, whatever its standard, ready for service in Bohemia by August 1813 was no mean achievement.[7] Certainly there were deficiencies, and Schwarzenberg himself was the first to recognize them. On 11 August, he wrote to the president of the Imperial War Council:

> With my own eyes, as the troops were moving into camp I unfortunately saw that the complaints rising from all sides were justified, and that not only was

there a significant shortage of ammunition pouches, but even that many soldiers in the Kottulinsky and Czartoryski infantry regiments had no trousers... The extraordinary inconvenience that results from this for His Majesty's service in the coming season, when the nights will start to grow cold, is so obvious, that I feel it necessary to make Your Excellency aware of this straight away.[8]

These failings were confirmed by Sir Robert Wilson, a British colonel unofficially accompanying the Czar. Observing the Austrian troops marching through Bohemia, he saw that 'most of them [were] without shoes, many without greatcoats' in the pouring rain. Despite these hardships, he noted, they were 'marching with animated step'.[9] Wilson's colleague Sir Charles Stewart, the English minister to Berlin, painted a rosier picture. After attending a review of the Austrian army on 19 August, he reported enthusiastically: 'The composition of this army was magnificent, although I perceived a great many raw recruits: still, the system that reigned throughout, and the military air that marked the soldier... must ever fix it in my recollection as the finest army on the continent. The Russians may possess a more powerful soldiery, of greater physical strength and hardihood, but they cannot equal the Austrians in discipline or military *maintien*.'[10]

The truth probably lies somewhere between Stewart's glowing praise and Schwarzenberg's gloomy complaints. It is clear that the Austrian army had major problems of supply and equipment, but this did not undermine its fighting spirit—soon to be amply demonstrated when it went into battle. The fact that so many of its soldiers were young recruits was a significant handicap, since they were unused to long marches and adverse weather. As a result, the Austrians soon acquired the unenviable reputation of being the slowest marchers of all the allied troops.[11] Of course Napoleon's army also contained many new recruits, but they had already been toughened by the spring campaign. In terms of composition and tactics, the Austrian army as a whole remained old-fashioned. There had been some military reforms after 1805, but they had been nowhere near as thoroughgoing as the recent Prussian ones.[12] To enumerate these deficiencies is to miss the point. The Austrians' main contribution to the allied cause was the simple fact of their presence. They gave the allied armies a clear numerical advantage over the French and thus greatly aided the unfolding of the Trachenberg plan. If Napoleon remained on the defensive, he would be overwhelmed by superior forces; if he took the offensive he risked overextending himself, exposing weak spots that his opponents could exploit.

In one crucial area, Schwarzenberg had a dilemma that Napoleon did not have to face. Although in theory he was commander-in-chief, in practice it remained unclear whether his allies would tamely accept his orders. The most obvious problem was Alexander I. He accepted Schwarzenberg's nomination with good grace, and covered him with compliments when he met him at the review on 19 August. 'He kissed and pummelled me as often and as eagerly as if I was his long-lost brother,' Schwarzenberg told his wife.[13] Yet it was highly unlikely that Alexander would now consent quietly to fade into the background. He had just won a major military and moral victory on his native soil, had committed himself to the liberation of Europe, and commanded the most effective and battle-hardened army in the coalition. He also had a record of overruling his generals, most recently—and near-disastrously—at Bautzen. It was thus hardly surprising that the first mission Schwarzenberg gave Clam after Austria entered the war was to report on the situation at Russian headquarters.

Clam's 'Recollections' vividly depict his first impressions of the Russian army. 'The impressive results of its great material resources and the monarch's passion for all things military', he wrote

> seemed to me inextricably entangled with the organizational defects of an Asiatic horde, and the moral defects that are unavoidable when court and army headquarters, court favourites and fighting soldiers, influence and merit, merge into one. Once the war had been carried onto foreign soil, it had lost all its patriotism and national character, discipline had weakened, and the army had become a theatre of intrigue, a battleground for the passions, interests and pride of its leaders and most capable officers.[14]

Many of these problems were of Alexander's own making. While he wished to lead his army personally, he was also indecisive, which made him highly vulnerable to the various military cabals competing for his ear. As Clam commented acidly: 'The Czar, thirsty for martial glory, but without any of the qualities of a commander, became easy prey to all those who praised his own ideas with most eloquence, and won him over most skilfully to their own strategic plans.' The greatest rivalry was between Barclay de Tolly, the senior Russian commander, and a faction led by Wittgenstein, whom he had replaced, and General von Toll, the quartermaster-general, whose advice Alexander often sought. A talented soldier but a difficult colleague, Toll was one of the principal architects of the Trachenberg plan, and the chief Russian representative at Schwarzenberg's headquarters. Clam disliked him deeply: 'With patriotic phrases always tripping off his tongue, he was really nothing but an egoist whose unbridled ambition made him ubiquitous.'[15]

Clam, of course, is only one source, but his words have a wider significance. Since Schwarzenberg never wrote memoirs of his own, Clam's 'Recollections' fill in some of the gaps, and act as a guide to his chief's views and actions in these crucial years. Since they were not written for publication, they were also not polished or tailored for an audience. Above all, they underline the difficulties the rivalries at Russian headquarters created for Schwarzenberg. He had no desire to get involved, but if this was unavoidable, his only course was to choose the faction most likely to co-operate with him. In practice, this meant supporting Barclay, who though cold and reserved, was at least efficient and straightforward. 'With all his faults', Clam commented, 'Barclay was far more agreeable to Schwarzenberg than Wittgenstein or Toll.'[16] Yet even having Barclay on his side did not protect Schwarzenberg from being constantly harassed by the Czar's hangers-on. As late as September 1813, he was writing to his wife: 'It really is awful what I have to put up with, surrounded by weaklings, fops, peddlers of crackpot schemes, intriguers, blockheads, gasbags, nit-pickers; in a word, innumerable vermin torment me and gnaw into the marrow of my bones.'[17]

Just before the campaign began, Alexander's entourage was joined by a figure who posed a particularly serious threat to Schwarzenberg. This was the former French general Jean-Victor Moreau, a long-standing enemy of Napoleon and the only one with a great military reputation of his own. A republican, Moreau had helped Napoleon come to power, but had swiftly become disillusioned with his policies. In 1803 he had been approached by royalist conspirators to help overthrow Napoleon, but while happy to take power himself, had drawn the line at a restoration of the monarchy. Tried for treason, he had been acquitted but exiled to America, and had been living since then in Morrisville, New Jersey. Now Alexander invited him to return to Europe, join the Russian general staff and act as his military adviser. Moreau accepted, and by mid-August was in Germany.[18]

The Czar's motives in recruiting Moreau are still not wholly clear. Partly they were indeed military. Moreau was a celebrated general who had made his career in the very army Russia was now fighting, and his insights into its strategy, tactics, and organization could be enormously useful. More generally, even after the retreat from Moscow the allies remained in awe of Napoleon's genius, and felt more secure with his greatest French rival on their side. It may even be that Alexander originally intended Moreau to be the allied commander-in-chief, but was foiled by Austria imposing Schwarzenberg instead—further reason for Schwarzenberg to distrust the newcomer. Yet the deeper reasons for the invitation to Moreau may well have been political. The general retained a following in France, especially among republicans. Strikingly, Malet had named him as the head of the provisional government in the forged *senatus-consultum* that had launched his coup d'état. It was rumoured, and with some basis, that Moreau was the Czar's candidate to lead France if and when Napoleon was overthrown.[19]

It may seem extraordinary that the most autocratic monarch in Europe was thinking of reintroducing a republican form of government in France. Yet with Alexander, the extraordinary often becomes commonplace. He had been given an extremely liberal education based on the precepts of the Enlightenment by his grandmother Catherine the Great, who had appointed as his tutor the Swiss republican philosopher La Harpe. For eleven years, La Harpe had been a formative influence on Alexander, up to his dismissal in 1795 by Catherine, who in the wake of the French Revolution had come to regard him as a dangerous radical. As a result, even after he became Czar, Alexander retained a predilection for republican principles, as long as they stopped at the Russian border. More practically, working towards a moderate republic in France in the event of Napoleon's fall was in many ways shrewd politics. A regency under Marie-Louise would give Austria too much power, and the exiled Bourbons showed little sign of grasping the immense changes that had transformed France since 1789. A friendly republic led by a military hero who was prepared to keep the peace might offer the best chance for a stable European settlement.

Moreau had arrived too late to help shape the Trachenberg plan, but he was happy to endorse it. It now remained to be put into operation. The allied armies would move concentrically on Napoleon's position, taking care to avoid a battle with him in person until they had united and enjoyed an overwhelming superiority. Blücher would advance from the east and Bernadotte from the north, while the largest army, Schwarzenberg's, would attack north-west from Bohemia, heading for Leipzig to outflank Napoleon's right wing. On 17 August, it began its march. For his part, Napoleon had already decided on his own strategy. It was very similar to that of the previous spring. The Emperor was still determined on a strong offensive northward, to capture Berlin and outflank the allies' own right wing. He detached almost a third of his army—120,000 men—under Marshal Oudinot for this purpose. He himself, with the remaining 300,000 troops, would stay on the defensive around Dresden and wait for the advancing allies to make a mistake which he could exploit.[20]

This plan has generally been criticized by historians, and with good reason.[21] Napoleon was again violating his own principle of concentrating his forces to strike a knockout blow when the moment arose. He was also unwisely dividing them in the face of a numerically superior enemy. It was possible that the northern detachment would be too small to take Berlin, but large enough to be sorely missed by the main body when Schwarzenberg's attack came. Napoleon made this outcome more likely by placing his northern forces under the command of Oudinot. Forty-six in 1813, Oudinot had the distinction of having received more wounds than any other marshal—twenty-two in all, including three recently in Russia. As this record suggests, he was an extremely brave fighting soldier, and had performed well as a divisional commander. However, when operating outside the Emperor's immediate supervision, he tended to lose confidence and make mistakes. Napoleon himself later commented that while Oudinot was 'a decent fellow, he was not very intelligent'.[22] It would have made more sense to entrust such an important task to the far more capable Soult, but he had been sent to stabilize the Spanish front after Vitoria. The need to shore up far-flung positions was whittling down the number of competent marshals available, and the results were becoming plain.

By 18 August, Oudinot had moved north and was just three marches away from Berlin. Each of his corps took a separate route: his own advanced on the left, that of General Reynier in the centre, and that of General Bertrand on the right. Emerging from thick forest on the morning of the 23rd, Bertrand and Reynier, to their surprise, found themselves faced by a smaller Prussian force occupying the villages of Blankenfelde and Gross-Beeren. Bertrand immediately attacked Blankenfelde on the right, but made only limited progress in the face of heavy artillery fire. On his left, Reynier only advanced on Gross Beeren some hours later, but had taken it by 3 p.m. After this, both men assumed that the day's fighting had ended, and their men began to bivouac and prepare their supper.[23]

What they did not realize was that a few miles to the north, the Prussian General von Bülow, commanding a much stronger force of 38,000, had heard the cannon fire at Gross Beeren. He immediately marched to the sound of the guns, and heavy rain ensured he was able to get close to the French before the alarm was given. After a devastating artillery duel, the Prussians assaulted Gross Beeren, using their bayonets because conditions were too wet for them to fire their muskets. Amid savage fighting, they stormed both the village and a strategic height just to the west. All subsequent French attempts to retake these positions failed, and that evening Reynier withdrew down the road. A few hours later he met Oudinot and informed him that his corps was in no condition to fight again next day. Discouraged and worried that his army might now be outnumbered, Oudinot ordered a general retreat, and his attack on Berlin came to an ignominious end.[24]

The battle of Gross Beeren was an ominous foretaste of what could happen once Napoleon's subordinates were given independent command. Oudinot acted both unimaginatively and over-cautiously. It is unclear whether his forces were sufficient to take Berlin, but his defeat on the 23 August was entirely avoidable. Had he mounted a coordinated instead of a piecemeal attack with his three corps, he would almost certainly have gained a victory. Even after his defeat, his losses—approximately 3,000 men, relatively modest for the campaign—did not warrant a full-scale retreat. Oudinot's corps commanders did not perform much better. The normally competent Reynier attacked too late in the day, and having done so neglected to send out scouting parties that could have warned him of von Bülow's advance. Yet the real fault lay with Napoleon for choosing Oudinot at all. As a result, all his drive on Berlin had achieved was to weaken his main army in the face of Schwarzenberg.

While Oudinot was being checked in the north, Napoleon headed eastwards from Dresden, to get closer to the advancing allied armies, observe them and profit from any mistakes they might make. At this stage he thought the main allied force was the one facing him under Blücher, and planned to attack and destroy it before the flanking armies to the north and south could come to its aid. However Blücher, scrupulously following the Trachenberg plan's order not to engage Napoleon personally, retreated before him. By 23 August, Napoleon had realized that the largest enemy concentration was not in front of him, but to the south in Bohemia under Schwarzenberg. This threat was all the more serious since Schwarzenberg had now changed his objective. Hearing of Napoleon's advance and fearing he might get between himself and Blücher, he had abandoned his march on Leipzig. Instead, he turned north, through the mountains of the Erzgebirge, towards Dresden itself, held by only 20,000 men under Marshal Gouvion Saint-Cyr. At best Schwarzenberg hoped to take it and deprive Napoleon of his main base; at the least he aimed to force him to turn back, relieving the pressure on Blücher. This second aim was swiftly achieved: early in the morning of 26 August, Napoleon gave up pursuing Blücher and returned to aid Saint-Cyr.[25]

By this time, after a horrendous march through the Bohemian mountain passes, the main allied army had already reached Dresden. At 9 a.m. on 25 August, Alexander, Frederick William, and Schwarzenberg stood on the Racknitz heights overlooking the city from the south. The weather was good, and they could see Dresden spread out before them. The new town, or Neustadt, lay on the north bank of the river Elbe, and the old town, the Altstadt, on the southern bank closest to the allied positions. The Altstadt had three lines of defence: a ring of redoubts, the barricaded garden walls of the suburbs, and finally the old city wall. These had been strengthened by Napoleon, but were still in no condition to withstand an attack by a numerically superior force. In front of these lines to the east Saint-Cyr's troops occupied a substantial walled park, the Grosser Garten, while the mountainous country sloping down to the western sector was bisected by a steep-sided river, the Weisseritz, which afforded the French right flank some protection. From the Racknitz heights, however, it was clear that Saint-Cyr's garrison was far inferior to Schwarzenberg's army, and that if Napoleon did not soon arrive to reinforce it Dresden would fall.

The battle of Dresden was Napoleon's last great victory, and a disastrous initial setback for Schwarzenberg. This was largely the result of the allies' mistakes, and since all their leaders attempted to evade responsibility for them, it remains very difficult to work out what decisions they took and when. It should have been obvious to the allies that Dresden could have been taken if attacked immediately, and the first mystery is why they failed to do this. Eyewitness accounts are contradictory. One Russian staff officer, Danilievsky, later claimed that Alexander had wanted to attack straight away but that Schwarzenberg, concerned that many of his troops were still struggling through the mountain passes and would be exhausted on arrival, advised against the idea. Another Russian officer, Svinin, recalled that it was Schwarzenberg who proposed attacking, only to be opposed by Moreau and Toll, who eventually won Alexander over to their point of view.[26] This version of events is supported by Schwarzenberg himself, writing to his wife ten days later: 'Between ourselves, Dresden was not attacked as I ordered, on the day I wanted, but on the following day.'[27] It is hard to believe that Schwarzenberg would have lied to his wife, to whom he was devoted.

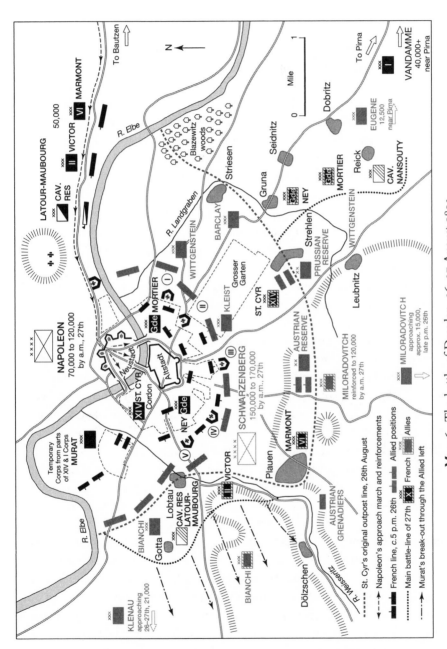

Map 6. The battle of Dresden, 26–27 August 1813.

Whatever the reason, by 2 p.m. it had been decided not to storm Dresden that day. Instead, the allies inched closer, keeping their options open and postponing further deliberations for tomorrow. However, by the following morning the situation was clearly changing. French reinforcements could be seen approaching, and around midday a rumour swept through allied headquarters that Napoleon himself had arrived in Dresden. In fact, outstripping his troops, Napoleon had mounted his horse on the edge of the battlefield and galloped the last few miles into the city, narrowly avoiding Russian cannonballs fired from the other bank of the Elbe. He then stationed himself at the entrance to the main bridge over the river, directing his troops to their positions as they passed over.

The allies' next decision is the most disputed of all, since it helped turn a lost opportunity into a bloody defeat. The key question before them was whether to proceed with the postponed attack, now scheduled for 4 p.m., or to withdraw in the face of the enemy reinforcements and the news of Napoleon's presence. Most sources claim that the Czar was convinced by Moreau and Toll that the attack should be definitively shelved and that after a long argument he brought Schwarzenberg, who wished to fight, round to his view. From this point on, however, accounts differ. According to one, Schwarzenberg was unable to find his staff officers, who were on a different part of the field, in time to countermand the previous orders. Another holds that he did find them, and that they persuaded him to ignore Alexander's wishes. Either way, the agreed signal for the attack, four cannon shots, was given at 4 p.m., and the allies found themselves committed to the one course of action the Trachenberg plan aimed to avoid, a confrontation with Napoleon before all their forces were united.[28]

Clam, however, gives another version of events, and since he was close to Schwarzenberg and his evidence has been unused until now, it should be taken seriously. His 'Recollections' flatly contradict the received view, and claim that Schwarzenberg's primary aim was never to capture Dresden. Instead, Clam writes, Schwarzenberg marched on the city simply to force Napoleon to return and thus relieve the pressure on Blücher. Only if Napoleon did not disengage from Blücher did he wish to mount a serious attack and 'punish [Napoleon] for this neglect by the loss of Dresden'.[29] Once it had become clear that the allied troops were in no state to assault Dresden on the 25th, and that Napoleon was almost certainly hurrying back to defend it, Schwarzenberg advised withdrawal. In his view, Clam recalled:

the strategic aim of the operation had been achieved, Napoleon had been separated from Blücher and forced back along his lines of communication,

Blücher had been put in a position to strike a blow against the French corps left behind, and the main army enabled to concentrate its strength on the 26th for the defence of Bohemia. Schwarzenberg took this view, and it underlay the opinion he expressed at the council of war held on the afternoon of the 25th, that the capture of Dresden should not be the main object, but a secondary one that circumstances now made impossible, and arguing that a successful result had already been achieved with Napoleon's return, he proposed retreat. Alexander and Moreau, however, wanted to fight, and the attack was fixed for the 26th.[30]

Clearly Clam was defending his chief and shifting the blame onto the Czar, whom he regarded as an incompetent soldier, and Toll, whom he detested. Yet this does not mean his testimony should be dismissed. It fits with Schwarzenberg's record as an extremely cautious commander, which the rest of the war would only confirm. In addition, since Schwarzenberg's main contribution to the Trachenberg plan had been to insist that the allies should only fight Napoleon once all their forces had been united, he is more likely on this occasion to have argued for retreat. Clam's evidence is certainly not conclusive, but it does challenge the previously held assumption that Schwarzenberg bears the main responsibility for the attack.

Meanwhile, in Dresden itself the inhabitants realized with alarm that their city was about to become a battleground. An eyewitness, the Saxon artillery officer Heinrich Aster, later recalled: 'In the suburbs many people took advantage of this last opportunity to find a more secure refuge than their houses afforded ... Everybody was extremely fearful, when they saw how few French troops there were to defend them.'[31] Having remained loyal to Napoleon, the Dresdeners knew they could expect harsh treatment if the allies won a victory. They feared the Austrian and Prussian soldiers, but were terrified of the Russians, stories of whose 'strength, brutality and rapacity' were whispered everywhere with horror. Anxiety turned to relief, however, with the news of Napoleon's arrival. 'There is Napoleon,' Aster heard many citizens saying. 'Things will be soon be very different.'[32]

Once the four cannon shots had sounded, the allied army approached Dresden in five columns. On the extreme right Wittgenstein's Russians advanced close to the Elbe, on their left Kleist's Prussians entered the Grosser Garten, in the centre the Austrians under Colloredo and Chasteler attacked the French-held redoubt no. 3 and the nearest suburbs, and on the left wing, beyond the river Weisseritz, more Austrians under Bianchi and Meszko moved on the village of Lobtau. The fighting was particularly savage around redoubt no. 3. Whole ranks of the oncoming Austrians were cut down by murderous cannon and musket fire, and two assaults were beaten back. Then, with ammunition running low, the fusillade began to slacken, and the Austrians stormed forward into the ditch and began to tear down the palisade. At this point Sir Robert Wilson, watching from his post near the Czar, decided to join the fray. As he rather vaingloriously put it in his journal:

> I remembered what I owed to Austria, England, and myself. I dismounted, climbed over the palisades, with extreme difficulty reached the crest of the parapet, sprang on it, took off my cap and gave three cheers . . . and then leapt into the battery. My cheers had been answered by all around me of all ranks, and instantly hundreds mounted and manned the redoubt. This being accomplished, I descended.[33]

By 6 p.m. the allied advance had reached its furthest point, the outskirts of the Dresden suburbs. As well as redoubt no. 3, the Grosser Garten had also been cleared of the French after furious fighting. Yet even though Napoleon was still heavily outnumbered, he felt he now had sufficient reinforcements to mount a counterattack. He sent his troops forward at all points of the line, and himself rode onto the battlefield to direct them. In fierce hand-to-hand combat the Prussians were pushed back to the central avenue of the Grosser Garten, and the Austrians driven from redoubt no. 3. On the flanks the French made less progress, but by nightfall they had regained almost all the ground they had lost during the day. Around midnight the weather, which had been fine, broke, and it began to rain heavily, soaking the weary soldiers on both sides as they settled down to get some rest.

Although they had not held on to their gains, the Austrian troops had fought well in their first battle of the war. Their performance reveals that they contributed much more than mere numbers to the allied cause. They had advanced bravely in the face of withering fire, and had stormed heavily fortified positions. They had done so after a punishing march through the Bohemian mountains which had cruelly exposed the deficiencies in their equipment. Aster later paid tribute to them in his recollections: 'The dreadful roads and weather, inadequate clothing and above all the lack of shoes, [had already] exhausted them. These circumstances can hardly have raised the morale of the ordinary soldiers. Anybody who has themselves experienced such conditions can only admire the brave conduct of these men on the 26th August.' Sir Robert Wilson was more succinct: 'The intrepidity of the Austrians could not be excelled, nor the perfection of their dispositions, but they were required to do that which was physically impossible.'[34]

So far the contest had reached stalemate, but the scales were tipping in favour of Napoleon. All through the night reinforcements streamed into Dresden, bringing his forces to 125,000—still less than the allies' 150,000, but a great improvement on the previous day's odds. Conversely, the allies had frittered away their advantage. They had manoeuvred poorly, failing to bring their superior numbers to bear, and now Napoleon was on the scene. They now had to decide whether to continue the battle or, contenting themselves with having separated Napoleon from Blücher, retreat the way they had come. A council of war was convened, but was interrupted at 1 a.m. by ominous news. On his way back to Dresden two days before, Napoleon had detached a corps of 40,000 men under the tough and experienced General Vandamme to outflank the allies on their right flank and cut their main line of retreat, the road leading from Königstein back into Bohemia via Peterswalde. Now the allies learned that Vandamme was close to cutting this road, which was only held by 13,000 men under Prince Eugen of Württemberg.[35]

Given this peril, a retreat would have been prudent. Yet this course was not taken. Instead, it was decided that the army would stay in its present position. Again, the thinking behind this decision is not entirely clear. The intention may have been to tempt Napoleon into an attack with inferior forces that could be defeated, but equally the fact that the allies reinforced their centre and centre-left during the night implies they themselves had not ruled out taking the offensive. It may simply be that, after hours of argument and counter-argument, staying put was adopted as the path of least resistance. Whatever the reasoning, the consequences were disastrous.

Accounts of Schwarzenberg's role in these discussions are once more contradictory. Several secondary sources portray him as arguing for a retreat in view of the lack of provisions and the exhaustion of the troops. Yet he himself later claimed that he supported attacking, and was only persuaded to withdraw during the afternoon of the 27th. This uncertainty over his stance probably stems from the confusion reigning at allied headquarters that night, with some generals urging retreat, others a defensive battle, and the Czar hesitating between them. For Clam, this chaos was the real reason for Schwarzenberg's indecision and mistakes. 'It would be unfair', he wrote,

> not to stress the extreme pressure he was under from all sides, which had to be seen to be believed, and is impossible to convey. All the problems with which the commander of any allied army must grapple came together at once and became more obvious and dangerous by the hour. Czar Alexander's unfortunate compulsion to meddle in military decision-making, the insolent, denigrating presumption of twenty different advisers who buzzed around the field-marshal and literally shouted him down, from Moreau and Toll... down to the most insignificant officers who thronged round the Czar, the ill-will of the Russians, their appalling insubordination, created a truly dreadful scene... in short, it was hardly possible to wield a field-marshal's baton under unluckier circumstances, than Schwarzenberg did in his first great battle.[36]

The French advance began, in pouring rain, at 6 a.m. on 27 August. Instead of attacking in the centre, as he usually did, Napoleon changed his strategy and threw his forces against both wings of his opponents' army. In heavy fighting, Mortier's and Ney's corps pushed back the allied right from the Elbe, further jeopardizing its communications with Bohemia. The village of Reick was taken at midday after a ferocious hand-to-hand struggle and bombardment that set it on fire in several places; there were horrible scenes as many of the wounded perished in the flames. The Russians and Prussians fell back, and the French penetrated close to the allied centre. Urging his soldiers on himself, Napoleon commandeered a horse artillery battery and ordered it to fire on a cluster of enemy horsemen nearby. Though he did not know it, he was taking aim at the allied commanders and their staff. What happened next was described by Sir Robert Wilson, who was riding with them:

> as the Emperor [Alexander], General Moreau, Lord Cathcart, myself and suite were passing on the right of the centre in the wake of a French battery that still played, a ball came and struck something about us. For a few seconds no effect was seen or heard, but then General Moreau cried 'Oh!' and I perceived him, for I was next upon his left, struggling and endeavouring to dismount. I immediately said: 'Sire, General Moreau is wounded'. And almost at the instant I saw him throw himself from his horse, with one leg shattered and the inside of the left knee all mangled. His horse which had stood firm till the General fell, now staggered and threw himself down close to his master... Moreau then lifted himself up a little, looked at his legs, and said: '*C'est passé avec moi! Mon affaire est faite.*'[37]

Moreau was carried to a nearby farmhouse, where both his legs were amputated by the Czar's surgeon. His death a week later, coupled with the courage with which he bore his injuries, excited grief and admiration. Clam, however, was less sentimental. 'Aside from the sympathy which the end of a remarkable and upright man must inspire', he commented, 'his death was perhaps a blessing, since he was a great obstacle to the unity of our command.'[38] Moreau's removal also had significant political consequences. Had he lived, he could well have been a contender for the leadership of France, with the major advantage of Alexander's backing. In this light, it is eerily appropriate that the battery which killed him was commanded by Napoleon himself.

If the allied right was hard pressed, their left was in still worse straits. Manned by the Austrian divisions of Generals Weissenwolf and Meszko, it was particularly vulnerable because so many troops had been taken from it to reinforce the centre. It was also isolated from the rest of the army by the gorge of the river Weisseritz. In the course of the morning it was attacked by four strong French columns under Marshal Murat, the king of Naples. By midday the Austrian line had been broken in two places. Meszko's soldiers attempted to retreat in square formation, but this proved useless as the rain soaked their powder and made it impossible for them to fire their muskets. Some of the squares were ridden down by the French cavalry, and the rest surrendered, with Meszko himself being taken prisoner. Further east, the Austrian troops were pinned against the Weisseritz gorge. The key position here was the village of Dölzschen; having cleared it of the enemy, the French discovered its well-stocked wine cellars and swiftly drank them dry. By the early afternoon the allied left wing had collapsed, and huge numbers of prisoners—probably 15,000—had been taken. Napoleon was poised to roll up his opponents' army from both wings.

The only course now open to the allies was retreat, and the order to withdraw was given at around 3 p.m. Their combined armies had suffered a brutal setback, with 14,000 men killed and wounded and 24,000 in total taken prisoner, compared to 10,000 French casualties. Schwarzenberg claimed to his wife that he tried to resign his command, but that Francis I had refused to allow him to do so.[39] At 4 p.m., wet through from the rain, his soaking cocked hat drooping around his ears, Napoleon rode back into Dresden in triumph. Behind him followed a thousand of his prisoners, three captured Austrian generals including Meszko, fifteen Austrian standards and twenty-six guns. Napoleon had won a great victory in the tradition of Austerlitz and Friedland. It was to be his last.

The human cost of this triumph was all too visible outside the city. The next morning Aster walked out over the battlefield, which was 'covered with wounded, and heaped with dead where the fighting had been fiercest. Men and horses mutilated in every way stretched as far as the eye could see.' Aster then performed one small good deed:

> I went into the Grosser Garten . . . Everything was still and lonely, and the dead lay all around me. Suddenly I heard a groan that came from the garden's western exit; I looked around, but nothing moved, there were only the dead. After a pause the sound was repeated, and I walked over to the garden gate, from where the moaning seemed to be coming. As I came round the pillars of the gate, I found in one of them a small recess, presumably used to store tools, and in which a Prussian and a Russian, both badly wounded, had been lying quite hidden. I immediately ran back to the city and was lucky enough in a short time to find two men with a wheelbarrow . . . I went back with them and had the Prussian, who was lying in front, brought out first onto the wheelbarrow, and then the Russian.[40]

For his part, Schwarzenberg ordered his army to pull back along three roads through the mountains into Bohemia. The Russians and Prussians under Barclay de Tolly would take the easiest eastern route through Peterswalde and the Austrians would withdraw in the centre along the difficult road via Dippoldiswalde and in the west towards Kommotau. Yet the retreat posed the allies considerable dangers. The most serious was the threat to their communications. Indeed, just as Moreau was wounded the news had been received that Vandamme had cut the vital road back to Peterswalde. If he pushed aside Eugen of Württemberg and was immediately supported by Napoleon, he would be able to outstrip his opponents struggling along the inferior roads to the west and block them as they emerged from the mountain passes. If that happened, the war could well come swiftly to an end.

With the allied withdrawal in such jeopardy it was clear that Eugen of Württemberg urgently needed reinforcing. He was sent 6,700 elite troops of the 1st Russian Guards Division and, rather less helpfully, a new commander, Count Ostermann-Tolstoy, a cousin of Leo Tolstoy. Barclay de Tolly had already been directed to withdraw down the Peterswalde road and come to Eugen's aid. Yet at this critical juncture an incident occurred that still remains mysterious. Barclay, fearing that he would be trapped between Vandamme to his front and Napoleon to his rear if he took the

Peterswalde road, disobeyed orders and switched instead to the Dippoldiswalde route, which was unable to cope with this influx of extra soldiers and
became completely clogged.[41]

When the first histories of the campaign were written, a controversy arose
over whether Barclay had acted on his own initiative, or at the urging of
Toll, representing Russia at Schwarzenberg's headquarters.[42] Here Clam is a
crucial witness. In his manuscript recollections, he voiced the suspicion that
Toll had secretly altered Schwarzenberg's plans and sent Barclay a private
message to change routes. Even more discreditable was the motive Clam
ascribed to Toll—to trick Barclay into disobeying orders so as to destroy
him. 'Whether it was a case of jealousy and hate towards Barclay', he wrote,

> or whether [Toll] was innocent of this error and Barclay's obstinacy was the
> only cause, I have never been able to work out. But it is certainly true that
> several Russians . . . encouraged [Schwarzenberg] to proceed harshly and with-
> out mercy against Barclay, and assured him that if he wished, he could make
> Barclay pay for his insubordination with his command and even with his life.
> The vehemence of these urgings betrayed the clear intention to ruin Barclay,
> so this must raise the suspicion of premeditation.[43]

According to Clam, Schwarzenberg did not take any action against Barclay,
because he found him easier to work with than Toll and his faction, who
would have replaced him had he been dismissed—or worse. If accurate, the
story raises the disturbing possibility that one Russian general at least was
prepared to dice with the security of the allied army to bring down a rival.
There clearly was hostility between Barclay, Toll, and their respective
factions, and Schwarzenberg discussed it in his letters to his wife. Yet
Clam is only one source, and in the chaos of the retreat he may have
misinterpreted Toll's actions. Exactly what prompted Barclay to disobey
orders will probably never be known.

Meanwhile, although Ostermann-Tolstoy had remained with Eugen of
Württemberg, without Barclay's help the two were in a very dangerous
position. By the morning of the 29 August they had been pushed down the
Peterswalde road as far as the village of Kulm, where they made a stand.
They were heavily outnumbered by Vandamme, but by the early afternoon
the urgent requests for help they had sent back to headquarters were
beginning to bear fruit. The Czar, on the Dippoldiswalde road, could see
the battle developing to the east and began to rush reinforcements to the
scene. The nearest troops were an Austrian division commanded by General

Count Colloredo, who refused to obey Alexander's orders because they did not come via Schwarzenberg. But Metternich was on the scene and, remarkably, he assumed a military role. On his own responsibility he despatched Colloredo towards the scene of the fighting.[44]

Throughout the day Kulm and the surrounding villages witnessed furious combat as they were successively taken and retaken by the French and Russians. The Russian General Krapowitski was killed, and Ostermann-Tolstoy's left arm was blown off by a round shot. The Russian troops held firm, aided by the fact that instead of concentrating his forces, Vandamme committed them piecemeal to the battle. Yet the Russians were still outnumbered two to one, and it was only in the evening that the tables began to turn. By then the Czar, the king of Prussia, Schwarzenberg, and even Barclay had arrived on the field, and 50,000 reinforcements were expected the following day. At 5 p.m., Vandamme launched a powerful attack, but at the last moment his regiments were charged in the flank by Russian heavy cavalry and beaten back.

The next morning, 30 August, the battle resumed along a north–south axis following the Peterswalde road. The allies now had enough troops to take the offensive against Vandamme, pushed his left wing off the road and began to envelop it. The French had been checked, but their line of retreat north back to Dresden was still open. Shortly afterwards, however, the situation changed dramatically. The Prussian General von Kleist, struggling with his corps through the mountains to the west, had received urgent orders to turn and make for Kulm, and had done so by taking a forest path unmarked on the map that his cavalry scouts had discovered. At around 11 a.m. the Prussians emerged on the road to the north of Vandamme, cutting off his retreat. The French tried to fight their way out but failed, and those who were not killed or dispersed were taken prisoner, including Vandamme himself. With 5,000 French casualties and perhaps 10,000 captured, the battle of Kulm was a major victory for the allies, which considerably sweetened the bitter pill of defeat at Dresden.

The responsibility on the French side for the disaster of Kulm has been much debated by military historians.[45] An argument can be made that Vandamme advanced too far, hoping to gain an independent victory, and got more than he bargained for. Yet the striking fact is Napoleon's failure to support him effectively at any point after the battle of Dresden ended. In the past, Napoleon had been famous for his ruthless pursuit of a defeated enemy, and in this case there was the added incentive that if he helped Vandamme

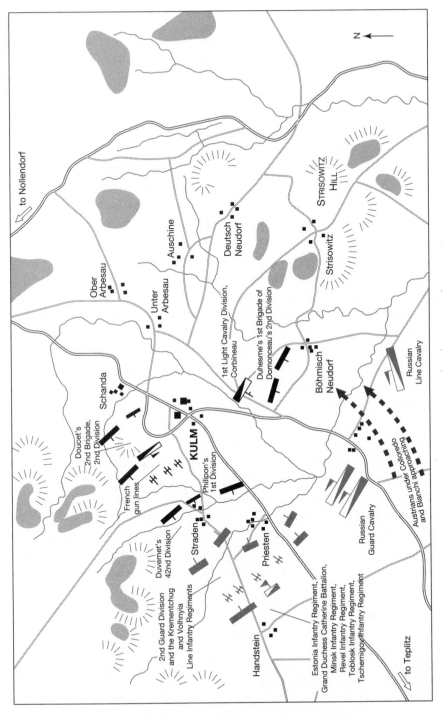

Map 7. The battle of Kulm, 29–30 August 1813.

To the map labels:

to Nollendorf

N

Ober Arbesau

Schanda

Unter Arbesau

Auschine

Deutsch Neudorf

STRISOWITZ HILL

Strisowitz

1st Light Cavalry Division, Corbineau

Duhesme's 1st Brigade of Domonceau's 2nd Division

Böhmisch Neudorf

Russian Line Cavalry

Austrians under Colloredo and Bianchi approaching

Doucet's 2nd Brigade, 2nd Division

French gun lines

KULM

Philipon's 1st Division

Duvernet's 42nd Division

Straden

Priesten

2nd Guard Division and the Krementchug and Volhnyia Line Infantry Regiments

Handstein

Russian Guard Cavalry

Estonia Infantry Regiment, Grand Duchess Catherine Battalion, Minsk Infantry Regiment, Revel Infantry Regiment, Toblosk Infantry Regiment, Tschernigov Infantry Regiment

to Teplitz

secure the vital Peterswalde road he could cut the retreating allies off from their base in Bohemia. He was certainly hampered by his lack of cavalry, and also worried by the news of Oudinot's repulse at Gross Beeren. Yet he did nothing to help either Oudinot or Vandamme. On the morning of 28 August he rode out with the Young Guard to Pirna, a little way out of Dresden on the Peterswalde road, but ordered these troops to proceed no further, and himself returned to Dresden that afternoon.

If evidence were needed of a decline in Napoleon's powers, this behaviour offers a good example. At Dresden he had displayed all his old military genius, but seemed unable to sustain it as in the past, and in the following days relapsed into listlessness. Conceivably this could have been a further sign of a long-term pituitary condition, but there may also have been more short-term causes. Several witnesses claim that on the evening after the battle Napoleon had a violent attack of vomiting and diarrhoea. He himself apparently ascribed it to food poisoning, and being soaked to the skin during the day cannot have helped.[46] According to these sources, it was this indisposition that forced Napoleon to turn back from Pirna to Dresden the next day rather than pursuing Schwarzenberg. Yet this story cannot be verified, and other accounts contradict it. The fact remains that after the battle of Dresden the Napoleon of 1813 let slip an opportunity that the Napoleon of 1805 would immediately have seized.

Whether, or to what extent, Napoleon's sluggishness had begun to worry his commanders is unclear. There is evidence that at least one of Vandamme's divisional generals spoke openly about the problem. Eight months later at Fontainebleau, just after the Emperor's abdication, Clam was discussing the events of 1813 with a group of senior French officers. One lamented the 'fatality' that had dogged the campaign, and ascribed the failure to support Vandamme at Kulm to the fact that the cannon-fire from the battlefield could not be heard at Dresden or Pirna. At this point General Corbineau, who had actually managed to cut his way out through Kleist's corps, rounded on his colleague. 'What do you mean, talking about "fatality"?', he exploded.

> The Emperor's insouciance, his stubborn belief in no-one but himself, that's the only fatality! Does one wait for the sound of cannon before following the most elementary rules of war and reinforcing an exposed detachment? Didn't the Emperor know how to make war? Didn't he have a legion of aides-de-camp and other good-for-nothings around him; had he forgotten to send out patrols? Isn't this the way to get brave men massacred? This constant habit of despising the enemy, this dreadful obstinacy, has ruined him.[47]

If the allies' tactics at Dresden had been disastrous, the overall strategy they had worked out at Trachenberg remained in place. Its greatest vindication came a hundred miles to the east, on 26 August, on the banks of the river Katzbach. After Napoleon's return from his eastward march to face Schwarzenberg, Marshal Macdonald had been left with 100,000 men to contain Blücher's Army of Silesia. Macdonald's instructions were to drive Blücher east beyond the town of Jauer, but then to take up a defensive position. He moved forward, assuming that Blücher would continue to retreat—a foolish assumption with such a fiery opponent as the old Prussian. Born in France of Scots Jacobite descent, Macdonald was an upright and honourable man, but only a mediocre commander.[48] This showed in his strategy. He dissipated his numerical strength by advancing on Jauer in three widely dispersed columns, and detached a fourth, under General Puthod, far to the south to guard against a Russian corps that posed no serious threat. In front of him lay the junction of two rivers, the Katzbach and the Wütende (or 'Roaring') Neisse. As the prefix 'roaring' suggests, in bad weather the second stream could easily become a raging torrent.

For his part Blücher, hearing of Napoleon's departure west with over half of his troops, decided to launch an attack himself. The two armies blundered into each other on the morning of 26 August, in pouring rain that severely limited visibility and prevented the infantry from firing their muskets. Like Kulm, the battle developed on a north–south axis. Blücher placed his centre and right on a steep-sided plateau, with its front protected by the Wütende Neisse and its northern flank by the Katzbach. His left wing, to the south, was slightly advanced, on the other bank of the Wütende Neisse. Macdonald sent two infantry columns across the river against the plateau, but they were slowed virtually to a standstill by rain, mud, and the narrow roads. General Souham's corps, which was meant to support them, arrived late on the field and played almost no part in the fighting.

As a result of these mishaps, the French were never able to deploy their full strength on the plateau, and were outnumbered by the Prussians and Russians waiting for them. The infantry fought each other ferociously with bayonets and clubbed muskets; at one point the French cavalry looked menacing, but were charged and broken by Russian dragoons and Cossacks. Eventually the whole French force was driven off the plateau amid scenes of chaos; many fugitives who attempted to swim to safety across the Wütende Neisse, now in full spate, were drowned. Meanwhile Blücher's left flank, which had been withdrawing before the French advance and now saw the rout on their right, launched a counterattack and put their adversaries to flight. By nightfall Macdonald's army was in full retreat everywhere, and Blücher had achieved a major victory.[49]

The French had been badly mauled, but worse was to follow. The Russian and Prussian troops were much fresher than they were, had far more cavalry, and harassed their fleeing opponents mercilessly. As Dominic Lieven observes, 'this was by far the most successful pursuit of a defeated enemy in 1813.'[50] The French rearguard formed squares to repel the allied cavalry, but since their muskets were still useless because of the rain they were swamped. To the south, General Puthod, now completely cut off, was forced to surrender on 29 August with 4,000 men and sixteen guns. In all, by the time he reached safety in Saxony Macdonald had lost probably 35,000 men, the vast majority prisoners. With his customary honesty he took full responsibility for the disaster. On 8 September, he wrote stoically to his daughter:

> War is often a matter of luck, and it has not favoured us. The main cause has been the bad weather; if any mistakes have been made they are entirely my own fault, and I blame nobody else. I have never grudged attributing glory to others or sharing it with them, but errors must be shouldered by the commander alone.[51]

By attacking precipitately and on too wide a front, Macdonald had certainly blundered. Yet his misfortunes were only part of a wider picture. By September 1813, it was becoming clear that the overall allied strategy was working, and the French was not. At Dresden the allies, for reasons that remain controversial, broke the cardinal rule of the Trachenberg plan, attacked Napoleon before all their forces were united, and were soundly beaten. Elsewhere, however, the plan worked excellently, as the Emperor's subordinate commanders were successively isolated and defeated at Gross Beeren, Kulm, and the Katzbach. The result was that, despite Dresden, the French now found themselves on the defensive, even more outnumbered than before, with their advancing enemies closing the net around them. For this deteriorating situation Napoleon was ultimately to blame. At Prague he had spurned negotiation and chosen, in Schwarzenberg's words, 'to accept the risks of war'.[52] His challenge had been accepted, and his chances of victory were rapidly receding.

8

The Battle of the Nations

The autumn campaign of 1813 now entered its second phase. Napoleon had thrown back Schwarzenberg but without gaining any lasting strategic advantage. To achieve this, he needed to destroy at least one of the three armies facing him. Schwarzenberg's forces were battered but intact, Blücher was advancing from the east, and the Army of the North had defeated the French thrust at Berlin. Napoleon was incensed that his victory at Dresden had been nullified by the mistakes of his subordinates. On 4 September, riding out to face Blücher, he stopped at the village of Hochkirch, and saw for himself what a rabble Macdonald's beaten soldiers had become. A dog appeared and began barking at him. In a rage he aimed a shot at it; when the pistol misfired, he threw it at the animal.[1]

Obeying the Trachenberg plan, as soon as Blücher realized Napoleon was in front of him, he withdrew. This left Napoleon in the same dilemma as before, uncertain in which direction, and against which opponent, to move. Eventually he returned to his original plan of marching on Berlin, to link up with the besieged garrisons of Hamburg and Stettin, and menace the Russians with an attack into Poland. If he had put all his weight behind this attack and led it himself, this would have made sense, and conformed to his own principles of warfare. Instead, he returned to Dresden to reorganize the troops defeated at Kulm and the Katzbach. Ney was ordered to replace Oudinot and advance on Berlin with just 58,000 men. Oudinot was demoted to the command of a corps serving under Ney, creating a recipe for jealousy and insubordination.[2]

On 2 September, Ney's army began its march north-east towards the Prussian capital. Opposing him was Bernadotte with his Army of the North, composed of Prussians, Russians, and Swedes. Bernadotte aimed to halt the French with his advance guard around the village of Zahna, then pivot and fall on their left with his main force. On the afternoon of 5 September, his advance guard, under the Prussian General Tauentzien, was attacked by Oudinot's corps at Zahna, and driven down the road to the small village of Dennewitz. The next morning, the battle began in earnest. It was fought on a sandy plain interspersed with woods and small hills. Tauentzien was soon in a very dangerous position, assailed by a strong French corps. Fortunately for him, the skilful and experienced General von Bülow, commanding the Prussian 3rd corps a few miles to the west, had been alerted to the developing situation. Bülow immediately marched east, and by midday on the 6th his leading troops were on the field, taking the pressure off Tauentzien.

Like Gross Beeren and Kulm, Dennewitz was not an orderly battle. Each corps was thrown piecemeal into combat as it arrived, adding to the general confusion. This was increased by poor weather conditions; not torrential rain this time, but a strong wind that raised thick clouds of sand and dust and significantly reduced visibility. On the whole this affected the French most, since they were coordinating an offensive in unfamiliar country. Yet it was they who were attacked at first, by the Prussian reinforcements who pushed them east out of Dennewitz. Then the Prussians in turn came under threat, from Oudinot's and General Reynier's corps emerging onto the field from the south. By 4 p.m., Reynier had stormed the village of Golsdorf that stood in his path, and was poised to roll up his opponents from their flank.

The Prussians were saved by a blunder of Ney's. Blinded by the swirling dust, and too close to the fighting himself, he failed to see the opportunity before Reynier and Oudinot on his left wing, and resolved to attack the Prussians on his right beyond Dennewitz. At this critical moment, he ordered Oudinot to disengage on the left and march to the right. Still furious at being superseded by Ney and quite happy to see him compromise himself, Oudinot obeyed, even though he could see how mistaken the order was and despite Reynier's pleas for him to remain. This decided the battle. Without Oudinot's support, Reynier succumbed to a renewed attack by Bülow, and Oudinot failed to reach the right wing in time to prevent its own offensive being broken. The French fell back in disorder, and fled some miles before they could be rallied. While the Prussians had slightly more casualties than their opponents—10,000 to the French total of 8,000— they took 13,500 prisoners and 53 guns.[3]

The allies had won another important victory, but the immediate consequence was a burst of internal recrimination. This centred on the role of Bernadotte during the battle. Although he commanded the Army of the North, Bernadotte had been slow to aid Bülow, and had only arrived with his Russians and Swedes in the final stages of the battle. He added insult to injury by publishing an official bulletin of the battle that gave them most of the credit and minimized the part played by the Prussians. Bülow was furious; he felt that Bernadotte had left him and his troops to fight all day against heavy odds, and was now trying to snatch away the laurels of victory.[4]

Bernadotte's actions at Dennewitz, and indeed during the entire war, remain controversial. The first historians of the 1813 campaign argued that though he was a cautious commander, he always supported his allies.[5] Yet Michael Leggiere's more recent verdict is much harsher: 'Bernadotte's unrestrained personal considerations, dynastic concerns and political machinations strangled and almost suffocated the Prussian war effort.'[6] This sums up the central charge against Bernadotte, that throughout the war he acted as a politician rather than as a general. He had only joined the allies on condition that they would help him wrest Norway from Napoleon's ally Denmark. If he failed to achieve this and returned home empty-handed, his domestic position could become precarious. The suspicion at the time, echoed today by scholars like Leggiere, was that Bernadotte deliberately kept his Swedes out of action in Germany because he needed them later for the conquest of Norway.

The death of Moreau at Dresden added a further twist to Bernadotte's calculations. Although Bernadotte was crown prince of Sweden, there is evidence that he had his eye on a greater prize—the leadership of France once Napoleon had been overthrown. At first he appears to have seen himself as Moreau's colleague at the head of a moderate republic. He even wrote to that veteran of 1789, Lafayette: 'If Moreau, you and I fell out of a cloud into the middle of the Place Vendôme, we might find it awkward at first, but who knows if the result might not be a revolution?'[7] Moreau's removal necessarily changed this scheme. Bernadotte was far too canny openly to declare himself, but several witnesses alleged that he now aimed, with the Czar's backing, to become king of France. One of them attributed to him some remarkable words: 'Bonaparte is a rascal, he has to be killed; as long as he lives, he will be the curse of the world; there must be no emperors, this is not a French title; France needs a king, but a soldier-king; the Bourbon dynasty is exhausted and will never return. Who could suit the French more than me?'[8]

Whether the French crown really was Bernadotte's chief goal at this juncture is probably impossible now to tell, but the rumours that he did provided another plausible explanation for his lacklustre commitment to the

allied cause—as a future king of the French, he did not want to be seen
fighting them as an enemy general.[9] Bernadotte always claimed to have
sound strategic reasons for his cautious conduct. Yet distrust of him became
so widespread that discreditable political motives were regularly ascribed to
his military actions. This did nothing for the unity of the coalition.

Paradoxically, Bernadotte's hesitations provoked the allies' boldest decision
of the campaign. In the first days of September Schwarzenberg, still reeling
from his repulse at Dresden, became concerned that Napoleon might advance
south and attack him in Bohemia. He decided that Blücher should reinforce
him with 50,000 men from his Army of Silesia, and secured Alexander's and
Frederick William's consent to this plan. Blücher, however, was determined
to keep his army intact and independent. In a crucial letter to the Czar of 11
September, he fiercely opposed Schwarzenberg's order, and his main argument was the need to keep an eye on Bernadotte. His own proposal was to
link up himself with Bernadotte, and attack with their combined forces over
the Elbe. This would at once expose Napoleon to a powerful thrust from the
north, and deprive Bernadotte of any excuse for hanging back.[10]

The French defeat at Dennewitz clinched Blücher's case, and decided his
chiefs to accept his scheme as part of a renewed offensive. This would be
two-pronged: Blucher and Bernadotte would advance from the north over
the Elbe, and Schwarzenberg would outflank Napoleon from Bohemia by
marching not on Dresden as before, but on Leipzig, sixty-five miles to the
west. The reinforcements Schwarzenberg was demanding would now come
from the Russian Army of Poland, advancing in reserve from the east under
General von Bennigsen.

Meanwhile at Dresden, Napoleon had lapsed into an indecisive, slightly
dissociated state. According to Marshal Saint-Cyr, he received the news of
Dennewitz 'with all the coolness he would have brought to a discussion of
events in China or the previous century'.[11] He did indeed contemplate an
advance on Schwarzenberg in Bohemia, and with this in mind carried out a
reconnaissance to the south between 9 and 17 September, but was discouraged by the strength of the allied position and returned to Dresden. It was
not until three weeks later that the news Blücher and Bernadotte had
crossed the Elbe spurred him into action. He decided to march north-
west to Torgau to face them, destroy their forces, then turn back and deal
with Schwarzenberg. October would clearly be a month of battles.[12]

It was now that Napoleon made his greatest mistake of the campaign, and he did so as much for political as military reasons. Having decided to move north, he concluded that the moment had come to abandon all his positions east of the Elbe. These were now too exposed and gave him too large an area to defend. He also resolved to abandon Dresden, too far forward to remain his forward base. Saint-Cyr later wrote that Napoleon had informed him of this at a late-night meeting on 6 October. Just twelve hours later Napoleon changed his mind, and ordered Saint-Cyr to remain at Dresden with two army corps, consisting of 30,000 men.[13] To garrison a position that was now of secondary importance was a terrible error. As a result, Napoleon deprived himself of a substantial section of his army that could have made all the difference on the battlefield. As F. L. Petre puts it in his classic study of 1813: 'It is impossible to see in this decision to hold on to Dresden anything but a vast deterioration in Napoleonic strategy.'[14]

What prompted Napoleon to take such a false step? Part of his motivation was certainly territorial. To abandon Dresden, his centre of operations for the last five months and the capital of his most faithful ally, was symbolically to renounce his possession of Germany, and he could not bring himself to do this. Yet beneath this reluctance lay something deeper, a rooted inability to give up anything he had gained. This trait had been disastrous before, and would be so again. Caulaincourt noted it with great acuity: 'As at Moscow, and every time it became necessary to retreat, [Napoleon] made the decision too late and at a moment when the enemy, strengthened by reinforcements, could crush him by sheer weight of numbers.'[15] This failing was not only visible on campaign, but in Napoleon's diplomacy. Time and again in 1813 and 1814, he held out too long and made concessions too late. Had he compromised at the Congress of Prague just four days earlier, he might have secured peace.

Napoleon's obstinacy had one further, dangerous consequence. With the failure of the Prague negotiations, political unease had begun to spread to the marshals. Berthier's doubts had long been known to the Emperor, but his colleagues now took them up with less discretion. The most significant intervention came from Murat, whose status as king of Naples and Napoleon's brother-in-law carried particular weight. A renowned cavalry general, famous for his flamboyant uniforms, particularly on the battlefield, Murat had little political talent. This quality was amply supplied by his wife, Napoleon's younger sister Caroline, an intelligent and hard-headed woman with a taste for power. The Murats were not a harmonious couple; he resented the fact that he owed his crown to her, while she had

had an affair, among others, with Metternich. What united them was a determination to retain their throne, regardless of Napoleon's own fate. By the summer of 1813 they had begun negotiations with Austria to join the allies in exchange for a guarantee they would keep Naples.[16]

Double-dealing did not come naturally to Murat, and he was soon assailed by doubts and scruples. After the Russian disaster, he had retired to Naples, but was unable to resist an appeal from his old comrades-in-arms, Berthier and Ney, to return to the colours. Yet this was only part of Murat's motivation. After the victories of Lützen and Bautzen, it seemed possible that Napoleon might yet still triumph over his enemies. Rejoining the army also offered Murat a last opportunity to make Napoleon see reason and return to the negotiating table. If this succeeded, then both he and Napoleon would survive; if not, he had discharged his duty to his brother-in-law and could save himself by whatever means necessary, including joining the allies. Murat nowhere explicitly stated this, but it is the only interpretation that explains his actions over the next months.

Murat arrived at Dresden on 14 August, and saw Napoleon three days later. He had coordinated his actions with Berthier and Caulaincourt, since he met with them the day before, and both were present at his interview with Napoleon, though they remained silent. Clearly aware of the Austrian terms at Prague, Murat urged a peace that would secure the Rhine frontier for France, with Westphalia and Holland remaining in her sphere of influence and—naturally—the status quo in Italy. His conclusion was blunt: 'Sire, everybody wants peace because it would be honourable, and the army fears a continuation of the war.'[17] This was a very loaded phrase. Murat was setting out the army's concerns, and implying that under some circumstances its interests might differ from Napoleon's.

This was not yet mutiny, but Napoleon knew how carefully any sign of military disaffection needed to be handled. Beneath the sarcasm of his riposte, there was a note of anxiety: 'So the army reasons! What is it saying?' At this point, in another move clearly concerted beforehand, Murat's friend and chief of staff General Belliard, just returned from a mission in France organizing army supplies, was brought into the room. 'What should we do?' Napoleon asked him. 'Peace, Your Majesty,' Belliard replied, 'and then they will carry you in triumph.'[18] This was a telling response, from a senior officer just back from the home front, reflecting not only the army's concerns but also what the prefects in France had been reporting about civilian opinion for several months.

Napoleon may have had to listen to Murat, but he had no intention of taking his advice. The king of Naples left the meeting empty-handed, and deeply frustrated. Talking things over later with Belliard, he let his anger show: 'Ah, the wicked man, he'll sacrifice the army and France, and get us all killed! Berthier, Caulaincourt and I set out to him all the advantages of an honourable peace, but we couldn't move him. He heard us out with absolute calm, and we came away with nothing.'[19] The meeting had at least satisfied Murat's conscience; having issued his warning to his brother-in-law, he now felt free to strike out on his own path. The other marshals were not so fortunate. Equally concerned by the prospect of losing everything if Napoleon was defeated, but without kingdoms of their own to retire to, they remained tied to France and to the army, and their alarm and discontent grew steadily.

By October, the marshals' disaffection had become so open that it began to affect Napoleon's strategic decisions. On the 10th, he was at Düben, north of Leipzig, preparing to strike at Blücher and Bernadotte. Yet instead of attacking, he stayed put for the next four days in the pleasant moated country house he had made his headquarters, agonizing over his next move. Many historians have seen this as further evidence of Napoleon's declining powers. He was clearly unsure of Blücher's and Bernadotte's exact location and worried about the approach of Schwarzenberg's army towards Leipzig from the south, but the Napoleon of old would have assessed and reacted to the situation far more quickly. Instead, one witness records him sitting at his desk doodling letters in Gothic script on a sheet of paper.[20]

Some unpublished notes of Caulaincourt's reveal that there were other factors at work. Napoleon's initial plan at Düben was to cross to the right bank of the Elbe, destroy the bridges Blücher and Bernadotte had thrown over the river, and cut them off from the rear. This strategy carried a risk that his own lines of communication to the west could be cut off, and this was too much for the marshals. As Caulaincourt recalled:

This project, which would separate us from France, hampering if not breaking entirely our communications with her, appealed to nobody ... [Berthier] who had been told about the plan in Dresden did everything he could to get it changed, and the other commanders did as well. Ney, whom the Emperor summoned and talked to because of his popularity with the soldiers also tried to make him understand that the state of opinion within the army demanded that he take another direction and move back towards France, whose frontiers and security were already seen as menaced.[21]

Napoleon defended his plan, but the marshals stuck to their position. The impasse was only broken by news that changed the strategic picture. Blücher and Bernadotte had struck further west than anticipated, towards Halle, and were already menacing the French rear. Then Murat, commanding the French forces to the south around Leipzig, reported that Schwarzenberg was advancing fast on the city. This finally determined Napoleon to pull back to Leipzig, concentrate his forces there and fight a decisive battle. According to Caulaincourt, he took this decision 'less by conviction that it was the right course than a realization that he had to bow to the general opinion'.[22]

This incident is very revealing. It shows that Napoleon's hesitation at Düben was caused not only by his own lethargy, but by a confrontation with his increasingly recalcitrant marshals. The result was that he lost four crucial days in which he could have destroyed the armies of Blücher and Bernadotte before turning south to face Schwarzenberg. It also underlines the increasing role of Ney, who in the coming months was to become the most consistent and visible spokesman for the army and its grievances. For Napoleon, these were ominous signs. If the army he had so often led to victory was now developing a mind of its own, then a central pillar of his regime was crumbling.

Napoleon took his decision to withdraw to Leipzig early in the morning of 13 October. Having issued his orders, he left Düben at 7 a.m. the next morning, and was in Leipzig by midday. By then, fighting had already begun. The first allied attacks were launched against Murat, who was defending the low but strategic heights south of the city between the villages of Markkleeberg and Liebertwolkwitz. This soon turned into the biggest cavalry battle of the campaign, as Murat threw 5,000 dragoons and cuirassiers against his opponents. 'Like a great, shining snake', wrote one eyewitness, 'the massive column of horsemen burst out of the smoke and bore down on the allies.'[23] Murat was in the thick of the fighting. Highly visible in a gold-embroidered velvet uniform and a hat with tall ostrich plumes, he came very near to being captured. A Prussian officer rode up close to him and called on Murat to surrender, but was shot down just in time by a member of Murat's household. As evening fell, the French still held the heights, and the conflict had reached a stalemate. The losses on both sides were heavy: 1,500 dead and wounded for the French, and 2,500 for the allies.

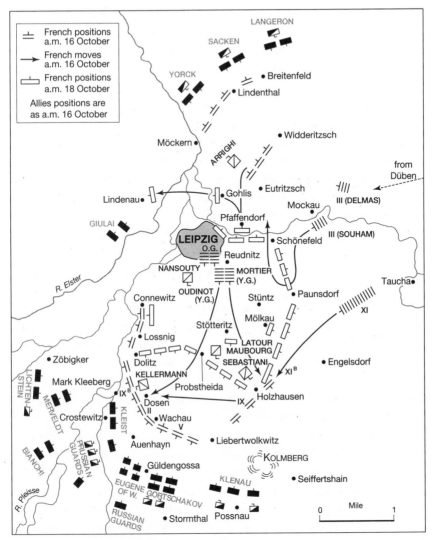

Map 8. The battle of Leipzig, 16–19 October 1813.

If the battle was fatal for several thousand soldiers, it was also a disaster for the local inhabitants. Throughout the day, thousands of peasants struggled into Leipzig, fleeing from the hostilities. Even before the action began, their situation had become intolerable; soldiers from both sides had plundered their food and possessions, and ripped out the timber in their houses to make fires and shelters. Those who chose to remain had an even more unpleasant experience. A resident of Liebertwolkwitz later wrote down his recollections of 14 October, which make harrowing reading. At 10 a.m., the first cannon shots provoked a general stampede for safety to the church, whose thick walls offered some protection. For six hours the villagers cowered as the windows were shot out by musket fire and the surrounding streets were set ablaze. During a lull in the engagement, a French officer arrived and, speaking German, 'expressed his amazement that anyone could have decided to take refuge in a building in the middle of a battle'. He promised to warn them if the fighting intensified, which it duly did, with cannonballs thudding into the church walls. Braving the bombardment, the daughter of the local saddler went outside to search for her mother, only to find her shot dead in her own garden.[24]

The next day saw a pause as the commanders drew up their battle plans. Napoleon realized he had to strike a decisive blow quickly. At present he was only slightly outnumbered. He had 191,000 men available compared to the allies' 200,000, but was heavily outgunned by their artillery. Napoleon knew, however, that within a few days Schwarzenberg would be reinforced by Bernadotte's Army of the North, Bennigsen's Army of Poland, and a further Austrian contingent, whereas he himself could only expect 14,000 fresh troops. This would give the allies a massive superiority of 130,000. Eventually all these forces were indeed deployed on the field, making Leipzig the bloodiest battle in history until the first day of the Somme.

Napoleon anticipated that Schwarzenberg would begin by attacking, so initially proposed to fight on the defensive. He then aimed to counterattack as he had done at Bautzen. Macdonald would turn the allies' right wing, forcing them to weaken their centre right, which would be stormed by the Imperial Guard supported by Marmont and heavy artillery fire. This plan had one flaw. Napoleon was convinced that Blücher, approaching from the west, would not arrive in time to throw the French offensive off-balance. Strikingly, he made exactly the same mistake two years later at Waterloo, when he obstinately refused to believe that Blücher would march so swiftly to support Wellington. On both occasions he seriously underestimated Blücher, 'that madman', as he contemptuously called him.[25] He failed to realize that the old Prussian, for all his eccentricities, was the allied commander who had most thoroughly absorbed his own military principles of speed, mobility, and relentless offensive spirit.

If Napoleon's strategy was faulty, Schwarzenberg's was potentially disastrous. He relied heavily on the local knowledge of his quartermaster-general, von Langenau, who had recently defected from the Saxon to the Austrian army. Langenau persuaded him that the most suitable sector for an attack would be on the left, and Schwarzenberg initially assigned 140,000 men to this task. Yet in reality the ground was completely unsuitable; it was swampy and overgrown, and shut in between two rivers, the Elster and the Pleisse, making deployment extremely difficult. All this gave the defenders a major advantage, and it remains baffling why Langenau advocated striking here. Had his plan gone ahead, it could well have given Napoleon the crushing victory he needed by significantly weakening the allies' right and right centre, exactly where he planned his own attack. However, the Russians, and particularly the Czar, protested so heatedly that after a fierce argument Schwarzenberg was forced to back down. The attack between the Elster and the Pleisse was scaled down, with Blücher now to advance from the northwest rather than the west, and troops were shifted across to reinforce an offensive in the centre.[26]

The battle began at 9 a.m. the next day, with this allied frontal assault on the French line. It succeeded in taking Markkleeberg, but failed to advance further in the teeth of a stubborn defence and heavy artillery fire. Meanwhile on the left the Austrian general Gyulai proceeded with what was to have been the main attack between the Pleisse and the Elster, but the French position was too strong and he made no headway. By 11 a.m., Napoleon felt ready to launch his counteroffensive. Advancing on the right into murderous gunfire, Macdonald's corps took an important redoubt on the Kolmberg and drove the Austrians from Liebertwolkwitz. An anonymous sergeant-major, a German schoolteacher conscripted into the French infantry earlier in the year, later described the ferocity of the fighting:

> The Emperor came past us on his grey horse . . . at such a gallop as I have never seen a horse travel. The cannonballs ploughed into the ground to the left and right in front of and behind him so that the earth was thrown over his head. He held his reins in his right hand and with his left clutched his hat to his head. Every moment we expected him to be hit but he rode on through it all.

> We stood in square in a dreadful hail of shot . . . Within fifteen minutes the battalion had at least a hundred men killed and wounded . . . We now moved down into a meadow in a valley. Before us was a hill; behind us a stream. Shells came over the hill. One of the skirmishers, Heinen, who came from Bonn, had an apple; he cut it in two and gave me half, saying: 'Here, my dear sergeant-major, let's eat this together; who knows if we'll be here tonight.' The apple was not eaten when a cannonball came down the valley and took off the heads of five skirmishers in the third rank on the left wing, including

that of my good Heinen. As I was standing behind him, I was so covered with his blood and brains that I could scarcely see. I had the bodies taken to the rear and went down to the stream to clean up my uniform as best I could.[27]

Amid this horror, the main French counterattack went in and penetrated deep into the allies' right centre. The Prussians were driven back to the village of Crobern. Then a heavy cavalry division was unleashed, breaking the Russian infantry before them and capturing twenty-six guns. They were now dangerously close to the small hill from which the Czar and the king of Prussia were watching the action. In the nick of time, two Russian cavalry charges, one in the front and one in the flank, caught the French off guard and scattered them. The frontal attack was led by Schwarzenberg himself, who mounted and led forward the Cossacks of the Russian Imperial Guard. These last-ditch measures had the necessary effect. By the late afternoon, though the allies' line had been pushed back, it had not been broken.

A major reason for this lay in developments to the north-west of Leipzig. Napoleon needed Marmont's corps, which was holding this sector, to clinch the main attack, and at 7 a.m. he ordered it to head south-east to support Macdonald. Having seen the sky to the west lit up by enemy camp fires the previous night, Marmont was concerned that Blücher was very close. Napoleon dismissed his fears as 'absurd'. As F. L. Petre comments, this is 'a remarkable instance of Napoleon's growing habit of making the wish father to the thought'.[28] Marmont's troops were just moving off when the Prussians began to advance. Marmont realized that if he carried out his orders he would leave the entire French rear exposed, so he stopped, turned round, and took position around the village of Möckern. As a result, he never arrived to support Macdonald. By underrating Blücher, Napoleon had fatally compromised the offensive that was meant to bring him victory.

Marmont was now committed to defending Möckern against a formidable Prussian assault. Blücher sent in Yorck's corps first, and stood by the side of the road praying aloud as they marched past. The fighting was notably savage; the French defended themselves with great determination, but Yorck's men attacked with terrifying ferocity. In the course of the afternoon Möckern was taken and retaken several times. Prince Karl of Mecklenburg, directing a bayonet charge, had two horses shot from under him by cannonballs. By the time a fresh brigade advanced, at 5 p.m., the Prussian artillery had been brought up to within 700 yards of the French line. Amid this murderous exchange of point-blank fire, the Prussians wavered and fell back and Marmont ordered his men forward in pursuit. At this moment, in one of the critical decisions of the battle, Yorck threw in the only reserve he had left—his cavalry. Seven regiments charged furiously against the advancing French infantry. They rode down two battalions, and their impetus carried them up to the main French gun battery in the village. Marmont's troops were finally thrown out of Möckern, leaving thirty-five guns, eight ammunition wagons, four hundred prisoners, and two standards behind. Both sides paid a very high price in casualties: almost half of Yorck's corps were killed or wounded. But their charge had turned the tide of the entire battle. The French line of retreat to the north had been cut off, and they were almost surrounded.[29]

Napoleon had failed to win the quick decisive victory he needed, and his enemies now had the advantage. Both sides were too exhausted to do much fighting on 17 October, but during the afternoon Bennigsen arrived on the field and Bernadotte's troops were expected the next day, giving the allies almost a two-to-one superiority over the French. Leading a division in Bennigsen's army was Bubna, who had now exchanged diplomacy for warfare. Faced with these lengthening odds, the logical option for Napoleon was to prepare an orderly withdrawal. In the course of the 17th, he seems in principle to have decided on this course, but then did virtually nothing to put it into practice. Now that Blücher was blocking escape to the north-west, Napoleon had a choice of three routes heading back to Erfurt and Jena. However, they were only accessible by a single road west from Leipzig crossing the river Elster by a bridge and the marshes beyond by a long causeway to the village of Lindenau. Prudence dictated throwing more bridges across the Elster and its tributary the Pleisse to relieve pressure on the existing one, but Napoleon did nothing. It was a further striking illustration of his psychological inability to retreat that Caulaincourt so shrewdly underlined.

What Napoleon finally did do that day was to pull back and shorten his line to aid a smooth departure from the field. It now stretched from Lindenau in the west, through Probstheida in the centre, to Paunsdorf and Schoenefeld in the north-east. His other preoccupation that day was not military at all. In the fighting on the 16th, a senior Austrian general, Count Merveldt, had been captured. Extremely short-sighted, he had mistaken some French troops for Prussians, and been promptly surrounded. Like Schwarzenberg and Bubna, Merveldt was a diplomat as well as a soldier, whom Napoleon had got to know as far back as 1797 during peace negotiations with Austria. At 2 p.m., the Emperor sent for him and—half-way through the bloodiest battle of the age—discussed with him reopening negotiations with the allies. Even now his terms differed little from those of his counter-proposal to Metternich at Prague. He was still not prepared to renounce the protectorate of the Rhine Confederation, though he was ready to give up Hamburg and Lübeck, and grudgingly agreed to reconsider the future of Holland. He also accepted that Italy should become independent of France, though clearly wished to place his stepson Eugène de Beauharnais at its head. Precious time that Napoleon could ill afford passed in this discussion, and early the next morning Merveldt was sent back to the allied lines with the offer. Francis, Alexander, and Frederick William immediately rejected it, and did not even send an answer.[30]

The battle of Leipzig resumed at 7 a.m. on 18 October. Schwarzenberg's strategy was straightforward: a general attack in six columns on the French in all sectors. The allies now had 1,360 cannon on the field, more than double their opponents' total, and they opened a deafening bombardment. The French held on tenaciously. On their western flank, General Bertrand broke out of Lindenau, drove back the surrounding Austrians and gained valuable space around Napoleon's line of retreat. To the east, Bennigsen captured some of the outlying French positions but could advance no further since Bernadotte, due to support him on the right, had still not arrived.

The battle reached its peak in the afternoon. Prussian and Russian troops mounted a succession of furious assaults on Probstheida, which formed the pivot of Napoleon's line. They managed to penetrate to the centre of the village, but were eventually forced out with heavy losses on both sides. In this action alone, four French generals were killed. Further east Bennigsen had more success, largely because the leading corps of Bernadotte's army were finally beginning to appear. Concentrated artillery fire and repeated infantry attacks led by Bubna drove the French out of Paunsdorf. Of the sixty-six houses standing before the battle, half were completely demolished and the other half seriously damaged. At the same time the allies captured Schönefeld, by now a blazing ruin. In this sector they were helped by a remarkable auxiliary, a British battery from the Royal Artillery using the recently-developed Congreve rockets. It was commanded by Captain Richard Bogue, who was killed in the thick of the action. Its modern-day successor, O Battery of the Royal Horse Artillery, is the only British unit to carry 'Leipzig' as a battle honour.[31]

As the French held on desperately in Paunsdorf, two brigades of their Saxon cavalry were stationed in the fields beyond. Early in the afternoon, their officers held an impromptu conference, ordered the men to sheath their sabres, and led them over to the Russians. A few hours later, a division of Saxon infantry followed suit. Their motivation was a mixture of German patriotism and a conviction that the French cause was lost and Saxony should not be dragged down with it. Napoleon later claimed that the Saxons' change of sides had cost him the battle. This argument is unsustainable, since at the most 4,000 troops were involved, and their actions did not lead to an allied breakthrough.[32] The real significance of the defection was to demonstrate, in the most dramatic way, that even Napoleon's staunchest German allies were now abandoning him.

While the soldiers were slaughtering each other, the unfortunate civilians who had not fled continued to suffer. One was the vicar of Plaussig, a village to the north of Paunsdorf, who later set down his experiences. On 17 October he and his family watched as Prussian volunteers were billetted in his vicarage, destroying his library in the process, before being replaced by Russians. Worse was to follow next day:

> The battle began at nine o'clock. The gunfire was so heavy that the earth shook. The windows rattled so hard that we thought they would smash. All around us were Russian soldiers shouting and running to and fro. There was scarcely any room for us to stand. In the south and south-west, wherever we looked, we saw burning villages. The flames from Schoenefeld were blown towards us by the strong winds ... We had been told that the Russians loved children; trusting to this, my wife hid some baby clothes under our eleven-week-old infant in his basket-work crib. As soon as the Russians came in, they rushed to the crib, threw the baby out onto the floor and took the clothes.[33]

As evening fell, it was clear that Leipzig would be an allied victory. The French had not been routed, but were clearly in retreat, particularly in the north-east sector with the loss of Paunsdorf and Schönefeld. During the night, Napoleon gave the order to withdraw, and troops streamed back into the city, causing bottlenecks and confusion in the unlit streets. Marmont and Generals Souham and Durutte were assigned to defend Leipzig and cover the evacuation, with three corps under Macdonald to act as a rearguard. The Elster bridge was to be mined, and blown up as soon as Macdonald had passed over it to hinder pursuit.

At 7 a.m. on 19 October, in bright autumn sunshine, the allies moved in to storm the city. Leipzig, with a population of roughly 30,000, consisted of

Figure 6. The battle of Leipzig: Schwarzenberg announcing the victory to the allied monarchs, 19 October 1813, by Johann Peter Krafft.

Figure 7. The battle of Leipzig: fighting at the Grimma Gate.

lightly fortified outer suburbs, then a solid defensive wall with four gates enclosing the old town. By 11.30, the French had been driven from the suburbs, and the final assault began. From the north, Blücher himself led the assault on the Halle gate. With tremendous energy and courage, he urged his men on, shouting 'Forwards! Forwards!...Hit them hard and keep hitting!' The attackers broke through and, after bitter house-to-house fighting along the narrow streets, reached the city centre. To the east, there was a furious struggle as the Swedes and Russians stormed the Grimma gate. It ended in a ghastly massacre, since the defenders manning the gate itself had been ordered under no circumstances to open it, and their comrades outside were mercilessly cut down. With very few exceptions, no prisoners were taken.[34]

Napoleon had left Leipzig at 11 a.m. to organize the retreat. Eyewitness descriptions of his demeanour are contradictory: some claim he looked visibly depressed, others that he maintained his habitual calm in a crisis. The chaos on the road west can hardly have improved his mood. According to one observer, 'Ammunition wagons...cannon, cows and sheep, women, grenadiers and soldiers, the healthy, the wounded and the dying, all were... crushed together in a great mass.' Ominously, there were none of the usual cheers as Napoleon rode by. General de Marbot later recalled that 'the army was angry at the lack of care with which its retreat from the battlefield had been organized.' Progress was painfully slow, but eventually Napoleon got over the Elster bridge and the causeway beyond to Lindenau. He set up his headquarters in the local mill, then climbed upstairs and went to sleep.[35]

The final act of the tragedy now began. Explosive charges had now been placed under the Elster bridge by the experienced engineer Colonel Montfort. By an extraordinary oversight, however, Montfort was not told which would be the last unit to cross before the detonation should take place. As the hours went by, he became increasingly concerned, and finally decided to go over to Lindenau himself to get the information, leaving a corporal named Lafontaine in charge of the bridge. Montfort got to Lindenau, but found that pushing his way back against the tide of fugitives was impossible. Meanwhile, some Russian skirmishers had reached the meadows to the north of the bridge, and began firing into the crowd struggling over it. Just before 1 p.m., Corporal Lafontaine lost his nerve and, with the bridge still packed, lit the fuse. Marshal Marmont, who had just reached the far bank, described what happened next:

A terrible explosion suddenly drowned out all the noises of the retreat: the shouts and cries and the rumbling of the wagons. Beams, planks, stone blocks, men, carts and equipment were hurled up into the air to crash down again. A huge cloud of smoke billowed up.[36]

The premature destruction of the Elster bridge turned a French defeat into a disaster. Napoleon's rearguard was now trapped in Leipzig, and shortly afterwards surrendered; 12,000 men were taken prisoner and eighty guns captured. Marshal Poniatowski tried to ride his horse through the river and drowned; Macdonald got three-quarters of the way across on a tree his engineers felled, then swam to safety on the other bank. By the time the French army regrouped, it numbered just 80,000. Estimates vary, but between 14 and 19 October it probably lost between 40,000 and 50,000 killed and wounded, and 15,000 prisoners. The allied losses were equally terrible: approximately 50,000 dead and wounded, and 4,000 captured.[37] Casualties on this scale would not be seen again until World War One.

At 1 p.m., the Czar, Frederick William, and Schwarzenberg rode into Leipzig's market square with military bands playing. Shortly afterwards they were joined by Bernadotte, Bennigsen, and Blücher. The citizens, transported with joy, crowded every window and even climbed onto the roofs to cheer them. It was an extraordinary moment. The allies' battle tactics had hardly been inspired, but by avoiding major mistakes and bringing overwhelming numbers to bear, they had decisively defeated Napoleon and ended his dominion in Germany. The next day Blücher, who had contributed so much to the victory, wrote a triumphant letter to a friend:

> We have just had two great, beautiful days; during the 18th and 19th the Great Colossus fell like an oak tree in a storm. He, the Great Tyrant, has saved himself, but his henchmen are in our hands . . . Goodbye; I am so tired I am shaking all over.[38]

Plate 1. Napoleon as first consul, by Antoine-Jean Gros.

Plate 2. Napoleon in March 1812, by Anne-Louis Girodet.

Plate 3. Armand de Caulaincourt, 1808, by Jean-Baptiste Isabey, from the Austerlitz Table.

Plate 4. Prince Metternich, 1815, by Sir Thomas Lawrence.

Plate 5. Marie-Louise and the king of Rome, by François Gérard.

Plate 6. Louis-Alexandre Berthier, 1808, by Jacques Augustin Catherine Pajou.

Plate 7. Alexander I, 1814, by François Gérard.

Plate 8. Francis I, 1841, by Anton Einsle.

Plate 9. Prince Carl Philipp zu Schwarzenberg, by François Gérard.

Plate 10. Count Carl Clam-Martinic, portrait at Burg Clam, Austria.

Plate 11. Prince Blücher, engraving from a sketch by Major General Birch Reynardson, 1814.

9
Natural Frontiers

The retreat from Leipzig was a ghastly trial for the French army. Given the need to outstrip the victorious allies, it was conducted by forced marches. Unable to keep up with the pace, thousands dropped by the wayside. Advancing in their wake, their pursuers found the woods on each side of the main road filled with dead and dying stragglers, and abandoned wagons and cannon everywhere. The scene was not as terrible as the retreat from Moscow, but it carried unmistakeable echoes of that calamity.[1]

As the army struggled west to the Rhine, Napoleonic Germany collapsed around it. Westphalia was occupied by Russian troops and its king, Napoleon's youngest brother Jérôme, fled to Düsseldorf. In early November Jérôme's father-in-law, King Frederick of Württemberg, deserted the French cause. He was following the example set by Bavaria, which had signed the Treaty of Ried with Austria just before Leipzig.[2] The defections of Württemberg and Bavaria were personal triumphs for Metternich, who had shrewdly guaranteed that both states could keep the considerable territorial gains they had made under Napoleon if they now switched allegiance. The fate of the King of Saxony was a stark warning of the dangers of staying with the losing side. The one major German monarch to stay faithful to Napoleon, the king was captured at Leipzig and taken as a prisoner to Berlin, and his country put under allied administration.

Bavaria's change of camp had one immediate military consequence. Her army, previously under Napoleon's command, now marched north from the Danube to cut off his retreat to France. However, it was pushed aside at the battle of Hanau, just east of Frankfurt-am-Main, on 30 October. Despite this success, the French were still too disorganized to halt and regroup at Frankfurt, and continued their flight. On 2 November, they crossed over the Rhine at Mainz, leaving just three bridgeheads on the right bank, opposite Mainz and Strasbourg further south, and at Wesel to the north. For the first time since 1793, France herself was threatened with invasion.

If a compromise settlement to end the war was to be reached, now was the moment to revive negotiations, with Napoleon defeated and the heartland of his empire under threat. Accompanying the allied armies on their advance through Germany, Metternich pondered the overture Napoleon had made at the height of the battle of Leipzig and now, from a position of strength, decided to respond to it. To do so, he had the perfect instrument to hand. On 24 October, the French minister to Weimar, the baron de Saint-Aignan, had been captured by a Cossack raid on the town. He had then spent two uncomfortable and alarming days in Russian custody, fearing he would be sent back to Russia as a prisoner. Metternich rescued him from this plight, and not just from humanitarian motives. Saint-Aignan was the brother-in-law of Caulaincourt, whose desire for peace was widely known, and also close to Talleyrand. If released and sent home, Saint-Aignan could both transmit Metternich's proposals to Paris and help mobilize powerful support for them.[3]

Metternich first discussed peace with Saint-Aignan on 26 October. He spoke in very general terms, regretting that a settlement had not been reached at Prague, blaming Napoleon's intransigence for this, and raising the possibility of resuming negotiations. The next day he convinced the Czar and the English ambassador to Vienna, Lord Aberdeen, to support a peace proposal in principle. The Prussians were not consulted. Why Alexander, with his well-known reluctance to deal with Napoleon, agreed to Metternich's plan is not entirely clear. Probably he feared disrupting the alliance, and probably Metternich reassured him, as before, that Napoleon was certain to reject any reasonable offer. Whatever the truth, Metternich was able to confide his scheme to Schwarzenberg in a letter written that evening, and to add: 'I have arranged this matter with the Emperor Alexander.'[4]

Over the next few days, secret diplomacy was interrupted by a grand public event. The allied army arrived in Frankfurt on 4 November, and on the morning of the 6th Metternich escorted Francis I into the city. It was a deeply symbolic moment. Here, twenty-one years before, Francis had been crowned Holy Roman Emperor. For over a thousand years, the Holy Roman Empire had united the states of Germany and central Europe in a loose federation, until abolished in 1806 and replaced by Napoleon's Confederation of the Rhine. Now, in the person of its last ruler, it was triumphing from the grave over its upstart successor, ruined in just a few weeks. Writing that evening to his current mistress Wilhelmine von Sagan, Metternich lyrically described the scene:

> Imagine, my friend, a hundred thousand people crowding the streets, filling every window from cellars to attics, all drunk with joy. What cheering—what holy enthusiasm! The crowned head of the Holy Roman Empire returning as a conqueror to the place that scoundrels had besmirched—never was the triumph of truth over falsehood, of good over evil, of the majestic over the absurd—so vividly displayed.[5]

It was in Frankfurt that Metternich put the finishing touches to his new peace initiative. At 9 p.m. on 9 November, he summoned Saint-Aignan to an interview, and said that he had just agreed with the Czar a secret peace overture to Napoleon. Saint-Aignan would be released, return to Paris and present it verbally to the Emperor. Nesselrode entered the room and confirmed Metternich's words. Saint-Aignan then took down, at Metternich's dictation, the proposal. It stated that 'the allied sovereigns were unanimously agreed on the power and preponderance that France should retain in all their integrity, by confining herself to her natural limits, which are the Rhine, the Alps and the Pyrenees.' The German and Italian states, as well as Holland, were to be completely independent. In addition, England 'was ready to make the greatest sacrifices for a peace on this basis and to recognize that freedom of commerce and navigation which France has a right to claim'.[6]

The offer of France's 'natural limits' was highly significant, and astutely calculated. The concept had a long history. Julius Caesar in his *Gallic Wars* had first stated that ancient Gaul had originally extended to the Rhine, the Alps, the Atlantic, and the Pyrenees. The extent to which regaining these 'natural' frontiers shaped the foreign policy of the French kings remains controversial.[7] What is clear, however, is the central role it had come to occupy in revolutionary and republican rhetoric after 1792. On 31 January 1793, just ten days after Louis XVI's execution, the great orator Georges-Jacques Danton rose in the Convention to give the idea its most famous and lapidary expression: 'The limits of France are marked out by nature. We shall attain them at each of their four points: at the Ocean, the Rhine, the Alps and the Pyrenees.'[8] After immense efforts these frontiers had indeed been gained. They had been confirmed by the treaties of Campo Formio in 1797 and then Lunéville in 1801, the second of which Napoleon himself had

Map 9. The 'historic' and 'natural' frontiers of France.

signed. Conceding the 'natural limits' again in 1813 gave Napoleon a chance to claim to the French that he had concluded peace with honour—his empire may have been swept away, but the greatest territorial gain achieved by the Republic had been preserved.

Associating England with these terms was also a shrewd tactic. Metternich knew that the prospect of its inclusion in a general peace would be an extremely tempting bait for Napoleon. The fact that only a continental peace had been on offer at the congress of Prague had been a major reason for its failure. The statement that England was now prepared to make the greatest sacrifices for a settlement was, however, far from accurate. Her government was determined that Antwerp, the best-placed base for a cross-channel invasion, and which Napoleon had substantially strengthened, should be removed from French control. Yet Antwerp lay at the mouth of the river Scheldt, itself part of the Rhine delta, arguably situating it within France's 'natural limits'. Above all, England had always refused to make any concessions on her so-called 'maritime rights', the complex system of regulations that underpinned her naval blockade of the French empire and imposed draconian restrictions on neutral shipping. Indeed, her uncompromising insistence on upholding these restrictions had led the USA, whose commerce was suffering considerably from them, to declare war on her in June 1812.[9]

For Metternich, the solution to this dilemma lay with George Gordon, Earl of Aberdeen, the newly appointed English ambassador to Vienna, who had also travelled to Frankfurt. In fact, Cathcart as ambassador to Russia and Stewart as minister to Berlin were also at Frankfurt, but Aberdeen enjoyed Castlereagh's confidence more than they did. Metternich had been cultivating Aberdeen since his arrival, with considerable success. Aberdeen was a highly intelligent and civilized man, but he was only 29, on his first diplomatic mission, and no match for Metternich's diplomatic guile.[10] Aberdeen was all the more sympathetic to peace proposals since he had just had his first experience of war; he had ridden over the field of Leipzig just after the battle and been horrified by the carnage.[11] Metternich had already secured Aberdeen's agreement, along with the Czar's, to the peace approach to Napoleon at the meeting of 27 October. Significantly, Cathcart and Stewart were not present, and were told nothing of the initiative.

The next, extremely delicate, stage was to associate Aberdeen with the maritime concessions in the terms dictated to Saint-Aignan. In a carefully choreographed scene, Aberdeen was ushered into the room after Saint-Aignan had finished writing, and the document was read aloud. It has been claimed that Aberdeen had difficulty understanding the wording because his French was so poor, but this is unlikely, since his written French was perfectly adequate. The language barrier certainly did not prevent him from objecting to the extent of the sacrifices to which England was presented as consenting. In particular, he warned 'against supposing that any possible consideration could induce Great Britain to abandon a particle of what she felt to belong to her maritime code'. But he did not actually demand that the offending phrases be altered and that, for Metternich, was the essential point. The next day Saint-Aignan set off on his mission to Paris.[12]

The 'Frankfurt proposals', as they came to be known, remain perplexing on several counts. Could Metternich and Nesselrode really have thought that the English cabinet, when it understood the sleight-of-hand practised on Aberdeen, would not swiftly repudiate him and take back concessions that had never really been made? Metternich provided an answer in his memoirs—the question did not arise, since the Frankfurt terms were never sincerely meant. Instead, they were simply meant to drive a wedge between Napoleon and French public opinion. If the Emperor rejected them, which it was assumed he would, he would appear intransigent, and in the unlikely event that he accepted them various pretexts could be found to withdraw the offer.[13]

Here again Metternich's memoirs, presenting him after the event as the architect of Napoleon's fall, are economical with the truth. Throughout 1813 he wanted to rescue Napoleon, not destroy him, because it finally seemed possible that his power could be reduced to manageable proportions. Metternich's real fear was of victorious Russia, now the strongest state on the continent and an increasingly menacing presence on Austria's eastern border.[14] The best way of countering this threat, he felt, was by balancing Russia in the west by a chastened but still formidable France, led by a Napoleon who had learned his lesson. If this was Metternich's motivation at the beginning of 1813, it was doubly so by the end of the year, with Napoleon driven back to the Rhine and Russian strength and prestige greater than ever. However Metternich chose to portray them later, the Frankfurt proposals clearly reflected this motivation.

This still leaves the problem of how Metternich thought the English government could be persuaded to accept his plan. Castlereagh and his colleagues were considerably more experienced than Aberdeen, and backed by a press and public opinion determined to preserve England's maritime rights. Metternich no doubt hoped to create a momentum they would find impossible to resist. Despite their anger at the trick played on Aberdeen, if Napoleon swiftly accepted the proposals they would find it difficult to defy France, Austria, and Russia. They would find themselves isolated, and appear the only obstacle to peace. Once again everything depended on Napoleon. If he rejected the overture, or even delayed replying, Austria would have dangerously alienated a key ally whose subsidies were essential to the war effort, and gained nothing in return. The fact that Metternich was prepared to take this risk shows how desperate he still was, at the eleventh hour, for a compromise settlement.

The military context was also critical. On 7 November, just as the Frankfurt proposals were being prepared, the allies convened a council of war that lasted for three days. Before it lay two crucial questions—whether to cross the Rhine, and if so, when. Resolving them laid bare deep divisions, not just between the allied governments, but within them as well. Blücher and his chief of staff Gneisenau wanted to advance on Paris as quickly as possible, but Frederick William III was strongly opposed. 'This wretched invasion of France that's planned makes me tremble,' he wrote. On the Russian side, Nesselrode had deep reservations about an invasion of France. The Czar, however, remained determined to press ahead. As Castlereagh shrewdly observed: 'He has a *personal* feeling about Paris, distinct from all political or military combinations. He seems to seek for the occasion of entering with his magnificent guards the enemy's capital, probably to display, in his clemency and forbearance, a contrast to that desolation [which had been visited on Moscow].'[15]

As commander-in-chief and also an experienced diplomat, Schwarzenberg played a pivotal part in both military and political decision-making. He was careful to coordinate his strategy with Metternich's diplomacy. On 3 November, just before he arrived in Frankfurt, he wrote to him: 'I must base my plan of operations on circumstances as they arise; but before presenting it to Czar Alexander it's essential that we agree on its principles.'[16] Unfortunately, once Schwarzenberg and Metternich were in Frankfurt, they no longer needed to correspond, and no record exists of their discussions. Yet it is clear that both men favoured an invasion of France within weeks. Metternich thought the allied advance should continue, to force Napoleon to accept suitable peace terms. He was convinced that the armistice during the Congress of Prague had benefited the French, and was determined not to repeat the mistake. Just after dictating the Frankfurt proposals to Saint-Aignan, he noted: 'Our first condition was that there should be no question of a truce.' For his part, Schwarzenberg wished to strike immediately, before Napoleon could regroup his forces and rally the French nation behind him. He was also concerned that if his army stayed where it was, it would soon run out of food and supplies.[17]

On 9 November, the council of war thrashed out a draft plan of campaign. Schwarzenberg's army would invade France from Switzerland, Blücher would attack through Belgium, and Bernadotte would occupy Holland. From this point on, however, the picture becomes murkier. That evening Schwarzenberg made an appearance at the meeting with

Saint-Aignan just as it was ending. He made obvious his approval when Metternich emphasized how welcome Caulaincourt's appointment as French negotiator would be to Austria. This was a clear signal to Saint-Aignan, and through him to Napoleon, that the allied military and diplomatic strategies were identical.[18]

The next day, Schwarzenberg informed the council of war that he wished to revise the invasion plan. Now he proposed that his army should strike into southern France, unite with Wellington who was currently crossing the Pyrenees, and with this combined force advance on Paris. Blücher, meanwhile, would remain in reserve to guard the allies' flank and rear. It is tempting to conclude that these changes were connected with the interview with Saint-Aignan the previous night, but the link, if it existed, was not straightforward. If it had been, Schwarzenberg would surely have pressed for a delay in invading, to give time for negotiations to start, but he did not. Blücher's relegation to a support role, however, may well have been inspired by the meeting. The fierce old Prussian passionately believed that Paris should be taken and Napoleon overthrown. If he was allowed to attack independently, he could become difficult to control. Schwarzenberg and Metternich fully supported an invasion, but only one that was carefully planned, firmly under their command, and a safe distance from Paris.[19]

Four days later Saint-Aignan arrived back in Paris, and presented the Frankfurt proposals to Napoleon. For the next two days Napoleon shut himself away with the duc de Bassano working on a reply, which was sent on the 16th. It was short, vague, and non-committal. It simply stated that 'a peace based on the independence of all nations, both on the continent and at sea, had always been the object of the Emperor's wishes and policy.'[20] It went on to propose the calling of a peace conference at Mannheim, and named Caulaincourt as the French plenipotentiary. This was not a formal rejection of the Frankfurt terms, but it was far from the swift and clear acceptance of France's 'natural limits' necessary for Metternich to convince his allies to persevere with his plan. By his own account, it dismayed even the ultra-loyal Bassano. In notes made for memoirs he never completed, he wrote that the first draft he prepared explicitly accepted the Frankfurt proposals, but that Napoleon then altered it.[21] Apparently this was because he was suspicious of the informality of the overtures, with their use of a captured opponent as a go-between. He was conveniently forgetting he had employed Merveldt in exactly the same way during the battle of Leipzig.

The exchange between Napoleon and Metternich did not stay secret long. Saint-Aignan lost no time in recounting his experiences to his brother-in-law Caulaincourt and his friend Talleyrand, both longtime enemies of Bassano. Soon the Paris salons were buzzing with the news of the Frankfurt proposals and the government's evasive reply. At court, a powerful faction led by Berthier, Savary, and Pasquier pressed for Bassano's dismissal, accusing him of inspiring the unsatisfactory response of 16 November. This charge was unfair, since Napoleon bore the final responsibility. However, Bassano's lack of independence, and his well-known inability to moderate the Emperor's aggression, told against him. Within a few days of the letter being sent, it became clear that his position was untenable.[22]

In fact, Napoleon had been thinking for some weeks of replacing Bassano. At Mainz after the retreat from Leipzig, he had asked Caulaincourt directly if he would agree to become foreign minister. Well aware of the difficulties of serving a master like Napoleon, Caulaincourt refused, with the excuse that he was much better suited to court functions. 'Seeing my reluctance,' Caulaincourt later wrote,

> the conversation about my own future ended there. [Napoleon] added that, since he was unable to keep [Bassano], with whom however he was satisfied . . . he had to find a successor . . . After several minutes silence, he gave me a penetrating gaze and said: 'You want me to take back Talleyrand . . . Everybody wants me to.'[23]

This was indeed Caulaincourt's aim. Just two months short of his 60th birthday, Talleyrand enjoyed the greatest reputation of any living French diplomat. He was also capable of standing up to Napoleon. These qualities made him eminently suitable for negotiating a compromise peace. Yet Napoleon was deeply suspicious of Talleyrand's methods and his ultimate aims. Although unaware that he had betrayed state secrets to Metternich and the Czar in 1808, he did know that Talleyrand had hoped for his death in Spain that year, and had schemed to secure the succession for Murat. He also knew that Talleyrand was personally corrupt, and surrounded by a clique of intriguers and speculators. 'He's in the hands of the vilest people,' Napoleon told Caulaincourt. 'He's the man with the most ideas, the most flair, but he's gold mixed with shit.' This was a slight improvement on calling Talleyrand 'a shit in a silk stocking', as he had to his face four years before.[24]

While he did not want him back at the foreign ministry, Napoleon knew he could not afford to alienate Talleyrand and his powerful political allies. 'Berthier swears by him, so do Savary, the police, Pasquier,'[25] he remarked. His solution was to make a show of offering Talleyrand the post, but privately to impose conditions that made acceptance impossible. The day after the reply to the Frankfurt proposals was sent, Napoleon summoned Caulaincourt again and ordered him to negotiate Talleyrand's return to the ministry. He laid down two stipulations: Talleyrand should separate not only from his shady entourage, but also from his wife. Mme de Talleyrand was a woman of flexible virtue, whose scandalous past had embarrassed the diplomatic corps when her husband had previously been foreign minister. However, repudiating her in this way would be a deep personal humiliation for Talleyrand, and he firmly refused to do so. When Caulaincourt reported this, Napoleon's response was terse: 'Between her and me, France and a whore, the choice shouldn't be difficult!'[26]

As Napoleon had hoped and expected, Talleyrand's refusal removed Caulaincourt's main excuse for not taking the foreign ministry himself. On 20 November, he renewed his offer to Caulaincourt, and made it clear he would not accept a refusal. Even now Caulaincourt tried to remonstrate, but to no avail. That evening, his appointment was made official. The nomination reflected Napoleon's deep ambivalence about the course he should take. He was making the acknowledged leader of the peace party foreign minister, but four days before had baulked at endorsing the actual peace proposals. To underline this fact, Bassano did not leave the government. Instead, he simply switched jobs, becoming secretary of state, responsible for transmitting Napoleon's orders to the other ministers. This meant that from the start Caulaincourt faced a rival smarting from his demotion, who still enjoyed constant access to the Emperor. It was not a happy augury.

Caulaincourt fully supported the Frankfurt proposals, and knew that their terms were the best France could now expect. His first task was to undo the damage caused by the response of 16 November. On the 25th, a reply to this arrived from Metternich, expressing satisfaction at Napoleon's general willingness to negotiate but insisting that first he should explicitly accept the proposals. For six days Napoleon argued with Caulaincourt over how to respond. Finally Caulaincourt got his way, and on 2 December announced to Metternich the Emperor's adhesion to 'the general and summary bases' for peace that the proposals set out.[27]

Getting Napoleon this far was a considerable achievement. Its fragility, however, is underlined by a remarkable, and to my knowledge, unpublished document in the French foreign ministry archives. These are the draft instructions Napoleon gave Caulaincourt as his plenipotentiary to the peace congress that he assumed would now open at Mannheim. They have the same date, 2 December, as Caulaincourt's letter to Metternich, and must have been drawn up alongside it over the previous six days. They run to fifty pages, and prescribe the French position on every subject of negotiation in minute detail. They are clearly the quid pro quo Napoleon extracted from Caulaincourt as the price of accepting the Frankfurt proposals.[28]

From the start, the document qualified this acceptance so stringently as virtually to negate it. It did so by stating two central principles. Firstly, it insisted that the fate of none of the conquered lands given up by France could be settled without her consent. Secondly, it proposed that the independence of all states should be guaranteed, as well as the freedom of the seas.[29] This was a transparent attempt both to prevent the victorious allies from dominating the continent, and England from controlling the sea. It had been prefigured by Bassano's letter of 16 November, advocating 'a peace based on the independence of all nations, both on the continent and at sea'.

Napoleon's plans for the future of the relinquished territories revealed just how much influence he intended to wield even after his empire had been dismantled. He set out their premise quite bluntly: '[The plenipotentiary's] first priority must be to ensure that as much as possible of these lands passes to princes of the [Bonaparte] dynasty, to leave as little as possible in the hands of rival powers . . . and to divide and enfeeble what remains outside France's orbit so it can never unite and become dangerous to her.'[30] By these indirect means, France would remain the dominant power on the continent.

This aim was clearest in the proposals for Italy and Germany. The kingdom of Italy, whose crown Napoleon wore, would simply pass to its viceroy, his stepson Eugène de Beauharnais, and his descendants. The Pope, currently under house arrest in France, could return to Rome, but purely as a spiritual leader, with all his temporal power removed. Following the Frankfurt proposals, the French and Austrian borders with Italy would be set in Piedmont for the former, and at either the river Isonzo or the river Adige for the latter. Murat and his descendants would keep the kingdom of Naples, whose former king would retain only Sicily. The King of Sardinia would stay on the island, renouncing all his possessions on the mainland.

As a result, the extended Bonaparte family would continue to rule the most important parts of Italy.[31]

Germany, with its crucial position on France's eastern border, was to be kept even weaker than Italy. Napoleon accepted the dissolution of the Rhine Confederation, and hence also the end of his protectorate, but was determined that no similar body, this time under allied control, should replace it. Hence the only link between the various German states should be the law of nations, and no individual state should become sufficiently powerful to unite them and pose a threat to France. As to the actual territorial settlement, each country 'should be maintained as it was before the reunion of the [north German] departments beyond the Rhine' in 1810.[32]

This proposal ensured that kingdoms like Saxony, Bavaria, and Württemberg, which were still or which had recently been French allies, remained much as they were. Its main purpose, however, was to keep Napoleon's youngest brother Jérôme as king of the crucial client state of Westphalia. To reconcile this with the expected allied demands in Germany, a complicated series of exchanges was envisaged. In accordance with the terms previously set out at Prague, the Prussian lands annexed by Westphalia would be returned to give her 'a tenable frontier' on the Elbe. Hanover, also annexed to Westphalia, would be restored to England. In compensation, Westphalia would receive the territories of another client state, the Grand Duchy of Berg, strategically placed on the right bank of the Rhine and ruled from Düsseldorf.[33]

If Westphalia was shifted south-east to the banks of the Rhine, this was no coincidence. Henceforth she would be the guardian of France's eastern 'natural frontier'. To buttress her in this role, Napoleon demanded total French control of the navigation and policing of the river itself. He also aimed to keep the three important bastions on the right bank he still occupied—Kehl opposite Strasbourg, Kastel opposite Mainz, and Wesel close to the Dutch border. Napoleon anticipated the allies' objection that 'no state whose barriers [to invasion] are removed can be secure, that Germany's barrier is the Rhine, that it is . . . the only one, and that it would not exist at all if France kept . . . bridgeheads on the right bank from which her forces could penetrate into the heart of Germany.'[34] His answer was that since communications with and between these bridgeheads would pass through France, they posed no threat to German security. This was hardly convincing, and made even less so by a further statement in the instructions: 'It is . . . essential carefully to forestall and skilfully to avoid anything that could give the impression that the frontier between France and Germany is fixed.'[35] These were ominous words. Their main aim was to ensure French possession of the Rhine itself, but they left the door open to future conquests beyond.

The Low Countries, where the Rhine approached the sea, were even more important to Napoleon. 'No sacrifice could be harder for France', he wrote,

> than to give up any part of Holland. There is nothing she should not be prepared to do to avoid this sacrifice, or, if this proves impossible, to limit its extent. This is, for her, the most important and delicate part of the whole negotiation. It is here that the terrain should be disputed with the most skill and obstinacy, and where concessions, if they become inevitable, should only be made in the last extremity.[36]

Here Napoleon's most formidable adversary was England, for whom French possession of the Dutch and Belgian coast meant a constant threat of invasion. He hoped to disarm her by offering her all the Dutch colonial possessions in exchange for France keeping Holland itself. If England refused, he was determined to hang on to as much of Holland as possible. His preferred frontier was the river Ijssel, the farthest-flung tributary of the Rhine running into the sea, which would have reduced an independent Holland to a tiny rump state. If this too proved unattainable, the furthest Napoleon was prepared to retreat was to the river Waal, which would still have left him with almost half the country. Underlining their importance, Caulaincourt was not to make any of these concessions without his specific authorization. Napoleon also ruled out any restoration of Holland's traditional rulers, the house of Orange, presumably because they could form a rallying-point for national resistance to France. Instead, Holland would revert to what it had been between 1795 and 1805, a small powerless republic taking her orders from Paris.[37]

A further axiom of the instructions was that French sacrifices on the continent should be compensated by England's return of all the French colonies it had captured during the war, including Guadeloupe, Martinique, and trading posts in India. Captured Dutch possessions, especially the Cape of Good Hope, would also be restored. Napoleon also planned to exploit to the full the concessions over England's 'maritime rights' Aberdeen had made at Frankfurt. He did this through a draft declaration of the freedom of the seas to be included in any final treaty. In peacetime, it stated, ships of any nation should be able to sail wherever they wished and carry on trade if the local laws permitted it. In wartime the same rule should apply, except if a ship was carrying arms or munitions for one of the belligerents, or attempting to enter a besieged or blockaded port. If arms were found on a trading ship, they could be removed, but otherwise its cargo or crew could not be touched. This would have left English 'maritime rights', with the extensive powers of search and confiscation they currently granted, in tatters, and went far beyond what even Aberdeen had conceded.[38]

Napoleon showed particular concern for the rights of French subjects or adherents in the relinquished lands. Through the 'extraordinary domain', his own private war-chest formed from the loot of his conquests, large numbers of his servants had been rewarded with estates and titles and revenues throughout Europe. This had been particularly true of the marshals, whose loyalty was so important. Amazingly, Napoleon intended that they should keep these possessions even after the countries where they were located had been renounced. It is difficult to see how any of the states concerned could have accepted this. Napoleon also insisted that the local inhabitants who had collaborated with French rule in these countries should be protected from reprisals by a special clause in a future treaty. One way of achieving this, he proposed, was that they be given the status of French citizens. On the surface, this appears principled and generous, but another motive can easily be discerned. The condition of unpopular minorities abroad possibly enjoying French citizenship would form a standing pretext for intervention throughout large swathes of Europe.[39]

Finally, Napoleon's gaze extended to the smaller islands of the Mediterranean. He designed an intricate exchange to encourage England to give up the key naval base of Malta. If she did, France would cede in return the Ionian islands to the kingdom of Italy; if she did not, Napoleon would keep them. If Malta was given up, it would be handed to Sicily. Napoleon was also precise about the future of Elba off the Tuscan coast, 'which whatever happens must remain French'.[40] As it turned out, this wish would be fulfilled, though not in the way he anticipated.

The Frankfurt proposals had accepted that France should continue to exercise influence beyond her borders after her empire had disappeared, but Napoleon's instructions stretched this principle well beyond its outer limit. One cannot imagine the continental powers agreeing to Jérôme Bonaparte continuing to rule Westphalia, to the existence of the three French bridge-heads over the Rhine, or to French subjects and supporters abroad receiving the rights and revenues that Napoleon proposed. Metternich might have conceded a kingdom of Italy ruled by Eugène de Beauharnais, but it is far from clear that his allies would. Above all, Napoleon's terms fell far short of England's demands. Far from creating the 'Dutch barrier', that strengthening of Holland against future French aggression so important to Castlereagh, they reduced it, at best, to half its former size. They also left Antwerp in French hands, though England considered this the single greatest threat to her national security. Finally, it is inconceivable that the English government would have consented to limit maritime rights it regarded as nonnegotiable.

Napoleon's instructions shed a highly revealing light on his attitude towards peace at the end of 1813. They show that even after the disaster of Leipzig, he was still not reconciled to losing his empire. Instead of seizing on the Frankfurt proposals with alacrity, as almost all his advisers urged him, he did so only grudgingly, and after a delay that ultimately proved fatal. If Napoleon did accept the 'natural frontiers' it was only a line behind which he absolutely refused to retreat. Beyond this limit he was determined to preserve a cordon of satellite states ruled by members of his family, and keep his other neighbours sufficiently weak and divided to ensure continuing French domination of Europe. On this basis, if a congress had opened at Mannheim in December, it is difficult to see how any settlement could have been reached.

Why was Napoleon, even at this late stage, so obdurate? Part of the reason was no doubt his psychological inability to retreat, and his deep aversion to giving up any territory unless forced to by military defeat. But his espousal of the 'natural frontiers' as the point of no return was also extremely significant. Attaining these had been one of the French Revolution's greatest achievements, mapped out by Danton and confirmed by successive peace treaties. To abandon them was, in a sense, to betray the Revolution, and Napoleon was determined not to risk that accusation. Caulaincourt described his state of mind with his customary insight. Napoleon had begun the 1813 campaigns, he wrote, 'with the aim of... making war with all his resources, and finally, if the war went badly, he was determined to sacrifice himself and his army on the frontiers that the Republic had bequeathed to the Empire'.[41]

Napoleon's hesitations doomed the Frankfurt proposals. Between their arrival in Paris and Caulaincourt's eventual positive response, which Metternich received on 5 December, two events occurred that substantially altered the diplomatic landscape. First, it became clear that the English government would repudiate Aberdeen's concessions. When Castlereagh heard of them he was deeply alarmed, and instructed Aberdeen to write a formal protest emphasizing that there could be no compromise either on England's maritime rights or the need to strengthen Holland.[42] Had Napoleon immediately accepted the Frankfurt proposals, it is just possible that Metternich could have called a peace conference in time to present England with a fait accompli. Now England's suspicions were thoroughly aroused, and the moment had passed. All Metternich could now do was to reply to Caulaincourt that before negotiations could open he must once more consult his allies, which in effect meant just England.

Second, for several weeks from mid-November a crisis erupted between Austria and Russia. Its focus was the planned invasion of France. The attack into southern France that Schwarzenberg favoured necessitated marching through Switzerland. This suited Austria for a number of reasons, both political and military. It kept the main allied advance away from Paris, giving Napoleon time to see reason and start negotiating seriously. It also enabled Austrian forces to be detached for a drive due south, to gain the favourable frontier in northern Italy that Metternich desired. Here a highly personal factor intervened. Switzerland was officially neutral; it was also the home of the philosopher César de la Harpe, the Czar's old tutor whom he venerated, and who strenuously lobbied his old pupil for his country's neutrality to be respected. A compromise solution would have been for the Swiss government to grant the allies free passage, but on 18 November it formally ruled this out.

If the Austrian strategy was to be carried out, there was now no alternative to violating Swiss neutrality, and this fact put Metternich on a collision course with Alexander. The Czar refused to allow a march through Switzerland, and even warned he would regard this as an act of war against Russia itself. The main casualty of this confrontation was the Frankfurt proposals. Despite his reluctance to negotiate with Napoleon, Alexander had reluctantly let them go forward. The Swiss crisis infuriated him, and he withdrew his support. This presented Metternich with a stark choice. If he did not withdraw or substantially modify the proposals, he would lose his main continental ally, Russia.

In the first week of December, Metternich made his choice. For some time he had been working on a declaration that would be issued just before France was invaded. This aimed to drive a wedge between Napoleon and domestic public opinion, by reassuring the French people that the allies were not making war on them, but only on 'that preponderance that, to the misfortune of Europe and France, the Emperor . . . has for too long exercised beyond the limits of his empire.' According to Aberdeen, Metternich had at first intended to publish the document straight after the meeting with Saint-Aignan, and include in it the offer of France's 'natural limits'. Now, with relations with Russia and England so strained, he did not dare. In place of this, the declaration merely promised France 'a greater extent of territory than she has ever known under her kings'.[43]

The Declaration of Frankfurt, as it swiftly became known, appeared on 7 December. When it reached Paris, both Napoleon and Caulaincourt were shocked. Having finally accepted the proposals transmitted through Saint-Aignan, they expected a settlement to be reached swiftly on the basis of the 'natural limits'. Instead, they received a propaganda announcement that substitued fine-sounding phrases for concrete terms. Understandably, they began to suspect that Metternich's initiative had been a trick from the start, just one more attempt to divide the French people from their Emperor through vague promises that the allies had no intention of fulfilling. In fact Metternich had been sincere, but his position weak. His proposals were undermined not by his own duplicity, but the delay in the French response which gave his allies, dubious about them from the start, time to think again. The first major peace effort since the congress of Prague had ground to a halt.

The invasion of France was the next step, but the question of Swiss neutrality remained. Unable to budge the Czar, Metternich took the risky step of outwitting him. He opened secret negotiations with a pro-Austrian faction in the Swiss government, to ensure that the allies would tacitly be welcomed into the country and meet no resistance. Then, when Alexander had left headquarters for a few days to visit his wife's family in Karlsruhe, he persuaded Francis I to order his troops into Switzerland. The plan worked; on the night of 20–21 December, the Swiss forces guarding the vital bridge across the Rhine at Basel withdrew, allowing Schwarzenberg to cross the river. Informed by Metternich after the event, Alexander was horrified. 'You have grieved me in a way you can never repair,' he exclaimed. Austrian strategy had triumphed, but relations between Metternich and the Czar were never the same again.[44]

Partly for symbolic reasons, but also no doubt to gain time to calm down, the Czar postponed crossing the Rhine himself until 13 January 1814, New

Year's Day according to the Russian calendar. To make up for the delay, he made it a suitably splendid occasion. The three allied monarchs rode over the bridge at Basel at the head of the army's elite troops, the Russian and Prussian Guards. Sir Charles Stewart, accompanying them, was deeply impressed. He later described the scene:

> It is impossible by any description to give an exaggerated idea of the perfect state of these troops...when one considered what they had endured, and contemplated the Russians, some of whom had emerged from the steeps of Tartary bordering the Chinese empire, traversed their own regions, and marched, in a few short months, from Moscow across the Rhine, one was lost in wonder, and inspired with a political awe of that colossal power.[45]

Stewart was right to be awestruck by the courage and endurance of these Russian soldiers, who had advanced over a thousand miles from their capital and forced the greatest general of his age back to his own borders. Their journey also gave the war begun in 1812 a striking symmetry. Just fourteen months before, Napoleon had been at the gates of Moscow. Now Alexander was approaching the gates of Paris.

10

Challenge from Within

Leipzig was not only a military disaster, it also caused a crisis of morale within France itself. The steady stream of prefects' reports describing public discontent and the desire for peace became a flood. The news of the defeat, wrote the prefect of the Rhône to Montalivet on 4 November, 'has discouraged people to the greatest possible degree'. His words were echoed next day by the prefect of the Indre: 'I cannot hide from you, Monseigneur, that the information in the last official bulletins has made the worst possible impression, and that peace is generally and desperately desired.' In the normally docile department of the Doubs, the prefect noted that 'the wish, the need for peace is becoming more intense each day and is expressed with an impatience and even a despair that I have never seen up till now.'[1]

It was clear that continuing the war would bring higher taxes and a fresh round of conscription, and this duly came about. The *droits réunis*, a series of indirect taxes, were increased, and the salt and property tax were doubled. Napoleon calculated that these measures would raise 500 million francs, but this turned out to be a substantial overestimate. Then, on 15 November, a *senatus-consultum* called 300,000 new conscripts to the army. It was small consolation for them that 150,000 of these would be held in reserve and only sent to the front if France was invaded, since this was obviously imminent. The recruitment bureaux went to work in an atmosphere of fear and distress. In many towns, this was compounded by the arrival from the front of columns of wounded or sick soldiers, who filled the local hospitals and religious establishments. This only increased the alarm of families about the possible fate of their loved ones sent to the army, and added to the inevitable pain of separation.[2]

Despite all this suffering, the numbers recruited were meagre. The lists of those previously rejected as unfit for service were ransacked, but to little avail. 'The register for 1813 of those turned down for not being tall enough or having weak constitutions has yielded very little', reported the prefect of the Côte d'Or. 'It is painful in the extreme to have to recruit in this way. One wastes one's time for no result. I hope however that we will get together 1400 or 1500 good soldiers, though many of them will be very small.'[3]

Conscription was not only a huge upheaval for those called up, but had a major impact on those left behind. In rural areas in particular, the departure of so many able-bodied young men created a crippling labour shortage. The prefect of the Doubs described this graphically in a report of 10 November:

> Agriculture is suffering from lack of workers, large families are exhausted, the current round of conscription is removing the last few unmarried men able to bear arms. I can vouch for this having seen with my own eyes on a journey of seventy leagues I have just made to revise the recruitment lists; the dearth of men is so great that women are doing all the work in the fields.[4]

In many departments, the response to the privations caused by conscription and extra taxation was simply resignation, but in others there were the beginnings of resistance. In several towns, seditious writings started to appear. In Bordeaux, they began with anti-government graffiti scrawled on walls with red crayon; shortly afterwards the mayor received anonymous death threats. On the night of 6 November, copies of a placard were distributed around the city centre attacking Napoleon for imposing, and the Senate for accepting, the recent tax rises. It ended: 'Down, a thousand times down with these monsters, and especially [the Emperor] who has shat down on us the *droits réunis!*'[5] Similar material circulated around Dijon in December, and the prefect received a three-page anonymous letter eloquently denouncing him for implementing the new conscription law:

> It is in vain that you try to execute such an odious measure ... Are you so blind as to think that heads of families will meekly abandon their wives, their children, their aged fathers ... have you been unmoved by the tears and cries of mothers about to be separated from their husbands? Do you think these women will not remind their men, with their natural eloquence, their persuasive tears, of the terrible experiences of the past ... of the millions of Frenchmen butchered to serve the ambition of one man? ... Funeral crepe is now our only adornment, and we would rather die a thousand times than serve the plans of the *cannibal* who does not hesitate to order you to burn our towns, ravage our countryside, in a word reduce us to despair, to frustrate an enemy who cannot be crueller than himself.[6]

By the end of November, in some areas, words were giving way to deeds. In the Doubs, previously solidly loyal, disturbances broke out in mid-November at Pontarlier. 'Before there was any question of [the new conscription law]', wrote the town's sub-prefect, 'feeling was already running high, but as soon as this measure was announced here the alarm became general, and murmurings against our august Emperor were publicly expressed.' As in Dijon and Bordeaux, the main target was the local authorities, but this time in person as well as in writing. 'In the countryside and in town', continued the sub-prefect, 'members of the municipal council have been menaced... placards full of invective and threats have been posted on their doors and in the public squares; some have even been insulted in the street.' Significantly, the agitation was non-political, and caused simply by war-weariness; the sub-prefect could detect no 'party-spirit', though he was constantly on the watch in case any developed. He urged his superiors to despatch the local brigades of gendarmes to the area, but it was some weeks before order was fully restored.[7]

Events took a more dramatic turn in Hazebrouck, in the department of the Nord. At 9 a.m. on 22 November, the local sub-prefect, César de Ghesquière, arrived at his offices to organize the departure of a column of conscripts. He had just begun his work when the two gendarmes guarding the sub-prefecture's main door were pushed aside by several of the new recruits, all armed with clubs. Ghesquière went to reason with them, and saw a crowd of young men beyond that he estimated at two thousand. He reminded them that they were being called up to defend their country, but this was greeted by shouts of: 'And who will feed our mothers and sisters?' He was then forced to retreat by a shower of stones. With some courage he went upstairs to put on his uniform and fetch his sword, then returned and once again tried to restore order. The crowd now invaded the building, ransacked the offices and his living quarters, and chased him from room to room until he finally managed to take refuge in the attic.[8]

Over the next few days the rebellious conscripts were joined by others from neighbouring towns and villages. They split up into different groups, often with a local leader, but no clear strategy. By this time the departmental gendarmerie, unable to cope with the scale of the upheaval, had been reinforced by 300 troops of the line. There was a pitched battle at the village of Estaires on 26 December; three rebels were killed and twenty wounded. There were no casualties on the government side, but two unfortunate bystanders died in the crossfire. After this check the insurgent bands split up, dodging the forces of repression sent after them. A new prefect, comte Beugnot, was sent to the scene from Paris. By early January 1814, through a combination of severity and judicious amnesty, he had restored a degree of calm.[9]

However primitive and disorganized, the Hazebrouck revolt was no minor riot. For over a month, bands of rebels numbering several thousand ranged across two departments of northern France, large parts of which were beyond the authorities' control. As at Pontarlier, the movement was spontaneous, and had no political overtones. It was simply a further sign that the burdens of conscription and taxation were testing the French people to breaking point. Beugnot made the point as strongly as he dared in his final report:

> It would be wrong to seek any outside influence, or conspiracy, in the disorders around Hazebrouck. The outward cause is the real one. The levies of conscripts have been too frequent and too numerous in [the department of the Nord], which in filling its quota of the target of 300,000 men, will this year have contributed 22,000 recruits, a heavy but inevitable burden.[10]

If the peasants and artisans of the Nord who took up their clubs to protest had been asked what message they wished to send the government, it would surely have been one word: peace. Few of them cared whether they were ruled by Napoleon, Louis XVIII or even Bernadotte. What they objected to was being marched off to fight in a war in which they no longer believed, leaving their fields and workshops untended and their families threatened with poverty. Napoleon was convinced that the French would reject any peace without victory. Ironically, the exact opposite was true; the only domestic threat to his regime came from the increasing numbers of French people desperate for an end to war and exasperated by his refusal to accept this. Had Napoleon made a settlement on almost any terms in late 1813, his throne would have remained secure. The prefect of the Côte d'Or made the point eloquently to the interior minister Montalivet that December:

> Peace, Monseigneur, peace! That is the cry of the towns and the countryside. Everyone desires it. Peace alone can heal all our wounds, and win back from the people that confidence which was so complete fifteen months ago, and which has been shaken by misfortune, but only seeks the occasion to return. All the officials of every class, I might even say of all parties ... all reasonable people, all those who have just reflected for a moment, are devoted to His Majesty. All would lay down their lives for him and for his dynasty, the majority through attachment and conviction, the rest because they feel that the greatness and even the survival of France depend upon him and on his

dynasty, but in the lower classes of society a pronounced indifference is evident; people think only of living from day to day, and only peace and the happiness it brings will revive their enthusiasm.[11]

At this time there was still no coherent opposition to Napoleon. Some ministers and marshals could deplore his unwillingess to make peace, and even tell him so, but however exalted, they were still only individuals. Peasants in the Nord and the Doubs could rebel in despair against conscription, but they could be dispersed by troops if necessary. Yet in December 1813, these disparate voices of protest were joined by another that could not be ignored. This was the Legislative Body, which although somnolent for thirteen years and elected on a tiny franchise, still had an unchallengeable right to represent the people.

The Legislative Body's awakening owed much to Napoleon's mishandling of it. This stemmed in turn from his mishandling of the Frankfurt proposals. Napoleon had summoned the assembly for 2 December to present the budget for 1814, but then postponed the opening to the 19th. This was because he hoped that by then, having accepted the Frankfurt terms, he would be able to inform the deputies that peace negotiations had started. As it turned out, the only reply he received from Metternich was the statement that Austria would have to consult her allies. All Napoleon could do when the deputies met was tell them, rather lamely: 'Negotiations have been opened with the allied powers. I have accepted the preliminary bases which they have offered. I had therefore hoped that before the beginning of this session the congress of Mannheim would have met, but new delays which are not attributable to France have deferred this moment which all the world desires.'[12]

The delay in the opening of the session had a further damaging consequence. Having arrived in Paris from their home departments, the deputies now found themselves idle in the capital for over a fortnight. This gave them time to meet and talk together and, by comparing their experience of their different localities, to realize how widespread desire for peace was throughout the country. They also picked up a great deal of gossip from the court and the great Paris salons about Napoleon's initial inadequate reply to the Frankfurt proposals of 16 November, and the damaging delay it had caused in the negotiation. Thus by the time Napoleon convened them, many deputies were already predisposed to think that his obstinacy was jeopardizing an excellent chance to end the war. In this mood, they paid little attention to the subtle revision of the offer of the 'natural frontiers' in the allied declaration of 1 December. In any case, even if they had, the majority probably would have cared little, provided the conflict ceased.[13]

Napoleon was well aware that one of the aims of the allied declaration was to make him appear the major obstacle to peace, and so drive a wedge between him and French public opinion. In his speech from the throne, he launched a riposte to this. He announced that he would make available all records of the negotiations undertaken since Saint-Aignan had brought the Frankfurt proposals to Paris, to separate commissions elected by the Senate and the Legislative Body. This was intended to dispel any doubts about his commitment to reaching a settlement. Reassured, the deputies and senators would then present public addresses endorsing Napoleon's position and demonstrating to the allies that the French nation still stood solidly behind him.

Within a few days the Senate had obediently voted a suitable address. Matters were very different, however, in the Legislative Body. Napoleon had compounded the deputies' frustrations by nominating as their president not a candidate from a list submitted by themselves, as was the custom, but one of his own ministers, the elderly and ailing Claude Régnier, duc de Massa. This achieved the worst of both worlds: Massa was both a provocation to the assembly, and incapable of controlling it if it got out of order. It was thus predictable that when they came to elect the five commissioners to examine the record of the peace negotiations, the deputies chose men with strong reputations for independence from the government. They were the philosopher François-Pierre Maine de Biran, the lawyers Pierre-François Flaugergues and Joseph Lainé, the playwright François Raynouard, and a former diplomat and friend of Talleyrand, Jean-Antoine Gallois. Several had had brushes with authority in the course of their careers. Flaugergues had protested against the execution of Louis XVI in 1793 and been forced into hiding for a period, while Raynouard had a personal grudge against Napoleon, who had banned one of his plays after its first night.[14]

Lainé swiftly emerged as the leader of the group, which chose him to draft the report to form the basis of its address to Napoleon. A thin, bookish bachelor of 45, Lainé was a native of Bordeaux, where he had been admitted to the bar in 1789. At first an enthusiastic supporter of the Revolution, he had been horrified by its descent into violence, and when the Terror came to Bordeaux had used his influence to save several prisoners from the guillotine. First elected to the legislative body in 1808, he had proved

Figure 8. Joseph Lainé.

himself a diligent if not particularly outstanding deputy, and had been rewarded with the legion of honour two years later.[15]

It was later alleged that Lainé had royalist sympathies, but in 1813 at least there is no evidence of this. What he did care about, and which motivated his actions throughout the following months, was liberty. It was symbolic that his estate at Saucats, just outside Bordeaux, adjoined the château de la Brède, where the great Enlightenment philosopher Montesquieu, one of the founders of French liberalism, had lived, and which his grandson still occupied. During the Terror Lainé had helped save Montesquieu's papers from destruction, hiding them for a time in his own house. Montesquieu's condemnation of despotism and tyranny, and endorsement of constitutional government guaranteed by the separation of powers, were the foundation of Lainé's political convictions.[16]

Lainé's papers, now appropriately kept alongside Montesquieu's in the Bibliothèque Municipale de Bordeaux, offer remarkable insights into his character and opinions. They formed the basis of a two-volume biography by Emile de Perceval in 1926, but have rarely been used since. They reveal Lainé as a highly erudite man, steeped in literature, history, and the classics, and are full of notes of his reading, from works as diverse as Mably's *De la Législation*, Volney's *Voyage en Syrie et en Egypte*, and a history of the Roman emperors. British authors are also represented, with Hume's *History of Great Britain* and Mrs Macaulay's *History of England*. In line with his cosmopolitan outlook, Lainé also worked hard to teach himself Dutch and English. He does not seem to have got far with his English, but his efforts to write simple sentences are touching: 'There is a house in the fields. I had a dog and two hogs . . . You have some houses in the town. The towns are handsome in this country. Your horse is handsome, but the horses of the king are much handsomer.'[17]

Lainé used his considerable learning to comment extensively on the politics of his own day. He did so mostly in the form of notes and aphorisms, which act as a guide to his developing thought over the years. In particular, they provide a subtle and original critique of Napoleon, shrewdly linking his pursuit of glory abroad to his despotism at home. By 1813, Lainé had become convinced that Napoleon was cynically using the necessities of war to justify domestic tyranny. Typically, he illustrated this by referring to the wartime Roman dictator Marius. 'Marius', he noted, 'replied to those who accused him of flouting the laws: "I can't hear you above the sound of battle!"' Lainé's condemnation of these words—'What ironic sophistry! What a bad citizen!'—applied to Napoleon as much as to Marius. His distaste for war, and awareness of how easily it could be exploited for dubious political ends, is encapsulated elsewhere in an even pithier phrase: 'Better let the people sleep than awaken them with victories.'[18]

For Lainé, if war and dictatorship were inextricably linked, it followed that the only remedy was peace and liberty. In 1813, peace was obviously desirable for its own sake. But Lainé also saw it as a means to an end— curbing Napoleon's abuse of power and restoring the liberties he had confiscated to the French people. His election to the commission gave him the chance to translate this aspiration into reality. As he later recalled, he and his colleagues 'felt that in the interests of France, the legislative body needed to regain respect, and that one of the best ways of doing this was to show that the deputies were ready to echo the people's cry for peace and her murmurings against oppression. That is why the commission sought . . . to widen its remit by including in it the expression of certain grievances.'[19]

In this context, Lainé's use of the word 'grievances' [*doléances*], was highly significant. In May 1789, the deputies to the estates-general, called by Louis XVI to resolve France's financial crisis, had arrived at Versailles armed with *cahiers de doléances* [literally, 'notebooks of grievances'] listing all the abuses in the state their constituents wished to see curtailed. The frustration of these hopes for reform by an indecisive king had led directly to revolution two months later. In 1813, representatives of the people were once again trying to exploit circumstances to limit the powers of a much more thorough despot than Louis XVI. In a striking way, the experience of Lainé and his colleagues bore comparison with that of their revolutionary predecessors twenty-four years before.[20]

On Friday 24 December, the first meeting of the commission to examine the diplomatic correspondence about the Frankfurt proposals was held. It was chaired by Cambacérès as arch-chancellor, the duc de Massa attended as president of the legislative body, and the papers were presented by two councillors of state. The commissioners soon realized that some of the documents were being held back, which hardly increased their confidence in the proceedings. Nonetheless, within four days a draft report had been hammered out. Although Cambacérès and the councillors of state toned down some of its harsher criticisms of excessive conscription and taxation, they did not remove them all, leading Lainé to suspect they tacitly agreed with many of them. 'We thought we could read in the eyes of these exalted figures', he noted, 'that they were delighted to have found a mouthpiece through which to speak the truth and beg for peace.'[21]

At 3 p.m. on Tuesday 28 December, Lainé rose to his feet and gave the commission's report, in the form of a speech, to the legislative body sitting in closed session. A second reading was requested, which he gave the next day. By this time, however, the authorities were getting cold feet. No drafts of the speech survive, but if a transcription made from memory by one of the deputies who heard it is accurate, one can see why it caused alarm. It was not just a passionate plea for peace, but a frank and devastating critique of Napoleon's arbitrary rule. It is difficult to believe that this text could have been approved by Cambacérès and the councillors of state, even if they did privately endorse some of its sentiments. Possibly the commissioners had always intended to make a much stronger report than the government was prepared to permit, or, conceivably, Lainé simply improvised as he was speaking.

Lainé's initial argument was that it was perfectly possible to make peace with honour on the terms offered by the allies. This was a shrewd tactic, since he correctly sensed that Napoleon's acceptance of the Frankfurt proposals was half-hearted at best, and that even then the Emperor 'was preparing ways of eluding them'. Had he seen Napoleon's draft instructions to Caulaincourt for the planned congress at Mannheim, his suspicions would have been amply confirmed. Lainé stated, in terms that could not be ignored, that a settlement on the basis of France's 'natural frontiers' would fully satisfy national pride. He went further, and flatly condemned the conquests made beyond them since 1794. He made all these points with great, and often flowery, eloquence:

> Our enemies, carried by victory to the banks of the Rhine, have offered our august monarch peace on terms that a hero previously accustomed to such success might find presumptuous. But if up until now noble and heroic sentiments have dictated refusal before France's deplorable present state was sufficiently realized, it would be imprudent to repeat this refusal now that the enemy has crossed our legitimate frontiers. If shameful terms were being offered, His Majesty would only need reply by exposing these foreign schemes to his people; but on the contrary the object is only to contain us within the limits of our own territory, and to check that aggression, that ambitious activity, that has for twenty years been so fatal for the peoples of Europe . . . These proposals seem [to the commission] honourable for the nation, since they prove that the foreign powers fear and respect us . . . The Pyrenees, the Alps and the Rhine enclose a vast realm many of whose provinces were never part of [the old monarchy], and yet at that time France's royal crown was more glorious and majestic than any other.[22]

At this point, there was an interruption. Massa, beside himself, burst out: 'What you are saying is unconstitutional!' But Raynouard immediately riposted: 'The only unconstitutional thing here is your presence!' This allowed Lainé to proceed, daring to advise Napoleon not only to renounce the protectorate of the Rhine Confederation, but also Holland and Belgium. He then moved on to the crucial link between foreign war and domestic tyranny:

> Let us not deceive ourselves: our misfortunes overwhelm us . . . commerce is destroyed, industry is dying, there is not a Frenchman whose family or property has not been affected.

> What are the causes of this ineffable misery? A vexatious administration, excessive taxes, the deplorable method of collecting them, and the even crueller abuses of the recruitment system for the army . . .

Conscription has become an odious curse for the whole of France, since it has always been brutally executed. For the last two years young men have been harvested three times a year.

A barbarous and pointless war periodically engulfs our youth, tearing them away from education, agriculture, commerce and the arts. Have the tears of mothers and the sweat of the people become the monarch's only resource?[23]

The deputies were first amazed, then delighted. By a massive vote of 223 to 51, they voted next day to publish the speech, making clear it had their full approval. But Lainé was already thinking ahead. The commission's report was meant to serve as the basis for a public address to Napoleon, demonstrating to the allies the unity of the French people's deputies with their Emperor. Cambacérès and the councillors of state had insisted that this should not contain any criticism of Napoleon's domestic rule. The compromise reached underlined the parallels with 1789. The criticisms would not appear in the address itself, but instead in a list of grievances—which was actually termed a *cahier de doléances*—to be presented to Napoleon at the peace. Lainé's notes at the time showed the problems this posed. 'What should we put in the *cahier*?' he mused. 'That's the difficulty. Dare we say everything?'[24]

In fact Lainé had a very good idea of what the *cahier* should contain. He intended it to be no less than a blueprint for a properly constitutional political system. Its foundation should be 'that type of liberty compatible with monarchy, especially civil liberty, which extends to the lowest classes who are always the most exposed to oppression'. Central to this was the principle, championed by the Revolution but since subverted by Napoleon, that taxes required the consent of the nation. 'Peace', Lainé wrote, 'should make possible a reduction in taxation, which should never be levied except by vote of the legislative body meeting in annual session.' Even during wartime, taxes should never be raised by generals using military means, as Napoleon's commanders had often done.[25]

Lainé recognized Napoleon's achievement in establishing religious freedom and uniform laws: 'There is little to demand in relation to liberty of religion . . . in general legislation is fairly impartial.' The real problem lay elsewhere, in the overweening power of the executive and the weakness of the other organs of state. Lainé was scathing about the 'incoherence' of France's institutions, and particularly the judiciary's lack of independence. A commission should be drawn from the Legislative Body, the Senate, and the Council of State, he argued, 'to coordinate our institutions with morality, religion, and a strongly monarchical constitution'. Napoleon would probably never have agreed to such a transfer of power from his hands to those of the legislature. Yet Lainé certainly had no thought of dethroning him. 'The legislative body', he concluded, 'has no intention of overthrowing [the regime]; it simply wishes for reform and less suffering.'[26]

Lainé's plans for the address and *cahier de doléances* were never realized. Within hours of the deputies' vote to publish his speech, the machinery of repression swung into action. At 9.30 that evening, a police official arrived at the printer's, took away one of the printed copies and brought it to Napoleon. Reading it, the Emperor became furious, and decided it was a clear call to sedition. That night he called his council, and took two drastic decisions. Publication of Lainé's speech was banned, and the Legislative Body was dissolved.

At midday the next day the commissioners, who had already been working for hours on the draft address, received a note from Savary as minister of police summoning them immediately. Convinced they were about to be arrested, they decided to seek safety in the Legislative Body, which they assumed was currently meeting. Reaching the assembly chamber, they found the doors locked, and notices posted announcing the suspension of the session. The arbitrary government they had denounced was showing its claws.

For these men, so familiar with the events of the Revolution, the echoes of 1789 were deafening. In June of that year, the deputies to the national assembly at Versailles had also been locked out of their chamber, but had gathered in a nearby indoor tennis-court and sworn an oath not to separate until they had drawn up a constitution. This option was not open to Lainé and his colleagues, since their own assembly had already been dissolved by the time they reached it. They decided to obey Savary's summons, to give the government no pretext for 'rigorous measures' against them. This was not a glorious act of defiance like the national assembly's, but the commission's actions over the previous days had shown it was fighting the same battle.[27]

Receiving them in his study, Savary harangued the commissioners, himself invoking 1789. 'You have tried to imitate the [national] assembly,' he claimed. To do so at such a moment, with the enemy poised to invade France, was to betray their mandate. Clearly suspecting Lainé's motives, he questioned him closely about his loyalty to the regime: 'How is it, Monsieur, that all the ill-intentioned people are using your name as a rallying-point? . . .

What do you want to achieve?' Lainé replied, tactfully, that he only wished Napoleon would 'extend his hand to raise up a nation that had become too subservient'.[28]

Despite the Legislative Body's dissolution, an invitation had been issued for its members to attend the Emperor's customary New Year's Day reception at the Tuileries. Most went, but the five commissioners prudently decided to stay away. They were right to do so. Napoleon was in a towering rage, and turned furiously on the deputies present. Various versions exist of what he said, but they all agree on its key themes and phrases. He accused Lainé of being an enemy agent, working for England and corresponding with the Prince Regent. But he also made a more substantive point. Like the dictator Marius evoked by Lainé, he insisted that war and national emergency justified the inroads made on individual liberty. In this moment of crisis, he asserted, he alone represented the state, and to claim otherwise verged on treason. 'Don't you realize', he stormed,

that in a monarchy the throne is inseparable from the person of the monarch? What is the throne? A piece of wood covered in velvet; but, in the language of monarchy, I am the throne! You speak of the people; don't you realize that it is I above all who represent them? You cannot attack me without attacking the nation itself. If abuses exist, is this the moment to come to me with remonstrances, when two hundred thousand Cossacks are invading our frontiers? Is this the moment to quibble about individual rights and liberties, when the priority is to save political liberty and national independence? The ideologues in your ranks demand guarantees against state power, when the whole of France only wants security against the enemy.[29]

When Lainé heard of Napoleon's allegations against him, he assumed that his liberty and possibly his life were in danger. The next day he wrote a letter to Savary, for transmission to the Emperor, defending himself passionately against the charge of treason. He had received less than ten letters from England in the whole of his life, he claimed, and all had related to his legal work. He protested his loyalty in extravagant terms, regretting that he had incurred 'the most dreadful misfortune that can befall a subject: the displeasure of his sovereign'.[30] He was later accused of truckling to Napoleon. This is hardly fair, since despite all his self-exculpation, he at no point retracted any of his speech. He was naturally alarmed for his personal safety, but he still did not betray his principles.

What Lainé really wanted to know was whether he would be detained in Paris or be allowed to return home with the other deputies, and he asked

Savary's advice on this. To his great relief, Savary replied that he could leave if he wanted. Shortly afterwards, he set off for Bordeaux, stopping off en route at Orléans. His fear of arrest was greatest here, since he could have been detained with less publicity than in Paris, and before he reached Bordeaux where his friends could have protected him. Yet he was able to proceed without incident, and was back on his family estate a few days later.[31]

Napoleon made several errors in dealing with Lainé. His allegation that Lainé was working for England was baseless, and clearly the product of anger. Although his decision not to imprison Lainé did him credit, Napoleon also made a mistake in letting him return to Bordeaux. This was because he ignored one final reason why Lainé had acted as he did—concern for the plight of his native city. As an important local notable, Lainé was horrified by the effect on Bordeaux's economy of the war and continental blockade. As an Atlantic port heavily dependent on colonial trade, Bordeaux had suffered disastrously from the embargo. Lainé was personally affected by this. As a member of the city's central bureau of charity, he helped distribute basic necessities to the destitute, whose numbers were increasing sharply. A calculation drawn up for the bureau's meeting of 19 December 1812 estimated these as 3,261 at the lowest, and 8,681 at the highest. Although Lainé had gone into the law, his family were merchants, and by 1812 his brother Honorat's trading house, Dubedat and Lainé, was in severe financial difficulties.[32]

Lainé had powerful economic as well as political motives for opposing the war. He made these clear in his notes for the commission's draft address. 'Above all, we must insist on freedom for commerce and industry', he wrote, '[and prove] that this is in the government's and the treasury's interest . . . Since peace will bring to an end the great project of closing the continent [to foreign trade], we must turn our attention to the sea, whose resources have become useless to us.'[33] By letting Lainé go back to Bordeaux, Napoleon was allowing a leading symbol of opposition to return to his home town, whose acute economic distress was bound to gain him many sympathizers. As the prefect's reports made clear, this distress was already spilling over into political discontent, with the posting of seditious placards. Lainé's presence could only accelerate this process.

Lainé was remarkable because he combined political courage with intellectual distinction. These qualities made him an exceptionally shrewd observer of the last phase of Napoleon's rule. They also gave him a penetrating insight into Napoleon's own character and motivation. In particular, his argument that the Emperor preferred war to peace because it preserved his dictatorship is powerful and plausible. Napoleon was well aware that peace would bring questioning of the high taxation, censorship, and conscription which gave him such tremendous resources, and his outburst at the New Year's Day reception of 1814 shows he did not welcome this. Conquest and glory had become essential ingredients of his rule, and he was unwilling, and perhaps incapable, of governing without them.

Alongside simple unwillingness to give up power, Napoleon's old fears persisted. These became very clear the moment France was invaded. The last time this had happened, in 1793, the republican government had decreed a massive military mobilization, the *levée en masse*, the conscription of all able-bodied men without exceptions. But conscription was indelibly associated with the other traumas of that year—popular violence and terror. Napoleon could have invoked this precedent, but was noticeably reluctant to do so. Did he fear unleashing an armed and radicalized population that might attempt to revive the republic? In an unpublished section of his memoirs, Caulaincourt commented perceptively on this:

> Napoleon did not dare to demand the *levée en masse* of the French people. Such an action would no doubt have sufficed to terrify Europe, and destroy all [the allies'] hopes, but this immense resource could only be wielded by the irresistible will of a republican nation. The empire was based only on the genius of one man.[34]

Fear of reviving revolutionary spectres also marked Napoleon's attitude to the National Guard. This had first been formed as a popular militia in 1789 at the moment of the storming of the Bastille. At its height during the Revolution all active citizens had been required to join it. Napoleon, however, had reduced it to purely ceremonial functions on coming to power. The reverses since Russia had necessitated changing this policy, and many of those eligible for National Guard service had been called up and sent to the army. On 17 December 1813, a decree formed those remaining into a 'sedentary' home guard. Significantly, the only place where units were not raised was Paris. Napoleon was unable to forget the role the capital's National Guard had played in the Revolution—it had led the attack on the Tuileries in August 1792. When Pasquier urged him to include the Paris guard in the decree, he replied: 'Who will answer to me for the attitude of [these troops]? If it's bad, will I regret leaving in my rear a force like this?'[35]

With the allied invasion, the issue resurfaced, and was discussed at length at a council meeting in early January 1814. It became clear that many of the ministers shared Napoleon's fears. Savary, who was present, wrote that all recalled that the Paris guard 'had been the most powerful instrument at the disposal of political agitators during the Revolution, and that it would be dangerous to return it to their hands'. He noted a further telling detail: 'It was a remarkable fact that all the members of the council who had acquired fame during the Revolution were at first against raising the Paris national guard.' Eventually a compromise was reached: 30,000 men were called up, but the poorer and presumably more radical Parisians were rigorously excluded, and the political reliability of their officers was to be carefully monitored.[36]

Napoleon's suspicions of the National Guard were palpable, but it was still useful for propaganda purposes. On 23 January, just before returning to the front, he staged a symbolic ceremony at the Tuileries. Accompanied by Marie-Louise and his 3-year old son, dressed for the occasion in a miniature National Guard uniform, he made a speech to the force's assembled officers: 'I entrust the Empress and the King of Rome to the courage of the national guard.'[37] The next day, he once again confirmed Marie-Louise as regent, aided by a council headed by his elder brother Joseph and, as before, the loyal and efficient Cambacérès. At 6 the following morning, he left Paris. He never saw his wife and son again.

11

The Congress of Châtillon

While Napoleon was organizing his war effort and confronting the Legislative Body, the allied armies, almost 200,000 strong, were advancing deep into eastern France. Along the whole front they were only opposed by 70,000 French troops, who prudently retreated before them. By 18 January, Blücher had reached Joinville on the river Marne, while to the south Schwarzenberg, with the main body, had occupied the strategic plateau around Langres.[1]

This easy progress had a powerful effect at allied headquarters, and particularly on the Czar, who arrived in Langres on 22 January. Alexander saw his ultimate goal, a triumphal march on Paris and the overthrow of his great enemy Napoleon, within his grasp. He even began to look beyond this, and revived his old idea of placing Bernadotte, who would be an obedient Russian client, on the French throne. His determination to press on was mirrored by Blücher. The Prussian commander was burning to avenge Prussia's humiliating defeats by Napoleon in 1806 by crushing him and seizing his capital. 'The drive goes on to Paris', he wrote on 14 January. '... I believe we will be strong enough to deliver a decisive blow that will decide everything.'[2]

These perspectives filled the Austrians with alarm. Their aim remained, as it had been at Frankfurt, to negotiate a compromise peace well before they reached Paris. Their desire to preserve Napoleon was only reinforced by their distaste for the replacement Alexander had in mind for him. 'We have no interest in sacrificing a single soldier to put Bernadotte on the French throne,' Metternich wrote to Schwarzenberg on 16 January. 'You think I'm mad? Well, I'm not; this is the plan!' Schwarzenberg was equally horrified. 'I've received your letter,' he replied, '... and ever since I can't get B[ernadotte] out of my mind. What! The world has witnessed an alliance

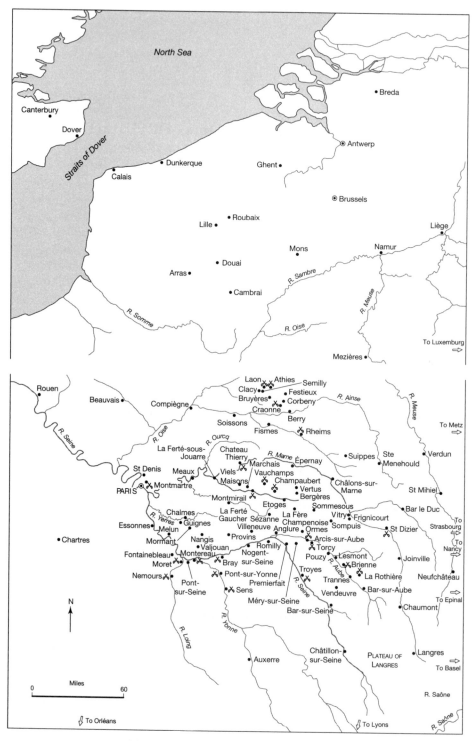

Map 10. The campaign of France, 1814.

between the greatest sovereigns of Europe to arrive at such a scandalous result!!! Impossible! I count on you [to avoid it].'[3]

At this critical moment, Metternich was reinforced by a powerful new ally. On 18 January, the English foreign minister, Lord Castlereagh, joined him at Basel after a gruelling three-week journey from London in freezing winter weather. Temperamentally, the serious, taciturn Castlereagh was very different from his extrovert Austrian counterpart, but politically both men were cautious and pragmatic, and to Metternich's delight soon found common ground on the questions before them. 'I cannot praise Castlereagh enough', Metternich wrote on 30 January. 'His attitude is excellent and his work as direct as it is correct . . . his mood is peaceful, peaceful in *our* sense.'[4]

The essential point was that Castlereagh found the prospect of Bernadotte as king of France as unacceptable as did Metternich. The two differed about the alternative: Castlereagh supported a Bourbon restoration as the best guarantee of peace, whereas Metternich's preferred option remained a Napoleonic France reduced to acceptable limits. Faced with the threat of Bernadotte, however, they swiftly arrived at a compromise. They decided that there were only two choices to rule France—Napoleon or the Bourbons. Which one was a matter for the French people. If the allies were seen to interfere, it could cause a patriotic backlash which Napoleon would be sure to exploit. In the meantime, unless and until Napoleon's authority was successfully challenged from within, the allies should continue to negotiate with him.[5]

Other critical questions were discussed in the same spirit of cooperation. Castlereagh's main aim was to ensure, in the wake of Aberdeen's blunder at Frankfurt, that England's maritime rights were maintained intact in any peace settlement. Recognizing the English government's intractability on this point, Metternich gracefully conceded it. On the issue of France's future borders, however, there was a wider gap. Metternich had endorsed the 'natural frontiers' at Frankfurt, while Castlereagh followed the policy set out by his mentor Pitt the Younger nine years before. This favoured returning France to her 'former limits' of 1792, before the revolutionary wars.[6]

Both men, however, were prepared to make concessions. With the crossing of the Rhine, France's 'natural frontiers' had already been breached, and Metternich realized that it was now probably impossible to obtain them in their entirety. Castlereagh too was willing to be flexible, provided Antwerp was taken from France and a solid 'barrier' created in the Low Countries to protect England from future invasion. This was perfectly in keeping with Pitt's policy, which had been less committed to imposing France's 'former limits' than is generally acknowledged.[7] Even Pitt had accepted that this could prove impossible in practice, and that part of the Netherlands and the left bank of the Rhine might have to remain in French hands.

On this basis, in the course of a week in Basel, Metternich and Castlereagh discussed the outline of new frontiers for France, marking a compromise between her 'natural' and her 'former' limits. She would lose Mainz, but retain a substantial chunk of territory on the left bank of the Rhine up to the river Moselle. Holland would be given a strong barrier against France, including Antwerp. No precise line for the future Franco-Dutch border was mentioned, but shortly afterwards Castlereagh proposed that it should be the river Meuse. These discussions were soon overtaken by events, but show that Castlereagh was at least prepared to consider a significantly more generous settlement for France than her pre-1792 boundaries.[8]

More immediately, the Czar's plan for an immediate drive on Paris to dethrone Napoleon had to be scotched. On the night of 22 January, Metternich and Castlereagh left Basel, and arrived at Langres three days later. There they found Schwarzenberg thoroughly angry and upset. He was still committed to Metternich's plan for a limited invasion of France and compromise peace well before Paris was reached. For three days Alexander had given him no peace, constantly pressing him to change his strategy and march on the capital. Schwarzenberg held firm, but his exasperation with the Czar was obvious. 'We should make peace here; that's my opinion,' he wrote to his wife on 26 January, 'any advance on Paris would be against all military principles... but Czar Alexander has had another of those fits of buffoonery that often seize him. This is an absolutely decisive moment; may Heaven protect us in this crisis.'[9]

The same day, Schwarzenberg sent Francis I a long memorandum setting out the case for and against an offensive on Paris. He nowhere stated, but it is highly likely, that it had been concerted beforehand with Metternich and Castlereagh. He awaited Francis' decision whether to remain on the plateau of Langres or 'descend into the plain and begin the struggle', but made his own preference clear. He needed time to rest his troops, bring up reinforcements, and establish closer contact with both wings of his army. In the flat lands between the plateau and the capital, there were no obvious points where his forces could halt and regroup. Langres was therefore the last position from which peace with Napoleon was possible. Furthermore, as the allies advanced deeper into France, the likelihood of a popular rising against them would increase. For Schwarzenberg, the dangers of going forward far outweighed the benefits.[10]

Although Schwarzenberg was careful to concentrate on military matters, the issues he raised were clearly political. Staying put implied negotiating with Napoleon; advancing would be a long step towards his overthrow. Francis sent the memorandum to Metternich for his views. These, along with his own decision, he then forwarded to Alexander, Frederick William, and Castlereagh. Metternich concluded his comments with a series of questions designed to pin down the Czar. The most important were whether the allies wished to negotiate peace with France on the basis of the natural frontiers, whether they aimed to change her ruling dynasty, and if so whether in favour of the Bourbons or another candidate. Francis' answers were clear—the allies should leave the dynastic question to the French themselves, and begin peace talks with Napoleon. They should also swiftly decide how far, if at all, France should be allowed to retain the natural frontiers. Of the other allied monarchs, only Alexander clearly opposed these proposals.[11]

On two successive evenings, on 27 and 28 January, Metternich had long interviews with the Czar. Both were stormy. Alexander argued fiercely against a Bourbon restoration. Instead, once Paris had been captured, he proposed to call a representative assembly. In this way the French people themselves could choose their form of government and ruler, but on the understanding that both a republic and Napoleon would be excluded. Bernadotte was not directly mentioned, but a Parisian parliament sur-rounded by Russian troops was unlikely to choose any other candidate.

Metternich's reply was forthright. Calling an assembly in Paris would simply revive the instability and factionalism of the revolutionary era, and could under no circumstances be considered. He even made the ultimate threat available to a coalition partner: if Alexander persisted with his plan, Austria would withdraw. Faced with this, the Czar was forced to concede, and a compromise was reached. The idea of an assembly, and by implication Bernadotte, was dropped. Instead Caulaincourt, who had already left Paris expecting a negotiation, would be invited to a peace conference at Châtillon-sur-Seine, between Langres and the capital. However, in accord-ance with the Czar's wishes, the allied advance would resume. By insisting on this Alexander showed considerable acumen. If fighting continued, the peace terms would vary according to the fortunes of war. The decision would shift from the conference table to the battlefield and here, the Czar was confident, the allies' numerical superiority would ensure Napoleon's defeat and overthrow.[12]

With these questions resolved, the ministers of the four Powers met the next morning to discuss the most important remaining issue—that of France's future borders. Having pondered his previous conversation with Metternich, Castlereagh felt that the territories to be allowed to France beyond her 'former limits' needed to be reduced. Unwilling to alienate such a useful ally, Metternich acquiesced. However he still urged, as Castlereagh described it, 'some concession to France, neither extensive nor important in itself, beyond the ancient limits . . . [indicating] some portion of the flat country of Savoy and possibly some portion of territory on the left bank of the Rhine.'[13] This showed that Metternich realized the importance of the Rhine and the Alps to Napoleon. If the allied peace terms made a gesture, if only a symbolic one, towards them, he could still proclaim that national honour had been saved. The meeting accepted Metternich's proposal.

Over the next few days, events turned sharply in the allies' favour. Arriving at the front on 26 January, Napoleon decided to exploit the gap between the two invading armies and turn on Blücher. The first engagement, however, was indecisive. It took place on 29 January at Brienne, at whose military academy Napoleon had spent his schooldays. The Prussian and Russian troops finally withdrew, but in good order, and not before Napoleon had almost been captured by a party of Cossacks, and Berthier wounded in the head and knocked from his horse. Worse followed for the French three days later. Reinforced by Schwarzenberg, Blücher went on the offensive, and caught Napoleon by surprise. At La Rothière just outside Brienne, in blizzard conditions, 40,000 French faced 53,000 allies, whose numbers rose during the day to 110,000. By the afternoon the French right wing was starting to give way, and Napoleon had no option but to retreat. His losses were roughly equal to his opponents'—6,000 dead and wounded—but he had clearly been defeated.[14]

The news of La Rothière caused jubilation at allied headquarters. Napoleon had been beaten on his native soil, and the road to Paris seemed to lie open. However, Caulaincourt had now been invited to a peace conference, and this promise had to be honoured. On 3 February, the allied representatives arrived at Châtillon—for Austria Stadion, Metternich's predecessor as foreign minister; for Prussia Humboldt, who had already taken part in the congress of Prague; for Russia Count Razumovsky, a known

Figure 9. *Campaign of France, 1814,* by Jean Louis Meissonier.

Francophobe; and for England no less than three envoys, Cathcart, Stewart, and Aberdeen. Caulaincourt was waiting for them, having arrived at Châtillon a fortnight before. Underlining how desperately most French people wanted the war to end, in the towns en route from Paris he had been acclaimed by crowds shouting 'Long live peace!'[15]

The envoys and their substantial entourages were billeted around the town. Caulaincourt was assigned the largest house, that of M Etienne, a rich merchant. The conferences were held in the mansion of a local noblewoman, Mme de Montmaur. Châtillon itself, being in a war zone, was a ghost town. The peasants had fled, there was no market, and hence no food. 'We are bringing our own provisions as if we were travelling to the Indies,' wrote Stadion to his wife. In this depressing atmosphere, the congress opened on 5 February, only to be adjourned after twenty minutes because Razumovsky claimed that his instructions had not yet arrived. Then, as soon as Caulaincourt had left the room, Castlereagh declared to his allies that even if Napoleon accepted all their terms, England could not sign until all aspects of the settlement, even those unconnected with France, had been agreed. However accommodating Caulaincourt proved to be, there would still be a significant delay before any treaty was concluded.[16]

At this moment Caulaincourt's main concern was not the other Powers, but his own master. He was desperately worried that even in defeat Napoleon might still risk his future in battle rather than entrust it to diplomacy. Once again, he joined forces with Berthier to make the Emperor see reason. 'Bring the truth home to His Majesty,' he wrote to the marshal on 3 February, 'convince him how serious the situation is, and how much any delay will risk to no advantage. Tell me truthfully . . . do you still have an army? Can we discuss conditions for a fortnight or should we accept them straight away? If no-one has the courage to tell me where we really stand, I am left with . . . no idea what I should do.'[17]

In these perilous circumstances, what Caulaincourt needed were pleni-potentiary powers, enabling him to sign a peace without referring the terms back to Napoleon. On 4 February he wrote the Emperor begging for these. Initially, Napoleon brushed the request aside. Discussing it with the Duke of Bassano, he pointed at a passage from Montesquieu's *Grandeur et Déca-dence des Romains* at his elbow. This described Louis XIV's attitude when France was invaded in 1709: 'I know of nothing so magnanimous as the resolution taken by one recent monarch, to bury himself beneath the ruins of his throne rather than accept proposals that no king should have to hear.' Yet Bassano, in a courageous outburst that belied his reputation as a warmonger, threw the quotation back at Napoleon: 'I know of something even more magnanimous—to throw down your glory to close the abyss into which France risks falling with you!' Throughout most of the night he argued with the Emperor, and finally extracted a letter giving Caulaincourt *carte blanche* to sign whatever terms he saw fit, which was sent the next day. It was Bassano's greatest contribution to peace in 1813–14.[18]

The crucial session of the congress opened at midday on 7 February. To his horror, Caulaincourt found that the offer of the natural frontiers no longer held. Instead, the allied representatives demanded the 'former', pre-revolutionary, frontiers of France. All that was left of the Frankfurt proposals were 'arrangements of mutual convenience concerning portions of territory on both sides of these limits'—a phrase Metternich had inserted into the instructions for the conference, presumably indicating the 'flat lands of Savoy' and parts of the left bank of the Rhine he was prepared to concede. Shocked, Caulaincourt could only reply: 'Today's stipulations differ so

greatly from the bases proposed to M de St Aignan [at Frankfurt] . . . that
they are completely unexpected.'[19]

Having recovered, Caulaincourt sought one crucial clarification. If he
accepted the terms, he asked, would a treaty be signed immediately, ending
the bloodshed? This was precisely the issue the allies wished to avoid.
Castlereagh's stipulations two days before had made a delay inevitable,
and it was clear that the Russians were in no hurry to make peace
with Napoleon, especially since they believed his fall to be imminent.
Razumovsky had just received a letter from Nesselrode, telling him of the
capture of several strategic French towns and instructing him to slow down
the negotiations. Caulaincourt thus received an evasive answer, and asked
for time to reflect, which was willingly granted. The session resumed at 8 p.m.,
but broke up with no further decision reached.[20]

Caulaincourt now had the *carte blanche* he wanted, but hesitated to use it.
He had expected to sign peace on the basis of France's 'natural frontiers',
but now found that only her 'former limits' were on offer. Accepting
these immediately was a fearful responsibility, and he baulked at it. They
had never been discussed with Napoleon, who might well disavow him.
Caulaincourt decided he could only accept the terms with Napoleon's
express permission. Immediately after the evening session ended, he sent a
despatch detailing the proposals to his master, asking for further instructions.
He could only hope that Napoleon would accept the seriousness of the
situation, and give a swift and positive answer.[21]

On 7 February, Napoleon arrived at Nogent-sur-Seine, north-west of
Châtillon, and received Caulaincourt's report late that same evening. He
read the letter, then went into his room without a word and shut the door.
Berthier and Bassano joined him shortly after and found him at his desk with
his head in his hands. He showed them the terms, and after a long silence
they both urged him to accept them. Napoleon's response was a passionate
tirade:

> What! You want me to sign such a treaty, and trample underfoot my coron-
> ation oath? Unprecedented defeats may have forced me to promise to
> renounce my conquests, but to abandon those of the Republic! To betray
> the trust placed in me with such confidence! To . . . leave France smaller than
> I found her! Never! . . . What will the French people think of me if I sign their
> humiliation? What shall I say to the republicans in the Senate when they ask
> me once more for their Rhine barrier? . . . You fear the the war continuing,
> but I fear much more pressing dangers, to which you're blind.[22]

The coronation oath to which Napoleon referred bound him to 'maintain the territorial integrity of the Republic', which meant above all the natural frontiers. If he broke it and returned to the pre-revolutionary limits, he feared that his regime might not survive. This was the 'pressing danger' that alarmed him more than the prolongation of the war. He even named the men who would lead the movement against him—the 'republicans in the Senate' like Sieyès, Garat, and Grégoire, who had never forgiven him for returning to a form of monarchy and would seize this chance to take their revenge. The empire would be overthrown and the Republic restored, under the banner of a patriotic war to regain the boundary of the Rhine.

In a gesture of despair, Napoleon threw himself on his bed, and continued to argue furiously with Berthier and Bassano. Eventually, after several hours, they managed to wear him down. It was agreed to accept the terms, giving up Belgium first and then, if this did not satisfy the allies, surrendering the left bank of the Rhine as well. Napoleon and his advisers also recognized that Germany and Italy were now irretrievably lost. In the early hours of the morning, Bassano left the Emperor's bedside to draft the necessary instructions to Caulaincourt.

In his manuscript notes, Lainé had argued that Napoleon's unwillingess to make peace was entirely cynical, since war abroad gave him an excuse to maintain his tyranny at home. Napoleon's behaviour on 7–8 February offers compelling evidence that even if this was partially true, it was not the whole story. That night Napoleon appeared in genuine agony, convinced that if he accepted the terms before him, he would exchange the prospect of military defeat for one he feared more, domestic upheaval. After dismissing Berthier and Bassano, he tried to sleep, but was unable to do so, calling in his valet ten times, either to bring him a light or to take it away. His thoughts turned to death, both his own and his son's. At four in the morning, he wrote a melodramatic letter to his brother Joseph in Paris:

> Paris will never be taken while I am alive . . . If news arrives of my defeat and death, you will be told before the rest of my household: send the Empress and [my son] the King of Rome to Rambouillet . . . Never let the Empress and the King of Rome fall into the enemy's hands . . . That would destroy everything . . .
>
> I would prefer my son's throat to be cut than to see him raised in Vienna as an Austrian prince.
>
> I have never seen a performance of *Andromaque* without pitying the fate of Astyanax [the son of Hector, captured after the fall of Troy] outliving his family, and without thinking that he would have been better off dying with his father.[23]

Then, at around 7 a.m., there was a dramatic reversal of fortune. A messenger arrived from Marshal Marmont with news that Blücher, in his haste to reach Paris, had allowed the four army corps he commanded to become widely separated. Napoleon leaped out of bed; this was the chance he had hoped for, and he immediately began to plan exploiting it. When Bassano, who had been working the rest of the night writing up Caulaincourt's instructions, arrived to have them signed, Napoleon waved him away: 'Oh, there you are! Things have moved on. I'm facing down Blücher! I'll beat him tomorrow or the day after; everything's going to change. Let's not hurry anything. There'll be plenty of time to take the peace on offer later!'[24] The diplomatic humiliation he dreaded had receded, and he was returning to the place where he felt happiest, the battlefield.

At Châtillon, there were no conferences on 8 or 9 February, as the allied diplomats discussed how to respond to Caulaincourt's request for an immediate signature of peace. On the 9th, Engelbert von Floret, Stadion's deputy, visited Caulaincourt to keep him informed. He was greeted with a diatribe showing that at least one of Napoleon's servants shared his fears that a harsh settlement would reignite the French Revolution. 'Ha, M de Floret,' Caulaincourt burst out, 'you are preparing great misfortunes for us and for yourselves. You saw the need to end the Revolution, you did so in the noblest way by marrying an Archduchess to [Napoleon], and now you're in danger of rekindling it with all its horrors.' Later that day Caulaincourt's assistant Rayneval spoke to Floret in similar terms: 'Your policy could have terrible consequences. Today you can still avoid them, but soon . . . this will be beyond your power. You are lighting a fire that you will be unable to put out and which could spread further than you think. It's not the Bourbons I fear, they have no chance, but disorder, a new overthrow of the social order.'[25]

Floret was impressed by these warnings. 'Unfortunately', he wrote, 'I could think of little to say in reply to them.' His concerns were not shared by his Russian colleague. Convinced that Napoleon was about to fall, Razumovsky pressed for the congress to be temporarily halted. Stadion, however, strongly opposed this. The deadlock was broken on 8 February when Razumovsky received instructions from the Czar, saying that he did not feel able at present to answer Caulaincourt's request for an immediate peace treaty, and that the conferences should cease until further notice. The next day Razumovsky read out this letter to the other allied envoys, who were completely taken aback; Stadion especially was furious. But little could be done. Alexander was clearly determined to march on Paris, and for the moment could not be gainsaid. On 10 February, the negotiations were suspended.[26]

This brought about a second and even more furious clash between Alexander and his allies. Metternich and Castlereagh rightly sensed he was making a second attempt, emboldened by military success, to overthrow Napoleon and replace him by Bernadotte. They swiftly coordinated a counterattack. On 11 and 12 February, Castlereagh had two long meetings with the Czar, at which he argued strongly for continuing negotiations with Napoleon. At a ministerial conference on the 13th, Metternich again played his trump card, bursting out that 'Austria would not tolerate this [Russian] tyranny, and would withdraw its army from the coalition and make a separate peace with Napoleon.' He then proposed an ingenious comprom- ise: a preliminary treaty with France. This had two advantages. Though it still meant a settlement with Napoleon, it was less binding than a full treaty and thus answered Castlereagh's doubts about signing a complete settlement immediately. Also, since it did not entail an armistice, the Czar could go on hoping that the war could still topple Napoleon. The basis of the prelim- inaries would, once again, be France's former limits. Realizing he was isolated, Alexander gave way. The preliminary treaty was drafted, and sent for discussion at Châtillon.[27]

At Troyes, the allies were looking forward to military victory, but as they were discussing and arguing, it was slipping from their grasp in the field. On 9 February, Napoleon had left Nogent-sur-Seine and headed north-east, aiming to catch Blücher's army strung out on the march. The next morning he caught the most isolated corps, commanded by the Russian General Olsufiev, at Champaubert. It was overwhelmed, and Olsufiev experienced the humiliation of being captured in a wood by a 19-year-old French conscript. With his own troops concentrated in the middle of the scattered enemy forces, Napoleon was now able to pick them off at will. The next day he moved west to attack General von der Osten-Sacken's corps at Montmirail. The day was decided by a charge of six battalions of the Imperial Guard led by Ney, which sent the allies reeling back, and was completed by a ferocious pursuit. On 14 February, Napoleon defeated Blücher himself, who was hurrying westwards to retrieve the situation, at Vauchamps. Blücher's right wing was broken by a crushing French cavalry charge, and he had to make a fighting retreat. In just six days, he lost a third of his total force.[28]

This extraordinary week re-established Napoleon's military reputation after La Rothière, and remains one of his most brilliant displays of generalship. However to the south the French forces, under Marshals Victor and Oudinot, were being pressed hard by Schwarzenberg. Napoleon now turned to face this threat, and on 18 February attacked one of Schwarzenberg's corps, commanded by Prince Eugen of Württemberg, at Montereau. After a heavy artillery duel, the French stormed the main allied position on the plateau of Surville, with Napoleon himself helping to position the guns to exploit this success. When Schwarzenberg heard of this reverse, he was shaken. Always a cautious general, he pulled his whole army back behind the river Seine.

The series of allied defeats spurred Schwarzenberg to a further action, which was highly significant and which he seems to have taken on his own initiative. He went to Alexander and Frederick William, who were at his headquarters, and proposed an armistice. This was an extraordinary move, since it cut completely across the decision taken at Troyes just three days before, to work instead for a preliminary treaty. It betrayed Schwarzenberg's exasperation with the slowness of the diplomats at Châtillon. Even more extraordinary, Alexander and Frederick William immediately agreed to the plan. This was a measure of their consternation at Napoleon's resurgence, and of how brittle their earlier confidence had been. As a result, having first been unsure about whether to negotiate with Napoleon at all, the allies now found themselves committed to not one, but two, peace overtures towards him, the first aiming at a preliminary peace, the second at an armistice.[29]

Yet an armistice had one advantage, which reveals Schwarzenberg's shrewdness in suggesting it. It would end the fighting, so that diplomacy would no longer be at the mercy of the events of war. Up until now, both sides had been gambling on outright military victory, altering their terms and delaying conferences in accordance with news from the battlefield. With these temptations removed, negotiations could become simpler and more straightforward. Schwarzenberg's initiative thus offered the best available hope of peace.

At Troyes, Metternich was furious that his own policy had been upstaged, but could do little about it. With Alexander, Frederick William, and Schwarzenberg ranged against him, he had to accept that for the moment the congress of Châtillon was eclipsed. Castlereagh was also angry, but equally impotent. The diplomats convened just once at Châtillon on 17 February to present the preliminary treaty to Caulaincourt, who replied that he would have to consider it and consult Napoleon. The conferences then adjourned once again, as attention shifted to the armistice negotiations.[30]

Caulaincourt had temporized with good reason, since he no longer had *carte blanche* to conclude an agreement. Five days before, buoyed up by his victories at Champaubert and Montmirail, Napoleon had written to him that the only possible basis for peace now was the natural frontiers, and that any other treaty 'would be merely a truce'. On 17 February, he formally rescinded Caulaincourt's powers, and instructed him 'to sign nothing without my order, since I alone know my position'.[31] Ironically, this placed the allies in exactly the same situation Napoleon had been in two weeks before, desperate for a settlement that their opponent was unwilling to accord. Napoleon's change of stance should not have been unexpected. He had only momentarily considered abandoning the natural frontiers under extreme pressure, on the night of 7–8 February. Now, with the military situation restored, he returned to them as his *sine qua non* for peace. As the heir of the Revolution, with all that entailed, he felt he could retreat no further.

Further proof of Napoleon's renewed intransigence soon followed. On 21 February, he sent a long letter to Francis I, invoking family ties and attempting to divide him from his allies. 'I propose to Your Majesty', he wrote, 'that, without delay, we sign a peace on the bases you yourself established at Frankfurt, and which I and the French nation have adopted as our ultimatum.' He blocked every avenue of compromise on these conditions: 'I shall never cede Antwerp or Belgium.' To deter Francis from advancing on the capital, he shamelessly conjured up the spectre of the Revolution and the *sans-culottes*: 'There are 200,000 men under arms in Paris.' The letter, with its hectoring tone, had the opposite effect on Francis than the one intended. It alienated him, and made him despair of any meaningful negotiation with his son-in-law.[32]

After Schwarzenberg proposed the armistice to Berthier, as Napoleon's chief of staff, he was kept waiting five days. Berthier then sent him a blustering reply, clearly dictated by Napoleon himself, vaunting the strength of the French army and its latest victories. He also did not fail to mention 'the armed population' of Paris. Schwarzenberg persevered, and armistice negotiations began on 24 February at Lusigny a few miles east of Troyes, but the first French condition was that the natural frontiers be explicitly recognized as the basis of any future treaty. Since the allied representatives were all soldiers rather than diplomats, they replied, quite reasonably, that this was beyond their competence. They referred the matter back to their head-quarters, and were told firmly that all political questions should be kept out of the talks.[33]

Fortune might have swung back to Napoleon's side, but he did not feel strong enough to break off the discussions just yet, and agreed that the natural frontiers should not be mentioned. Instead, the issue simply reappeared in a different form over the question of the armistice demarcation line. Napoleon saw this as a means of staking his claim to the natural frontiers in a final settlement, and was determined that it should follow them as closely as possible. In the words of his secretary Baron Fain, he 'sought to profit from the occasion to lay the basis of a definitive peace. He wanted to keep Antwerp and the Belgian coast: this was the reward he expected for his recent successes.' For the same reason, he also wanted to keep Savoy on the French side of the line. The allied envoys refused to accept this, and on 5 March, after several days of fruitless wrangling, the Lusigny negotiations broke up.[34]

The failure of Lusigny was a body blow to moderates on both sides. One reason why Schwarzenberg pressed for an armistice was probably because it meant dealing with his friend Berthier, whom he knew to favour a swift peace. Berthier's letter to Schwarzenberg had been uncompromising, but since it had obviously been inspired by Napoleon it did not have to be taken at face value. One sign that Berthier genuinely wanted a settlement was that he sent as the French representative to Lusigny his own adjutant, General Charles de Flahaut, Talleyrand's illegitimate son and another member of the 'peace party'. Flahaut did everything he could to keep the talks alive. Certainly he was seen as an ally by the Austrian envoy, General Duka, Francis I's personal military adviser. Duka several times spoke to Flahaut in private, and his words could unofficially be taken as those of his master. As Flahaut related in a confidential report:

> He told me of the Emperor of Austria's sincere desire to end the war. He said that his master had never [wished] to march on Paris. He cited as proof how slowly Prince Schwarzenberg was advancing. He repeated several times that he had no doubt peace could swiftly be concluded, if we could put a stop to the fighting, that the Emperor of Austria wanted this, and that [his peace terms] would be very reasonable. He returned to this subject every day, asking bluntly that we help the Emperor of Austria to make peace. 'Ensure that hostilities end on the 28th,' he told me, 'give us the means of making peace: I swear to you that the Emperor of Austria and England wish it to be *honourable* for France.'[35]

On the evening of 28 February, all three allied representatives came to Flahaut and echoed Duka's words, saying that if only an armistice could be agreed a moderate peace would certainly follow. Flahaut was later blamed for not signing then and there on his own authority, but this is unfair. Like Caulaincourt at Châtillon a fortnight before, he was in a dreadful position; he knew that the only way to make peace was to go against his master's wishes. Tragically, in these crucial months no-one in Napoleon's entourage was prepared to do this, ensuring that the only solution left would be a military one.[36]

Schwarzenberg's initiative was in ruins, but it had alarmed Castlereagh enough to take counter-measures. For the last year, the allies had been linked together by a complicated set of bilateral treaties, which had given Austria considerable leeway to pursue a separate policy towards Napoleon. Castlereagh proposed to reinforce these by a single general alliance between England, Austria, Russia, and Prussia. At Chaumont, where the monarchs and ministers now had their headquarters, after a week of intense discussions his plan was accepted. On 10 March, the treaty of Chaumont was signed, binding the allies not to make any separate peace until their common war aims had been achieved.[37]

The last act at Châtillon could now begin. On 28 February, the conferences resumed; Caulaincourt again asked for more time to consider the preliminary treaty, and was given a deadline of 10 March. At 9 that morning he read out to the assembled diplomats a long memorandum repeating that the natural frontiers offered the only acceptable formula for peace. A long silence followed. Stadion and his colleagues realized the end had come, but they made one last effort. Caulaincourt was asked to produce a detailed counter-project to their own proposals, which he did five days later. This took the form of a full draft treaty, which still ceded almost nothing of the natural frontiers: Holland was given a barrier to the south, but France would retain Antwerp, most of Belgium, the left bank of the Rhine and Savoy. Beyond her borders, the kingdom of Italy would go to Eugène de Beauharnais, and the king of Saxony would lose none of his territories. All the allied diplomats rejected this, and on 19 March the congress of Châtillon was formally closed. The last peace negotiation between Napoleon and his opponents had failed.[38]

In an unpublished manuscript preface to his memoirs, Caulaincourt posed three basic questions: '*Did the Emperor Napoleon want peace at Châtillon, could I have achieved it, and was it possible?*' To the first his answer was categoric: 'The Emperor's real plan, his constant determination, was always summed up in the words "abdicate or die rather than leave France smaller than I found her".' Again, strikingly, Caulaincourt linked this to Napoleon's fear that abandoning the natural frontiers would give the republicans a powerful propaganda weapon against him. 'The Emperor did not want peace', he continued, 'not because he did not see its necessity, but because he thought the one under discussion was incompatible with his [here the word "honour" is erased and replaced, significantly, with "survival"], and with the establishment of [his] new dynasty which, as he said, should not have to blush in front of our old republicans, having appealed to the pride and to the glory of the nation.'[39]

Caulaincourt's second answer was equally clear. In his view, if he had used his *carte blanche* to sign any peace not based on the natural frontiers, he would simply have been disavowed by his master. Besides, to do so would have been to betray Napoleon's trust, 'and if betrayals can sometimes be useful, they are never honourable'.[40] Caulaincourt was particularly sensitive on this point, since within his lifetime he was reproached for not immediately accepting the terms presented on 7 February, and letting slip a major chance for peace. His first accuser, ironically, was Bassano, whom he had so often portrayed as a warmonger. In his notes for his memoirs, not published until long after his death, Bassano was categoric: 'If, on the 7th, 8th or 9th February, [Caulaincourt] had given up Antwerp, Belgium, and the Rhine for the sake of peace, it would have been assured. He undermined the negotiation . . . by not accepting immediately, using his unlimited powers, the [allied] declaration of the 7th as a basis [for this].'[41]

Both Caulaincourt's and Bassano's versions rest on an imponderable: even if Caulaincourt had signed a treaty in early February, would either Napoleon or the allied leaders have ratified it? Here the evidence is contradictory. Castlereagh and the Russians initially wished to delay, but by the 14th, alarmed by Napoleon's string of victories, they had changed their minds and were ready to make an immediate peace. The crucial question, therefore, is whether Napoleon would have followed suit. For a brief moment, he did contemplate settling for France's former limits, though he never actually sent Caulaincourt instructions to that effect. Yet just a week later he wrote that if he had been presented with a fait accompli, he would have accepted it. 'If the allies had agreed to your proposals on the 9th', he told Caulaincourt, '[I would have stopped fighting]; I would not have risked everything when the smallest defeat would have ruined France.'[42]

Admittedly, Napoleon was writing after the event, but had he been presented with a treaty ratified by the allies, he would have been under tremendous pressure, not least from his own entourage, to sign it. It is thus probable, though ultimately impossible to know for certain, that between 7 and 9 February Caulaincourt did miss an opportunity to end the war.

Finally, though he refused to shoulder any blame for its failure, Caulaincourt maintained that the congress of Châtillon could in principle have succeeded. 'As to the third question: was peace possible?' he wrote, '... Yes at the beginning, but only with Savoy and some rectifications of the old frontier... It is probable, or at least I think so, that immediately after they resumed [on 17 February] the negotiations could... have led us to [this] result.'[43] The first reason Caulaincourt gave, which Metternich's actions confirm, was that Austria would have supported such a solution. The second was the series of allied defeats, which put Paris out of immediate danger. While it rests in part on speculation, overall this seems a fair assessment.

The fact remains that Caulaincourt felt unable to sign such a peace without a specific order from his master, and that this was never sent. This was because, as Caulaincourt perceptively wrote, Napoleon felt that not only his honour, but his survival, required him not to send it. The reasons why Napoleon felt this were complex, and ingrained in his character and beliefs. Central to them was the fear he expressed with such passion and vehemence on the night of 7 February—that dishonour would bring revolution.

12

The Beginning of the End

When Napoleon asserted that the French people would reject peace without victory, he was thinking above all of the people of Paris. In 1792, he had witnessed their ferocity in the face of defeat, and assumed that they would react the same way in 1814. Were Napoleon's fears justified, or merely based on his grisly memories of the Revolution?

Whereas in the provinces public opinion was monitored by the prefects, in the capital this was the job of the police, and Pasquier, the prefect of the Paris police, wrote Napoleon daily reports. These survive, and are a mine of information about Parisian opinion in the last months of Napoleon's regime.[1] The picture that emerges bore little relation to the Emperor's preconceptions.

Unlike those of the provincial prefects, Pasquier's bulletins do not deal with public opinion under a separate heading. Instead, references to it are scattered through the main sections: on the theatres, notable events (usually murders or suicides), surveillance of barracks, and the operations of the Bourse, the Paris stock exchange. The reasons for this are unclear, but the likeliest is that Pasquier was strongly in favour of peace, and known to be so.[2] Including in his bulletins all available evidence that the Parisians felt the same way was an obvious means of steering Napoleon in this direction. Yet Pasquier could not do this too openly, otherwise the Emperor, always suspicious of being manipulated, might take serious offence.

This helps explain the reports' most striking feature—most of the material on public opinion comes in the sections on the Bourse. On one level, this had a clear logic. In the crisis conditions of spring 1814, the Bourse was packed. 'In these circumstances', Pasquier concluded, 'the stock market becomes a barometer—if admittedly often an inaccurate one—of opinion.'[3] On another level, presenting public opinion in the guise of reporting on the Bourse allowed Pasquier to make his points effectively, but not too obtrusively. It was worthy of his skill and subtlety to smuggle everything his master did not wish to hear into some inoffensive paragraphs on stocks and shares.

All the bulletins portray the Bourse as desperate for an end to the war. Most obviously, the share index rose at any news that peace was likely to be signed, and fell when this prospect receded. On 8 January, Pasquier reported that 'the fall in share prices would have been steeper, according to observers, if there was not still some hope of peace.' In contrast, two days later he noted: 'the rise in consolidated stocks is attributable to new transactions and to sustained rumours of peace.' More concretely, on 20 January he wrote that 'today's rise can be credited to an article in the *Moniteur* saying that [Cau-laincourt] has received his passports to attend [a peace conference] in Basel.'[4]

The Bourse was probably the best-informed public place in Paris. In fact, as the crisis continued and business declined, it seems to have functioned more as a clearing-house for news than as a forum for commercial transac-tions. On 9 March, for example, it was 'so crowded that it was difficult to move; the numbers of the curious grow daily and business is almost at a standstill.' On the 12th, apparently, commerce virtually stopped: 'people were principally occupied chasing the latest news.' Inevitably in such a febrile crowd, there was much unsubstantiated rumour as well as hard fact. When on 3 February some countrywomen arrived in Paris from Vincennes, claiming to have encountered on the road thirty armed men with long beards speaking bad French, traditional fears of brigands revived. In fact, the thirty bandits turned out to be eight bedraggled deserters from the army. What this did illustrate was the level of alarm and anxiety in the capital, whose effects, if one report is to be believed, could be fatal in themselves. On the morning of 8 March, a story went round the Bourse that 'among the people fleeing Montereau for Paris, several had died of fear in the stagecoach.'[5]

From 2 February, the Bourse's attention was fixed on the negotiations at Châtillon. Initially, the news received was sparse. No word, for example, seems to have leaked out about the allied demand for France's former limits. However, the session of the congress on the 17th, coupled with the French victories of the previous week, caused hopes to rise sharply. That day, a report circulated that Marie-Louise had just received a letter from Napoleon announcing that the allies had made him 'improved offers of peace', and share prices rose as a result. Two days later, optimism reached a peak. 'It is said', Pasquier reported, 'that the signature of peace preliminaries depends on just one article that would make Antwerp a free city.'[6] Given Napoleon's determination to keep Antwerp French at all costs, this smacks of wish-fulfilment. It is further evidence of the role of rumour in reflecting the public's most urgent desires.

When the preliminary peace did not materialize, hopes were revived by the armistice talks at Lusigny. Significantly, they were swiftly linked to Berthier; on 22 February, the talk was that he had left Paris the previous night to draw up the demarcation lines. Over the next few days, speculation mounted that both an armistice and peace preliminaries were being agreed. On the 26th, it was believed that an armistice had actually come into force. In another example of desire becoming reality, it was also said that at Châtillon, Stadion, with his Francophobe reputation, had been replaced as the Austrian representative by the more moderate Prince Liechtenstein, and that the preliminaries would be signed by 10 March. 'All thoughts are turned towards peace,' concluded Pasquier's spies.[7]

When the armistice too proved an illusion, confidence slumped, and this time it did not recover. On 3 March, Pasquier noted that 'today's fall in share prices is attributable to the lack of official news and above all to the dwindling hope of peace now talk of negotiations has ceased.' There was no sense of panic, only a weary resignation. By mid-March the bulletins described 'an atmosphere not of bitterness, but of increasing sadness'. By the 24th, it was generally accepted that the congress of Châtillon had broken up, and that the war would continue to the end. The police spies loyally reported unbreakable confidence in Napoleon's military genius, but the general mood of fatalism belied this.[8]

The Bourse strongly favoured peace, since it was founded on commerce, and peace and commerce are generally linked. Did it represent Parisian opinion as a whole? The evidence is very patchy. The only other place in Paris that Pasquier monitored as closely as the Bourse was the eastern quarter, the Faubourg Saint-Antoine. The comparison, however, is reveal-ing. If the Bourse was bourgeois and capitalist, the Faubourg Saint-Antoine was solidly working-class, and had a long radical tradition. During the Revolution it had been the sans-culottes' greatest stronghold, from where the crowd had marched on the Tuileries on 10 August 1792. In the event of a 'dishonourable' peace, if a popular backlash could be expected anywhere it was here.[9]

In fact, nothing of the sort transpired. By 1814, the Faubourg Saint-Antoine too was weary of war and its attendant hardships—conscription, taxation, and high food prices. On the night of 20–21 January, many of the conscription notices posted in the district were torn down. Six weeks later, discontent and protest were being openly expressed. 'The misery of the suburbs, and particularly of the Faubourg Saint-Antoine, is becoming painfully obvious', warned Pasquier's bulletin of 3 March. 'The people are strongly expressing their bitterness, and ardently hoping for peace as the only remedy for their ills.'[10] Ironically, by prolonging the war Napoleon was bringing closer the one outcome he feared most—upheaval on the Paris streets.

Despite its importance, Paris did not lead France in 1814. This role fell to another city far to the south-west. By early March, Bordeaux was poised to fall to an invading British army. Five months before, Wellington had crossed the Pyrenees into France. His advance had been impeded by atrocious weather, but now its pace was quickening. To Wellington's 135,000 troops Marshal Soult, facing them, could only oppose 33,000. On 27 February, at the hard-fought battle of Orthez, Soult was defeated and decided to retreat eastwards towards Toulouse. This left Bordeaux, to the west, virtually undefended. A week later, Wellington detached two divisions under General Beresford to capture the city. It was clear they would face little opposition. On 11 March, the prefect of the Gironde wrote a despairing letter to the minister of the interior Montalivet: 'We estimate the enemy's numbers at 12,000 to 15,000. We have only six or seven hundred, with not one cannon. My men have no muskets.'[11]

The prefect ended on an even more ominous note, if that were possible: 'I must, with great regret, inform your excellency that we cannot count on the loyalty of the citizens. Yesterday I had the two imperial decrees of the 5th March posted; no sooner had they been put up than they were torn down.' This was no surprise, since opinion in Bordeaux had now swung sharply against the regime. The collapse of trade caused by the war and continental blockade remained the main factor, with its grim repercussions of poverty and unemployment. The circumstances were tailor-made for sedition. However, in contrast to the Marseilles and Toulon plots of 1812–13, in Bordeaux this took a royalist direction.[12]

By the spring of 1814, the city had become one of the most important centres of a pro-Bourbon secret society, the *Chevaliers de la Foi*. This had been set up five years before by a group of well-connected young noblemen determined to overthrow Napoleon. It was extremely well-organized, and recruited chiefly among aristocrats who had refused to rally to the Emperor, and Catholics horrified by his arrest and imprisonment of the Pope in 1809. Its secrecy makes it difficult to assess its strength accurately, but its networks were most powerful in Brittany, Languedoc in the south-west, and Franche-Comté in the east. It also had many sympathizers in Paris and Toulouse. In Bordeaux, it had perhaps 400 members, but by late 1813 it had linked up with another royalist group, the paramilitary *Garde Royale*, whose composition was more bourgeois and working-class. This gave it both a popular base, and a presence on the streets. It had also recruited the mayor, Count Jean-Baptiste Lynch, and three of his key subordinates.[13]

With these instruments, the *Chevaliers'* leaders faced a fluid and paradox-ical situation. The allied invasion posed an unprecedented, and possibly a fatal, threat to Napoleon. However, it was far from clear that the allies favoured a Bourbon restoration. The elderly, gouty Louis XVIII, currently holding court at Hartwell House in Buckinghamshire, inspired little confi-dence as an effective replacement for the Emperor. The Czar personally disliked Louis, and the Austrians did not want Napoleon replaced at all. Only the English inclined to Louis, because they thought that as France's pre-revolutionary dynasty, the Bourbons would be content to retreat to her pre-revolutionary borders. All the Powers agreed that unless the Bourbons could demonstrate clear popular support for their cause, their return was out of the question.[14]

The *Chevaliers* responded with an extremely shrewd strategy—the only one available in the circumstances. They did not have sufficient manpower for a full-scale rising. What they could do was mount a demonstration for just long enough to convince the allies that the Bourbons did have a large following in France, and could safely be endorsed. As one of them percep-tively put it, they aimed to create 'a surface appearance of royalism which could prove decisive at the right moment'.[15] Bordeaux was ideally suited for this purpose. The *Chevaliers* already had a strong presence there, and it was strategically placed between the other royalist strongholds of the Vendée to the west and Languedoc to the east. Above all, it lay in the path of a British army, whose government was notably more sympathetic than its allies to the Bourbons, and currently sheltering Louis XVIII himself.

Then, in early February, the *Chevaliers* gained a trump card. Louis XVIII was too infirm to travel far, but as soon as France was invaded he had demanded that the British government allow his younger brother, the comte d'Artois, and his two sons to join the allied armies. He was discreetly supported by Wellington, who thought that, if nothing more, the Bourbon princes might prove useful auxiliaries against Napoleon. The prime minister, Lord Liverpool, agreed. The comte d'Artois was despatched to the allied headquarters in eastern France, and his eldest son, the duc d'Angoulême, to the British army in the south-west. On 3 February, Angoulême arrived at Wellington's headquarters. He was physically unprepossessing and suffered from nervous tics, but this was unimportant. The royalists had their rallying point, a focus for the faithful and a magnet for the wavering.[16]

On 11 March, the French troops evacuated Bordeaux. All remaining authority was now in the hands of the *Chevaliers'* ally, Lynch, the mayor. The conspirators had already sent a messenger to inform the British of their plans. At 10 a.m. the next day, Lynch and his senior colleagues set off in two coaches to meet Beresford's advancing troops and negotiate the city's surrender. With them went a large escort mostly recruited from the *Garde Royale*. As soon as the first British soldiers came into sight, Lynch stopped his coach and got out. He then ripped off his tricolour sash and *Légion d'Honneur* ribbon he was wearing, shouted 'Long live the king!', produced a sash and cockade in Bourbon white, and put them on. His companions immediately followed suit.[17]

Beresford did not need to react, only to let events take their course. He accompanied Lynch back to Bordeaux, and into the midst of the *Chevaliers'* planned demonstration. Responding to royalist organizers and to the sheer drama of the occasion, a large crowd gathered crying 'Long live the king! Long live the Bourbons!' The royal flag was unfurled over the city hall, and moments later appeared on every bell-tower. At 3 p.m., Angoulême entered the city. Acclaimed on all sides, he made his way through the packed streets, to a hastily organized *Te Deum* in the cathedral.[18]

How genuine were these cheers for the Bourbons? Beyond the hard core of *Chevaliers* and their sympathizers, it is hard to judge. Many no doubt came from sheer relief that Bordeaux had been spared the horrors so familiar on the other side of the Pyrenees. Here the Bourbons' British allies helped them considerably; unlike the French army, they were scrupulous in paying for what they took. Wellington dealt ferociously with looters, and when his Spanish troops began plundering the countryside, he disbanded them. Yet the Bourbons' greatest weapon was provided by Napoleon himself, and his refusal to end the war. This gave them a golden opportunity to present themselves to a France exhausted by conflict as its best hope of peace. They played on this theme with great skill; when Angoulême addressed crowds on the march to Bordeaux, he did not talk about divine right, but uttered a simple slogan: 'No more wars! No more conscription! No more oppressive taxes!' The strategy reaped its reward, and was the single greatest factor in the royalists' success.[19]

One notable adherent it gained was Lainé, who for the last two months had been living quietly at his home outside Bordeaux. The treatment he had received in December, he considered, absolved him from any duty of loyalty to Napoleon. The Bourbons, he now felt, offered the best chance of achieving what he cherished most—peace and constitutional government. Very discreetly, he made contact with the *Chevaliers*. In February, he composed a pamphlet for them, proclaiming that the Bourbons would end the war, respect political and civil liberty, end conscription, and reduce taxation. However, he remained detached from the *Chevaliers'* main activities, and it is probable that they were keeping him in reserve. As a courageous opponent of Napoleon who had now turned to royalism, Lainé had great propaganda value for them, and they did not want him compromised. He was kept in ignorance of Lynch's machinations, and taken by surprise by the upheaval on 12 March. His return to the public stage only came a fortnight later, when Angoulême appointed him as Bordeaux's new prefect.[20]

The 'event of Bordeaux' was a tremendous blow to Napoleon. For the first time, there was now a rival authority to his own on French soil. For the moment, it was confined to the south-western corner of France, but its psychological impact travelled far beyond. It showed the French that the Bourbons, dismissed for twenty years as irrelevant exiles, were a political force with a realistic chance of power. It also altered the allies' calculations. Deeply divided over the prospect of peace with Napoleon, they had reached a compromise: to negotiate with him as long as the French people continued to support him. Bordeaux showed that this could no longer be assumed, undermining the main reason for keeping talks alive. By mid-March 1814, with diplomacy in tatters and the Bourbons resurrected, Napoleon's throne was beginning to totter. His only hope of saving it now lay on the battlefield.

As the odds mounted against him, Napoleon was already planning his next offensive. Once again, Blücher offered the most tempting target. Despite his successive defeats in February, the tough old veteran was still determined to keep advancing on Paris. He aimed first to circle north, unite with two further corps in the region of Rheims, and then strike east for the capital. Although Schwarzenberg promised to support him if he ran into difficulties, this left a gap between the two allied armies that Napoleon was quick to exploit. Assuming that Blücher had been taught a lesson and that his move north was simply a retreat, he set off in hot pursuit. As before, he hoped to catch his opponent on the march and destroy his units in detail. He had no idea that Blücher, secretly encouraged by the Czar, who admired his fighting qualities, was quite prepared to turn and give battle. Once again Napoleon, in his contempt for 'that madman' Blücher, had seriously under-estimated him.[21]

Skilfully, Blücher evaded the French on his tail, and on 5 March linked up with his reinforcements at Soissons. He now had 100,000 men to Napoleon's 50,000, and was ready to fight. Yet Napoleon still could not believe that he would do anything but retreat. As a result, when he made contact with the enemy on the morning of 9 March, in thick fog near the town of Laon, he was convinced he was only facing a rearguard. When the fog lifted to reveal Blücher's entire army, even Napoleon must have been disconcerted. He still decided to attack, but his troops could make no headway against the enemy, who were not only far stronger but drawn up in a formidable position on a steep-sided plateau. By the evening fighting had petered out.

Shortly afterwards, disaster struck. Marshal Marmont, who had been operating some way to the east, had arrived in the early afternoon on the extreme right of the French position. When the battle died down he dismissed his troops for the night, but failed to take sufficient precautions against surprise. Blücher's scouts spotted this negligence, and at 7 p.m., in the dark, the Prussians launched a sudden attack against the French, who were foraging for their supper. Marmont's panic-stricken soldiers turned and bolted down the road, sweeping their commander along with them. They were only saved from encirclement and destruction by a small detach-ment of the Imperial Guard, which bravely kept open their line of retreat.[22]

The next morning Napoleon's position was dire, with his right flank in tatters and his opponents poised to advance. He was saved by a rare stroke of luck—the nervous breakdown of their commander. Blücher was fiery and energetic, but he was 72, and had already had one serious mental collapse. Now, under the tremendous strain of campaign and battle, this recurred.

On the morning of 10 March, his eyesight gave way and he began hallu-
cinating once more that he was pregnant with an elephant. Command
devolved onto his chief of staff, General von Gneisenau, a distinguished
military thinker, but lacking his chief's aggressive drive. Instead of attacking
immediately, as Blücher would have done, he hesitated, unable to grasp
how vulnerable his enemies were. After some hours of inconclusive skir-
mishing, he allowed the French to withdraw and did not pursue them.[23]

Although his elephant and his chief of staff robbed him of a decisive
victory, Blücher had nonetheless defeated Napoleon in person. In defiance
of the Trachenberg plan, he had done so with only part, and not the whole,
of the allied army. The effect was both practical and psychological. It broke
Napoleon's string of victories, and correspondingly lowered the morale of
his remaining men. It also left him with a narrowing range of options. If
Blücher's troops started after him, they and Schwarzenberg could trap him
between them. All Napoleon could do was try and keep them apart. At this
moment, luck again came to his aid. The pivot between Blücher's and
Schwarzenberg's forces was a 12,000-strong Russian corps under General de
Saint-Priest, a French émigré. On 12 March, Saint-Priest advanced and
captured Rheims, isolating himself dangerously from both armies. The
next night, at 10 p.m., Napoleon pounced. The Russians were routed,
Saint-Priest was killed, and the French reoccupied the town.

From this central position, Napoleon could now strike at either Blücher's
or Schwarzenberg's communications. He chose the latter, since Schwarzenberg was steadily pushing Macdonald, who was facing him, back towards
Paris. First, Napoleon planned to force Schwarzenberg into retreat by
attacking his right flank. Then he aimed to drive east, relieving his garrisons
at Metz and Verdun, and cutting his opponents off from the Rhine. It was a
brilliant strategy, but a desperate one. It assumed that the allies would stand
still, hypnotized by his speed and daring. In particular, it underestimated
Schwarzenberg.[24]

The allied commander-in-chief was keeping his nerve and his temper,
but with difficulty. His relations with the Czar, whose demands for an
advance had become even more strident, had reached breaking-point. At
midnight on 12 March, while Schwarzenberg was absent at his headquarters, Alexander called an emergency meeting to speed up help to Blücher.
In a fury he turned to Metternich and asked if Schwarzenberg had been
secretly ordered not to fight and instead to retreat over the Rhine. Frederick
William then joined in, accusing the Austrians of letting Blücher be

destroyed, and of being in league with Napoleon. When Schwarzenberg heard of this, he was outraged. 'Between [the Czar's] august character and mine', he wrote sarcastically to Metternich, 'the difference is like night and day. As to the King [of Prussia], he is not worthy to be judged by men of honour; he suspects every vice in others, because, if he had enough courage and energy, he would have them all himself.' But the confrontation took its toll. Schwarzenberg took to his bed with 'stress, exhaustion and vexation', and for several days after his recovery travelled not on horseback but in a specially made carriage.[25]

In these dire circumstances, Schwarzenberg made a crucial decision. He had begun to pull back when Napoleon advanced from Rheims, but now he turned to fight. Partly this was a product of the Czar's pressure, but also because in his own military judgement the time was right. He felt his communications were secure for the moment, further retreat would discourage his troops, and Blücher needed support. He ordered his army forward, to meet Napoleon on the river Aube. This action dramatically changed the situation. The great historian of 1814, Henry Houssaye, even argues that it saved the campaign for the allies. Had Schwarzenberg continued to withdraw, the gap between himself and Blücher could have widened dangerously, damaging allied unity beyond repair.[26]

On the morning of 20 March, Napoleon approached the town of Arcis-sur-Aube, which was held by an allied force. Unable to believe that Schwarzenberg would do anything other than retreat from him, he assumed this was a rearguard. This seemed to be confirmed when the garrison promptly abandoned the town. Ney's infantry occupied Arcis and repaired its partly demolished bridge over the Aube, and General Sébastiani's cavalry fanned out beyond. In fact, Schwarzenberg was hurrying towards Arcis as quickly as he could. Suddenly, a substantial advance guard of allied cavalry appeared. It bore down on Sébastiani's horsemen, scattering them, and penetrated almost as far as the bridge. A division of the Imperial Guard rushed forward to plug the gap, but defeat was staring the French in the face.

Napoleon himself was at the bridge, rallying Sébastiani's battered cavalry and trying to prevent their alarm spreading to the other troops. As he well knew from experience, a dramatic gesture was needed, and the moment provided it. A shot from an enemy howitzer landed a few feet in front of his line, with its fuse sputtering. Seeing that some soldiers were backing away, Napoleon deliberately rode his horse over the shell. There was a deafening explosion, the horse was blown apart, but when the smoke cleared, amazingly, Napoleon himself was unhurt. The line moved forward, and the Emperor's reckless act of courage had done its work.

Napoleon may have had a darker motive. He was struggling against tremendous odds, and reaching the limits of his endurance. The allies had rejected the natural frontiers and thus any prospect, in his view, of an honourable peace. He had written to his brother Joseph of possible death in battle, and it may be that he secretly welcomed this. It is conceivable that his bravery at Arcis was not simply to encourage his men, but a disguised attempt at suicide. There is some evidence to confirm this. A few weeks later, Napoleon admitted to a confidant: 'At the battle of Arcis...I did everything I could to find a glorious death.' Another source cites a comment of General Sébastiani. When some soldiers tried to rescue Napoleon from the fighting at the bridge, Sébastiani muttered to them: 'Can't you see he wants to make an end of it?' This is not conclusive proof that Napoleon sought his own death at Arcis, but, given his state of mind at the time, it makes it likely.[27]

Napoleon's gesture and the Imperial Guard's arrival stabilized the situation. By nightfall the French had driven the allies out of the town and back into the plain beyond. The respite, however, was short-lived. As Ney and Sébastiani advanced the next morning on what they thought was the last of the allied rearguard, they found Schwarzenberg's whole army drawn up before them. It numbered 80,000; the French only 28,000. Napoleon had made exactly the same miscalculation as at Laon. His only option was to retreat. This he did with great skill, helped by Schwarzenberg's slowness in mounting an attack. By 6 p.m., the French had withdrawn through Arcis to the opposite bank of the river Aube, and blown up the bridge to delay pursuit. In contrast to Leipzig, this was done after, not before, the last troops were across.

Napoleon's next decision ushered in the last phase of the campaign. The prudent course was to fall back on Paris, swell his ranks with its garrison and National Guard, and make his stand there. Possession of the capital would also underline his legitimacy, and discourage disloyalty among the Parisian elites. Instead, Napoleon chose to stick to his previous plan, to march east and link up with his forces on the frontier. This carried the tremendous risk of leaving Paris exposed. Yet Napoleon calculated that as soon as the cautious Schwarzenberg saw his communications menaced by the French offensive, he would immediately turn back. Napoleon also reckoned that even if the allies ignored him and pressed on to Paris, the city could hold out long enough for him to relieve it.

The fact that Napoleon chose to take this gamble is very revealing. To do so was second nature to him. He loathed the idea of retreat, and for him attack was always the best form of defence. Yet to assume that a lunge forward would automatically send the allies scurrying back to protect their communications ignored all the evidence of the past fortnight. Blücher had turned and fought at Laon; even the cautious Schwarzenberg had taken the offensive at Arcis. Napoleon believed they would not call his bluff now because he wanted to believe it. As David Chandler remarks: 'his capacity for self-delusion was very marked at this time.'[28]

Napoleon's miscalculation may well have been magnified by sheer exhaustion. Napoleon was not an old man, but his physical health had been declining for some time, and he was in a desperate situation. The day after the battle of Arcis, Marshal Macdonald wrote laconically to his daughter in Paris that the Emperor was 'very tired'.[29] Psychologically, too, Napoleon was at the end of his tether, possibly to the point of suicide. In this state of mind, his latest plan was really a despairing bid to end his agony in one way or another. It was summed up by the revolutionary slogan of his youth: 'Victory or death!' The chances of victory, however, were slim, leaving death as the more likely prospect.

On 22 March, Napoleon started east, concealing his movements with a substantial screen of cavalry. Initially, as intended, the allies were confused. They did not remain so for long. That evening a party of Cossacks captured a French courier heading for Paris. He carried a note from Napoleon to Marie-Louise telling her of his plan. This was valuable information, but the details were vague, and at first the allied leaders reacted cautiously. They decided there was no point turning around, since Napoleon was now well ahead of them and to retreat two days after a successful battle would demoralize their troops. They kept to the strategy they had agreed right after the battle, to move north, meet Blücher, and fight Napoleon with their combined forces.

The next morning, the weary soldiers began their march. En route more intercepted letters were brought to the allied commanders. Several made it clear that Paris was in a poor state of defence. The most important was from Savary to Napoleon, expressing doubts about whether its loyalty to the regime could withstand a siege. Then, in the evening, came the news that Bordeaux had declared for the Bourbons. It was these developments, rather than Napoleon's note to Marie-Louise, that proved decisive. They revealed both that Paris could be taken and that Napoleon's domestic authority was beginning to crumble. Alexander had been given the ammunition he needed. He proposed to Schwarzenberg and Frederick William, who were with him, that the army make for the capital. Both men swiftly agreed.[30]

On 25 March, the allies turned west. Blücher's army proceeded to join the main body, making a massive combined force of 180,000. Blücher himself was emerging from his breakdown, and rode alongside his troops in a carriage. In a typically eccentric touch, he wore a lady's large green silk hat to protect his sore eyes from the sun. Schwarzenberg, however, felt sufficiently restored to abandon his own carriage and return to horseback.[31] There was a world of difference between the two convalescent commanders, but over the last months they had undergone the same trials and kept Napoleon at bay. Now the road to Paris lay open, and victory was close.

13

Talleyrand

As the allied armies approached, Paris was in no condition to withstand them. Some fortifications had been hastily improvised, but they were wholly inadequate. Joseph Bonaparte, in command of the city as his brother's deputy, made regular tours of inspection, but this impressed nobody. As he was setting off on one of them, a staff officer asked where he was going. General Dejean, accompanying Joseph, replied: 'To visit an incomplete and useless defence system dreamt up by incompetents.' To man these inadequate lines, Joseph had just 42,000 men—30,000 of these were regular troops under Marshals Marmont and Mortier. The rest were National Guard, 3,000 of whom were armed only with pikes. The disappointing numbers of National Guard were an inevitable consequence of the decision taken two months earlier to limit their recruitment to middle- and upper-class citizens.[1]

In these circumstances, the only effective way to defend Paris was to distribute weapons to the population. Yet a government that had baulked at including workers in the National Guard was hardly likely to take this far more radical measure. With its memories of the Revolution, it feared arming the Parisians even more than being overwhelmed by the invaders. On 16 March, Pasquier wrote to the interior minister Montalivet: 'Above all we must avoid stirring up the population of Paris. There is no knowing where this might lead. Once roused it could easily be led astray by all sorts of factions. It is in great distress. It would be very easy to encourage it to acts of despair against the government, and there is no lack of people ready to exploit these feelings.'[2] It was perhaps no coincidence that Pasquier's father had been guillotined in Paris during the Terror.

In fact, Pasquier need not have worried, since most Parisians were in no mood to fight anybody. Instead, their dominant emotion was fear. They knew that a large part of the enemy army was Russian, and were terrified that it might take revenge for the destruction of Moscow by burning Paris to the ground. Their alarm was heightened by the increasing flood of refugees from the surrounding countryside, with tales of wild Cossacks and their depredations. In late March, Marshal Macdonald's daughter Nancy wrote to her father at the front:

> This morning the gates of Paris were swamped by farm animals and peasants' carts carrying furniture. Everyone on the road from Meaux . . . is arriving and spreading consternation; but the weather is so fine that it gives us courage, and the approach of the enemy and the horrors they are committing have been talked of so much that we're getting used to it. But if a shell landed on Paris and even if we heard the sound of cannon, which we might tonight, that would be very frightening. What will become of us? I still trust in Providence, which will not permit the centre of civilization to be swallowed up or conquered by the barbarians.[3]

Amid the panic and confusion, one man in particular kept his nerve and his head—Talleyrand. The former foreign minister occupied an ambiguous position, deeply distrusted by Napoleon, but still a grand dignitary of state, and as such sitting on the regency council. His role in the crucial

Figure 10. Cossacks on campaign in France, 1814.

days of March and April 1814 was pivotal, and remains controversial. He is generally depicted as working throughout this time for a Bourbon restoration, having decided that Napoleon was a lost cause.[4] Yet this view ignores considerable evidence that up to a very late stage his preferred option was not the return of the king, but a regency exercised by Marie-Louise on behalf of Napoleon's infant son. Talleyrand had certainly decided that peace was impossible with Napoleon as head of state. On a personal level, he had been in semi-disgrace since 1809, and had nothing more to hope for from the Emperor himself. A regency, on the contrary, had considerable attractions. It was far more compatible with post-revolutionary France than the Bourbons, and Talleyrand himself was the obvious candidate to become Marie-Louise's prime minister. In this role, he would be following an illustrious precedent—that of Cardinal Mazarin, who had steered the policy of another Habsburg-born regent of France, Anne of Austria, during Louis XIV's minority.

The most solid source for Talleyrand's intrigues to bring about a regency is Caulaincourt. Not only was he an old friend and protégé of Talleyrand, he was also close to Talleyrand's most important collaborator at the time, the councillor of state Eméric, duc de Dalberg. Although Caulaincourt was at Châtillon and then at Napoleon's headquarters in March 1814, Dalberg was in Paris throughout and gave him detailed information on the events there for his memoirs.[5] Reports also reached Caulaincourt that Talleyrand's machinations extended beyond Paris. An undated note in his papers reads:

> Before the 21st March, it is said, Talleyrand's agents told leading citizens of Lille that everything was ready for a regency, that it was agreed, that it was impossible that the Emperor would not be killed in the continuous fighting, and that the regency would be proclaimed, with a council composed of Cambacérès, Talleyrand, and three others.[6]

The expectation of Napoleon's death in battle this note evokes is telling. The major problem facing the partisans of a regency was how to dispose of the Emperor. Alive, he would be a major obstacle to the scheme. Only the direst circumstances would persuade him to abdicate in favour of his son. Even if he did and went into exile, he would remain a constant presence in the wings, attempting to direct his successor's actions. The most convenient solution was an enemy bullet or sabre, and Talleyrand clearly hoped that this would resolve his dilemma. On 20 March, in a letter that chimed exactly with the rumours Caulaincourt was picking up, he wrote to his niece the duchesse de Dino: 'If the Emperor were killed, his death would guarantee the rights of his son ... The regency would satisfy everyone because a council would be named that would satisfy all shades of opinion.'[7]

Talleyrand's manoeuvres are always difficult to follow, and he complicated them further by making discreet contact with both the Bourbons and the allies. Through his confidante Aimée de Coigny, connected to the *Chevaliers de la Foi* through her lover Bruno de Boisgelin, he first sent a message to Louis XVIII assuring him of his goodwill. Then, in early March, he despatched a friend of Dalberg, the royalist agent the baron de Vitrolles, to allied headquarters with the advice to march directly on Paris. Neither action committed Talleyrand to anything; he was careful to act only through go-betweens, and committed nothing to paper himself. The overture to the Bourbons was a sensible insurance measure, since they were the obvious alternative if the regency should prove impossible. As for urging the allies to make straight for the capital, this was the shortest way to achieving Talleyrand's primary goal, the downfall of Napoleon.[8]

Whether Napoleon was killed or not, the chances of establishing a regency depended on Marie-Louise and her son remaining in Paris. However brilliantly the Emperor fought, Talleyrand was certain that he was doomed, and that the allies would soon capture the capital. At that moment, it was vital that they find the Empress and the king of Rome firmly installed there, as the legitimate rulers of France. This would make it very difficult for the allies, and particularly for Marie-Louise's father Francis I, to avoid recognizing the regency. For his part, Napoleon was fully aware of Talleyrand's aims. Discussing them retrospectively with Caulaincourt a few weeks later, he observed:

> I am certain that Talleyrand wanted ... the regency; this form of government would have suited both him and M de Metternich, who was always his ally. You can be sure that Talleyrand had long ago prepared his arrangements were I to die at the head of the army. Since no bullet found me, he still wanted to act as if I was no longer there. This no doubt was his reason for wishing to keep Marie-Louise in Paris; he would have made her his instrument and his protectress.[9]

Most rulers feel uncomfortable when others plan for the event of their demise. Yet Talleyrand was at least trying to keep the Bonaparte dynasty in power. Remarkably, Napoleon saw this as a betrayal equivalent to declaring for the Bourbons. In his desperate letter to his brother Joseph of 8 February, he added: 'If Talleyrand supports the argument that the Empress should stay in Paris if our troops have to evacuate it, then treason is being plotted.'[10] Clearly, Napoleon's definition of treason included any attempt to save his son's throne while he himself was still alive.

The decisive moment came at a meeting of the regency council on 28 March. That day the allied army reached Meaux, just over thirty miles east of Paris, and the question of Marie-Louise's departure could no longer be deferred. There are several accounts of what happened at the council, but the most detailed is an unpublished one by Caulaincourt. This claims that of the twenty-two members present, nineteen voted for Marie-Louise to stay, including Talleyrand, Cambacérès, and Savary. Talleyrand was particularly eloquent. According to Caulaincourt, 'he went up to the Empress during a pause in the meeting and begged her to weigh the consequences of the decision she was being urged to take . . . What was there to fear in Paris with loyal troops whose example would galvanize all classes of citizens? The worst thing would be to abandon them . . . to deprive them of the rallying-point that had been entrusted to their courage.'[11]

At this juncture, with the overwhelming majority present in favour of staying, Joseph Bonaparte intervened. First he read out Napoleon's letter of 8 February insisting that his wife and son leave the capital if it seemed about to fall, then a second one confirming this, written on 16 March. The reaction round the table was first shock, then anger. 'Why bother to consult us', burst out several councillors, 'if the Emperor's orders leave us no choice?' Caulaincourt adds that everyone at the meeting was aware of Napoleon's reasoning, and most disagreed strongly with it:

> It was known that the Emperor, who was aware that there had been talk of and even some plans for a regency that would remove him and put his son in his place, had ordered: *Treat as a traitor anyone who proposes that the Empress should stay in Paris.* Most of the ministers deplored the fact that the Emperor's suspicions were depriving the capital and the empire of their only hope of salvation.[12]

Talleyrand still tried to fight back even after the council had broken up, going to Marie-Louise and urging her to stay despite Napoleon's instructions. The empress's own instinct was to remain. But she did not feel able to disobey a direct order from her husband. The next day she and the 3-year-old king of Rome left the Tuileries for Blois, in a lumbering convoy including the imperial coronation coach covered with a cloth. As Caulaincourt damningly put it, 'her departure had all the pomp of a funeral'.[13]

Marie-Louise's flight had the worst possible effect on the capital. As Pasquier put it in his daily bulletin, it caused 'the most painful sensation'.[14] To the Parisians preparing to withstand a siege, it sent a message that the government had given up the fight in advance. It also profoundly alienated the Senate. When Cambacérès notified them that the empress had left, the senators made their disapproval plain. They also felt slighted by the curtness of the announcement, which was not accompanied, as was usually the case, by a detailed report. This mishandling of the Senate had important consequences. Had its members not been angry at being treated so cavalierly, they might not have acted the way they did a few days later.[15]

The news that Marie-Louise had abandoned Paris was brought to Talleyrand at his house in the Rue St Florentin, as he was talking with Dalberg and the banker Perregaux. According to Dalberg, Talleyrand 'was silent for a short while, then, resting his knee on a chair by the window, observed that everything was lost. "[The Empress] hasn't understood how important it was for her to stay. This departure changes everything. It's a great event", he repeated several times.'[16] It was at this moment, and not before, that Talleyrand switched his allegiance to the Bourbons. His efforts to save the Bonaparte dynasty through a regency had compromised beyond repair his relations with Napoleon. If the Emperor managed to relieve the capital, Talleyrand would probably be arrested. Now Marie-Louise, on whom the regency plan depended, had removed herself from the stage. For self-preservation as much as policy, Talleyrand had no choice but to rally to Louis XVIII.

From this point on Talleyrand had two aims: to make himself indispensable to a Bourbon restoration, and to ensure his own safety. To achieve them, it was essential that he himself stayed in Paris, and that Napoleon did not return. Joseph and the government had been ordered to follow Marie-Louise to Blois, and left the capital on 30 March. Talleyrand avoided doing so by a manoeuvre that was transparent but which served its purpose. That evening he presented himself at the city gates, having secretly arranged beforehand to be turned back by the National Guard. He could thus claim that he had tried to follow Napoleon's instructions, but had been prevented from doing so by over-zealous officials. He then returned to the Rue St Florentin to await, and attempt to shape, events.[17]

Talleyrand's next step was to communicate his thoughts to his inner circle. The reaction was at best lukewarm. His friends expressed grave doubts about restoring the Bourbons, arguing that the family had not learned the lessons of the Revolution, and citing as evidence references to divine right in Louis XVIII's previous proclamations. Talleyrand replied rather airily that the comte d'Artois might have such notions, but that Louis XVIII, 'having always had more liberal ideas and having lived in England would return with the desired opinions'. In the heat of the moment, Talleyrand was making a dangerous assumption. As it turned out, the Bourbons would prove less tractable and 'constitutional' than he expected.[18]

The same day the allies launched their assault on Paris from the north. Initially, Marmont's troops managed to contain it around the outlying villages of Pantin and Romainville. However, the main allied attack, delivered at 3 p.m. with forces more than double those of the defenders, was impossible to withstand. One and a half hours later, the French lines had been broken, and the strategic heights of Montmartre taken. The capital was now at the invaders' mercy, and Marmont and Mortier felt they had no option but to surrender. At two the following morning, 31 March, the capitulation of Paris was signed. The struggle for its possession had cost each side 9,000 casualties. With the outcome a foregone conclusion, it was the bloodiest, and most useless, battle of the 1814 campaign.[19]

Within hours Marmont's and Mortier's soldiers had evacuated the city. A brief, eerie calm fell on its deserted streets. It was broken at 7 a.m. by the appearance of three horsemen—the Russian foreign minister Nesselrode, accompanied by two Cossacks.[20] They made straight for the Rue St Florentin, to Talleyrand's house. The discreet message of support Talleyrand had sent had been noted by the allies, and they had decided that they needed his expertise on their side. Nesselrode informed Talleyrand that during his time in Paris the Czar wished not only to take Talleyrand's political advice but also to stay in his house, making it the allied headquarters. The question of who would now rule France would be decided under Talleyrand's own roof.

While Talleyrand was preparing to deal with the Czar, Napoleon was rushing back to save the capital. Having realized three days before that the allies had called his bluff, he had abandoned his attack on their communications, and was now doubling back in the hope that Paris would manage to hold out for just long enough for him to relieve it. At Troyes he left his troops behind and dashed ahead with just a small escort, aiming to get into the city himself and galvanize its defence. Then, in the early hours of 31 March, at a post-house called La Cour de France just a few miles south of his destination, he saw a column of French cavalry coming towards him. It was the advance guard of Marmont's and Mortier's army, which had just signed the capitulation and was evacuating Paris. Napoleon was thunderstruck by the news. For two hours, walking up and down in the road and then at a table in the post-house, he bombarded his staff with different plans to recover the situation. At first he wanted to lead Marmont's and Mortier's soldiers back to fight in the city, in defiance of the capitulation, but his companions refused to countenance this. Then he talked of withdrawing south to the river Loire and continuing the struggle from there.[21]

Eventually, the Emperor decided on a less dramatic course of action. He would fall back a few miles to Fontainebleau, unite his own forces with those of Marmont and Mortier, and await events. Meanwhile Caulaincourt, who was with him, would go to Paris and make a final attempt to reach a negotiated settlement. This would be a thankless task, since even in this extremity Napoleon remained reluctant to concede France's pre-revolutionary borders. It is probable that, even while accepting the loss of Belgium and the left bank of the Rhine, he still hoped to keep a last remnant of the natural frontiers, in the form of Nice and Savoy. Just before 4 a.m., with a heavy heart but once more following his duty, Caulaincourt departed for the capital.[22]

His first aim was to see the Czar. Arriving at the Hôtel de Ville at 7 a.m., he was told that the allied headquarters were at Bondy, a few miles northeast of the city, and immediately made his way there. Alexander received Caulaincourt with great courtesy, but gave little away. He warned him, however, that he and his allies were determined to treat no further with Napoleon himself, who had completely forfeited their trust. This was confirmation that the regency now offered the only hope of saving the Bonaparte dynasty. The Czar also advised Caulaincourt to go and see Schwarzenberg, who was currently the chief Austrian representative in the absence of Francis I at his headquarters in Dijon.

To Caulaincourt's shock, Schwarzenberg's reception of him was 'icy'. At first sight, this seems bizarre, since as commander-in-chief over the past few months he had done everything possible to further a settlement that would keep Napoleon on the throne. The reason for this change soon became clear. The previous month, Schwarzenberg had gone to immense trouble to set up the armistice talks at Lusigny. With some justification he had seen these as the only remaining way to achieve a compromise peace. He had been infuriated by Napoleon's rejection of these efforts, and from that moment had decided that he was a lost cause. As Caulaincourt later recalled, Schwarzenberg 'reproached the Emperor Napoleon with never having listened to the voice of prudence, and of having rejected the proposals made at Lusigny . . . [He] added that he had had huge difficulty in persuading his allies to agree to an armistice; that I had no idea of all the problems and opposition that he and Metternich had overcome to open for us this route to safety.' Schwarzenberg also revealed the damage caused by the arrogant letter Napoleon had written at the same time to Francis I: 'He complained bitterly about [this] letter . . . which had only too clearly exposed his insane pretensions, his schemes to divide the allies, and how much he still held to his old ideas and . . . ambitions.'[23]

Rebuffed by the Powers, Caulaincourt returned to Paris. He met with Pasquier, who assured him that the city was calm, and that there was no sign yet of disloyalty to the regime. He then visited Talleyrand, who was preparing to receive the Czar as his house-guest, and was very surprised to be faced by Napoleon's foreign minister. Talleyrand emphasized that it was now too late to save Napoleon: 'You will soon find out', he told Caulaincourt, 'that I did everything possible, two days ago, to save his throne, to keep the Empress and her son here, but [he] gave secret orders that wrecked everything; he trusts nobody; his letter to his brother ruined everything.'[24] Shortly afterwards, several Russian dignitaries arrived, and Caulaincourt thought it best to leave.

By this time, the Czar had left his headquarters to ride into the capital. He was accompanied by Frederick William, Schwarzenberg, and a glittering suite of 2,000 officers, followed by the allied army. At the capitulation he had declared that he wished 'to preserve Paris for the sake of France and . . . the whole world', and the citizens' relief and gratitude were obvious. This was probably the high point of Alexander's life, the fulfilment of everything he had dreamed of since the burning of Moscow. As he entered the city through the Porte St Martin, the streets were packed and the windows crowded with cheering spectators. He headed for the Champs-Elysées, where a grand military review was held. Along his route, a few cries of 'Long live the Bourbons!' rang out. These came from a small group of *Chevaliers de la Foi*, perhaps no more than forty in all, trying to recreate that 'surface appearance of

Figure 11. The entry of the allies into Paris, 31 March 1814, by Jean Zippel.

royalism' that had succeeded so well in Bordeaux. According to eyewitnesses, Alexander was impressed by the demonstration.[25]

At 6 p.m., the Czar arrived at Talleyrand's house, and an impromptu conference was held in the great salon on the first floor. It included, apart from Alexander himself and Talleyrand, Frederick William, Schwarzenberg, Nesselrode, and Dalberg. Ironically, the fullest account of what happened again comes from Caulaincourt, who naturally was not there, but got the details from Dalberg. The Czar began by emphasizing that as long as Napoleon was excluded, 'any monarchical government acceptable to France which promised stability would be sure of the allies' support'. This left, he declared, three choices: the regency, any other suitable sovereign apart from Napoleon, or the Bourbons. According to Caulaincourt, the regency 'seemed to suit most of those present', but the obstacle to it was the fact that Napoleon was still alive. As to the second option, several people favoured Louis-Philippe, duc d'Orléans, Louis XVIII's younger cousin, who combined royal blood with an acceptance of the changes wrought by the French Revolution.[26]

It was left to Talleyrand to put the case for the Bourbons. He did so by outlining a concept that was to shape much of European politics for the next thirty years, that of legitimacy. Napoleon and his empire, he argued, could only be replaced 'by invoking a principle; only a right hallowed by tradition . . . could vanquish one based on conquest and reinforced by glory'. In his view, the Bourbons alone could lay claim to this principle. Compared to this the duc d'Orléans, however worthy a king he might make, would be nothing more than a usurper. Schwarzenberg supported Talleyrand, but Alexander was less convinced. He 'believed the nation and the army so strongly opposed to this restoration', commented Caulaincourt, 'that he spoke little of it, and then with the reserve of a man who fears to challenge ingrained prejudices . . . "Is this the wish of France?", [he] asked in astonishment.' The gathering broke up at 10 p.m. without agreement. Talleyrand did manage to extract a declaration that the allies would no longer deal with either Napoleon or his family, but as events were to prove, even this did not end the prospects for a regency.[27]

To bolster his position, Talleyrand now played the card whose importance he had noted fifteen months before when General Malet attempted his coup—the Senate. He had been struck then by the success of Malet's ruse of forging a Senate decree announcing Napoleon's death and the installation of a provisional government. Now he adapted this for his own purposes. He was friendly with many senators, and had over several days discreetly discussed with them the necessity for Napoleon's removal. His task was made easier by their continuing anger at the mishandling of Marie-Louise's departure, and their feeling that Napoleon's government had abandoned them.

Having taken these soundings, Talleyrand now took an extraordinarily daring step. As soon as the meeting in his salon ended, he convoked the Senate on his own authority, though he had no right to do so. Of the ninety senators present in Paris, sixty-four answered his summons. On 1 April, they elected a five-man provisional government, whose principal figures were Dalberg and Talleyrand himself. The next day, in the evening, they voted for the deposition of Napoleon and his dynasty. Malet and Talleyrand had both understood that, despite its years of servility to Napoleon, the Senate offered the only remotely constitutional means of dethroning him. Malet had forged one of its decrees to this end, and failed. Talleyrand obtained the genuine article, and succeeded.[28]

If Talleyrand exceeded his authority by convening the Senate, using it to end Napoleon's rule made legal and political sense. Having made Napoleon

Emperor, by the *senatus-consultum* of 18 May 1804, it was the only body which could claim the power to depose him. The senators have often been reproached with abandoning Napoleon, who had loaded them with favours, in order to save as much as possible of their own wealth and status. Yet, as Pierre Serna has shrewdly argued in a recent work, they did have constitutional grounds for their actions. By detaining political prisoners without trial, raising taxes illegally, making ministers responsible only to him, and destroying press freedom, Napoleon had violated the constitution he had sworn to uphold and created instead a dictatorship. All these points were forcefully made in the decree that justified the abolition of the empire.[29]

One section of the decree was particularly striking. Although it cited numerous examples of Napoleon's domestic tyranny, it reserved its greatest condemnation for his bellicosity. It did so in terms that showed clear awareness of the opportunities for settlement he had missed from Prague to Châtillon. 'Instead of reigning solely to advance the interests, happiness and glory of the French people', it asserted, 'Napoleon has put the finishing touches to his country's misfortunes, by rejecting peace terms that the national interest required and which left intact the honour of France.' These words laid bare the extent of Napoleon's self-delusion. He thought that the Senate would depose him if he made peace too readily; in reality, it deposed him because he refused to end the war.[30]

Throughout these dramatic events, Caulaincourt was a constant presence in the wings, desperately fighting for Marie-Louise and her son. He managed to have two further interviews with the Czar, on the afternoons of 1 and 2 April. He had one major weapon to deploy: the army. As far as was known, it remained solidly loyal to Napoleon. It had now been reinforced by Marmont's and Mortier's troops from Paris, and it was rumoured that Napoleon was planning to march on the capital. If this was true, the allies risked being caught between two fires. Although the Parisians had been quiescent so far, there were signs that this might be changing, with large numbers beginning to gather in the streets. Ominously, when ordered to exchange their tricolour cockades for ones in Bourbon white, the National Guard refused. The capital's fearsome reputation as a revolutionary city magnified the allies' fears. With his usual prudence, Schwarzenberg began to consider withdrawing from Paris, and drew up orders for his troops to pull back east to Meaux.

In his meetings with the Czar, Caulaincourt exploited these factors to the hilt. Only the regency, he claimed, could put an end to the conflict, which could otherwise become a French civil war. His arguments made a visible impression on Alexander. At the next conference in Talleyrand's salon, on the morning of 2 April, he appeared half-converted to the cause of Marie-Louise and her son. Talleyrand, who was planning for the Senate to dethrone Napoleon and his family that evening, was seriously alarmed. For a moment, he and his allies 'thought that their cause . . . was lost without hope.' In the nick of time General Dessolles, the new commander of the National Guard, intervened. He reminded the Czar that several leading figures, including himself, had only declared for the Bourbons because they thought he was committed to a restoration, and that to switch policy now would be to betray them. This appeal to his honour stopped Alexander pronouncing for the regency on the spot, but the decision was merely postponed to a further conference. The future of France—and the fate of several prominent Frenchmen—remained in the balance.[31]

At this dangerous moment, it is probable that Talleyrand began to plan Napoleon's assassination. It would not be too surprising if he had, since Napoleon's continuing existence was now putting his own life at risk. If there was a reversal of military fortune, Talleyrand could expect no mercy. Meanwhile, the Emperor's presence at the head of his army was Caulaincourt's most powerful argument for a regency. There is no direct evidence that Talleyrand endorsed killing Napoleon, but it is clear that some of his most trusted collaborators did. During these days his confidential agent, Roux-Laborie, contacted an acquaintance, the self-styled comte de Maubreuil, a 30-year-old cavalry officer with a royalist background and a reputation for ruthlessness, and met with him in the Rue St Florentin. Maubreuil later claimed that Roux-Laborie proposed to him, on behalf of Talleyrand, recruiting a band of assassins, riding to Fontainebleau, and murdering Napoleon there. The fact that Talleyrand was not present does not in itself undermine the story. If he had indeed authorized such a discreditable operation, he would have done so on a 'deniable' basis.[32]

Maubreuil was an extremely untrustworthy character, and changed his version of events several times subsequently during his long and chequered life. More solid evidence for the plot comes in the memoirs of the reliable Pasquier. On the morning of 2 April, Pasquier recalled, he went to Talleyrand's house, presumably after the conference in the salon had broken up. He saw Dalberg, and expressed fears about what might happen if Napoleon took the offensive. 'You're right', replied Dalberg, 'which is why extra precautions are needed . . . Measures have already been taken; we will

Figure 12. The 'comte' de Maubreuil.

forestall the possibility we fear'. 'He then explained to me', Pasquier continued, 'that a certain number of determined individuals, led—in his words—by a tough customer, would disguise themselves as *Chasseurs* of the Imperial Guard...and either before or during the coming battle would approach Napoleon...and deliver France from him.'[33]

Pasquier claimed that he was so shocked by this plan that, even though he had by now gone over to the Bourbons himself, he wrote to the duc de Bassano at Fontainebleau warning him that Napoleon should be on his guard. As it was, the operation was never launched, since within two days it had been overtaken by events. Maubreuil was switched to other clandestine duties in the countryside around Paris, which he combined profitably with highway robbery. However extraordinary his story may seem, the logic of the situation, and Pasquier's supporting testimony, make it highly plausible. If Talleyrand did consider having Napoleon killed, this simply reflected the extreme perils of April 1814, and the vital interests at stake.

14
The End of Glory

On the evening of 2 April, Caulaincourt returned to Fontainebleau, where Napoleon had set up his headquarters in the vast Renaissance chateau. He reported that while the chances for a regency were good, the allies insisted on the Emperor's own abdication. In response, Napoleon made it clear that he intended to march on Paris and decide his future in battle. At midday the following day he reviewed the Imperial Guard. He then made a short speech, announcing that he planned to recapture Paris from the allies and the French traitors who were collaborating with them. This was greeted with a huge cheer of 'Vive l'Empereur! A Paris! A Paris!' Orders were issued for the army to advance, and for Napoleon's command post to be moved to the Château de Tilly, further up the road to the capital.[1]

If the soldiers were enthusiastic, the marshals were dismayed. They were well aware of what was happening in Paris, and were increasingly convinced that Napoleon himself was doomed. The prospect of a battle in the city, where many of them had families and all had property, was deeply unappealing. Above all, like the rest of France, the marshals were desperate for peace. None desired it more than Berthier, but he still felt unable openly to oppose Napoleon. Others had fewer inhibitions, especially Ney, whose disaffection had been growing since before Leipzig, and Lefebvre, who at almost 60 was unwilling to continue fighting indefinitely. The marshals simply refused to contemplate an attack on Paris. On 4 April, they finally acted. During the changing of the guard, they gathered close to Napoleon, muttering ominously. While the soldiers cheered, Ney exclaimed, loudly enough for the Emperor to hear, 'Nothing but abdication can save us!'[2]

The next scenes were dramatic. Napoleon went back into his study to work with Berthier, Caulaincourt, and Bassano. Shortly afterwards, Ney, Lefebvre, and Marshal Moncey burst into the room. Ney acted as spokesman. He told Napoleon that the situation was desperate, and that his only course was to abdicate. The Emperor replied that he was going to advance and defeat the enemy. His temper rising, Ney burst out that the army would not march on Paris. 'The army will obey me!' Napoleon shouted. 'The army will obey its chiefs,' riposted Ney, directly challenging his master's authority. It was a dangerous moment for Napoleon; his obstinacy was making him almost as obstructive to his own marshals as to Talleyrand and the allies. There was the potential for violence in the room. Ney certainly felt it, for he tried awkwardly to defuse the situation. 'Don't worry,' he added, 'we're not going to act out a scene from St Petersburg'—a reference, in questionable taste, to the murder of Czar Paul I by his own officers thirteen years before.[3]

In the middle of this confrontation, Marshals Macdonald and Oudinot, who had just reached Fontainebleau with their troops, were announced. Napoleon hoped for support from Macdonald, who just four days before had advocated fighting to the end. But Macdonald, under pressure from his subordinate generals, had now changed his mind. When Napoleon asked him what his soldiers were saying among themselves, he replied: 'That you are ordering us to march on the capital ... and I've come to tell you, in their name, that they don't want to expose it to the same fate as Moscow.' This intervention was decisive. Napoleon's mood changed; he became calm and almost resigned. 'Ah well, gentlemen,' he said, 'since that's how things stand, I abdicate. I wanted to make France happy, I've failed; events have turned against me. I don't want to add to our misfortunes; but if I abdicate, what will you do? Do you want the King of Rome to succeed me, with the Empress as regent?' Everyone in the room signalled assent.[4]

Napoleon wrote out a short statement abdicating in favour of his son. He named three commissioners to take it to the allies in Paris—Caulaincourt, Macdonald, and Ney. Given his altercation with Ney just a few minutes before, his last choice may seem surprising. Ney, however, was extremely popular in the army, and his inclusion would send a powerful message to the victors that it supported the regency. Napoleon then threw himself on a sofa, looked around at his companions, and uttered some extraordinary words: 'Bah, gentlemen, let's drop all this and march out tomorrow; we'll certainly beat them!' Even now, he could not contain his gambler's instinct to stake his future on a final battle. The marshals swiftly stamped on the idea. 'No,' they replied, 'we've had enough, and beware that each passing hour doesn't make the commissioners' task more difficult.'[5]

Figure 13. The study at Fontainebleau in which Napoleon abdicated on 6 April 1814.

At 4 p.m. Ney, Caulaincourt, and Macdonald set off in two coaches for the capital. On the way, they stopped off at Essonnes to inform Marshal Marmont of Napoleon's abdication. Marmont's corps now formed the advance guard of the French army, just a few miles away from Schwarzenberg's troops further down the road, and it was essential to keep its commander abreast of the situation. But on entering Marmont's headquarters, the three commissioners immediately realized something was wrong. While they told Marmont about their mission, his staff looked on with concern, whispering among themselves. Finally the marshal, visibly embarrassed, told them some astonishing news. The previous day, he had received a letter from Schwarzenberg, announcing the political changes in Paris and urging him to join the allies and bring the war to a speedy end. On his own

authority, Marmont had agreed, on condition that Napoleon himself was
guaranteed his liberty and generous treatment. In this exchange, the regency
had nowhere been mentioned. Just before the commissioners arrived,
Schwarzenberg had sent a messenger accepting these terms.[6]

Of all the actors in Napoleon's downfall, Marmont has received the worst
press. He has even bequeathed a verb to the French language—*raguser*,
derived from his title of Duke of Ragusa—meaning 'to betray'. His action,
though admittedly a form of treason, has not even been credited with a
political motivation. Instead, it is usually seen as a product of pure bad
character: weakness, ingratitude, and vanity. Certainly negotiating secretly
with Schwarzenberg was a shabby way to repay Napoleon's trust. Just a few
hours before, the Emperor had remarked to Caulaincourt: 'I have more
confidence in Marmont than anybody.' Marmont may also have been
flattered that the allied commander-in-chief was treating him as an equal.[7]

Concentrating on his character flaws ignores the fact that Marmont
sincerely supported peace. In November 1813, at Mainz after the retreat
from Leipzig, he had spoken to Napoleon and, according to Caulaincourt,
'tried to make clear to him his position and the need for peace'. Marmont
himself added, in his memoirs, that at this time he, Berthier, and Caulaincourt 'did everything we could to persuade [Napoleon] to make peace'.[8]
Now, in April 1814, Marmont found himself in a unique position to end the
war without delay. Some of his motives were no doubt self-interested. In
contrast, his impatience for the conflict to stop was widely shared, and
perfectly consistent with his actions over the past five months. It led him
into treacherous waters, but was genuinely felt.

Marmont had assumed that Napoleon's next move would be to march on
Paris, and had seen Schwarzenberg's overture as one means of avoiding a
final bloody battle around the capital. Now the commissioners presented
him with a far more honourable way of achieving peace, by supporting
Napoleon's abdication. It meant breaking off his negotiations with Schwarzenberg, which would be awkward, but although an agreement had been
reached, it had not actually been signed, which gave him a little leeway.
Marmont agreed to accompany the commissioners to Paris, and on the way
to see Schwarzenberg and inform him of his decision. He told his divisional
generals that the pact with Schwarzenberg, of which they were aware, was
over, and that they should hold their positions until his return. He then
climbed into Caulaincourt's carriage and the party drove on to Schwarzenberg's headquarters at the Château de Petit-Bourg. The allied commander-

in-chief accepted Marmont's change of heart with good grace, and invited him and his companions to dinner before resuming their journey.[9]

Caulaincourt and the three marshals arrived at Talleyrand's house at 3 a.m. on 5 April. They were immediately ushered in to see the Czar. Alexander had been impressed by Caulaincourt's advocacy of the regency two days before. Now Caulaincourt was supported by three famous military commanders, underlining the fact that the alternative to the regency would probably be continued war. All the witnesses to the meeting agree that the Czar was 'shaken' by their arguments. He objected, rather weakly, that the Senate had already deposed Napoleon and his family, but the marshals replied by demanding to be allowed to address the assembly and force a retraction. After two hours of heated discussion, Alexander asked them to return at 9 a.m., by which time, he said, he would have made his decision. As the envoys left through the great salon, they encountered the members of the provisional government waiting there anxiously, and the two groups almost came to blows.[10]

At this moment the regency was within an ace of being agreed. The Czar had little sympathy for the Bourbons, and was unwilling to fight on to impose them on France. Furthermore, the French army appeared to be solidly behind the Bonaparte dynasty. The allies' military position was also far from ideal. If the war continued, they risked being caught between Napoleon attacking in their front and a possibly insurgent Paris at their back. Caulaincourt and the marshals assumed that when they returned to Talleyrand's house in a few hours' time, the Czar would support the proclamation of Napoleon II, with his mother as regent. As Ney later wrote: 'The negotiations seemed to promise the happiest results.'[11]

Macdonald felt the same way, and clearly expected to stay in the capital for some days helping organize the new dispensation. Just after seeing Alexander, he wrote to his daughter Nancy, who was still in Paris, with detailed instructions. He was particularly concerned that no details of his secret talks should leak out, which meant keeping his family close by him. 'If I still have any power over you,' he told Nancy, 'I demand absolutely that you dine with me every day you are free, excepting only your father-in-law [the duc de Massa, ex-minister of justice], that is to say you should have no visitors, and that I wish us to spend all our available time together.'[12]

The four men decided to go to Ney's house in the Rue de Lille for breakfast. They did not in fact return to Talleyrand's house at 9, probably because they were waiting for a formal summons to do so, which arrived in the late morning. They were still eating when Marmont was informed that his aide-de-camp Colonel Fabvier had appeared and wished to speak to him. Marmont left the room, and returned a few minutes later with unbelievable news: in his absence, his second-in-command General Souham had led his corps over to the allies. 'I am lost!' he stammered, 'I am in despair! What a terrible mistake!' Everyone at the table dropped their forks in shock.[13]

Souham's action, it later turned out, had been less premeditated treachery than the product of fear and suspicion. A few hours after Marmont had left with the commissioners, Souham had received an invitation to dine with Napoleon that evening. He already had a bad conscience that he had done nothing to stop Marmont's negotiations with Schwarzenberg. Now he jumped to the conclusion that Napoleon's invitation was a ruse to lure him to Fontainebleau and have him arrested. 'I may be tall,' he remarked to one of his colonels, 'but I don't want to make myself shorter by a head.' At 11 p.m., he ordered his troops to march, telling them simply that they were moving to a new position. In the dark, they did not see the Austrians, whom Souham had warned to make way for them. By the time dawn broke and they realized where they were, it was too late.[14]

Marmont was not wholly responsible for his 'treason', since he had tried to undo it once he heard that Napoleon had abdicated. It was General Souham, against his orders, who eventually carried it through. Yet Marmont's initial disloyalty set in motion a train of events he proved unable to control. Its first consquences were felt by the commissioners around Ney's breakfast table. The moment the Czar learned what had happened, their principal weapon, the French army's united support of the Bonapartes, would be useless. All they could do was rush to Talleyrand's house and hope to snatch Alexander's agreement to the regency before he heard the news. At first, they thought they would succeed. Receiving them, the Czar rehearsed his previous reservations, but gave ground before their counterarguments. At that moment, one of his aides-de-camp entered the room and, in order to conceal his message from the Frenchmen, spoke to Alexander in Russian. But Caulaincourt, who had been French ambassador to St Petersburg, understood enough to know that the subject was the defection of Marmont's corps. He turned to Macdonald next to him and whispered: 'Bad news . . . We are lost . . . He knows everything.'[15]

When Alexander turned his attention back to them, Caulaincourt and the marshals could see that everything had changed. The Czar announced briefly that the regency would be unworkable, and that the Bourbons offered the only hope of stability for France. 'The Emperor must abdicate unconditionally,' he concluded. 'He will be provided for; we will give him an independent state.' Devastated, the commissioners left to report the news to Napoleon. At the foot of the staircase, Caulaincourt was called back. Alexander wanted to know what territory he thought most suitable as Napoleon's future realm. After Corsica, Sardinia, and Corfu had been discussed and rejected, Caulaincourt suggested the small island of Elba, off the Tuscan coast. The Czar accepted the proposal.[16]

The exhausted envoys now returned to Fontainebleau, where they arrived at 2 a.m. on 6 April. Napoleon was fast asleep, so Caulaincourt went into his bedroom, shook him awake, and told him of the failure of their mission. Napoleon initially considered withdrawing to fight behind the Loire, but soon decided this would only lead to civil war, and that if he continued fighting more of his commanders might follow Marmont's example. Caulaincourt then left, leaving his master to his own thoughts. A few hours later, Napoleon summoned him, along with Ney and Macdonald, and told them he would abdicate unconditionally. He wrote out a short statement and handed it to Caulaincourt:

> The allied Powers having declared that the Emperor Napoleon is the sole obstacle to the restoration of peace in Europe, the Emperor Napoleon, faithful to his coronation oath, declares that he renounces, for himself and his successors, the thrones of France and Italy, and that there is no personal sacrifice, even that of his life, that he is not prepared to make in the interests of France.[17]

With those short lines, an extraordinary European empire came to an end. It had lasted for twenty years, and dominated the continent from Spain to the borders of Russia. Ultimately, it had been brought down by a revolt of army commanders driven to breaking-point by Napoleon's intransigence. Marmont's disobedience was the most critical; without it, Napoleon would still have been forced to abdicate, but his throne would probably have been saved for his son. The other marshals' refusal to fight on was also an act of mutiny, though less spectacular than Marmont's. This was underlined on the morning of 6 April, even before Napoleon had abdicated, when Ney, Macdonald, and Caulaincourt instructed Berthier, as chief of staff, to transmit no further orders from Napoleon to the troops.[18]

If the empire was dead, its funeral still had to be arranged. This was left to the commissioners. First, an armistice had to be signed. The details of

Figure 14. The table on which Napoleon wrote his abdication.

Napoleon's future, and that of his family, also needed to be settled. To draw up the armistice, the cooperation of Berthier, to whom command of the army now devolved, was essential. Berthier readily offered to help, since peace had been his dearest wish ever since the retreat from Moscow. However, he had no wish to be chosen as one of the commissioners required to implement the agreement. He was exhausted, and probably still suffering from the effects of the lance-thrust to his head in February. Just before the armistice was completed, he excused himself to Caulaincourt in a letter showing he was on the verge of a breakdown:

> I have just received the armistice announcement: I have distributed it to all the army corps and to the forward posts, and ordered the end of all hostilities. The most urgent thing is to nominate commissioners. You know I need a rest. Would it be possible to name someone other than me [as a commissioner]? . . . Who is the allied commissioner? Where must he report to? It seems to me that he should come to headquarters. Shouldn't we inform our garrisons of the armistice? Let me know, please, about all these things . . . Can one authorize troop movements before the commissioners arrive? This is

urgent, since we are camped so close together that supplies will soon run out... Can I give passes to those [officers] who want to go to Paris? How will we get money for the army? Who should one go to to get what it needs? What should my relations be with the [new] minister of war?... During the armistice, I think it would be best for either [Macdonald or Ney] to command the army. You know that I need a rest, at least for some time.[19]

At the time of writing, Berthier was clearly incapable of taking a decision about anything. The next day he rallied a little. He still refused to become a commissioner, but told Caulaincourt he would stay on for the moment as commander of the army. He had no intention, however, of going to Elba, even for a short time, and within four days had left Fontainebleau. He never saw Napoleon again. He was reproached at the time, and subsequently, for abandoning his old friend and patron. Caulaincourt was more sympathetic. 'Without doubt,' he wrote in his memoirs,

> [Berthier] would have done better not to leave until the Emperor had himself departed, but before judging him, one should in justice consider the thousand embarrassments and pitfalls of his situation. One should also remember the state he was in, suffering, tormented by the restlessness of the Emperor, who had been worrying him for some time, and even frightening him by proposing plans for which he feared he would be made responsible. The Emperor's feverish mood made Berthier genuinely ill... sleepless nights, fatigue, and age had been undermining [Berthier's] faculties for two years... The Emperor, who saw this change, sometimes treated him quite badly.[20]

Napoleon's own status, and that of his family, was resolved by the treaty of Fontainebleau, which was signed on 11 April. He retained the courtesy title of Emperor, and was given the sovereignty of Elba for life, with an annual income of two million francs to be paid by his Bourbon successors. He was also permitted a guard of four hundred of his own soldiers. Marie-Louise was given the three north Italian duchies of Parma, Piacenza, and Guastalla, which her son and his descendants would inherit. Napoleon's mother, brothers, sisters, nephews, and nieces were all accorded princely rank and substantial pensions. Even his ex-wife Joséphine was not forgotten; her divorce settlement was reduced slightly, but she remained an extremely wealthy woman.

On 12 April, Napoleon appeared calm, but exhausted and depressed. He talked to Caulaincourt for hours about the problems facing France, and the humiliations he foresaw for her. Twice he exclaimed: 'Life is unbearable to me!' Caulaincourt eventually left, but was summoned again at 3 a.m. Napoleon was lying in bed in semi-darkness, and told Caulaincourt to sit near him. In a weak voice, he said he was convinced that Marie-Louise and the king of Rome would not be allowed to join him on Elba, and that attempts would be made to assassinate him. He asked Caulaincourt to remain attached to his wife and son, and then began hiccuping and groaning in pain. Horrified, Caulaincourt asked if he had taken poison. Napoleon replied that he had swallowed a preparation of opium he had kept in a bag hung round his neck since the retreat from Moscow, when he had feared being taken prisoner.

Caulaincourt started for the door to get help, but Napoleon struggled desperately to prevent him. Eventually Caulaincourt broke free and alerted a servant. At this moment Napoleon began vomiting up the opium, which saved his life. As it had been kept for two years the poison had lost some of its potency, and given his body a chance to expel it. By 7 a.m. he was out of danger, but 'his face was extremely haggard, almost distraught, its features shrunken'. Two hours later, though still very weak, he was receiving visitors. His recovery was helped by an affectionate letter from Marie-Louise, written on the road from Orléans to Rambouillet. While some rumours of his attempted suicide leaked out, those who knew the truth kept it a close secret. It was only confirmed beyond doubt by the publication of Caulaincourt's memoirs in 1933.[21]

Meanwhile, Marie-Louise had been having troubles of her own. Since leaving Paris, she, her son, her brother-in-law Joseph, and the regency council had travelled to Blois, then Orléans. For some weeks, it is probable that Joseph had been attempting to seduce her. Rumours of this have occasionally been mentioned since, but much more solid evidence comes in unpublished notes of Caulaincourt's, which for reasons of discretion he did not include in his memoirs. Caulaincourt twice met and had long conversations with Marie-Louise towards the end of April, and she may well have confided in him then. He also claimed that Napoleon himself confirmed the story the following year. Napoleon, he recalled, told him that in March 1814

a phrase in a letter from the Empress Marie-Louise, which revealed that Prince Joseph had behaved badly to her but did no go into any further details, made the Emperor realize that [Joseph] had tried *to rape her*... A report from the minister of police gave details, which had been only too clear since the Empress in her indignation had complained of this to her household. The Emperor said to me: 'How can I trust people ... who behaved in this way in the situation we were in then? Joseph is ... without honour, as ambitious as he is incapable.'[22]

Figure 15. The bed in which Napoleon attempted suicide at Fontainebleau during the night of 12–13 April 1814.

This incident may well have had important political consequences, deciding Marie-Louise not to share her husband's exile. Napoleon's brothers and sisters had always treated her badly, particularly Jérôme and Pauline, Princess Borghese. In Caulaincourt's view, Joseph's conduct was the last straw. Had Marie-Louise not feared that Joseph and the rest of Napoleon's family might come to Elba too, he thought, she would have resisted much more fiercely the allies' efforts to separate her from her husband. 'The result of all these iniquities', Caulaincourt concluded,

> was [to give the Empress] a pronounced aversion for [the Bonaparte] family, and a secret reluctance to follow the Emperor to a place where she might meet them and suffer their malice. When the Empress learned the details of the abdication she announced she was ready to share the Emperor's fate and console him, but then she reflected . . . 'I don't want to go to Elba with Joseph and Jérôme; I don't want to see Princess Borghese again, they'd make me too miserable . . . She cried, lamented the Emperor's misfortune, repeated that that

she was willing to die with him, but not to go to Elba with him because of his family.[23]

On 12 April, the Bourbons took possession of Paris. Louis XVIII was immobilized in England by a sharp attack of gout, so his younger brother the comte d'Artois, who had been in eastern France with the allies since February, entered the city in his name as lieutenant-general of the kingdom. Mounted on a white horse, he rode up to the Porte de Pantin, where the provisional government had assembled to meet him. Talleyrand came forward and, leaning against Artois' horse to take the weight off his club foot, uttered some flattering words of welcome: 'Monseigneur, the joy we feel on this day of regeneration will be beyond all expression, if you accept, with the celestial goodness that distinguishes your august house, the homage of our profound emotion and respectful devotion.' Artois, who was seeing Paris for the first time in twenty-five years, was so moved he was unable to reply.[24]

Napoleon stayed at Fontainebleau for a further week, preparing his departure for Elba. It was now clear that Marie-Louise would not accompany him, but would return to Vienna with her father, taking her son with her. During this time four commissioners, one from each of the allied Powers, arrived to escort him to his destination and ensure his safety: General Koller for Austria, Count Shuvalov for Russia, Sir Neil Campbell for England, and General von Waldburg-Truchsess for Prussia. At midday on 20 April, Napoleon held his last parade, to say farewell to the Imperial Guard, in the Courtyard of the White Horse in front of the château. Of his entourage, only the diehards were left, including his secretary Fain and the duc de Bassano. Caulaincourt was absent, negotiating final details on his behalf in Paris. The scene has become legendary. Napoleon faced his veterans and made a short, emotional speech:

> Soldiers of my Old Guard, I have come to say goodbye. For twenty years, you have always followed the path of honour and glory. In these last days, as in those of our prosperity, you have never ceased to be models of courage and loyalty ... Do not lament my fate; if I have decided to go on living, it is to serve your glory. I wish to write the history of the great things we have done together! ... Farewell, my children! I would like to embrace you all; let me at least embrace your flag![25]

General Petit came forward with one of the standards, and the Emperor buried his face in its folds. By this time everybody present was in tears, from the Guardsmen to the allied commissioners. Napoleon tore himself away, walked quickly to the carriage drawn up at the gates of the courtyard, and took the road south.

A large convoy accompanied Napoleon into exile: four carriages for the commissioners, eight more for his household, and a detachment of the Imperial Guard. Its route lay down the valley of the Rhône, then eastwards through Provence to Fréjus, the point of embarkation for Elba. On the second day, at Nevers, it was joined by another allied representative, Carl Clam-Martinic. Nominally he travelled as General Koller's first aide-de-camp, but his real function was to check all the arrangements on behalf of Schwarzenberg and Metternich, and to report back to them. At first, all went well; in the towns along the route, crowds gathered and shouted 'Vive l'Empereur!' Then, just beyond Nevers, the Guard detachment turned back. It was meant to be replaced by Austrian and Cossack units, but Napoleon refused to travel surrounded by foreign troops, which would make him look, he claimed, like a prisoner. 'Besides', he remarked to the commissioners, 'you can see I don't need them.' The party moved off again without an escort. It was to prove a dangerous mistake.[26]

After Lyons, the welcoming citizens melted away. As Napoleon travelled down through the Midi, they were replaced by others, but far less friendly. Since the beginning of the Revolution, the region had had a strong royalist, and militant Catholic, tradition. Added to the widespread hardship and resentment caused by Napoleon's conscription and taxation, this made a combustible mixture. This first became clear when the convoy stopped at a post-house just outside Avignon. It was greeted by a large gathering shouting 'Long live the King! Long live the allies!... Down with the tyrant, the wretch, the wicked beggar!' The scene was ugly, and the crowd clearly on the verge of violence.[27]

With some bravery, the commissioners tried to defuse the tension. They managed to clear the mob jostling around Napoleon's convoy, but could not stop the invective hurled at it. The Prussian commissioner Waldburg-Truchsess, who kept a diary of the journey, later recalled: 'We could not persuade these frenzied people to stop insulting the man who, they said, had made them so unhappy, and whose only desire was to increase their misery.'[28] The situation was deeply ironic, though Napoleon, cowering in his carriage, had little time to ponder it. He was confronted with the fate he dreaded most, death at the hands of an angry crowd. Yet his attackers were not republican *sans-culottes*, outraged by the betrayal of national honour or a shameful peace. Some were royalists, but to judge by their words to the commissioners, many were ordinary men and women simply venting their fury at the privations caused by years of conflict. Napoleon had always thought his greatest danger would come from a dishonourable peace. The reality was exactly the opposite; it was his refusal to end the war that toppled his regime, and at Avignon threatened his life.

At the next stop, the village of Orgon, the crowds were even more menacing. They had had enough warning of Napoleon's approach to rig up a gallows in front of the inn at which he stopped. From it they hung an effigy dressed in a blood-soaked uniform, and pinned on it a placard reading 'Sooner or later this will be the tyrant's fate.' The villagers pushed up against the carriage window to hurl abuse at him. They only drew back when Count Shuvalov began to harangue them: 'Aren't you ashamed to insult a defenceless man? He's humiliated enough by the sad situation he's in... Contempt is the only weapon you should use against him, now he's stopped being dangerous. It would be beneath the French nation to take any other revenge!'[29] This impromptu speech had its effect; some people even applauded. The convoy was able to proceed.

It may seem paradoxical that a man who had shown such courage on the battlefield should be unnerved by the prospect of perishing at the hands of a mob. But Napoleon's reaction to the incident at Orgon underlined how much he feared this type of death. As soon as he had left the village, he hastily put on a shabby blue greatcoat and a round hat with a white Bourbon cockade, and rode in front of his carriage, posing as a courier. In this ignominious disguise, he reached the next way-station, a run-down hostelry at a hamlet called Les Calades. By this time, he was pale and shaking. His alarm was increased by a conversation with the landlady, who asked him if he had seen Bonaparte on the road. She added that the scoundrel would probably be butchered by the people, which was no more than he deserved. After she had left Napoleon begged his companions to do nothing that could give away his real identity. When the commissioners, who had been left behind in the scramble to get out of Orgon, arrived, they found him slumped in a back room, his face running with tears.[30]

When lunch was served, Napoleon had little appetite for it. Since his own cooks had not prepared it, he was afraid it might have been poisoned. Ashamed of showing his fear, he pretended to eat what was served to

Figure 16. Napoleon attacked at Orgon, 25 April 1814.

him, but surreptitiously threw most of it under the table. The only wine he drank was brought from his own carriage. He related in detail to the commissioners the atrocities committed in Provence during the Revolution, and said he was convinced that Bourbon agents had stirred up the local people to assassinate him. He then proposed to change his route, return to Lyons and from there travel due east into Italy, but his companions ruled this out. At the least noise, Waldburg-Truchsess observed, 'he gave a start and changed colour'.[31]

Meanwhile, another crowd had gathered outside, having heard rumours of Napoleon's arrival. It seemed more peaceful than the previous ones, but the commissioners decided to take no chances. They sent a messenger to the mayor of the next town, Aix-en-Provence, asking him to ensure the convoy's safety on the next stage of its route. The mayor swiftly replied that he would take the necessary measures, and sent a detachment of gendarmes to Les Calades to keep order. At this point, Napoleon decided that he would be safer if he dressed as an Austrian officer. He put on General

Koller's uniform, forage cap, and greatcoat, his companions formed up around him, and the little procession forced its way through the press of people to the waiting carriages. The worst was over. Along the rest of the route Napoleon was greeted by many cries of 'Long live the King!', but there were no more threats of violence.[32]

Having earlier disdained an escort of foreign troops, Napoleon was now delighted to learn that two squadrons of Austrian hussars were stationed nearby at Le Luc. They were there to guard his youngest sister Pauline, Princess Borghese, who had been staying in Nice and hurried inland to join him. Napoleon and Pauline met at the Château du Bouillidou, outside Le Luc, on the afternoon of 26 April. Pauline was horrified that her brother was wearing an Austrian uniform, and refused to embrace him until he had taken it off. After this, things went more smoothly. Despite her vanity and frivolity, Pauline was always fiercely loyal to Napoleon. She immediately offered to follow him into exile, and was gratefully accepted. She kept her word—having first taken the waters at Ischia, she arrived on Elba in November. She was the only one of Napoleon's siblings who made the journey.[33]

The next day the convoy, accompanied by the Austrian hussars, arrived in Fréjus. By now Napoleon had recovered his nerve, and with it his preoccupation with status. He was originally to sail to Elba on a corvette, to be made over to him by the new French government. To his fury, he found that a modest brig, not a corvette, was waiting for him in the harbour, and refused to go aboard. Rounding on its captain, M Montcabrié, he shouted: 'You can go and fuck yourself with your rotten brig!' Outraged, Montcabrié walked off and did not return. It was decided that Napoleon would travel instead on the English frigate *Undaunted*, which had been ordered to provide an escort. Mollified, he put himself out to charm the company at dinner, and also talked at length about the great plans he had left unfinished. He behaved, however, as if still surrounded by his court; as Waldburg-Truchsess remarked, 'he resumed all his imperial dignity'.[34]

The contrast between Napoleon's return to playing the Emperor and his state of panic two days before was underlined by Carl Clam-Martinic, who was present, in an unpublished letter written to Schwarzenberg the next day. Clam suspected that Napoleon put on the display at dinner precisely to efface the impression made by his behaviour at Orgon and Les Calades. His description sheds a remarkable light on the complexities and paradoxes of Napoleon's personality:

It would be difficult to imagine two more opposite and contradictory facets in one person, as Napoleon showed in the performances he gave us on the 25th [at les Calades] and yesterday [at Fréjus]. In the first, he hid in a lonely inn, pale and trembling, anxiously asking everyone's advice . . . begging them to give the landlady no suspicion by their behaviour that he was the Emperor, [and] jumping at every footfall. To see him there, in the ruins of his lost empire, was enough to make one take him, without exaggeration, for a wretched, cowardly usurper; but yesterday, we saw him again, as if he was weaving spells around us, inviting us to his table, expanding on the plans that would have made him master of Europe within two years, and which he had been preparing 'because I didn't know then that Fortune would desert me' . . . proving to the Russians that he had not been defeated by them, but only by his own mistakes, and assuring us all that he had made France the first Power in the world.[35]

At 8 p.m. on 28 April, Napoleon and his entourage embarked on the *Undaunted*. Waldburg-Truchsess and Shuvalov took their leave of him and prepared to return to Paris, while Koller, Clam-Martinic, and Sir Neil Campbell accompanied him to Elba. Throughout the five-day voyage, Napoleon was good-humoured and affable. However, he clearly remained embarassed by the fear he had displayed in Provence. 'I showed myself bare-arsed to you, my dear General,' he remarked to Koller, 'but tell me frankly, don't you think those scandalous scenes were secretly encouraged by the French government?' On 2 May, the *Undaunted* sighted Corsica, his birthplace, and hove to outside the port of Calvi. Napoleon came to the bridge and pointed out all the landmarks in view to his companions. As the frigate turned about, he took off his hat and saluted his native land. He never saw it again.[36]

On the afternoon of 4 May, Napoleon stepped ashore at Portoferraio, the capital of Elba. His newly designed flag, blue with a diagonal red band sprinkled with the Bonaparte golden bees, was run up over the town fort. The garrison gave it a hundred-gun salute, but the *Undaunted* allowed it only twenty-one. The mayor and municipality made their new Emperor speeches of welcome; he replied that he would always show them the tenderness of a father. The party proceeded to a reception in the town hall. One of the mayor's armchairs had been hastily converted into a throne with gilded papier-mâché and some scarlet drapes. As Napoleon entered, a quintet of three violins and two double-basses burst into a serenade. It was a long way from his coronation ten years before, with a glittering crowd

Figure 17. A travelling lamp given by Napoleon to Carl Clam-Martinic, April 1814.

throning Notre-Dame and the Pope in attendance. The vast empire he had once ruled had shrunk to a small Italian island.[37]

No better example than Napoleon exists of the importance of the individual ruler in an authoritarian regime. Economic distress, public opinion, and ideological opposition all contributed to Napoleon's overthrow, but his own decisions played the crucial part. Nowhere is this clearer than in his refusal to make a compromise peace after the Russian disaster. Had he done so at Prague, or seized the Frankfurt proposals three months later, he could have retained France's 'natural frontiers', and probably also her domination of Italy. His refusal led to the carnage of Leipzig, and the loss of all his empire beyond the Rhine.

Finally, at Châtillon, when the natural frontiers had been overrun, Napoleon rejected the offer of France's pre-revolutionary borders, which would at least have saved his crown. On the ship to Elba, his companions confessed their astonishment at this recalcitrance, 'when his situation had become so desperate'. Napoleon replied: 'I could not agree to make the empire smaller than when I ascended the throne; I had sworn to maintain its integrity.'[38]

Napoleon believed that peace on these terms would goad the French people to rise up and overthrow him. He was catastrophically wrong, and his mistake had terrible consequences for himself, and worse ones for the thousands of soldiers and civilians who perished in the last two years of his struggle. His advisers desperately tried to change his mind, but he turned a deaf ear. Ironically, their most eloquent spokesman was the Duke of Bassano, who was often regarded as a warmonger. In 1813, as the military position worsened, he expressed alarm to Napoleon that the old revolutionary slogan, 'Victory or death!' was being revived. 'The question for France', he wrote to him, 'is not so simple; nations cannot accept such alternatives. They never die; *they tire of the need for constant victory.*'[39] These were wise words, a compelling warning against the temptations of military glory. Yet Napoleon would not, or could not, heed them, and fought on blindly to the end.

Epilogue: The Hundred Days

On 3 May 1815, a Frenchman and an Austrian met at the Three Kings Inn in Basel. The Frenchman, Pierre Fleury de Chaboulon, was a secret agent of Napoleon. The Austrian, travelling under the assumed name of Henry Werner, was in fact the Baron von Ottenfels, one of Metternich's most trusted subordinates. Their mission could not have been more sensitive. After a year of peace, its purpose was to prevent a renewal of war between France and the allied powers.

The immediate cause of the crisis was one of the most spectacular reversals of fortune in modern history—the Hundred Days. On 26 February 1815, Napoleon had escaped from Elba, and landed three days later in the south of France, with just a thousand men, in a daring bid to regain his throne. He then marched north, taking care to avoid central Provence, where he had so nearly been lynched the previous spring. At first it seemed impossible that such a risky gamble could succeed. However, this ignored the fact that the restored Bourbon monarchy had, in less than a year, managed to alienate much of the army. At every stage of Napoleon's route the troops sent to apprehend him instead rallied to him enthusiastically, along with significant sections of the local population. After Lyons fell to him on 10 March, without a shot being fired, his progress became irresistible. On the night of the 19th March, Louis XVIII fled Paris for the Belgian border, and twenty-four hours later Napoleon entered the capital to a delirious welcome.[1]

The news of Napoleon's escape from Elba reached the allied monarchs and their ministers at the Congress of Vienna, which had opened six months before to decide the shape of post-war Europe. Their presence together in one place enabled them to react quickly. On 13 March, a week before Napoleon reached Paris, they issued a proclamation branding him an

outlaw, 'beyond the pale of civil society'. It was written by Talleyrand, who
was at the congress as Louis XVIII's representative. If Talleyrand had indeed
contemplated assassinating Napoleon in April 1814, he was now condoning
it in a public declaration. Placing Napoleon outside the law in this way in
effect permitted anybody to murder him and to face no legal consequences.
Britain, Russia, Austria, and Prussia also began preparing for war. On 25
March, they renewed the treaty of Chaumont of the previous year, mobil-
izing 150,000 men each for the common cause and pledging to make no
separate peace with France.[2]

If Napoleon wanted to preserve his throne and even his life, he urgently
needed to persuade the Powers that he was no longer a threat. On 4 April,
he sent them a circular letter assuring them of his peaceful intentions. He
even accepted what he had fought so hard to avoid in 1814, France's return
to her pre-revolutionary borders. The Bourbons had consented to this as the
price of their restoration, and reopening the question would unite the
whole of Europe against him. Napoleon also sought to prove that he had
abandoned any idea of ruling France as a dictator. On 22 April, he issued the
'Additional act to the constitutions of the empire', which dramatically
limited his former authority. No taxation or conscription would be legal
without the consent of parliament, censorship would be abolished, and the
electorate would be enlarged. Whether Napoleon would have maintained
these concessions, or revoked them at the first opportunity, is impossible to
know.[3]

Of all the Powers ranged against him, the one most likely to listen to
Napoleon's overtures was Austria. She had made great efforts to broker a
compromise peace in 1813 and 1814, and could perhaps be persuaded to
revive them as an alternative to further conflict. She also controlled Napoleon's future, since his wife and son were currently living in Vienna under
Francis I's protection. If Napoleon failed to secure their return to France, his
dynasty would be doomed. Yet his own obstinacy had ruined Austria's
previous attempts to rescue him, and it remained very unclear whether she
would be prepared to do so again. If she tried once more and failed, she
would alienate her allies and face complete isolation.

An occasion soon arose for Napoleon to test the waters. As soon as he was
back in Paris he formed a ministry composed of faithful servants: Cambacérès as justice minister, Caulaincourt at foreign affairs, and Bassano as
secretary of state. A notable exception was the veteran intriguer Fouché,
disgraced in 1810 for unauthorized peace talks with England, and now

restored to the ministry of police. In late April, without informing Napoleon, Fouché received a secret emissary from Metternich, an employee of the powerful Viennese bankers Arnstein and Eskeles. Caulaincourt got wind of the mission and alerted Napoleon, but was unable to find out its precise purpose.[4]

This development offered Napoleon the opportunity he had been seeking for establishing communications with Metternich. The luckless Austrian emissary was arrested and interrogated. He revealed that he had given Fouché a letter, and a verbal message that an agent of Metternich's named Henry Werner would arrive in Basel on 1 May to receive a response. With typical audacity, Napoleon decided to substitute for Fouché's envoy one of his own, who would travel to Basel and investigate the intrigue before Metternich realized he had been duped. As long as the ruse secured a first meeting, it mattered little if Metternich subsequently realized the trick. If he genuinely wished for peace with France, he would be happy to have established direct contact with Napoleon; if not, valuable insight into his plans would have been gained. Either way, Napoleon himself would lose nothing.

For this delicate task, Napoleon chose Pierre Fleury de Chaboulon. It was a shrewd decision. Fleury de Chaboulon was a middle-ranking civil servant who as sub-prefect of Rheims in 1814 had organized an effective local resistance to the allied invasion. More recently, he had played an important role in preparing Napoleon's return from Elba. In February 1815, Bassano, then living in retirement in Paris, had sent him to Elba with a message that the Bourbons were deeply unpopular and that their overthrow was feasible. It was this information that had decided Napoleon to embark for France. Fleury had then crossed to the Italian mainland to deliver some secret messages for Napoleon, before catching up with him on his march to Paris.[5]

In memoirs he wrote only four years after the event, Fleury gave a detailed account of his mission to Basel. His instructions, he recalled, were clear. First, he was to find out whether Metternich and Fouché were actually plotting to assassinate Napoleon. If this was not the case, Napoleon ordered Fleury 'to inform M de Metternich of my position and of my peaceful dispositions, and to try and bring about a rapprochement between myself and Austria'. On 3 May, Fleury arrived at the Three Kings Inn, to find Ottenfels, waiting for him. It quickly became clear that Metternich had no intention of having Napoleon assassinated; Ottenfels expressed horror at the very thought. The plan was simply to capture him in a coup d'état, and restore the Bourbons once more.[6]

This disclaimer enabled Fleury to move the conversation forward, test the strength of Austria's commitment to the Bourbons, and—very gingerly—raise the possibility of reconciliation with Napoleon. He insisted that the Bourbons had lost what support they once enjoyed, that it was the French people, not just the army, who had welcomed Napoleon back, and that they would fight rather than see him dethroned again. This shocked Ottenfels, since Fouché, who had ostensibly sent Fleury, was assumed to detest Napoleon. Ottenfels enquired whether, instead of Napoleon, France might accept either the regency, or a monarchy with the duc d'Orléans as king. Yet Fleury remained adamant: 'The only leader we want is Napoleon; not the conquering, ambitious Napoleon, but Napoleon tamed by adversity.' Ottenfels replied that he would take these views back to Metternich, and the two men agreed to meet again in eight days' time.[7]

Fleury's recollections of the meeting, however, are not entirely accurate. In particular, the Austrians were far less wedded to the Bourbons than he states. Metternich's instructions to Ottenfels make it clear that from the start he was quite prepared to replace them either by the duc d'Orléans or the regency. He was well aware of Louis XVIII's mistakes, especially the favour he had shown to the unpopular returning émigrés. If Louis was to return, he would have to make a fresh start. The allies, Metternich wrote, 'wish to help resolve the national question by marginalizing the émigrés and removing the obstacles that the king's entourage have put in the way of his reconciliation with the new order in France'.[8]

Metternich's lack of enthusiasm for Louis XVIII was underlined by his willingness to consider the merits of Louis' more liberal cousin the duc d'Orléans, though this may also reflect his awareness that Orléans was strongly rumoured to be Fouché's choice. Metternich backed this up with a remarkable promise: if the French wanted Orléans as their king, he wrote, 'the Powers will act as intermediaries to ensure that [Louis XVIII] and his line give up their own claim to the throne.' As for the regency, Metternich made it clear that Austria would not oppose this, though she was concerned that this could involve her too closely in French domestic affairs. The only completely unacceptable solution was Napoleon keeping his throne: Ottenfels was to transmit 'the Powers' firm resolution to have no dealings with Napoleon Bonaparte because they feel there would be no security in any transaction with him'.[9]

Fleury immediately returned to Paris to report the outcome of the meeting. Napoleon was encouraged by the fact that it had actually taken place, despite Austria's refusal to recognize his own rule. He suspected that this might not be her last word, but the first stage in a negotiation, and authorized Fleury to continue. It also turned out that in Fleury's absence Fouché, suspecting his intrigue with Metternich had been discovered, had made a clean breast of it to Napoleon, claiming that his only purpose had been to divide Austria from her allies. When Fleury went back to Basel, therefore, he was able to carry genuine letters from Fouché which removed any doubts that he might be an imposter.[10]

Meanwhile in Vienna, Fleury's words as recounted by Ottenfels had made an impression. Metternich's instructions for the next meeting contained no mention of either Louis XVIII or the duc d'Orléans. The veto on Napoleon continuing to rule was maintained, but in exchange the regency was explicitly endorsed: 'The Powers would not refuse their consent to the regency, if it was the preference adopted by the [French] nation.' As for Napoleon, he would be assigned 'a place of residence from where he could no longer trouble the world'.[11] No actual location was mentioned, but it was no doubt intended to be further away from mainland Europe than Elba. Still, it is unlikely that as the father of the new Emperor of the French, Napoleon would have been exiled to somewhere as remote as St Helena.

Most important, these instructions were signed not only by Metternich, but by Nesselrode on behalf of the Czar. This made the offer of the regency virtually official. Russia and Austria were the two major continental Powers; if they made peace with France on this basis, England and Prussia would have no incentive to fight on to impose either Louis XVIII or the duc d'Orléans. The clock had been wound back almost exactly a year to April 1814, when Napoleon had been faced with abdicating in favour of his son. This time, however, Alexander was not wavering, but actively supporting this solution. Now, as then, Napoleon himself was beyond the pale, but his dynasty was being given a chance of survival.

To add weight to the proposal, Metternich told Ottenfels that he could, if necessary, show Fleury the instructions signed by Nesselrode and himself at the next meeting. This took place in another inn at Basel, The Stork, on the afternoon of 15 May. Ottenfels did not in fact produce the instructions, but his words, as Fleury recalled them, were unambiguous:

The sovereigns feel that they cannot alter their resolution never to recognize Napoleon as ruler of France nor to enter into any negotiation with him; *but at the same time I am authorized to declare formally to you that they give up their intention of restoring the Bourbons to the throne, and that they consent to give you the young Prince Napoleon.* They know that France hoped for the regency in 1814, and they are happy to fulfil this wish now.[12]

Naturally, the question of Napoleon's own fate caused heated discussion. Ottenfels insisted that his exile would be comfortable and not rigorous. 'You can be certain', he told Fleury, 'that Napoleon will be treated with the respect due to his rank, his marriage to a Habsburg, and his misfortune.' This did not pacify Fleury. 'I see', he riposted, 'that the allies want Napoleon handed over to them bound hand and foot: the French would never stoop to such treachery.' He then attempted to reassure Ottenfels that Napoleon was no longer to be feared as in the past. Napoleon, he claimed, 'was no longer the absolute master he had been before; he had also become fat and flabby, heavy and sluggish, slept a great deal, and realized that what he needed now was peace and quiet'. This is further evidence that Napoleon's physical decline, whether from a pituitary condition or some other cause, had become obvious to those close to him.[13]

Psychologically, however, it soon became clear that Napoleon had not changed at all. When Fleury brought the Austro-Russian proposal back to him, he saw it not as an opportunity for compromise, but as a sign of weakness. 'These gentlemen', he remarked, 'are starting to come round, since they're offering me the regency; my firmness is making them respect me. In a month I'll no longer fear them.' This impression was reinforced by the allied declaration published on 12 May, between Fleury's first and second meetings with Ottenfels, stating that they would not impose the Bourbons on France against her will. Napoleon took this as further proof that the Powers now favoured the regency. 'Well, gentlemen,' he announced to his courtiers, 'they're already offering me the regency; it's up to me whether to accept it or not.'[14]

Ottenfels' mission thus had the opposite effect from the one intended. Instead of persuading Napoleon to make way for his son, it encouraged him to raise the stakes. Fleury and Ottenfels had arranged to meet again on 1 June, but Napoleon was reluctant to let Fleury go. What he needed now to secure his position, he felt, was a military victory, not further negotiations. He was also sure that his determination not to abdicate was now clear to Metternich, and that the secret discussions would be suspended. He was quite right; Fleury did return to Basel on 1 June, but Ottenfels never appeared.[15]

A fortnight later Napoleon led his troops into Belgium to confront the nearest allied army, the Anglo-Prussian force commanded by Wellington and Blücher. Yet his own obstinacy had already sealed his fate. Even had he defeated the armies facing him, he could never have won the war. Though he refused to accept it, the allies were determined to force him from his throne, and one French victory would not have shaken them. They could mobilize a million men, and Napoleon could muster at best half that number. As he was invading Belgium, Schwarzenberg was marching 210,000 Austrians to the Rhine, followed by 150,000 Russians. Had the war continued, thousands more soldiers and civilians would have died to no purpose.[16]

Curiously neglected by history, the Ottenfels mission offered Napoleon his best hope of avoiding this grim prospect. He would have had to step down, but his young son would have taken his place, with Marie-Louise acting as regent until his majority. Even the Czar now conceded that this regime offered France a better chance of stability than a second Bourbon restoration. Prussia would have followed his lead, and England, although sympathetic to Louis XVIII, could not have challenged the combined will of her continental allies. Naturally, Austria had a family interest in the regency's success. Yet Napoleon preferred to destroy his dynasty rather than relinquish his grip on power.

Napoleon's defeat was now a foregone conclusion, and the end was quick. The issue was decided in four dramatic and bloody days. Napoleon took the offensive on 15 June. Wellington and Blücher outnumbered him by 209,000 to 125,000, but their forces were scattered and separated by a gap in the centre. Napoleon aimed to exploit this gap, move between them, and defeat them one after the other. It was a brilliant strategy, and it nearly worked. By the next day Napoleon had split Wellington from Blücher, and turned the main weight of his army on the Prussians. In a hard-fought battle at Ligny, Blücher was forced to retreat with heavy losses. He himself was unhorsed and ridden over twice during a cavalry charge, and was extremely lucky not to be killed or captured. Napoleon was now free to march west and overwhelm Wellington.

Yet appearances were deceptive. The Prussians had been beaten but not destroyed, and soon rallied. Blücher, having treated his bruises by rubbing himself all over with garlic, was determined to keep the agreement he had previously made with Wellington, that each would aid the other if attacked. Within a day, he had re-formed his troops and was leading them south-west towards his ally. Meanwhile, Wellington had taken up a strong position on a low ridge south of the village of Waterloo.[17] At 11.30 a.m. on 18 June, the battle began. Throughout the day Napoleon was lethargic and indecisive. He may have been crippled by a bout of haemorrhoids, as his brother Jérôme, who was there, later claimed.[18] Equally, his lassitude may have been a further symptom of a pituitary disorder. Napoleon attempted no brilliant manoeuvres, but simply launched his forces in clumsy frontal assaults on Wellington's line.

With 140,000 men and 400 guns crammed onto a front only 1,500 yards long, the result was a bloodbath. By 7 p.m. both sides were exhausted. At this critical moment the Prussians arrived on the battlefield, menacing the French right flank and rear. Napoleon now took the last gamble of his military career and sent forward the Imperial Guard, hoping to smash the depleted British line before Blücher could link up with it. The Prussian advance, however, took some of the pressure off Wellington and enabled him to plug some dangerous gaps in his front in the nick of time. As the Imperial Guard neared the crest of the ridge it was met by withering volleys of musketry at a range of twenty yards from the Brigade of Guards and the 52nd Regiment. Its three columns halted, wavered, and finally broke. Wellington ordered a general advance, and the demoralized French army began to disintegrate. Within minutes it was in full flight.[19]

Napoleon himself was almost captured by the Prussian cavalry, but managed to flee south, outdistancing his retreating army. He arrived back in Paris at dawn on 21 June. He could have fought on, but only by decreeing a popular mobilization and draconian emergency measures on the model of 1793 and 1794. With his ghastly memories of the Revolution, Napoleon refused to do this. On 22 June, he abdicated once again. He then fled to Rochefort on the west coast, hoping to take ship for America. By this time, however, a British naval squadron was already in place outside the port. On 15 July, accepting the inevitable, Napoleon and his entourage surrendered to Captain Maitland of HMS *Bellerophon*.

The fact that it was Wellington who had crushed Napoleon and was now advancing across the French border also sealed Louis XVIII's restoration. Wellington, like his government, was convinced that only the return of the Bourbons was compatible with the peace of Europe. He invited Louis, in exile nearby at Ghent, to follow him into France, and the old king, who had feared he would not be given a second chance to rule, was happy to oblige. On 8 July, he re-entered the capital. In the short-term, his dash for Paris behind Wellington's army secured his throne. In the long-term, it associated him durably with foreign invasion and national humiliation.

Many Frenchmen realized the futility of the Hundred Days, and none more so than Napoleon's old chief of staff Berthier. The marshal did not rally to his old master, and instead followed Louis XVIII into Belgium. But his loyalties were deeply divided, and he was desperate not to be seen as an *émigré*. As soon as he decently could he left the Bourbon court in exile, and joined his family in Bamberg, the home of his father-in-law, a Bavarian royal duke. From there, in early April, he applied for a passport to return to France, but this was refused. He was 61, his health undermined by years of campaigning, and he became increasingly anxious and depressed.

On 1 June 1815, detachments of the Russian army, on the march towards France, paraded through Bamberg. Berthier went up to one of the rooms on the third floor of the palace where he was staying to get a better view. There he found his children and their governess, preparing to go for a drive in the park. He told them to hurry downstairs, since the carriage was about to leave, and shut the door behind them. Lingering for a moment on the landing, the governess heard him groaning and muttering 'My poor country!' The next sound was a loud crash. She rushed into the room and found the window open, and a chair in front of it. Berthier was lying on the cobbles below, dead from a fractured skull. The official story was that he had climbed onto the chair to get a closer look at the troops passing below, had overbalanced, and accidently fallen from the window. However, Berthier's mental state, and his despairing words overheard by the governess, make it far more likely that he committed suicide. The invasion of France the previous year had brought him to the edge; the prospect of a second destroyed him.[20]

Napoleon's other leading servants had varying fates, none as tragic as Berthier's. Caulaincourt retired discreetly into private life, but his fidelity to the Emperor made him a target of royalist hatred. He devoted himself to writing his memoirs, which remain one of the principal sources for the Napoleonic period. He died of stomach cancer in Paris on 17 February 1827, aged 54. His rival Bassano outlived him by twelve years, and even returned to politics after the fall of the Bourbons. In 1834, he became prime minister under King Louis-Philippe, for eight days. He died five years later, at the age of 75.[21]

Having orchestrated one Bourbon restoration, Talleyrand became the first prime minister of the second. Recalled from the Congress of Vienna, he joined Louis XVIII as he crossed back onto French soil on 23 June 1815. Yet his ministry only lasted until September, when he resigned rather than accept the harsh peace terms the allies presented to France. Fifteen years later, the Bourbons were toppled for good and their cousin Louis-Philippe, duc d'Orléans, candidate for the throne in 1814 and 1815, finally became king. Talleyrand became an important and much-respected adviser to Louis-Philippe, serving him as ambassador to London between 1830 and 1834. He died in Paris, lucid and controlled to the last, on 17 May 1838 at the age of 84.[22]

Metternich lived even longer than Talleyrand, and rose even higher. He became Austrian chancellor in May 1821, and over the next twenty-five years the leading statesman of Europe, a champion of conservative principles against radical and revolutionary doctrines. His political partnership with Francis I endured until Francis' death in 1835. Forced from power by the 1848 revolution, he went into exile in London, Brighton, and Brussels. The subsequent counter-revolution permitted him to return to Austria in 1851. He divided his time between the capital and his estates, and was often consulted by the new Emperor Francis Joseph. He died in Vienna, aged 86, on 11 June 1859.[23]

Schwarzenberg did not long survive the Napoleonic wars. He was loaded with honours, and became president of the Austrian war council. However, his health was poor, and in 1817 he suffered a stroke. By a strange and fitting coincidence he died of a second stroke while revisiting Leipzig in October 1820, almost exactly seven years after his victory there.[24] His protégé Carl Clam-Martinic carved out a highly distinguished career. In 1835, he was made adjutant-general, and the following year minister of war. In 1821, he had married an Irishwoman, Lady Selina Meade. A close collaborator of Metternich, he was spoken of as his successor, but fell suddenly ill in Vienna on 22 January 1840. A week later he died, aged only 47.

Napoleon's fall made Czar Alexander the most powerful monarch in Europe. This did not change his complex and contradictory nature. While shrewdly promoting Russian power, he also made a visionary attempt to construct a new international order based on Christian principles. He played the leading role in a series of European congresses that had some success in preserving peace on the continent. Yet in 1820, a series of revolutions in Italy and Spain, and further unrest in France, alarmed and disillusioned him. His policy grew steadily more reactionary, both at home and abroad. On a journey to southern Russia, he fell ill of typhus at Taganrog and died there on 1 December 1825, aged 47.[25] Nesselrode survived him by thirty-one years. He continued as foreign minister and in 1845 became Russian chancellor, retiring only in 1856. He died in St Petersburg, aged 81, on 23 March 1862.

Frederick William III of Prussia saw his country restored to great-power status at the Congress of Vienna, and strengthened by the acquisition of much of Saxony and the left bank of the Rhine. He remained a faithful ally of Russia up to and beyond the death of Alexander I, and died in Berlin on 7 June 1840, aged 69. As for Blücher, Waterloo made him almost as famous as Wellington. He became a German national hero, but celebrity held no attraction for him, and he retired to the substantial estate given him by Frederick William at Krieblowitz in Silesia. His hallucinations do not seem to have reappeared, and he returned to his favourite peacetime pursuits of hunting and gambling. Once he lost so much at cards that he had to ask Frederick William to pay his debt. When the king refused, Blücher's reply was withering: 'You have been gambling with my bones all these years, so now I have a right to gamble with your money.'[26] Blücher died peacefully at Krieblowitz, aged 76, on 12 September 1819.

Of those closest to Napoleon, Marie-Louise did her best to rebuild her life after his fall. Made Duchess of Parma on Napoleon's first abdication, she took up residence there in 1816 and proved herself a model ruler; liberal, conscientious, and much-loved by her subjects. The price she paid was to leave her son in Vienna, since Metternich felt that anywhere else he would become a focus for Bonapartist discontent. The former king of Rome was raised there as Francis Charles, Duke of Reichstadt. He grew into a highly intelligent, personable young man, fascinated by all things military. He did not, however, live to see a battlefield. Struck down by tuberculosis, he died on 22 July 1832 at the palace of Schönbrunn, aged just 21. Marie-Louise lived on for fifteen more years. She married twice more after Napoleon's death, each time to her court chamberlain, Count Adam von Neipperg in 1821 and Count Charles de Bombelles in 1834. She died in Parma on 17 December 1847, aged 56.[27]

Napoleon's own fate was tragic, and soon became the stuff of legend. He had hoped to be allowed to settle in England, but the sympathetic crowds that gathered to see him when the *Bellerophon* anchored off Plymouth alarmed the government. It was decided instead to send him to the island of St Helena, in the South Atlantic. On this beautiful but incredibly remote volcanic outcrop, Napoleon spent the last five years of his life. His major activity was dictating his memoirs, the *Mémorial de Ste-Hélène*, portraying himself as an enlightened ruler who would have united Europe on liberal principles had the forces of reaction not brought him down.[28]

The isolation and tedium of his surroundings soon began to tell. Napoleon became prone to depression, shutting himself away in his bedroom for days at a time. Inactivity, and the sub-tropical climate, undermined his health; he became obese and was often afflicted with liver complaints. In July 1820, he grew noticeably worse, and by the following March he was bedridden. He had stomach cancer, the disease which had killed his father. On 3 May 1821, he slipped into semi-consciousness, and died two days later, surrounded by his tiny court in exile. He was 51. It was a cruel end to such an extraordinary career, which he himself had made inevitable.

Figure 18. Ex-Empress Marie-Louise and her third husband, Charles de Bombelles, at Parma, 1838, by Giuseppe Naudin.

Notes

INTRODUCTION

1. A. J. F. Fain, *Manuscrit de 1814* (Paris 1825), p. 406.
2. R. A. Alexander, *Napoleon* (London 2001), p. 1.
3. G. Lefebvre, *Napoléon* (Paris 1935); J. Tulard, *Napoléon. Le mythe du sauveur* (Paris 1977); J. Holland Rose, *The Life of Napoleon I* (London 1901); A. Fournier, *Napoleon I: eine Biographie* (Vienna and Leipzig 1886–9), Eng. version *Napoleon I: A Biography*, trans. A. E. Adams (London 1911).
4. J. Tulard, *Le grand empire, 1804–1815* (Paris 1982); T. Lentz, *Nouvelle histoire du premier empire* (4 vols., Paris 2002–10); J.-O. Boudon, *Napoléon et les cultes. Les religions à l'aube du 19ᵉᵐᵉ siècle, 1800–1815* (Paris 2002); A. Forrest, *Conscripts and Deserters: The Army and French Society during the Revolution and Empire* (Oxford 1989); M. Broers, *The Napoleonic Empire in Italy, 1796–1814: Cultural Imperialism in a European Context?* (London and Basingstoke 2005); C. Esdaile, *Napoleon's Wars: An International History, 1803–1815* (London 2007).
5. D. Lieven, *Russia against Napoleon: The Battle for Europe, 1807–1814* (London 2009).
6. E. de las Cases, *Mémorial de Ste-Hélène*, ed. A Fugier (2 vols., Paris 1961), vol. 1, p. 229.

CHAPTER I

1. The best modern account of the Russian campaign is A. Zamoyski, *1812: Napoleon's Fatal March on Moscow* (London 2004). See also D. G. Chandler, *The Campaigns of Napoleon* (London 1966; 1978 edn), pp. 739–861; C. Duffy, *Borodino and the war of 1812* (London 1972); and J. Thiry, *La campagne de 1812* (Paris 1969). The first major history of the campaign, written by a participant, is Général Comte Philippe de Ségur, *Histoire de Napoléon et de la grande armée pendant l'année 1812* (Brussels 1825). For a memorable eyewitness account, see Sir Robert Wilson, *Narrative of Events during the Invasion of Russia* (London 1860).
2. See J. D. Klier, *Russia Gathers her Jews: The Origins of the 'Jewish Question' in Russia, 1772–1825* (Dekalb, Ill., 1986), pp. 14–15, 68–9.
3. *Mémoires du général Lejeune*, ed. G. Bapst (2 vols., Paris 1895), vol. 2, pp. 288–9.
4. A. J. F. Fain, *Manuscrit de 1812, contenant le précis des événements de cette année, pour servir à l'histoire de l'empereur Napoléon* (2 vols., Paris 1827), vol. 2, pp. 423–4.

5. *Journal du maréchal de Castellane, 1804–1862* (5 vols., Paris 1895–97), vol. 1, p. 202.

6. *Mémoires du général de Caulaincourt, duc de Vicence, grand écuyer de l'empereur*, ed. J. Hanoteau (3 vols., Paris 1933), vol. 2, pp. 205–349.

7. There are innumerable biographies and studies of Napoleon; seven important modern ones are G. Lefebvre, *Napoléon* (Paris 1935); J. M. Thompson, *Napoleon Bonaparte: His Rise and Fall* (Oxford 1952); J. C. Herold, *The Mind of Napoleon: A Selection from his Written and Spoken Words* (New York 1955); J. Tulard, *Napoléon. Le mythe du sauveur* (Paris 1977); S. Englund, *Napoleon: A Political Life* (Cambridge, Mass., 2004); P. G. Dwyer, *Napoleon: The Path to Power, 1769–1799* (London 2007); and *Citizen Emperor: Napoleon in Power, 1799–1815* (London 2013). There are two essential published primary sources: *Correspondance de Napoléon 1er, publiée par ordre de l'empereur Napoléon III*, ed. A. du Casse (32 vols., Paris 1858–70), and a new, revised edn: *Napoléon Bonaparte. Correspondance générale* (12 vols., Paris 2004–). For Napoleon's administrative reforms in France, see L. Bergeron, *L'Episode napoléonien. Aspects intérieurs, 1799–1815* (Paris 1972); and T. Lentz, *Nouvelle histoire du premier empire* (4 vols., Paris 2002–10), vols. 1 and 3. Important studies of his art of war are Chandler, *The Campaigns of Napoleon*; O. Connelly, *Blundering to Glory: Napoleon's Military Campaigns* (Wilmington, DE, 1987); G. Rothenberg, *The Art of Warfare in the Age of Napoleon* (London 1977); and C. Esdaile, *Napoleon's Wars: An International History, 1803–1815* (London 2007). Much of Napoleon's own writing on war has recently been collected in B. Colson (ed.), *Napoleon. De la guerre* (Paris 2011).

8. *Mémoires de Mme la duchesse d'Abrantès, ou souvenirs historiques sur Napoléon, la Révolution, le directoire, le consulat, l'empire et la restauration* (18 vols., Paris 1831–2), vol. 1, p. 255.

9. V. Cronin, *Napoleon* (London 1971), p. 113.

10. The most persuasive analysis of this facet of Napoleon comes in P. W. Schroeder, *The Transformation of European Politics, 1763–1848* (Oxford 1994; 1996 edn), pp. 371–95, 467–70.

11. J. Kemble, *Napoleon Immortal: The Medical History and Private Life of Napoleon Bonaparte* (London 1959), pp. 190–4, 201, 221–3.

12. Kemble, *Napoleon Immortal*, pp. 164–70.

13. P. Hillemand, *Pathologie de Napoléon* (Paris and Geneva 1970).

14. Dr Walter Henry's account of Napoleon's post-mortem examination, reprinted in Kemble, *Napoleon Immortal*, p. 283.

15. Hillemand, *Pathologie de Napoléon*, p. 84; Kemble, *Napoleon Immortal*, p. 170.

16. Earl Stanhope, *Notes of Conversations with the Duke of Wellington, 1831–1851* (London 1888; 1998 edn), pp. 59–60.

17. On the Duchy of Warsaw, see M. Handelsman, *Napoléon et la Pologne, 1806–1807* (Paris 1909); P. Wandycz, *The Lands of Partitioned Poland, 1795–1918* (Seattle, 1974); W. H. Zawadski, *A Man of Honour: Adam Czartoryski as a Statesman of Russia and Poland, 1795–1831* (Oxford 1993); and T. Lentz, 'Quelle place

pour la Pologne dans le système napoléonien?' in T. Lentz, *Napoléon diplomate* (Paris 2012).

18. For Prussia and Napoleon, see B. Simms, *The Impact of Napoleon: Prussian High Politics, Foreign Policy and Executive Reform, 1797–1806* (Cambridge 1997), and *The Struggle for Mastery in Germany, 1779–1850* (London and Basingstoke 1998); C. Clark, *Iron Kingdom: The Rise and Downfall of Prussia, 1600–1947* (London 2006); P. Paret, *Yorck and the Era of Prussian Reform, 1807–1815* (Princeton 1966); R. Berdahl, *The Politics of the Prussian Nobility: The Development of a Conservative Ideology, 1770–1848* (Princeton 1988); and M. Gray, *Prussia in Transition: Society and Politics under the Stein Reform Ministry of 1808* (Philadelphia 1986).

19. *Mémoires du général de Caulaincourt*, vol. 2, pp. 286–7.

20. *Mémoires du général de Caulaincourt*, vol. 2, pp. 324–5.

21. On the background to Napoleonic Germany and the Confederation of the Rhine, see T. C. W. Blanning, *The French Revolution in Germany: Occupation and Resistance in the Rhineland, 1795–1802* (Oxford 1983), and 'The French Revolution and the modernization of Germany', *Central European History*, 22:2 (1989); K. O. von Aretin, *Heiliges Römisches Reich, 1776–1806. Reichsverfassung und Staatssouveränität* (2 vols., Wiesbaden 1967); and J. Gagliardo, *Reich and Nation: The Holy Roman Empire as Idea and Reality, 1763–1806* (Bloomington, 1980). The Napoleonic Rhineland is analysed in M. Rowe, *From Reich to State: The Rhineland in the Revolutionary Age, 1780–1830* (Cambridge 2003). On the states of the Confederation, see the articles in the symposium 'State-Building in the "Third Germany"', in *Central European History*, 24:2–3 (1991): R. C. Anderson, 'State-Building and Bureaucracy in Early 19th-Century Nassau'; L. E. Lee, 'Baden between Revolutions: State-Building and Citizenship, 1800–1848'; L. J. Flockerzie, 'State-Building and Nation-Building in the Third Germany: Saxony after the Congress of Vienna'; and M. W. Gray, '"Modifying the traditional for the good of the whole": Commentary on State-Building and Bureaucracy in Nassau, Baden and Saxony in the Early 19th Century'. Also important are E. Kraehe, *Metternich's German Policy* (2 vols., Princeton 1963–83), vol. 1, *The Contest with Napoleon, 1799–1814*; L. E. Lee, *The Politics of Harmony: Civil Service, Liberalism and Social Reform in Baden, 1800–1850* (Newark, NJ, 1980): H. A. Schmitt, 'Germany without Prussia: A Closer Look at the Confederation of the Rhine', *German Studies Review*, 6:1 (1983); H. Berding, *Napoleonische Herrschafts-und-Gesellschaftspolitik im Königreich Westfalen, 1807–1813* (Göttingen 1973); and W. D. Godsey, *Nobles and Nation in Central Europe: Free Imperial Knights in the Age of Revolution* (Cambridge 2004).

22. The most important works for Napoleonic Italy are M. Broers, *The Napoleonic Empire in Italy, 1796–1814: Cultural Imperialism in a European Context?* (London and Basingstoke 2005), *Napoleonic Imperialism and the Savoyard Monarchy, 1776–1821: State-Building in Piedmont* (Lampeter 1997), and *The Politics of Religion in Napoleonic Italy: The War against God, 1801–1814* (London and

New York 2002); S. J. Woolf, *A History of Italy, 1700–1860: The Social Constraints of Political Change* (London 1979); J. A. Davis, *Naples and Napoleon: Southern Italy and the European Revolutions, 1780–1860* (Oxford 2006); and R. J. Rath, *The Fall of the Napoleonic Kingdom of Italy, 1814* (New York 1941).

23. For the concept of 'inner' and 'outer' empire, see M. Broers, 'Napoleon, Charlemagne and Lotharingia: Acculturation and the Limits of Napoleonic Europe', *The Historical Journal*, 44:1 (2001). For Spain, see C. Esdaile, *The Spanish Army in the Peninsular War: The Causes, Experiences and Consquence of Military Humiliation* (Manchester 1988), *The Peninsular War: A New History* (London 2002), and *Fighting Napoleon: Guerrillas, Bandits and Adventurers in Spain, 1808–1814* (New Haven and London 2004); J. R. Aymes, *La guerre d'indépendance espagnole, 1808–1814* (Paris 1973); and G. H. Lovett, *Napoleon and the Birth of Modern Spain* (2 vols., New York 1971). Major studies of the continental blockade are F. Crouzet, 'Wars, Blockade and Economic Change in Europe, 1792–1815', *Journal of Economic History*, 24:4 (1964), and *L'économie britannique et le blocus continental, 1806–1813* (2 vols., Paris 1958); G. Ellis, *Napoleon's Continental Blockade: The Case of Alsace* (Oxford 1981); E. F. Heckscher, *The Continental System: An Economic Interpretation* (Oxford 1922); and S. Marzagalli, *Les boulevards de la fraude. Le négoce maritime et le blocus continental, 1806–1813* (Paris 1999). J. Tulard, *Le grand empire, 1804–1815* (Paris 1982), pp. 245–7 discusses the north German annexations.

24. For the general history of the Napoleonic empire, analysing these reforms and the reactions they aroused, the most important works are Lentz, *Nouvelle histoire*, esp. vol. 3; Tulard, *Le grand empire*; J.-O. Boudon, *Histoire du consulat et de l'empire* (Paris 2000); J. Lovie and A. Palluel-Guillard, *L'épisode napoléonien. Aspects extérieurs, 1799–1815* (Paris 1972); M. Broers, *Europe under Napoleon, 1799–1815* (London 1996); S. J. Woolf, *Napoleon's Integration of Europe* (London 1991); A. Grab, *Napoleon and the Transformation of Europe* (London and Basingstoke 2003); O. Connelly, *Napoleon's Satellite Kingdoms* (New York 1965); G. Ellis, *The Napoleonic Empire* (London 1991); and C. Esdaile (ed.), *Popular Resistance in the French Wars: Patriots, Partisans and Land Pirates* (London and Basingstoke 2005).

25. Bergeron, *L'épisode napoléonien*, p. 52.

26. Ellis, *The Napoleonic Empire*, pp. 91–2.

27. Chandler, *The Campaigns of Napoleon*, p. 756.

28. *Mémoires du général de Caulaincourt*, vol. 2, pp. 249–51.

29. Two essential general works on France under Napoleon are Bergeron, *L'épisode napoléonien*; and Lentz, *Nouvelle histoire*, vol. 3, pp. 28–834. On the Paris residence of the kingdom of Italy's foreign minister and secretary of state, see Lentz, *Nouvelle histoire*, vol. 3, p. 731.

30. Lentz, *Nouvelle histoire*, vol. 3, pp. 35–6; and I. Collins, *Napoleon and his Parliaments, 1800–1815* (London 1979), pp. 10–11.

31. The best one-volume treatment of the Senate and Legislative Body is Collins, *Napoleon and his Parliaments*. For the Senate, see also J. Thiry, *Le sénat de Napoléon* (Paris 1932).

32. Lentz, *Nouvelle histoire*, vol. 3, p. 69 n. 3.

33. For Cambacérès, see his *Mémoires inédits*, ed. L. Chatel de Brancion (2 vols., Paris 1999); *Cambacérès. Lettres inédites à Napoléon*, ed. J. Tulard (2 vols., Paris 1973); and L. Chatel de Brancion, *Cambacérès. Maître d'oeuvre de Napoléon* (Paris 2001).

34. *Cambacérès. Lettres inédites*, vol. 2, p. 893.

35. The best biography of Louis XVIII is P. Mansel, *Louis XVIII* (London 1981). On French royalism under Napoleon, see J. Godechot, *La contre-révolution, doctrine et action: 1789–1804* (Paris 1961); J. Tulard (ed.), *La contre-révolution. Origines, histoire, postérité* (Paris 1990); and G. Lewis, *The Second Vendée: The Continuity of Counter-Revolution in the Department of the Gard, 1799–1815* (Oxford 1978).

36. On the *chevaliers de la foi*, see G. de Bertier de Sauvigny, *Le comte Fernand de Bertier (1782–1864) et l'énigme de la Congrégation* (Paris 1948); and B. Plongeron, *Des résistances religieuses à Napoléon, 1799–1813* (Paris 2006).

37. The two best biographies of Carnot are M. Reinhard, *Le grand Carnot* (2 vols., Paris 1950–2); and J. and N. Dhombres, *Carnot* (Paris 1997).

38. Three major studies of Sieyès are P. Bastid, *Sieyès et sa pensée* (Paris 1939); D. Bredin, *Sieyès. La clé de la Révolution française* (Paris 1988); and M. Forsyth, *Reason and Revolution: The Political Theory of the abbé Sieyès* (Leicester 1987).

39. For the abbé Grégoire, see R. Hermon-Belot, *L'abbé Grégoire: la politique et la vérité* (Paris 2000); R. F. Necheles, *The Abbé Grégoire, 1787–1831: The Odyssey of an Egalitarian* (Westport, CN, 1971); and A. G. Sepinwall, *The Abbé Grégoire and the French Revolution: The Making of Modern Universalism* (Berkeley, CA, and London 2005).

40. Archives Nationales, Paris, série F7 3688/24, police générale, Seine, 1808–14, dossier 293 a, 'Les ex-sénateurs Garat et Grégoire'.

41. Important studies of the Idéologues and the opposition to Napoleon are G. Gusdorf, *La conscience révolutionnaire. Les Idéologues* (Paris 1978); C. B. Welch, *Liberty and Utility: The French Ideologues and the Transformation of Liberalism* (New York 1984); and L. de Villefosse and J. Bouissounouse, *L'opposition à Napoléon* (Paris 1969). On Constant, see D. Wood, *Benjamin Constant: A Biography* (London 1993); P. Bastid, *Benjamin Constant et sa doctrine* (Paris 1966); S. Holmes, *Benjamin Constant and the Making of Modern Liberalism* (New Haven and London 1984); and G. A. Kelly, *The Humane Comedy: Constant, Tocqueville and French Liberalism* (Cambridge 1992). On Garat, see P. Lafond, *Garat. 1762–1823* (Paris 1899).

42. Despite his significance, Barras remains a neglected figure. His memoirs, *Mémoires de Barras, membre du Directoire* (4 vols., Paris 1895–6) are generally regarded as unreliable, distorted by his hatred of Napoleon. There are few

biographies of him; the best is J. P. Garnier, *Barras, le roi du Directoire* (Paris 1970).

43. For Cambon, see F. Bornarel, *Cambon et la Révolution française* (Paris 1905); and C. Sené, *Joseph Cambon (1756–1820). Le financier de la Révolution* (Paris 1987).

44. Talleyrand's not always reliable memoirs are published as *Mémoires du prince de Talleyrand*, ed. duc de Broglie (5 vols., Paris 1891–2). The best biography of Talleyrand is E. de Waresquiel, *Talleyrand, le prince immobile* (Paris 2003), followed by G. Lacour-Gayet, *Talleyrand (1754–1838)* (4 vols., Paris 1928–34); and D. Cooper, *Talleyrand* (London 1932).

45. The best studies of Fouché are L. Madelin, *Fouché, 1759–1820* (2 vols., Paris 1901); and J. Tulard, *Joseph Fouché* (Paris 1998).

46. Lentz, *Nouvelle histoire*, vol. 3, p. 316. Fouché's bulletins to Napoleon have been published by E. d'Hauterive and J. Grassion, *La police secrète du premier empire. Bulletins quotidiens adressés par Fouché à l'empereur, 1804–1810* (5 vols., Paris 1908–64); those of his successor as minister of police Savary by M. Gotteri, *La police secrète du premier empire. Bulletins quotidiens adressés par Savary à l'empereur, 1810–1814* (7 vols., Paris 1997–2004).

47. Lentz, *Nouvelle histoire*, vol. 3, p. 331.

48. Lentz, *Nouvelle histoire*, vol. 3, pp. 334, 339, 346–9.

CHAPTER 2

1. The principal studies of Malet and his conspiracy are E. Hamel, *Histoire des deux conspirations du général Malet* (Paris 1873); M. Billard, *La conspiration de Malet* (Paris 1907); F. Masson, *La vie et les conspirations du général Malet* (Paris 1921); and most recently T. Lentz, *La conspiration du général Malet. 23 octobre 1812* (Paris 2012).

2. Lentz, *La conspiration*, p. 78.

3. Savary and Pasquier left memoirs which are an important source for the period: *Mémoires du duc de Rovigo, pour servir à l'histoire de l'empereur Napoléon* (8 vols., Paris 1828), and *Histoire de mon temps. Mémoires du chancelier Pasquier* (6 vols., Paris 1893–5). The best study of Savary is T. Lentz, *Savary: le séide de Napoléon* (Paris 2001), and of Pasquier by J. K. Kieswetter, *Etienne-Denis Pasquier: The Last Chancellor of France* (Philadelphia 1977). For Lahorie, see L. Le Barbier, *Le général de La Horie, 1766–1812* (Paris 1904). There is no biography of Guidal.

4. *Mémoires du duc de Rovigo*, vol. 6, pp. 2–4.

5. *Mémoires du duc de Rovigo*, vol. 6, p. 7.

6. *Mémoires du duc de Rovigo*, vol. 6, pp. 11–12; Lentz, *La conspiration*, pp. 189–91.

7. Hamel, *Histoire des deux conspirations*, pp. 213–15.

8. Lentz, *La conspiration*, p. 191; Hamel, *Histoire des deux conspirations*, pp. 217–23.

9. Lentz, *La conspiration*, pp. 226–9.

10. See e.g. L. Bergeron, *L'épisode napoléonien. Aspects intérieurs, 1799–1815* (Paris 1972), p. 107.

11. *Mémoires du général de Caulaincourt, duc de Vicence, grand écuyer de l'empereur*, ed. J. Hanoteau (3 vols., Paris 1933), vol. 2, pp. 341–2.

12. *Mémoires du général de Caulaincourt*, vol. 2, p. 339.

13. Talleyrand to Caulaincourt, 24 and 26 October 1812, Archives Nationales, Paris, 95 AP (Fonds Caulaincourt) carton 22 'Correspondance du duc de Vicence 1804–1826', dossier 8 'Talleyrand'.

14. Talleyrand to Caulaincourt, 31 October 1812.

15. Napoleon to Savary, 17 January 1812, cited in Lentz, *La conspiration*, p. 150.

16. *Mémoires de Barras, membre du Directoire*, ed. G. Duruy (4 vols., Paris 1895–6), vol. 4, pp. 188, 197.

17. P. Gaffarel, *Les complots de Marseille et de Toulon, 1812–1813* (Aix-en-Provence 1907), pp. 9–12. Gaffarel's remains the most detailed work on the two conspiracies.

18. Councillor of state Pelet de la Lozère to Savary, 17 May 1813, AN série F7 (police générale) carton 6591, pièce 95.

19. Police commissioner Caillemer to Savary, 8 April 1813, AN série F7 6591, pièce 129.

20. Cited in Lentz, *La conspiration*, p. 150.

21. Gaffarel, *Les complots*, p. 16.

22. Pelet de la Lozère to Savary, 17 May 1813, AN F7 6591, pièce 95; Gaffarel, *Les complots*, pp. 23–4.

23. Pelet de la Lozère to Savary, 17 May 1813, AN F7 6591, pièce 95; Gaffarel, *les complots*, pp. 39–41.

24. J.-P. Garnier, *Barras, le roi du directoire* (Paris 1970), p. 321.

25. AN F7 6591, pièce 47.

26. M. Agulhon, *La vie sociale en Provence intérieure au lendemain de la Révolution* (Paris 1970), p. 449; Gaffarel, *Les conspirations*, pp. 61–2.

27. Pelet de la Lozère to Savary, 7 and 15, June 1813, AN F7 6591, pièces 89, 78.

28. Pelet de la Lozère to Savary, 17 May 1813, AN F7 6591, pièce 95.

29. Gaffarel, *Les conspirations*, p. 35.

30. Cited in Lentz, *La conspiration*, pp. 270–1.

31. G. de Bertier de Sauvigny, *Le comte Fernand de Bertier (1782–1864) et l'énigme de la Congrégation* (Paris 1948), p. 36; T. Lentz, *Nouvelle histoire du premier empire* (4 vols., Paris 2002–10), vol. 3, pp. 629–32.

32. Montalivet to Napoleon, 29 November 1812, AN F1c I 12, unnumbered fo.

33. 'Récapitulation: bruits communs à plusieurs départements', unnumbered fo. in dossier 'Minute: joint à la lettre à Sa Majesté du 29 novembre 1812', AN F1c I 12, unnumbered fo.

34. AN F1c I 12, unnumbered fo.; 'Récapitulations' in 'Compte des bruits pour les 10 derniers jours de décembre 1812' and 'Compte des bruits pour les 10 premiers jours de janvier 1813', AN F1c I 12, unnumbered fos.

35. There is a substantial literature on Napoleonic conscription and the varying popular reactions it evoked; the most important works are L. Bergès, *Résister à*

la conscription, 1798–1814. Le cas des départements aquitains (Paris 2002); A. Crépin, La conscription en débats ou le triple apprentissage de la nation, de la citoyenneté, de la république, 1798–1889 (Arras 1998); A. Forrest, Conscripts and Deserters: The Army and French Society during the Revolution and Empire (Oxford 1989), and Napoleon's Men: The Soldiers of the Revolution and Empire (London and New York 2002); A. Pigeard, La conscription au temps de Napoléon, 1798–1814 (Paris 2003); and I. Woloch, 'Napoleonic Conscription: State Power and Civil Society', Past and Present, 111 (May 1986). Other important studies with significant sections on conscription are J.-P. Bertaud, Quand les enfants parlaient de gloire. L'armée au coeur de la France de Napoléon (Paris 2006); and N. Petiteau, Les Français et l'empire (1799–1815) (Paris 2008).

36. T. Lentz, Nouvelle histoire du premier empire (4 vols., Paris 2002–10), vol. 2, p. 360.

37. Bergeron, L'épisode napoléonien, p. 144.

38. Petiteau, Les Français et l'empire, p. 215.

CHAPTER 3

1. For the scenes in Vilna, see A. Zamoyski, 1812: Napoleon's Fatal March on Moscow (London 2004; 2005 edn), pp. 525–9; and D. Lieven, Russia against Napoleon: The Battle for Europe, 1807–1814 (London 2009; 2010 edn), p. 286.

2. Alexander I continues to be neglected by historians. The most detailed biography remains N. Shil'der, Imperator Alexander I: ego zhizn'i tsarstvovanie (4 vols., St Petersburg 1897–8). Since it has not been translated I have relied on J. Hartley, Alexander I (London 1994); A Palmer, Alexander I (London 1974); and for Alexander's mysticism and religious beliefs, F. Ley, Alexandre Ier et sa Sainte-Alliance, 1811–1825 (Paris 1975). There is, however, an important new biography in French: M.-P. Rey, Alexandre 1er, le tsar qui vainquit Napoléon (Paris 2009).

3. Caulaincourt to Champagny, duc de Cadore (foreign minister), 19 September 1810, Les relations diplomatiques de la Russie et la France, 1808–1812, d'après les rapports des ambassadeurs d'Alexandre et de Napoléon (7 vols., St Petersburg 1905–14), vol. 5, pp. 138–40.

4. Alexander to Colonel Michaud, cited in Lieven, Russia against Napoleon, p. 241.

5. Ley, Alexandre Ier, p. 54.

6. C. Esdaile, Napoleon's Wars: An International History, 1803–1815 (London 2007), pp. 488–90.

7. Cited in Lieven, Russia against Napoleon, pp. 241, 287.

8. There is no biography of Nesselrode in English, but a selection of his papers has been published in French: Lettres et papiers du chancelier comte de Nesselrode, ed. A von Nesselrode (11 vols., Paris 1904–11).

9. Cited in A. Sorel, L'Europe et la Révolution française (8 vols., Paris 1885–1904), vol. 8, p. 10.

10. For the events at Tauroggen, see Sorel, *L'Europe et la Révolution française*, vol. 8, pp. 21–6; and M. V. Leggiere, *Napoleon and Berlin: The Napoleonic wars in Prussia, 1813* (Stroud, 2002), pp. 28–39.

11. Sorel, *L'Europe et la Révolution française*, vol. 8, pp. 26, 55–6. For Frederick William III's biography, see T. Stamm-Kuhlmann, *König in Preussens grosser Zeit. Friedrich Wilhelm III, der Melancholiker auf dem Thron* (Berlin 1992).

12. Leggiere, *Napoleon and Berlin*, p. 290.

13. Francis I still awaits a modern biographer. For this period, however, there is an extremely shrewd analysis of his character and policy in H. Kissinger, *A World Restored: Metternich, Castlereagh and the Problems of Peace, 1812–1822* (London 1957; 1973 edn), pp. 209–13.

14. Metternich to Engelbert von Floret (French chargé d'affaires in Paris), 9 December 1812, published in W. Oncken, *Österreich und Preussen im Befreiungs-skriege* (2 vols., Berlin, 1876–9), vol. 1, p. 384.

15. The standard biography of Metternich remains H. von Srbik, *Metternich, der Staatsmann und der Mensch* (3 vols., Munich, 1925–54), though Wolfram Siemann is currently preparing a major new biography, and has produced a short preliminary study, *Metternich. Staatsmann zwischen Restauration und Moderne* (Munich 2010). A thought-provoking recent study of Metternich and his era in English is A. Sked, *Metternich and Austria: A Re-evaluation* (London and Basingstoke 2008). Other helpful studies are G. de Bertier de Sauvigny, *Metternich* (Paris 1986); A. Palmer, *Metternich* (London and New York 1972); and C. Zorgbibe, *Metternich, le séducteur diplomate* (Paris 2009). A selection of Metternich's papers have been published: *Aus Metternichs nach-gelassenen Papieren*, ed. R. von Metternich-Winneburg and A. von Klinckow-ström (8 vols., Vienna 1880–9). Much, however, remains unpublished, in the Acta Clementina series of the Czech National Archives, Prague.

16. Srbik, *Metternich*, vol. 1, pp. 79–80.

17. G. de Bertier de Sauvigny, *Metternich et son temps* (Paris 1959), p. 57.

18. Cited in Zorgbibe, *Metternich*, p. 485; Kissinger, *A World Restored*, p. 8.

19. This correspondence is in Metternich's papers in the National Archives of the Czech Republic, Prague: Acta Clementina 12/33 sg. C 50 carton 5 and 12/34 sg. C 50 carton 5.

20. The major published sources on Schwarzenberg are H. Kerchnawe and A. Veltzé, *Feldmarschall Karl Fürst zu Schwarzenberg* (Vienna and Leipzig 1913); *Briefe des Feldmarschalls Fürsten Schwarzenberg an seine Frau, 1799–1816*, ed. F. Novak (Vienna and Leipzig 1913); and K. zu Schwarzenberg, *Feld-marschall Fürst Schwarzenberg, der Sieger von Leipzig* (Vienna 1964). The major part of his papers is in the Schwarzenberg family archive, State Regional Archives of Trebon, Czech Republic.

21. The first major works covering the Austrian mediation, Oncken, *Österreich und Preussen* and F. Luckwaldt, *Österreich und die Anfänge des Befreiungskrieges von 1813* (Berlin 1898) are still unsurpassed in depth and detail. Also important are

Kissinger, *A World Restored*, pp. 19–28 and 41–82; and E. Kraehe, *Metternich's German Policy* (2 vols., Princeton, NJ, 1963–83), vol. 1, pp. 147–86.

22. See e.g. Sorel, *L'Europe et la Révolution française*, vol. 8, *passim*; T. Lentz, *Nouvelle histoire du premier empire* (4 vols., Paris 2002–10), vol. 2, pp. 387–436; J. Thiry, *La chute de Napoléon 1er. Lützen et Bautzen* (Paris 1971), and *La chute de Napoléon 1er. Leipzig* (Paris 1972).

23. Lentz, *Nouvelle histoire*, vol. 2, p. 398.

24. 'Autobiographische Denkschrift', *Aus Metternichs nachgelassenen Papieren*, vol. 1, p. 128.

25. See Zorgbibe, *Metternich*, pp. 18–21.

26. There is a a particularly cogent summary of Metternich's thinking in this area in P. W. Schroeder, *The Transformation of European Politics, 1763–1848* (Oxford 1996 edn), pp. 460–1.

27. Cited in Sorel, *L'Europe et la Révolution française*, vol. 8, p. 35.

28. The Metternich–Schwarzenberg correspondence is in the State Regional Archives of Trebon, Czech Republic, Schwarzenberg family archive, carton 128, II-87. Those written between 23 October 1813 and 17 October 1815 have been published in *Österreichs Theilnahme an den Befreiungskriegen*, ed. R. von Metternich-Winneburg and A. von Klinckowström (Vienna 1887); those written between 5 April and 23 October 1813 have not.

29. Schwarzenberg family archive, Trebon, carton 128, II-45 2/7.

30. Oncken, *Österreich und Preussen*, vol. 1, pp. 381–6; Metternich to Schwarzenberg, 11 December 1812, Schwarzenberg family archive, Trebon, carton 128, II-45 2/16.

31. Berthier to Schwarzenberg, 24 December 1812 and Metternich to Schwarzenberg, 16 January 1813, carton 123, II-45 3/18 and carton 128, II-45 2/25, Schwarzenberg family archive, Trebon. The most substantial biography of Berthier is still Général V. B. Derrécagaix, *Le maréchal Berthier, prince de Wagram et de Neuchâtel* (2 vols., Paris 1905).

32. For Britain's policy at this juncture I have relied on C. K. Webster, *The Foreign Policy of Castlereagh, 1812–1815: Britain and the Reconstruction of Europe* (London 1931) and (ed.), *British Diplomacy 1813–1815* (London 1921); also R. Muir, *Britain and the Defeat of Napoleon, 1807–1815* (New Haven and London 1996).

33. The fullest account of Bubna's mission to Paris is in Oncken, *Österreich und Preussen*, vol. 1, pp. 56–69.

34. For Wessenberg's mission, see Luckwaldt, *Österreich und die Anfänge*, pp. 12–27.

35. Luckwaldt, *Österreich und die Anfänge*, pp. 97–109; Sorel, *L'Europe et la Révolution française*, vol. 8, pp. 46–50.

36. Luckwaldt, *Österreich und die Anfänge*, pp. 50–1; Metternich to Count Zichy, Austrian minister to Berlin, 30 January 1813, published in Oncken, *Österreich und Preussen*, vol. 1, p. 416.

37. Lentz, *Nouvelle histoire*, vol. 2, pp. 398–400.

38. Lentz, *Nouvelle histoire*, vol. 2, pp. 363–5.

39. Dated 14 April 1813, the report is published in Oncken, *Österreich und Preussen*, vol. 2, pp. 618–25.

40. Oncken, *Österreich und Preussen*, vol. 2, p. 624.

41. Oncken, *Österreich und Preussen*, vol. 2, p. 620.

42. Oncken, *Österreich und Preussen*, vol. 2, p. 622.

43. Oncken, *Österreich und Preussen*, vol. 2, p. 622.

44. Oncken, *Österreich und Preussen*, vol. 2, p. 623.

45. For the events of 10 August 1792 and their background, see R. Allen, *Threshold of Terror: The Last Hours of the Monarchy in the French Revolution* (Stroud 1999); M. Reinhard, *La chute de la royauté. Le 10 août 1792* (Paris 1969); Sorel, *L'Europe et la Révolution française*, vol. 2; T. C. W. Blanning, *The Origins of the French Revolutionary Wars* (London 1986); and M. Price, *The Fall of the French Monarchy: Louis XVI, Marie Antoinette and the Baron de Breteuil* (London 2002).

46. E. de las Cases, *Mémorial de Ste-Hélène*, ed. A. Fugier (2 vols., Paris 1961), vol. 2, p. 101.

47. See e.g. J. Tulard, *Napoléon, ou le mythe du sauveur* (Paris 1977), pp. 54–5; S. Englund, *Napoleon: A Political Life* (Cambridge, Mass., 2004), pp. 50–1.

48. H. de Balzac, *Oeuvres complètes* (24 vols., Paris 1869–99), *La comédie humaine*, vol. 3, *Scènes de la vie privée, La femme de trente ans*, p. 6.

49. Balzac, *Oeuvres complètes: La comédie humaine*, vol. 3, *Scènes de la vie privée, La femme de trente ans*, p. 8.

CHAPTER 4

1. M. Leggiere, *Napoleon and Berlin: The Franco-Prussian War of 1813* (Stroud 2002), p. 44.

2. Leggiere, *Napoleon and Berlin*, p. 22; C. Clark, *Iron Kingdom: The Rise and Downfall of Prussia* (London 2006), p. 374.

3. Leggiere, *Napoleon and Berlin*, p. 280.

4. M. Kühn, *Johann Gottlob Fichte. Ein deutscher Philosoph* (Munich 2012), pp. 556–7.

5. For Stein's life and work, see G. Ritter, *Stein. Eine politische Biographie* (Stuttgart 1958); and H. Duchhardt and K. Teppe (eds.), *Karl vom und zum Stein: Der Akteur, der Autor, seine Wirkungs-und-Rezeptionsgeschichte* (Mainz 2003).

6. J. Breuilly, 'The Response to Napoleon and German Nationalism', in A. Forrest and P. Wilson (eds.), *The Bee and the Eagle: Napoleonic France and the End of the Holy Roman Empire, 1806* (London and Basingstoke 2009), p. 263; M. Broers, *Europe under Napoleon, 1799–1815* (London 1996), p. 239.

7. Clark, *Iron Kingdom*, pp. 309–13, 355–7.

8. D. Lieven, *Russia against Napoleon: The Battle for Europe, 1807–1814* (London 2009; 2010 edn), pp. 296–305.

9. Leggiere, *Napoleon and Berlin*, p. 47.

10. Clark, *Iron Kingdom*, pp. 326–7; Leggiere, *Napoleon and Berlin*, pp. 288–9.

11. For Yorck's biography, see P. Paret, *Yorck and the Era of Prussian Reform, 1807–1815* (Princeton, NJ 1966). The best source in English on Bülow is Leggiere, *Napoleon and Berlin*.

12. The most detailed works on Blücher are still W. von Unger, *Blücher* (2 vols., Berlin 1907–8) and (ed.), *Blüchers Briefe* (Stuttgart and Berlin 1913). For Blücher's delusions, see *Erinnerungen aus dem Leben des General-Feldmarschalls Hermann von Boyen*, ed. D. Schmitt (2 vols., Berlin 1990), vol. 1, pp. 362–3. There is one biography of Blücher in English, R. Parkinson, *Hussar General: The Life of Blücher, Man of Waterloo* (London 1975).

13. Lieven, *Russia against Napoleon*, pp. 37, 313–14; F. L. Petre, *Napoleon's Last Campaign in Germany. 1813* (London 1912), pp. 123–4, 145; R. Friederich, *Die Befreiungskriege 1813–1815* (2 vols., Berlin 1911–12), vol. 1, pp. 223–4.

14. Lieven, *Russia against Napoleon*, pp. 102–9, 283.

15. T. Lentz, *Nouvelle histoire du premier empire* (4 vols., Paris 2002–10), vol. 2, pp. 398–404; Lieven, *Russia against Napoleon*, pp. 307–8.

16. Lentz, *Nouvelle histoire*, vol. 2, pp. 402–3; Lieven, *Russia against Napoleon*, pp. 306–7.

17. D. G. Chandler, *The Campaigns of Napoleon* (London 1966; 1978 edn), pp. 875–8.

18. Leggiere, *Napoleon and Berlin*, pp. 278–81.

19. P. Young, *Napoleon's Marshals* (London 1973), p. 133.

20. For the battle of Lützen, see Petre, *Napoleon's Last Campaign in Germany*, pp. 68–90; Chandler, *The Campaigns of Napoleon*, pp. 881–7; and Lieven, *Russia against Napoleon*, pp. 315–16.

21. *Mémoires du duc de Raguse* (9 vols., Paris 1857), vol. 5, p. 15.

22. Chandler, *The Campaigns of Napoleon*, pp. 886–7.

23. Caulaincourt to Narbonne, 4 May 1813, Archives Nationales, Paris, Fonds Caulaincourt, 95 AP (Archives privées) carton 12, p. 604.

24. Leggiere, *Napoleon and Berlin*, p. 51.

25. A. Sorel, *L'Europe et la Révolution française* (8 vols., Paris 1885–1904), vol. 8, p. 109.

26. W. Oncken, *Österreich und Preussen im Befreiungskriege* (2 vols., Berlin 1876–79), vol. 2, pp. 307–10.

27. Metternich's instructions for Stadion are published in Oncken, *Österreich und Preussen im Befreiungskriege*, vol. 2, pp. 640–4.

28. Oncken, *Österreich und Preussen im Befreiungskriege*, vol. 2, p. 644.

29. Oncken, *Österreich und Preussen im Befreiungskriege*, vol. 2, p. 644.

30. Metternich's instructions for Bubna are also published in Oncken, *Österreich und Preussen im Befreiungskriege*, vol. 2, pp. 645–8.

31. Sorel, *L'Europe et la Révolution française*, vol. 8, p. 117; Lentz, *Nouvelle histoire*, vol. 2, p. 412.

32. Oncken, *Österreich und Preussen*, vol. 2, p. 648.

33. Oncken, *Österreich und Preussen*, vol. 2, pp. 316–19; Sorel, *L'Europe et la Révolution française*, vol. 8, pp. 115–17.

34. Bubna's report to Metternich on his meeting with Napoleon is published in Oncken, *Österreich und Preussen*, vol. 2, pp. 649–56.These quotations are on pp. 649–50.

35. Oncken, *Österreich und Preussen*, vol. 2, pp. 652, 650.

36. Oncken, *Österreich und Preussen*, vol. 2, p. 657.

37. Oncken, *Österreich und Preussen*, vol. 2, p. 651.

38. Oncken, *Österreich und Preussen*, vol. 2, p. 656.

39. Schwarzenberg family archive, State Regional Archive of Trebon, Czech Republic, carton 128, 11-87 42.

40. There is a recent biography of Caulaincourt: A. d'Arjuzon, *Caulaincourt, le confident de Napoléon* (Paris 2012), but the best study of him remains Jean Hanoteau's detailed preface to his edition of Caulaincourt's memoirs, *Mémoires du général de Caulaincourt, duc de Vicence, grand écuyer de l'empereur* (3 vols., Paris 1933), vol 1, pp. 1–234.

41. *Mémoires du général de Caulaincourt*, vol 1, pp. 53–81, 91–3.

42. The fullest study of Bassano is still A. Ernouf, *Maret, duc de Bassano* (Paris 1878), which contains important notes made by Bassano for memoirs he never published. For Talleyrand's opinion of him, see E. de Waresquiel, *Talleyrand. Le prince immobile* (Paris 2003), p. 427; and d'Arjuzon, *Caulaincourt*, p. 191.

43. Waresquiel, *Talleyrand*, pp. 389–401, *Mémoires du général de Caulaincourt*, vol. 1, pp. 281–99.

44. 'Autobiographische Denkschrift', *Aus Metternichs nachgelassenen Papieren*, ed. R. von Metternich-Winneburg and A. von Klinckowström (8 vols., Vienna 1880–89), vol. 1, p. 157; *Mémoires du général de Caulaincourt*, vol. 1, p. 325.

45. AN 95 AP carton 12, pièce 560, pp. 1–2.

46. AN 95 AP carton 18, typescript of Caulaincourt's MS 'Campagne de Saxe', pp. 210–12.

47. Chandler, *The Campaigns of Napoleon*, p. 890; Petre, *Napoleon's Last Campaign in Germany*, pp. 106–9.

48. Sorel, *L'Europe et la Révolution française*, vol. 8, p. 123.

CHAPTER 5

1. F. Petre, *Napoleon's Last Campaign in Germany: 1813* (London 1912), p. 127; G. Nafziger, *Napoleon at Lützen and Bautzen* (Chicago 1992), pp. 217–18.

2. Petre, *Napoleon's Last Campaign*, pp. 122–3, 130.

3. There are two fairly recent biographies of Ney: E. Perrin, *Le maréchal Ney* (Paris 1993); and F. Hulot, *Le maréchal Ney* (Paris 2000).

4. X. de Courville, *Jomini, ou le devin de Napoléon* (Paris 1935; 1981 edn, Lausanne), pp. 194–6.

5. D. G. Chandler, *The Campaigns of Napoleon* (London 1966; 1978 edn), p. 896.

6. Petre, *Napoleon's Last Campaign*, p. 137. On the cost of Bautzen to the French army, see C. Esdaile, *Napoleon's Wars: An International History, 1803–1815* (London 2007), pp. 502–3.

7. Caulaincourt, 'Campagne de 1813', typescript of ms, AN 95 AP carton 18, p. 241.

8. The best study of Barclay is M. and D. Josselson, *The Commander: A Life of Barclay de Tolly* (Oxford 1980).

9. D. Lieven, *Russia against Napoleon: The Battle for Europe, 1807–1814* (London 2009; 2010 edn), p. 324.

10. Lieven, *Russia against Napoleon*, p. 326.

11. Caulaincourt, 'Campagne de 1813', AN 95 AP carton 18, p. 259.

12. There are two identical typescripts of this section of Caulaincourt's memoirs, entitled 'Campagne de 1813' in his microfilmed papers in AN 95 AP carton 18; I have used the first one.

13. AP carton 18, p. 305.

14. AP carton 18, pp. 301–2.

15. *Mémoires du général de Caulaincourt, duc de Vicence, grand écuyer de l'empereur*, ed. J. Hanoteau (3 vols., Paris 1933), vol. 3, p. 456.

16. *Mémoires du général de Caulaincourt*, vol. 3, p. 353.

17. Caulaincourt to Berthier, 3 June 1813, AN 95 AP carton 14, pièce 309.

18. See Lieven, *Russia against Napoleon*, pp. 327–8; Chandler, *The Campaigns of Napoleon*, p. 899; T. Lentz, *Nouvelle histoire du premier empire* (4 vols., Paris 2002–10), vol. 2, pp. 410–11.

19. *Mémoires du général de Caulaincourt*, vol. 1, p. 138. This question of Caulaincourt's 'treason' is discussed exhaustively here (pp. 135–50).

20. *Mémoires du général de Caulaincourt*, vol. 1, pp. 135–6, 143.

21. Schwarzenberg family archive, State Regional Archives of Trebon, Czech Republic, carton 128, II-87 35.

22. W. Oncken, *Österreich und Preussen im Befreiungskriege* (2 vols., Berlin 1876–79), vol. 2, p. 324.

23. The correspondence of Metternich and Wilhelmina von Sagan for this period has been published: *Clemens Metternich–Wilhelmina von Sagan. Ein Briefwechsel, 1813–1815*, ed. Maria Ullrichova (Graz and Cologne, 1966).

24. The fullest discussion of these meetings is still Oncken, *Österreich und Preussen*, vol. 2, pp. 334–42; see also A. Sorel, *L'Europe et la Révolution française* (8 vols., Paris 1885–1904), vol. 8, pp. 133–7; and the recent analysis by A. Zamoyski, *Rites of Peace: The Fall of Napoleon and the Congress of Vienna* (London 2007), pp. 63–73.

25. Oncken, *Österreich und Preussen*, vol. 2, pp. 336–7.

26. J. M. Sherwig, *Guineas and Gunpowder: British Foreign Aid in the Wars with France, 1793–1815* (Cambridge, Mass. 1969), pp. 294–6. This is the standard work on Britain's subsidy policy towards her allies during the Revolutionary and Napoleonic wars.

27. Oncken, *Österreich und Preussen*, vol. 2, pp. 351–3; Sorel, *L'Europe et la Révolution française*, vol. 8, pp. 137–9; 'Autobiographische Denkschrift', *Aus Metternichs nachgelassenen Papieren*, ed. R. von Metternich-Winneburg and A. von Klinckowström (8 vols., Vienna 1880–9), vol. 1, pp. 146–8.

28. Oncken, *Österreich und Preussen*, vol. 2, pp. 356–63.

29. There are many editions of Gentz's works, but the most recent and comprehensive is *Friedrich Gentz. Gesammelte Schriften*, ed. G. Kronenbitter (12 vols., Hildesheim, Zurich, New York, Olms, 1997–2004). See also G. Kronenbitter, *Wort und Macht. Friedrich Gentz als politischer Schriftsteller* (Berlin 1994), and G. Mann, *Secretary of Europe. The Life of Friedrich Gentz, Enemy of Napoleon*, trans. W. H. Woglom (New Haven, Conn., 1946).

30. Oncken, *Österreich und Preussen*, vol. 2, pp. 364–7.

31. Oncken, *Österreich und Preussen*, vol. 2, p. 672.

32. 'Autobiographische Denkschrift', p. 150; Metternich to Eleonore Metternich, 28 June 1813, National Archives, Czech Republic, Prague, Acta Clementina 12/33 sg C50, carton 5.

33. A. J. F. Fain, *Manuscrit de 1813*, vol. 2 (Paris, 1825), 36–44; *Récits de la Captivité de l'empereur Napoléon à Ste-Hélène, par M le comte Montholon* (2 vols., Paris 1847), vol. 2, pp. 493–8. The version in Metternich's memoirs is in 'Autobiographische Denkschrift', pp. 150–7; Metternich's report to Francis I is published in Oncken, *Österreich und Preussen*, vol. 2, 384–6. Caulaincourt's account is in AN 95 AP, carton 12, 'Conversation de M de Metternich avec l'Empereur Napoléon, telle que Sa Majesté me l'a racontée', in two identical copies: pièces 620 and 621. It was published by Jean Hanoteau as 'Une nouvelle relation de l'entrevue de Napoléon et de Metternich à Dresde', *Revue d'Histoire Diplomatique* (octobre–décembre 1933), 421–40. Metternich's letter of 28 June 1813 to Eleonore Metternich is in the Czech National Archives, Acta Clementina 12/33, sg. C 50, carton 5.

34. Sorel, *L'Europe et la Révolution française*, vol. 8, pp. 144, 146, 147; Oncken, *Österreich und Preussen*, vol. 2, p. 391.

35. AN 95 AP carton 12, pièce 621, fos. 6–7.

36. AN 95 AP carton 12, pièce 621, fos 7–8; 'Autobiographische Denkschrift', p. 155; Metternich to Eleonore Metternich, 28 June 1813, Czech National Archives, Acta Clementina 12/33, sg C50, carton 5.

37. AN 95 AP carton 12, pièce 621, fos.15, 11, 13, 17.

38. Sorel, *L'Europe et la Révolution française*, vol. 8, pp. 41–2.

39. AN 95 AP carton 12 pièce 621, fo.6.

40. The most powerful statement of this argument is P. W. Schroeder, *The Transformation of European Politics* (Oxford 1994; 1996 edn), pp. 470–1.

41. AN 95 AP carton 12, pièce 621, fo.10.

42. AN 95 AP carton 12, pièce 621, fo.10.

43. *Récits de la captivité*, vol. 2, p. 497.

44. Metternich to Eleonore Metternich, 28 June 1813, Czech National Archives, Acta Clementina 12/33, sg C50, carton 5.
45. 'Autobiographische Denkschrift', p. 157.
46. Sorel, *L'Europe et la Révolution française*, vol. 8, p. 148.
47. Czech National Archives, Acta Clementina 12/33, sg C50, carton 5. This letter has been partially published in Zamoyski, *Rites of Peace*, p. 78; and in full in M. Price, 'Napoleon and Metternich in 1813: Some New and Some Neglected Evidence', *French History*, 26:4 (2012), pp. 502–3.
48. Price, 'Napoleon and Metternich in 1813', pp. 502–3.
49. 'Autobiographische Denkschrift', pp. 159–62.

CHAPTER 6

1. Within this substantial literature, I have relied here for the Napoleonic period on N. Petiteau, *Les Français et l'Empire, 1799–1815* (Paris 2008); D. Reynié, *Le triomphe de l'opinion publique. L'espace public français du 16ème au 20ème siècle* (Paris 1998); for the press, A. Cabanis, *La presse sous le consulat et l'empire, 1799–1814* (Paris 1975), and J.-P. Bertaud, *La presse et le pouvoir de Louis XIII à Napoléon 1er* (Paris 2000). For background I have consulted A. Farge, *Dire et mal dire. L'opinion publique au 18ème siècle* (Paris 1992); K. M. Baker, *Inventing the French Revolution: Essays on French Political Culture in the 18th Century* (Cambridge 1990); R. Monnier, *L'espace public démocratique. Essai sur l'opinion à Paris, de la Révolution au Directoire* (Paris 1994); and R. Chartier, *Les origines culturelles de la Révolution française* (Paris 1990).
2. P. M. Jones, *Reform and Revolution in France: The Politics of Transition, 1774–1791* (Cambridge 1995), pp. 72–3; D. Roche, *France in the Enlightenment* (Cambridge, Mass., 1998), p. 659.
3. E. de las Cases, *Mémorial de Ste-Hélène*, ed. A Fugier (2 vols., Paris 1961), vol. 1, p. 229.
4. See e.g. Prouver, prefect of the Indre, to Montalivet, 8 December 1812, Archives Nationales, Paris, série F1c III, Indre 7.
5. They are collected in the F1c III series.
6. 'Rapport sur les bruits répandus et l'esprit public', January 1814, F1cIII Bouches-du-Rhône 12, pièce 67.
7. Barante to Montalivet, 6 June 1813, AN F1c III, Loire-Inférieure 11.
8. The departments analysed here are Aveyron, Bouches-du-Rhone, Calvados, Charente, Côte-d'Or, Doubs, Forêts, Gironde, Hautes-Alpes, Haute-Loire, Indre, Loire-Inférieure, Nord, Rhône, Seine, and Yonne. This includes the cities of Lyon, Marseille, Bordeaux, and Lille. For Paris, where the prefect of police submitted the reports on public opinion, see pp. 205–8.
9. Jourdan, prefect of Forêts, to Montalivet, 4 March 1813, AN F1c III, Forêts 6.
10. 'Département de la Charente, Etat de situation politique et morale, 1er trimestre 1813', AN F1c III, Charente 9.

11. Prouver to Montalivet, 18 February 1813, AN F1c III, Indre 7; Rougier de la Bergerie, prefect of the Yonne, to Montalivet, 2 March 1813, AN F1c III, Yonne 10; Barante to Montalivet, 5 March 1813, AN F1c III, Loire-Inférieure 11.

12. Chazal, prefect of the Hautes-Alpes, to Montalivet, 19 March 1813, AN F1c III, Hautes-Alpes 5.

13. 'Rapports sur les bruits répandus et l'esprit public', July 1813, AN F1c III, Bouches-du-Rhône 12, pièce 40; baron du Plantier, prefect of the Nord, to Montalivet, 14 June 1813, AN F1c III, Nord 14, pièce 139; Méchin, prefect of Calvados, to Montalivet, 10 July 1813, AN F1c III, Calvados 4; Barante to Montalivet, 6 June 1813, AN F1c III, Loire-Inférieure 11; Prouver to Montalivet, 8 June 1813, AN F1c III, Indre 7; Taillepied de Bondy, prefect of the Rhone, to Montalivet, 30 June 1813, AN F1c III, Rhone 9; Boissy d'Anglas, prefect of the Charente, to Montalivet, 7 June 1813, AN F1c III, Charente 12.

14. Du Plantier to Montalivet, 14 June 1813, AN F1c III, Nord 14.

15. Barante to Montalivet, 6 June 1813, AN F1c III, Loire-Inférieure 11.

16. *Lettres et papiers du chancelier comte de Nesselrode*, ed. A. von Nesselrode (11 vols., Paris 1904–11), vol. 2, p. 99.

17. W. Oncken, *Österreich und Preussen im Befreiungskriege* (2 vols., Berlin 1876–79), vol. 2, pp. 397–9.

18. For Bernadotte's role and policy in this period, see L. Pingaud, *Bernadotte, Napoléon et les Bourbons, 1797–1844* (Paris 1901); D. P. Barton, *Bernadotte, Prince and King, 1810–1844* (London 1925); and F. D. Scott, *Bernadotte and the Fall of Napoleon* (Cambridge 1934).

19. For the Trachenberg plan, see *Geschichte der Kampfe Österreichs: Kriege unter der Regierung des Kaisers Franz, Befreiungskriege 1813 und 1814* (5 vols., Vienna 1913), vol. 3, E. Glaise von Horstenau, *Feldzug von Dresden*, pp. 3–6; F. L. Petre, *Napoleon's Last Campaign in Germany: 1813* (London 1912), pp. 181–4; and A. Sked, *Radetzky: Imperial Victor and Military Genius* (London 2011), pp. 40–3.

20. The question of the exact paternity of the Trachenberg plan remains controversial, and will probably never fully be resolved. Of the most recent literature, Sked, *Radetzky*, p. 41, supports Radetzky's claim, while Lieven, *Russia against Napoleon*, p. 369, puts the case for Toll.

21. Cited in R. Friederich, *Geschichte des Herbstfeldzuges 1813* (3 vols., Berlin 1903–6), vol. 1, pp. 98–9.

22. For Humboldt's biography, see P. R. Sweet, *Wilhelm von Humboldt. A Biography* (2 vols., Columbus, Oh. 1978). There is no biography of Anstett. For Metternich's displeasure at Anstett's nomination, see Comte de Narbonne, French plenipotentiary at Prague, to Bassano, 11 July 1813, AN 95 AP carton 13, pièce 39, no. 2.

23. The original of Metternich's memorandum is in the Haus-Hof-und-Staatsarchiv, Vienna, Staatskanzlei 194, Vorträge 1813 (VI–VII) fos. 67–71, and is published in Oncken, *Österreich und Preussen*, vol. 2, pp. 402–8.

24. Oncken, *Österreich und Preussen*, vol. 2, p. 404.

25. A. Sorel, *L'Europe et la Révolution française* (8 vols., Paris 1885–1904), vol. 8, p. 138.

26. Oncken, *Österreich und Preussen*, vol. 2, pp. 407–8.

27. L. Lecestre, *Lettres inédites de Napoléon Ier* (2 vols., Paris 1897), vol. 2, p. 274. Oncken, *Österreich und Preussen*, vol. 2, p. 432.

28. Caulaincourt, '1813. Conversation de l'empereur Napoléon avec le duc de Vicence avant son départ pour Mayence, et celui du duc de Vicence pour Prague', AN 95 AP carton 12, pièce 623, p. 1.

29. AN 95 AP carton 12, pièce 623, p. 2.

30. AN 95 AP carton 12, pièce 623, pp. 6, 9.

31. AN 95 AP carton 12, pièce 623, pp. 9, 10.

32. AN 95 AP carton 12, pièce 623, pp. 11–12.

33. AN 95 AP carton 12, pièce 623, p. 13.

34. AN 95 AP carton 13, Congrès de Prague, dossiers 34–48, pièce 327.

35. AN 95 AP carton 13, Congrès de Prague, dossiers 34–48, pièce 327.

36. Caulaincourt, '1813. Conversation de l'empereur Napoléon avec le duc de Vicence avant son départ pour Mayence, et celui du duc de Vicence pour Prague', AN 95 AP carton 12, pièce 623, p. 14.

37. See e.g. Sorel, *L'Europe et la Révolution française*, vol. 8, p. 154: 'Le congrès de Prague ne fut qu'un solennel trompe-l'œil'; and A Zamoyski, *Rites of Peace: The Fall of Napoleon and the Congress of Vienna* (London 2007), p. 82, ch. heading: 'Farce in Prague'.

38. 'Premier rapport sur la marche de la négociation à Prague. Prague, le 28 juillet 1813', Haus-Hof-und-Staatsarchiv, Vienna, Staatskanzlei 194, Vorträge 1813 (VI–VII), fos. 6–9.

39. Archives du Ministère des Affaires Etrangères, Paris, série Mémoires et Documents France, vol. 667, fo. 23.

40. AN 95 AP carton 13, pièce 39, no. 16.

41. AN 95 AP carton 13, pièces 401, 382.

42. AN 95 AP carton 13, pièce 39, nos. 10, 16.

43. Caulaincourt, '1813. Conversation de l'empereur Napoléon avec le duc de Vicence avant son départ pour Mayence, et celui du duc de Vicence pour Prague', AN 95 AP carton 12, pièce 623, p. 14.

44. Sorel, *L'Europe et la Révolution française*, vol. 8, pp. 169–70.

45. Sorel, *L'Europe et la Révolution française*, vol. 8, pp. 171–2.

46. Published in Oncken, *Österreich und Preussen*, vol. 2, p. 682.

47. Caulaincourt to Napoleon, 8 August 1813, AN 95 AP carton 13, pièce 402.

48. Sorel, *L'Europe et la Révolution française*, vol. 8, p. 174; *Correspondance de l'empereur Napoléon Ier, publiée par ordre de l'empereur Napoléon III* (32 vols., Paris 1858–70), vol. 26, p. 23.

49. Oncken, *Österreich und Preussen*, vol. 2, pp. 455–7.

50. Bassano to Caulaincourt, 13 August 1813, AN 95 AP carton 13, pièce 429.

51. Oncken, *Österreich und Preussen*, vol. 2, p. 456.

52. Oncken, *Österreich und Preussen*, vol. 2, p. 684.

53. Sorel, *L'Europe et la Révolution française*, vol. 8, pp. 175–6.

54. Caulaincourt to Bassano, midnight, 11 August 1813, AN 95 AP carton 13, pièce 454.

55. Bassano to Caulaincourt, 13 August 1813, AN 95 AP carton 13, pièce 415.

56. Caulaincourt to Bassano, 15 August 1813, AN 95 AP carton 13, pièce 460.

57. AN 95 AP carton 13, pièce 460.

58. AP 95 AP carton 13, pièce 460.

59. Bassano to Caulaincourt, 13 August 1813, AN 95 AP carton 13, pièce 415.

60. Bubna to Metternich, 9 August 1813, published in Oncken, *Österreich und Preussen*, vol. 2, p. 686.

61. Caulaincourt to Bassano, 9 August 1813, AN 95 AP carton 13, pièce 449.

62. 'Rapport sur les bruits publics et l'esprit public', AN F1c III, Bouches du Rhône 12, pièce 40.

63. Baron de Valsuzenay, prefect of the Gironde, to Montalivet, minister of the interior, 7 August 1813, AN F1c III, Gironde 9, pièce 209. A copy of the handbill is attached to this as pièce 210.

64. Boissy d'Anglas, prefect of the Charente, to Montalivet, 7 August 1813, AN F1c III Charente 12; AN F1c III Gironde 9, pièce 211.

65. 'Rapport sur les bruits répandus et l'esprit public' AN F1c III Bouches du Rhone 12, pièce 36.

66. Boissy d'Anglas to Montalivet, 7 August 1813, AN F1c III Charente 12; Valsuzenay to Montalivet, 7 September 1813, AN F1c III Gironde 9, pièce 214.

67. Baron du Plantier, prefect of the Nord, to Montalivet, 17 September 1813, AN F1c III Nord 14.

CHAPTER 7

1. *Briefe des Feldmarschalls Fürsten Schwarzenberg an seine Frau, 1799–1816*, ed. J. F. Novak (Vienna 1913), pp. 327–8.

2. For Clam's biography, see E. Wertheimer, 'Clam-Martinitz, Graf Karl Joseph Nepomuk', *Allgemeine Deutsche Biographie* (vol. 47, Leipzig, 1903), pp. 490–6.

3. Papiere aus dem Nachlasse des Grafen Carl Clam-Martinic, Burg Clam, Austria, no. 12, pp. 75–102, 'Erinnerungen an die Campagne von 1813'.

4. 'Erinnerungen an die Campagne von 1813', p. 78.

5. 'Erinnerungen an die Campagne von 1813', pp. 80–1.

6. 'Erinnerungen an die Campagne von 1813', pp. 81–2.

7. *Geschichte der Kampfe Österreichs. Kriege unter den Regierung des Kaisers Franz. Befreiungskriege, 1813 und 1814* (5 vols., Vienna 1913), vol. 3, E. Glaise von Horstenau, *Feldzug von Dresden*, pp. 9–14; G. E. Rothenberg, *Napoleon's Great Adversaries: Archduke Charles and the Austrian Army, 1792–1814* (London 1982), pp. 174–9.

8. Glaise von Horstenau, *Feldzug von Dresden*, pp. 11–12.

9. *General Wilson's Journal, 1812–1814*, ed. Anthony Brett-James (London 1964), p. 165.

10. Lieutenant-general Charles William Vane (Stewart), marquess of Londonderry, *Narrative of the war in Germany and France in 1813 and 1814* (London 1830), p. 106.

11. D. Lieven, *Russia against Napoleon: The Battle for Europe, 1807–1814* (London 2009; 2010 edn), pp. 393–4.

12. Rothenberg, *Napoleon's Great Adversaries*, pp. 181–4.

13. *Briefe des Feldmarschalls Fürsten Schwarzenberg*, p. 330.

14. 'Erinnerungen an die Campagne von 1813', p. 83.

15. 'Erinnerungen an die Campagne von 1813', pp. 84, 85.

16. 'Erinnerungen an die Campagne von 1813', p. 99.

17. *Briefe des Feldmarschalls Fürsten Schwarzenberg*, p. 332.

18. For Moreau's biography, see E. Daudet, *L'exil et la mort du général Moreau* (Paris 1909); and F. Hulot, *Le général Moreau, adversaire et victime de Napoléon* (Paris 2001).

19. Daudet, *L'exil et la mort du général Moreau*, pp. 186, 206.

20. D. G. Chandler, *The Campaigns of Napoleon* (London 1966; 1978 edn), p. 902.

21. Chandler, *The Campaigns of Napoleon*, p. 902; M. V. Leggiere, *Napoleon and Berlin: The Franco-Prussian War of 1813* (Stroud 2002), pp. 136–7; Lieven, *Russia against Napoleon*, pp. 422–3.

22. Leggiere, *Napoleon and Berlin*, pp. 74–5.

23. Leggiere, *Napoleon and Berlin*, p. 164.

24. Leggiere, *Napoleon and Berlin*, pp. 166–73; F. L. Petre, *Napoleon's Last Campaign in Germany: 1813* (London 1912), pp. 260–2.

25. Chandler, *The Campaigns of Napoleon*, pp. 903–6.

26. Glaise von Horstenau, *Feldzug von Dresden*, pp. 158–61.

27. *Briefe des Feldmarschalls Fürsten Schwarzenberg*, p. 333.

28. Glaise von Horstenau, *Feldzug von Dresden*, pp. 196–209; Petre, *Napoleon's Last Campaign in Germany*, p. 203–4.

29. 'Erinnerungen an die Campagne von 1813', p. 92.

30. 'Erinnerungen an die Campagne von 1813', p. 95.

31. H. Aster, *Schilderungen der Kriegsereignisse in und vor Dresden, vom 7 März bis 28 August 1813* (Dresden and Leipzig, 1844), p. 187.

32. Aster, *Schilderungen der Kriegsereignisse in und vor Dresden*, p. 126; Petre, *Napoleon's Last Campaign in Germany*, pp. 201–2.

33. *General Wilson's Journal*, p. 167.

34. Aster, *Schilderungen*, p. 123; *General Wilson's Journal*, p. 168.

35. Petre, *Napoleon's Last Campaign in Germany*, p. 211.

36. 'Erinnerungen an die Campagne von 1813', pp. 95–6.

37. *General Wilson's Journal*, p. 170.

38. 'Erinnerungen an die Campagne von 1813', p. 99.

39. *Briefe des Feldmarschalls Fürsten Schwarzenberg*, p. 333.

40. Aster, *Schilderungen*, p. 155.

41. Lieven, *Russia against Napoleon*, pp. 400–4.

42. See T. von Bernhardi, *Denkwürdigkeiten aus dem Leben von kaiserl. russ. Generals der Infanterie Carl Friedrich Grafen von Toll* (4 vols., Leipzig, 1856–58), vol. 2, pp. 177–87.

43. 'Erinnerungen an die Campagne von 1813', pp. 98–9.

44. Petre, *Napoleon's Last Campaign in Germany*, pp. 233–4.

45. See Petre, *Napoleon's Last Campaign in Germany*, pp. 241–9; Lieven, *Russia against Napoleon*, pp. 417–18.

46. See J. Kemble, *Napoleon Immortal: The Medical History and Private Life of Napoleon Bonaparte* (London 1959), pp. 199–200.

47. 'Erinnerungen an die Campagne von 1813', p. 101.

48. On Macdonald, see his own memoirs, *Souvenirs du maréchal Macdonald, duc de Tarente* (Paris 1892); and A. Hankinson, 'His Outspokenness', in D. G. Chandler (ed.), *Napoleon's Marshals* (London 1987).

49. Petre, *Napoleon's Last Campaign in Germany*, pp. 256–8.

50. Lieven, *Russia against Napoleon*, p. 385.

51. Macdonald to Nancy [Macdonald], comtesse de Gronau, 8 September 1813, AN 279 AP, Fonds Massa, carton 8, dossier 'Lettres du maréchal Macdonald, 1813'.

52. Schwarzenberg to Metternich, 14th April 1813, published in Oncken, *Österreich und Preussen*, vol. 2, p. 625.

CHAPTER 8

1. F. L. Petre, *Napoleon's Last Campaign in Germany: 1813* (London 1912), p. 270.

2. M. V. Leggiere, *Napoleon and Berlin: The Franco-Prussian War of 1813* (Stroud 2002), pp. 190–2.

3. On the battle of Dennewitz, see Leggiere, *Napoleon and Berlin*, pp. 193–211; Petre, *Napoleon's Last Campaign in Germany*, pp. 272–8; D. Lieven, *Russia against Napoleon: The Battle for Europe, 1807–1814* (London 2009; 2010 edn), pp. 423–5.

4. Leggiere, *Napoleon and Berlin*, pp. 221–2.

5. See e.g. R. von Friederich, *Die Befreiungskriege, 1813–1815* (2 vols., Berlin 1911–12), vol. 2, pp. 139–44.

6. Leggiere, *Napoleon and Berlin*, p. 294.

7. A. Sorel, *L'Europe et la Révolution française* (8 vols., Paris 1885–1904), vol. 8, p. 154.

8. Sorel, *L'Europe et la Révolution française*, vol. 8, p. 190.

9. L. Pingaud, *Bernadotte, Napoléon et les Bourbons, 1797–1844* (Paris 1901), pp. 219–44.

10. Petre, *Napoleon's Last Campaign in Germany*, p. 292.

11. L. Gouvion Saint-Cyr, *Mémoires pour servir à l'histoire militaire sous le directoire, le consulat et l'empire* (4 vols., Paris 1831), vol. 4, pp. 150–1.

12. D. G. Chandler, *The Campaigns of Napoleon* (London 1966; 1978 edn), pp. 916–17.

13. Saint-Cyr, *Mémoires*, vol. 4, pp. 184–90.

14. Petre, *Napoleon's Last Campaign in Germany*, p. 305.

15. '1813. Départ de Dresde. Conversation et ordres de l'empereur', AN 95 AP carton 12, pièce 656.

16. The best modern biographies of Murat are J. Tulard, *Murat, ou l'éveil des nations* (Paris 1983); and J.-C. Gillet, *Murat* (Paris 2008).

17. Gillet, *Murat* pp. 318–19.

18. 'Conversation avec l'empereur au sujet du Traité de paix', in V. B. Derrécagaix, *Les états-majors de Napoléon. Le lieutenant-général comte Belliard, chef d'état-major de Murat* (Paris 1908), pp. 541, 542–3.

19. Derrécagaix, *Les états-majors de Napoléon*, p. 543.

20. Petre, *Napoleon's Last Campaign in Germany*, p. 313.

21. '1813. Projets ministériels au depart de Dresde; ce qui les changea. Séjour à Düben. Paroles de sentiment du général Bertrand en revoyant l'empereur après Leipsick pour qu'il passe le Saal', AN 95 AP carton 12, pièce 644.

22. AN 95 AP carton 12, pièce 644.

23. Cited in D. Smith, *1813: Leipzig: Napoleon and the Battle of the Nations* (London 2001), p. 49.

24. Cited in Smith, *1813*, p. 58.

25. 'Notes de M de Rumigny, sécrétaire du cabinet de l'empereur, sur ce que sa majesté et d'autres personnes lui ont dit lors des différentes missions que l'empereur lui a donné au congrès de Châtillon et sur ce que sa majesté l'a chargé de dire au duc de Vicence', AN 95 AP carton 14, dossier 20, pièce 23, fo. 4.

26. Lieven, *Russia against Napoleon*, pp. 440–2.

27. Cited in Smith, *1813*, pp. 128–9.

28. Petre, *Napoleon's Last Campaign in Germany*, p. 343.

29. Petre, *Napoleon's Last Campaign in Germany*, pp. 344–8; Smith, *1813*, pp. 138–51.

30. Sorel, *L'Europe et la Révolution française*, vol. 8, pp. 191–3; Smith, *1813*, pp. 161–4; R. Friederich, *Geschichte des Herbstfeldzuges 1813* (3 vols., Berlin 1903–6), vol. 3 pp. 117–18.

31. Smith, *1813*, pp. 210–11; Petre, *Napoleon's Last Campaign in Germany*, p. 364 n. 1.

32. Petre, *Napoleon's Last Campaign in Germany*, pp. 365–6.

33. Cited in Smith, *1813*, p. 217.

34. Smith, *1813*, pp. 248–9; C. Clark, *Iron Kingdom: The Rise and Downfall of Prussia, 1600–1947* (London 2006), pp. 369–70.

35. Petre, *Napoleon's Last Campaign in Germany*, pp. 379; *Mémoires du général baron de Marbot*, ed. J. Garnier (2 vols., Paris 1983), vol. 2, p. 522.

36. Smith, *1813*, p. 277.

37. Smith, *1813*, pp. 297–300.

38. Blücher to Otto von Bonin, *Blüchers Briefe*, ed. W. von Unger (Stuttgart and Berlin 1913), p. 187.

CHAPTER 9

1. *General Wilson's Journal*, ed. A Brett-James (London 1964), p. 212; F. L. Petre, *Napoleon's Last Campaign in Germany: 1813* (London 1912), p. 388.

2. See P. W. Schroeder, *The Transformation of European Politics, 1763–1848* (Oxford 1994; 1996 edn), pp. 478–82.

3. Saint-Aignan to Caulaincourt, 26 October 1813, AN 95 AP carton 14, dossier 2, attachment to pièce 1 no.4.

4. The original of Saint-Aignan's report, written on 15 November 1813, on the allied overtures made to him is in Archives du Ministère des Affaires Etrangères, série Mémoires et documents France vol. 668, fos. 10–15. It is published in A. J. F. Fain, *Manuscrit de 1814* (Paris 1825), pp. 49–56. Metternich to Schwarzenberg, 27 October 1813, published in *Österreichs Theilnahme an den Befreiungskriegen. Ein Beitrag zur Geschichte der Jahre 1813 bis 1815* ed. R. von Metternich-Winneburg and A. von Klinckowström (Vienna 1887), p. 770.

5. *Clemens Metternich–Wilhelmina von Sagan. Ein Briefwechsel, 1813–1815*, ed. Maria Ullrichova (Graz and Cologne 1966), p. 100.

6. Fain, *Manuscrit de 1814*, p. 56.

7. The idea that the French Revolution and Napoleon merely continued a policy of attaining France's 'natural' frontiers pursued by the French kings since at least the sixteenth century forms the guiding principle of A. Sorel, *L'Europe et la Révolution française* (8 vols., Paris 1885–1904), and is set out in most detail in vol. 1, pp. 244–337. Sorel's thesis was strongly challenged in the 1930s by Gaston Zeller, especially in his article 'La monarchie d'ancien régime et les frontières naturelles', *Revue d'histoire moderne*, 8 (1933), pp. 305–33. The question has been reassessed more recently by P. Sahlins, 'Natural Frontiers Revisited: France's Boundaries since the Seventeenth Century', *The American Historical Review*, 5:5 (Dec. 1990), pp. 1423–51.

8. *Discours civiques de Danton*, ed. H. Fleischmann (Paris 1920), p. 48. See also J. Smets, 'Le Rhin, frontière naturelle de la France', *Annales historiques de la Révolution française*, 314 (1998), pp. 675–98, esp. pp. 679–80.

9. C. K. Webster, *The Foreign Policy of Castlereagh, 1812–1815: Britain and the Reconstruction of Europe* (London 1931), pp. 183–5, and (ed.), *British Diplomacy, 1813–1815* (London 1921), p. xl; R. Muir, *Britain and the Defeat of Napoleon, 1807–1815* (New Haven and London 1996), pp. 232–4.

10. For Aberdeen's biography, see L. Iremonger, *Lord Aberdeen* (London 1978); and M. E. Chamberlain, *Lord Aberdeen, a Political Biography* (London 1983).

11. Chamberlain, *Lord Aberdeen*, pp. 134–5.

12. Fain, *Manuscrit de 1814*, p. 53; Aberdeen to Castlereagh, 9 November 1813, published in Webster (ed.), *British Diplomacy*, p. 110.

13. 'Autobiographische Denkschrift', in *Aus Metternichs nachgelassenen Papieren*, ed. R. von Metternich-Winneburg and A. von Klinckowström (8 vols., Vienna 1880–4), vol. 1, pp. 177–8.

14. Schroeder, *The Transformation of European politics*, pp. 460–3.

15. Sorel, *L'Europe et la Révolution française*, vol. 8, p. 213; Castlereagh to Lord Liverpool, 30 January 1814, published in Webster (ed.), *British Diplomacy*, pp. 144–5.

16. *Österreichs Theilnahme an den Befreiungskriegen*, p. 774.

17. Metternich to state councillor Josef von Hudelist, 9 November 1813, published in A. Fournier, *Der Congress von Châtillon* (Vienna and Prague 1900), p. 242; M. V. Leggiere, *The Fall of Napoleon: The Allied Invasion of France, 1813–1814* (Cambridge 2007), p. 23.

18. Leggiere, *The Fall of Napoleon*, pp. 25–6; Sorel, *L'Europe et la Révolution française*, vol. 8, p. 209.

19. Leggiere, *The Fall of Napoleon*, pp. 25–8.

20. Fain, *Manuscrit de 1814*, p. 58.

21. A. Ernouf, *Maret, duc de Bassano* (Paris 1878), pp. 606–7.

22. Sorel, *L'Europe et la Révolution française*, vol. 8, pp. 221–3.

23. '1813. Retraite de Leipzick', AN 95 AP carton 12, pièce 639.

24. E. de Waresquiel, *Talleyrand. Le prince immobile* (Paris 2003), p. 398; AN 95 AP carton 12, pièce 639.

25. AN 95 AP carton 12, pièce 639.

26. '1813. Proposition de ministre des affaires étrangères', AN 95 AP carton 12, pièce 642.

27. Fain, *Manuscrit de 1814*, p. 63.

28. 'Projet d'instructions générales pour le duc de Vicence, d'après une dictée de l'empereur, du 2 décembre 1813', AAE MDF fos. 38–62.

29. AAE MDF fo. 41.

30. AAE MDF fo. 42.

31. AAE MDF fos. 44–6.

32. AAE MDF fos. 47, 48.

33. AAE MDF fos. 50–1.

34. AAE MDF fo. 48.

35. AAE MDF fo. 53.

36. AAE MDF fos. 53–4.

37. AAE MDF fos. 54–5.

38. AAE MDF fos. 57–61.

39. AAE MDF fos. 56–7.

40. AAE MDF fo. 45.

41. AN 95 AP carton 18, dossier 2, 'Campagne de Saxe', pp. 92–3.

42. Castlereagh to Aberdeen, 7 December 1813, published in Webster (ed.), *British Diplomacy*, p. 116.

43. Leggiere, *The Fall of Napoleon*, p. 61.

44. 'Autobiographische Denkschrift', in *Aus Metternichs nachgelassenen Papieren*, vol. 1, p. 184.

45. Lieutenant-general Charles William Vane [Stewart], marquess of Londonderry, *Narrative of the War in Germany and France in 1813 and 1814* (London 1830), pp. 254–5.

CHAPTER 10

1. Taillepied de Bondy, prefect of the Rhône, to Montalivet, minister of the interior, 4 November 1813, AN F1cIII Rhône 9, dossier 1811–1814; Prouver, prefect of the Indre, to Montalivet, 5 November 1813, AN F1c III Indre 7, dossier 1806–1813; Debry, prefect of the Doubs, to Montalivet, 25 November 1813, AN F1cIII Doubs 8, dossier 1812–1819, pièce 10.

2. T. Lentz, *Nouvelle histoire du premier empire* (4 vols., Paris, 2002–10), p. 136; H. Houssaye, *1814* (Paris 1888; 1911 edn), pp. 8–9; Cossé-Brissac, prefect of the Côte-d'Or, to Montalivet, 14 November 1814, AN F1cIII Côte-d'Or 9, pièces 218, 238.

3. Cossé-Brissac to Montalivet, 7 November 1813, AN F1cIII Côte-d'Or 9, pièce 219.

4. Debry to Montalivet, 10 November 1813, AN F1cIII Doubs 8, pièce 11.

5. AN F1c III Gironde 9, pièce 220.

6. Anonymous to Cossé-Brissac, 12 December 1813, AN F1c III Côte-d'Or 9, pièce 225.

7. Micaut, sub-prefect of Pontarlier, to Debry, 22 November 1813, AN F1cIII Doubs 8, pièce 13.

8. AN F1c III Nord 14, pièce 180.

9. Beugnot to Montalivet, 30 December 1813, AN F1c III Nord 14, pièce 208.

10. Beugnot to Montalivet, 17 January 1814, 'Rapport sur la sédition de l'arrondissement de Hazebrouck', AN F1c III Nord 14, pièce 173.

11. Cossé-Brissac to Montalivet, 13 December 1813, AN F1c III Côte-d'Or 9, pièce 238.

12. J. Thiry, *La chute de Napoléon 1er* (2 vols., Paris 1938–9), vol. 1 p. 26.

13. Fain, *Manuscrit de 1814* (1825), pp.10–11; *Histoire de mon temps. Mémoires du chancelier Pasquier*, ed. duc d'Audiffret-Pasquier (6 vols., Paris 1893–5), vol. 2, p. 117; E. de Perceval, *Un adversaire de Napoléon. Le vicomte Lainé, 1767–1835* (2 vols., Paris 1926), pp. 189–90.

14. I. Collins, *Napoleon and his Parliaments* (London 1979), p. 135.

15. Perceval, *Lainé*, vol. 1, pp. 97–9, 181.

16. Perceval, *Lainé*, vol. 1, pp. 137–41.

17. Bibliothèque Municipale de Bordeaux, MS 2029 Fonds Lainé, carton 33 fos. 47, 53, 75; carton 34. 'Extrait de l'histoire de la maison de Stuart par Hume', unnumbered notes on 'Histoire d'Angleterre de Mme Makaulai'.

18. Cited in Perceval, *Lainé*; BMB MS 2029 carton 34, unnumbered notes.

19. 'Notice sur les événements de décembre 1813', BMB MS 2029 carton 106, fo. 294.

20. For the most comprehensive recent treatment of the *Cahiers de doléances*, see G. Shapiro and J. Markoff, *Revolutionary Demands: A Content Analysis of the cahiers de doléances of 1789* (Stanford, Calif., 1998).

21. 'Notice sur les événements de décembre 1813', BMB MS 2029 carton 106, fo. 296.

22. Perceval, *Lainé*, vol. 1, pp. 213–14.

23. Perceval, *Lainé*, vol. 1, p. 215.

24. 'Notes préparatoires', BMB MS 2029 carton 106, fo. 304.

25. BMB MS 2029 carton 106, fo. 304.

26. BMB MS 2029 carton 106, fo. 304.

27. BMB MS 2029 carton 106, fo. 297.

28. BMB MS 2029 carton 106, fos. 297–8.

29. A. J. F. Fain, *Manuscrit de 1814* (Paris 1825), p. 23.

30. Cited in Perceval, *Lainé*, vol. 1, p. 224.

31. Perceval, *Lainé*, vol. 1, p. 220, n. 1.

32. BMB MS 2029, Correspondance des Lainé, IV, 'Situation matérielle et morale à l'époque du 17 décembre 1812' (unnumbered).

33. 'Notes préparatoires', BMB MS 2029 carton 106, fo. 304.

34. 'Campagne de Saxe—1813', AN 95 AP carton 18, dossier 2, p. 94.

35. C. Jones, *The Longman Companion to the French Revolution* (London and Harlow 1988; 1990 edn), pp. 68, 143–4; *Histoire de mon temps. Mémoires du chancelier Pasquier*, ed. duc d'Audiffret-Pasquier (6 vols., Paris 1893–5), vol. 2, p. 132.

36. *Mémoires du duc de Rovigo, pour servir à l'histoire de l'empereur Napoléon* (8 vols., Paris 1828), vol. 6, pp. 294–5.

37. Lentz, *Nouvelle histoire*, vol. 2, pp. 531–2; Houssaye, *1814*, p. 32.

CHAPTER 11

1. D. G. Chandler, *The Campaigns of Napoleon* (London 1966; 1978 edn), p. 952; M. V. Leggiere, *The Fall of Napoleon: The Allied Campaign in France, 1813–1814* (Cambridge 2007), pp. 488–9, 518–19.

2. Blücher to General von Rüchel, 14 January 1814, *Blüchers Briefe*, ed. W. von Unger (Stuttgart and Berlin 1913), p. 219.

3. *Österreichs Theilnahme an den Befreiungskriegen*, ed. R. von Metternich-Winneburg and A. von Klinckowström (Vienna 1887), pp. 798, 800.

4. Metternich to state councillor Josef von Hudelist, 30 January 1814, published in A. Fournier, *Der Congress von Châtillon* (Vienna and Prague 1900), p. 252. For Castlereagh's biography, see C. J. Bartlett, *Castlereagh* (1966); J. W. Derry, *Castlereagh* (London 1976); W. Hinde, *Castlereagh* (London 1981); and J. Bew, *Castlereagh: A Life* (Oxford 2012). C. K. Webster, *The Foreign Policy of*

Castlereagh: Britain and the Reconstruction of Europe, 1812–1815 (London 1931) remains important.

5. Fournier, *Der Congress von Châtillon*, pp. 53–4.

6. See Pitt's state paper of 19 January 1805, which formed the basis of Castlereagh's continental policy, published in C. K. Webster, *British Diplomacy, 1813–1815* (London 1921), pp. 389–94.

7. Webster, *British Diplomacy*, p. 390.

8. Castlereagh to Lord Liverpool, prime minister, 22 January 1814, Webster, *British Diplomacy*, pp. 135–6; Fournier, *Der Congress von Châtillon*, pp. 206–7.

9. *Briefe des Feldmarschalls Fürsten Schwarzenberg an seine Frau*, ed. F. Novak (Vienna and Leipzig 1913), p. 369.

10. Cited in Leggiere, *The fall of Napoleon*, pp. 546–7.

11. Metternich's memorandum, dated 27 January 1814, is in the Haus-Hof-und-Staatsarchiv, Vienna, Staatskanzlei, carton 195, Vorträge 1814 (I–III), fos. 40–7. For Alexander's response, see A. Sorel, *L'Europe et la Révolution française* (8 vols., Paris 1885–1904), vol. 8, p. 253.

12. Sorel, *L'Europe et la Révolution française*, vol. 8, pp. 254–5; Fournier, *Der Congress von Châtillon*, pp. 67–8.

13. Castlereagh to Liverpool, 29 January 1814, published in Webster, *British Diplomacy*, p. 143.

14. Chandler, *The Campaigns of Napoleon*, pp. 958–64; V. B. Derrécagaix, *Le maréchal Berthier, prince de Wagram et de Neuchâtel* (2 vols., Paris 1905), vol. 2, p. 544.

15. A. d'Arjuzon, *Caulaincourt, le confident de Napoléon* (Paris 2012), pp. 262–3.

16. *Mémoires du général de Caulaincourt, duc de Vicence, grand écuyer de l'empereur*, ed. J. Hanoteau (3 vols., Paris 1933), vol. 1, pp. 170–1; Sorel, *L'Europe et la Révolution française*, vol. 8, p. 258; Fournier, *Der Congress von Châtillon*, pp. 91–2.

17. AN 95 AP carton 14, dossier 11, pièce 1.

18. A. Ernouf, *Maret, duc de Bassano* (Paris 1878), pp. 620–3.

19. Fournier, *Der Congress von Châtillon*, pp. 94–6.

20. Fournier, *Der Congress von Châtillon*, pp. 98–9.

21. Sorel, *L'Europe et la Révolution française*, vol. 8, pp. 265–6.

22. A. J. F. Fain, *Manuscrit de 1814* (Paris 1825), pp. 109–12.

23. Sorel, *L'Europe et la Révolution française*, vol. 8, pp. 269–70.

24. Ernouf, *Maret*, p. 623.

25. Floret's journal of the congress of Châtillon, published in Fournier, *Der Congress von Châtillon*, p. 377.

26. Fournier, *Der Congress von Châtillon*, pp. 102–3.

27. Sorel, *L'Europe et la Révolution française*, vol. 8, pp. 273–9.

28. Chandler, *The Campaigns of Napoleon*, pp. 966–76.

29. Fournier, *Der Congress von Châtillon*, p. 152.

30. Fournier, *Der Congress von Châtillon*, p. 150.

31. Sorel, *L'Europe et la Révolution française*, vol. 8, pp. 282–3.
32. *Correspondance de Napoléon 1ᵉʳ, publiée par ordre de l'empereur Napoléon III*, ed. A. du Casse (32 vols., Paris 1858–70), vol. 27, pp. 225–6.
33. Berthier to Schwarzenberg, 22 February 1814, AN 95 AP carton 14, dossier 11, pièce 3; Fournier, *Der Congress von Châtillon*, p. 164.
34. Fain, *Manuscrit de 1814*, p. 157.
35. 'Analyse de la négociation de l'armistice de Lusigny', AN 565 AP, Papiers Flahaut, carton 18–19, dossier 5, pièce 19.
36. 'Notes de M. de Rumigny', AN 95 AP carton 14, dossier 20, pièce 23.
37. Webster, *The Foreign Policy of Castlereagh*, pp. 225–9.
38. Fournier, *Der Congress von Châtillon*, pp. 223–5.
39. 'Préface pour mes mémoires', AN 95 AP carton 14, dossier 20, pièce 37, fo. 41.
40. AN 95 AP carton 14, dossier 20, pièce 37, fo. 41.
41. Ernouf, *Maret*, p. 626.
42. Fain, *Manuscrit de 1814*, p. 284.
43. 'Préface pour mes mémoires', AN 95 AP carton 14, dossier 20, pièce 37, fo. 44.

CHAPTER 12

1. They are in the Archives Nationales, Paris, série F7, carton 3835, 'Police générale, rapports de la préfecture de police, 1811–mars 1814'.
2. *Histoire de mon temps. Mémoires du chancelier Pasquier*, ed. Duc d'Audiffret-Pasquier (6 vols., Paris 1893–95), vol. 2, pp. 87–91.
3. Pasquier's report for 9 March 1814, AN F7 3835, unnumbered folio.
4. Pasquier's reports for 8, 10, and 20 January 1814, AN F7 3835, unnumbered folios.
5. Pasquier's reports for 3 February, 8, 9, and 12 March 1814, AN F7 3835, unnumbered folios.
6. Pasquier's reports for 2, 17, and 19 February 1814, AN F7 3835, unnumbered folios.
7. Pasquier's reports for 22 and 26 February 1814, AN F7 3835, unnumbered folios.
8. Pasquier's reports for 3 and 24 March 1814, AN F7 3835, unnumbered folios.
9. See particularly Pasquier's reports for 15, 18, 19, and 21 January 1814, AN F7 3835, unnumbered folios.
10. Pasquier's report for 3 March 1814, AN F7 3835, unnumbered folio.
11. C. Esdaile, *The Peninsular War: A New History* (London 2002), pp. 455–82; E. Longford, *Wellington, the Years of the Sword* (London, 1969), pp. 334–8; Baron de Valsuzenay, prefect of the Gironde, to Montalivet, minister of the interior, 11 March 1814, AN F1c III Gironde 9, pièce 155.
12. AN F1c III Gironde 9, pièce 155; T. Lentz, *Nouvelle histoire du premier empire* (4 vols., Paris 2002–10), vol. 3, p. 562; G. Ellis, *The Napoleonic Empire* (London and Basingstoke 1991), p. 96.

13. G. de Bertier de Sauvigny, *Le comte Ferdinand de Bertier (1782–1864) et l'énigme de la Congrégation* (Paris 1948), pp. 49–75.

14. P. Mansel, *Louis XVIII* (London 1981), pp. 162–3.

15. Bruno de Boisgelin, cited in Bertier de Sauvigny, *Le comte Ferdinand de Bertier*, p. 74.

16. Longford, *Wellington*, pp. 340–1; Mansel, *Louis XVIII*, p. 165.

17. E. de Perceval, *Un adversaire de Napoléon. Le vicomte Lainé, 1767–1835* (2 vols., Paris 1926), vol. 1, p. 242.

18. Bertier de Sauvigny, *Le comte Ferdinand de Bertier*, pp. 129–30.

19. Longford, *Wellington*, p. 337; Mansel, *Louis XVIII*, p. 167.

20. Perceval, *Lainé*, vol. 1, p. 255.

21. D. G. Chandler, *The Campaigns of Napoleon* (London 1966; 1978 edn), p. 984; D. Lieven, *Russia against Napoleon: The Battle for Europe, 1807–1814* (London 2009; 2010 edn), pp. 497–8.

22. Chandler, *The Campaigns of Napoleon*, pp. 988–90.

23. Lieven, *Russia against Napoleon*, p. 502.

24. Chandler, *The Campaigns of Napoleon*, pp. 992–4.

25. Schwarzenberg to Metternich, 13 March 1814, published in *Österreichs Theilnahme an den Befreiungskriegen*, ed. R. von Metternich-Winneburg and A. von Klinckowström (Vienna 1887), p. 815; Schwarzenberg to Maria Anna zu Schwarzenberg, 18 March 1814, published in *Briefe des Feldmarschalls Fürsten Schwarzenberg an seine Frau, 1799–1816*, ed. J. F. Novak, p. 385.

26. H. Houssaye, *1814* (Paris 1888; 1911 edn), pp. 304–5.

27. Chandler, *The Campaigns of Napoleon*, pp. 994–7; L. F. J. de Bausset, *Mémoires anécdotiques sur l'intérieur du palais et sur quelques événements de l'empire de 1805 jusqu'au 1er mai 1814, pour servir à l'histoire de Napoléon* (4 vols., Paris 1827–29), vol. 2, pp. 245–6; J. M. Rouart, *Napoléon ou la destinée* (Paris 2012), p. 281.

28. Chandler, *The Campaigns of Napoleon*, p. 996.

29. Macdonald to Nancy [Macdonald], comtesse de Gronau, 22 March 1814, AN 279 AP, Fonds Massa, carton 9, unnumbered folio.

30. Lieven, *Russia against Napoleon*, p. 507.

31. Lieven, *Russia against Napoleon*, p. 509.

CHAPTER 13

1. Caulaincourt, '1814. Evénements de Paris, le 31 mars et après', AN 95 AP carton 14, dossier 20, pièce 1; H. Houssaye, *1814* (Paris 1888;1911 edn), pp. 423–6, T. Lentz, *Nouvelle histoire du premier empire* (4 vols., Paris 2002–10), vol. 2, p. 556.

2. Cited in Houssaye, *1814*, p. 427.

3. Nancy [Macdonald], comtesse de Gronau, to marshal Macdonald, 28 March 1814, AN 279 AP, Fonds Massa, carton 15, unnumbered folios.

4. This interpretation is even echoed by Talleyrand's most recent and best biographer, Emmanuel de Waresquiel, *Talleyrand, le prince immobile* (Paris 2003), pp. 435–8.

5. See Dalberg to Caulaincourt, 18 and 21 February 1823, AN 95 AP carton 14, pièce 28, fos. 82–3.

6. AN 95 AP carton 14, pièce 28, fo. 52.

7. Cited in A. Sorel, *L'Europe et la Révolution française* (8 vols., Paris 1885–1904), vol. 8, p. 312.

8. Sorel, *L'Europe et la Révolution française*, vol. 8, pp. 297–301.

9. *Mémoires du général de Caulaincourt, duc de Vicence, grand écuyer de l'empereur*, ed. J. Hanoteau (3 vols., Paris 1933), vol. 3, p. 173.

10. Cited in Sorel, *L'Europe et la Révolution française*, vol. 8, p. 269.

11. '1814. Evénements de Paris, 31 mars et après', AN 95 AP carton 14, dossier 20, pièce 1.

12. '1814. Evénements de Paris, 31 mars et après', AN 95 AP carton 14, dossier 20, pièce 1.

13. '1814. Evénements de Paris, 31 mars et après', AN 95 AP carton 14, dossier 20, pièce 1.

14. Pasquier's report of 29 March 1814, AN F7 3835, unnumbered folio.

15. '1814. Evénements de Paris, 31 mars et après', AN 95 AP carton 14, dossier 20, pièce 1.

16. '1814. Evénements de Paris, 31 mars et après', AN 95 AP carton 14, dossier 20, pièce 1.

17. Waresquiel, *Talleyrand*, p. 440.

18. '1814. Evénements de Paris, 31 mars et après', AN 95 AP carton 14, dossier 20, pièce 38.

19. Houssaye, *1814*, p. 519; Lieven, *Russia against Napoleon*, pp. 513–15.

20. '1814. Evénements de Paris, 31 mars et après', AN 95 AP carton 14, dossier 20, pièce 1.

21. *Mémoires du général de Caulaincourt*, vol. 3, pp. 54–63.

22. 'Projet d'instructions', AN 95 AP carton 14, dossier 19, pièce 5; *Mémoires du général de Caulaincourt*, vol. 3, p. 65.

23. *Mémoires du général de Caulaincourt*, vol. 3, pp. 78–80.

24. *Mémoires du général de Caulaincourt*, vol. 3, p. 85.

25. Lentz, *Nouvelle histoire*, vol. 2, p. 564.

26. '1814. Notes sur la participation de M le prince de Bénévent', AN 95 AP carton 14, dossier 20, unnumbered folios.

27. AN 95 AP carton 14, dossier 20, unnumbered folios.

28. *Mémoires du général de Caulaincourt*, vol. 3, pp. 104–5; J. Thiry, *Le sénat de Napoléon, 1800–1814* (Paris 1932), pp. 307–19.

29. P. Serna, *La république des girouettes, 1789–1815 et au-delà, une anomalie politique: la France de l'extrême centre* (Paris 2005), pp. 149–56.

30. Lentz, *Nouvelle histoire*, vol. 2, p. 567.

31. '1814. Notes sur la participation de M le prince de Bénévent', AN 95 AP carton 14, dossier 20, unnumbered folios.
32. F. Masson, *L'affaire Maubreuil* (Paris 1907), pp. 97–103.
33. *Histoire de mon temps. Mémoires du chancelier Pasquier*, ed. Duc d'Audiffret-Pasquier (6 vols., Paris 1893–95), vol. 2, p. 286.

CHAPTER 14

1. H. Houssaye, *1814* (Paris 1888; 1911 edn), pp. 602–3.
2. Houssaye, *1814*, p. 604.
3. A. Sorel, *L'Europe et la Révolution française* (8 vols., Paris 1885–1904), vol. 8, pp. 325–6.
4. *Souvenirs du maréchal Macdonald, duc de Tarente* (Paris 1892), pp. 265–7.
5. *Souvenirs du maréchal Macdonald*, p. 267.
6. *Mémoires du général de Caulaincourt, duc de Vicence, grand écuyer de l'empereur*, ed. J. Hanoteau (3 vols., Paris 1933), vol. 3, pp. 193–4.
7. *Mémoires du général de Caulaincourt*, vol. 3, p. 188.
8. *Mémoires du général de Caulaincourt*, vol. 1, p. 161; *Mémoires du maréchal Marmont, duc de Raguse, de 1792 à 1841* (9 vols., Paris 1857), vol. 6, p. 8.
9. *Mémoires du général de Caulaincourt*, vol. 3, pp. 203–6.
10. Houssaye, *1814*, p. 619; *Souvenirs du maréchal Macdonald*, p. 278.
11. Cited in Houssaye, *1814*, p. 621 n. 1.
12. Macdonald to Nancy [Macdonald], comtesse de Gronau, 5 April 1814, AN 279 AP, Fonds Massa, carton 9, unnumbered folio.
13. 'Notes sur la participation de M le prince de Bénévent', AN 95 AP carton 14, dossier 20, unnumbered folio.
14. *Mémoires du général de Caulaincourt*, vol. 3, pp. 217–18.
15. *Mémoires du général de Caulaincourt*, vol. 3, p. 222.
16. *Mémoires du général de Caulaincourt*, vol. 3, pp. 224–6.
17. A. J. F. Fain, *Manuscrit de 1814* (Paris 1825), p. 389.
18. Houssaye, *1814*, p. 639.
19. Berthier to Caulaincourt, 9 April 1814, AN 95 AP carton 14, dossier 64, pièce 8.
20. *Mémoires du général de Caulaincourt*, vol. 3, pp. 352–3.
21. *Mémoires du général de Caulaincourt*, vol. 3, pp. 343, 357–73.
22. '1814: conduite inconvenante du roi Joseph vis-à-vis de l'impératrice régente, elle l'indigne et l'indispose et l'éloigne de ce qui tient à l'empereur', AN 95 AP carton 14, dossier 20.
23. '1814: l'impératrice pendant le séjour de Fontainebleau', AN 95 AP carton 14, dossier 20.
24. E. de Waresquiel, *Talleyrand. Le prince immobile* (Paris 2003), pp. 455–6.
25. A. J. F. Fain, *Manuscrit de 1814* (Paris 1825), p. 406.

26. F. L. von Waldburg-Truchsess, *Nouvelle relation de l'itinéraire de Napoléon de Fontainebleau à l'Ile d'Elbe* (Paris 1815), p. 19.
27. Waldburg-Truchsess, *Nouvelle relation*, pp. 22–3.
28. Waldburg-Truchsess, *Nouvelle relation*, pp. 23.
29. Waldburg-Truchsess, *Nouvelle relation*, pp. 24–5.
30. *1809–1815: Mémorial et archives de M le baron Peyrusse, trésorier-général de la couronne pendant les cent-jours* (Carcassonne 1869), pp. 226–7.
31. Waldburg-Truchsess, *Nouvelle relation*, p. 30.
32. Peyrusse, *Mémorial et archives*, p. 227.
33. F. Fraser, *Pauline Bonaparte: Venus of empire* (New York 2009), pp. 204–18.
34. Waldburg-Truchsess, *Nouvelle relation*, p. 43.
35. Clam to Schwarzenberg, 28 April 1814, Burg Clam, Papiere aus dem Nachlasse des Grafen Carl Clam-Martinic, Briefe und Berichte. An Fürst Schwarzenberg, no.13.
36. General Koller's account of the voyage from Fréjus to Elba, in Waldburg-Truchsess, *Nouvelle relation*, p. 50; Peyrusse, *Mémorial et archives*, p. 230.
37. Koller, in Waldburg-Truchsess, *Nouvelle relation*, pp. 52–3.
38. Peyrusse, *Mémorial et archives*, p. 231.
39. A. Ernouf, *Maret, duc de Bassano* (Paris 1878), p. 534.

EPILOGUE

1. The literature on the hundred days is vast. Two classics are H. Houssaye, *1815* (3 vols., Paris 1893–1905); and A. Chuquet, *Les cent jours: le départ de l'Ile d'Elbe* (Paris 1920; the first volume of an unfinished work on the subject). More recent important works are: E. de Waresquiel, *Cent jours: la tentation de l'impossible, mars-juillet 1815* (Paris 2008); T. Lentz, *Nouvelle histoire du premier empire* (4 vols., Paris 2002–10), vol. 4, *Les cent jours, 1815*; A. Schom, *One Hundred Days: Napoleon's Road to Waterloo* (London 1992); and D. de Villepin, *Les cent jours, ou l'esprit de sacrifice* (Paris 2001).
2. P. W. Schroeder, *The Transformation of European Politics, 1763–1848* (Oxford 1994; 1996 edn), p. 550; Waresquiel, *Cent jours*, pp. 165–6, and *Talleyrand: le prince immobile* (Paris 2003), pp. 493–4.
3. Lentz, *Les cent jours*, pp. 375–82.
4. Waresquiel, *Cent jours*, p. 411.
5. P. A. E. Fleury de Chaboulon, *Mémoires pour servir à l'histoire de la vie privée, du retour et du règne de Napoléon en 1815* (2 vols., London 1819–20), vol. 1, pp. vi, 77–258.
6. Fleury de Chaboulon, *Mémoires*, vol. 2, pp. 4–9.
7. Fleury de Chaboulon, *Mémoires*, vol. 2, pp. 10–17.
8. Metternich's instructions for Ottenfels, 14 April 1815, National Archives, Czech Republic, Acta Clementina 8/42 sg. C 29 carton 8, fo. 26.

9. National Archives, Czech Republic, Acta Clementina 8/42 sg. C 29 carton 8, fos. 25–6.

10. Fleury de Chaboulon, *Mémoires*, vol. 2, pp. 20–5.

11. Metternich's and Nesselrode's instructions for Ottenfels, 9 May 1815, National Archives, Czech Republic, Acta Clementina 8/42 sg. C 29 carton 8, fos. 33–4.

12. Fleury de Chaboulon, *Mémoires*, vol. 2, p. 26.

13. Fleury de Chaboulon, *Mémoires*, vol. 2, p. 27.

14. Fleury de Chaboulon, *Mémoires*, vol. 2, pp. 36, 42–3.

15. Fleury de Chaboulon, *Mémoires*, vol. 2, p. 42.

16. D. G. Chandler, *The Campaigns of Napoleon* (London 1966; 1978 edn), p. 1015.

17. The Waterloo campaign has been exhaustively studied. Among the best of the older works are: H. Lachouque, *Napoléon à Waterloo* (Paris 1965); Chandler, *The Campaigns of Napoleon*, pp. 1007–95; and E. Longford, *Wellington: The Years of the Sword* (London 1969), pp. 393–441. The most important recent books are A. Barbero, *The Battle: A New History of Waterloo* (New York 2005); P. Hofschroer, *1815: The Waterloo Campaign* (2 vols., London 2006), which emphasizes the German contribution to Wellington's victory; and A. Roberts, *Waterloo: Napoleon's Last Gamble* (London 2005).

18. G. Barral, 'La santé de Napoléon 1er', *La chronique médicale*, 7 (1900), pp. 39–42.

19. Chandler, *The Campaigns of Napoleon*, pp. 1087–90.

20. V. B. Derrécagaix, *Le maréchal Berthier, prince de Wagram et de Neuchâtel* (2 vols., Paris 1905), vol. 2, pp. 599–603.

21. *Mémoires du général de Caulaincourt, duc de Vicence, grand écuyer de l'empereur*, ed. J. Hanoteau (3 vols., Paris 1933), vol. 1, pp. 203–21; A. Ernouf, *Maret, duc de Bassano* (Paris 1878), pp. 657–84.

22. Waresquiel, *Talleyrand*, pp. 504–616.

23. For Metternich's career after the death of Francis I, see H. von Srbik, *Metternich, der Staatsmann und der Mensch* (3 vols., Munich 1925–54), vol. 2, *passim* and, for his last years, pp. 303–515.

24. K. zu Schwarzenberg, *Feldmarschall Fürst Schwarzenberg, der Sieger von Leipzig* (Vienna 1964), pp. 395–428.

25. J. Hartley, *Alexander I* (London 1994), pp. 139–203.

26. R. Parkinson, *Hussar General: The Life of Blücher, Man of Waterloo* (London 1975), p. 250.

27. For Marie-Louise's latter years, see *Correspondance de Marie-Louise, 1799–1847* (Vienna 1887), pp. 179–345; and M. Billard, *Les maris de Marie-Louise* (Paris 1908). For the duke of Reichstadt, see J. Tulard, *Napoléon II* (Paris 1992).

28. See E. de las Cases, *Mémorial de Ste-Hélène*, ed. A Fugier (2 vols., Paris 1961). Of the many works on Napoleon on St Helena, three significant modern ones are: J. Kemble, *St Helena during Napoleon's Exile* (London 1969); J.-P. Kauffmann, *The Black Room at Longwood: Napoleon's Exile on St Helena* (New York 1999); and B. Unwin, *Terrible Exile: The Last Days of Napoleon on St Helena* (London 2010).

Sources and Bibliography

PRIMARY SOURCES

Public holdings: France

Archives Nationales, Paris (AN)
Série F1c I 12: Esprit public, objets généraux, An VI–An IX.
Série F1c I 14: Esprit public, objets généraux, 1813–1830.
Série F1c I 26: Esprit public pendant les Cent Jours.
Série F1c III (Esprit public et élections): Aveyron carton 7; Bouches-du-Rhône cartons 3, 7, 12; Calvados cartons 4, 8, 13; Charente 4, 9, 12; Côte-d'Or carton 9; Doubs carton 8, Forêts carton 6; Gironde cartons 6, 9; Hautes-Alpes cartons 3, 5; Haute-Loire cartons 5, 8; Indre carton 7; Loire-Inférieure carton 11; Nord cartons 11, 14; Rhône cartons 5, 9; Seine carton 29; Yonne cartons 3, 10.
Série F7 (Police générale): cartons 3092, 3688/23, 3835, 4222, 6591.
95 AP (Fonds Caulaincourt): cartons 12, 13, 14, 16, 18, 22.
279 AP (Fonds Massa): cartons 8, 9, 15.
565 AP (Archives Flahaut): cartons 18, 19.

Archives du Ministère des Affaires Etrangéres, Paris (AAE)
Série Mémoires et Documents France: cartons 666, 667, 668, 669, 670, 671, 672.

Bibliothèque Municipale de Bordeaux (BMB)
Ms 2029 (Fonds Lainé): cartons II, IV, V, VI, XII, XXXIII, XXXIX, XL, XLI, XLII, XLIII, XLIV, XLV, XLVI, XLVII, XLVIII, XLIX, L, LI, LII, LIII, LIV, LV, LVI, LVII, LVIII, LIX, CVI, CVII, CVIII, CX, CXI, CXXV.

Czech Republic

National Archives, Prague
Acta Clementina: 1/1 sg. C1/1 carton 1; 1/23 sg. C 2/5-13 carton 2; 2/17 sg. C 7/2-5 carton 2; 2/22 sg. C 7/6 carton 3; 2/62 sg. C 10/6 carton 6; 3/4 sg. C 13 carton 1; 3/21 sg. C 12 carton 2; 3/32 sg. C 12 carton 2; 3/36 sg. C 12 carton 3; 8/22 sg. C 26 carton 3; 8/42 sg. C 29 carton 8; 9/29 carton 1; 10/48 3 carton 8; 10/49 2 carton 8; 10/50 8 carton 8; 10/52 9 carton 8; 10/71 carton 1; 12/33 sg. C 50 carton 5: 12/34 sg. C 50 carton 5; 13/76 carton 4.

State Regional Archives, Trebon
Schwarzenberg Family Archive (secundogeniture), 1539–1948: cartons 123, 124, 125, 126, 127, 128.

Austria

Haus-Hof-und-Staatsarchiv, Vienna

Staatskanzlei, cartons 194, Vorträge 1813 (VI–XII), 195, Vorträge 1814 (I–VIII);
Interiora, Korrespondenz carton 75; Grosse Korrespondenz carton 474.
Hausarchiv, Sammelbände cartons 44, 52.

Private holdings: Austria

Burg Clam

Papieren aus dem Nachlasse Grafen Carl Clam-Martinic: 'Erinnerungen an die
Campagne von 1813'; Briefe und Berichte: An Feldmarschall Fürst Karl zu
Schwarzenberg.

PRINTED PRIMARY SOURCES

*1809–1815: Mémorial et archives de M le baron Peyrusse, trésorier-général de la couronne
pendant les cent-jours* (Carcassonne 1869)
Aster, H., *Schilderungen der Kriegsereignisse in und vor Dresden, vom 7 März bis 28
August 1813* (Dresden and Leipzig 1844)
Aus Metternichs nachgelassenen Papieren, ed. R von Metternich-Winneburg and
A. von Klinckowström (8 vols., Vienna 1880–9)
Bausset, L. F. J. de, *Mémoires anécdotiques sur intérieur du palais et sur quelques
événements de l'empire de 1805 jusqu'au 1er mai 1814, pour servir á l'histoire de Napoléon*
(4 vols., Paris 1827–29)
Blüchers Briefe, ed. W. von Unger (Stuttgart and Berlin 1913)
Briefe des Feldmarschalls Fürsten Schwarzenberg an seine Frau, 1799–1816, ed. F. Novak
(Vienna and Leipzig 1913)
Cambacérès, J. J. de, *Mémoires inédits*, ed. L Chatel de Brancion (2 vols., Paris 1999)
Cambacérès. Lettres inédits à Napoléon, ed. J. Tulard (2 vols., Paris 1973)
Clemens Metternich-Wilhelmina von Sagan. Ein Briefwechsel, 1813–1815, ed. M. Ullrichova
(Graz and Cologne, 1966)
Correspondance de Marie-Louise, 1799–1814 (Vienna 1887)
Correspondance de Napoléon 1er, publiée par ordre de l'empereur Napoléon III, ed. A. du
Casse (32 vols., Paris 1858–70)
De las Cases, E., *Mémorial de Ste-Hélène*, ed. A. Fugier (2 vols., Paris 1961)
Discours civiques de Danton, ed. H. Fleischmann (Paris 1920)
Earl Stanhope, *Notes of Conversations with the Duke of Wellington, 1831–1851* (London
1888; 1998 edition)
Erinnerungen aus dem Leben des General-Feldmarschalls Hermann von Boyen, ed.
D. Schmitt (2 vols., Berlin 1990)
Fain, A. J. F., *Manuscrit de 1812, contenant le précis des événements de cette année, pour
servir à l'histoire de l'empereur Napoléon* (2 vols., Paris, 1827)
Fain, A. J. F., *Manuscrit de 1813* (2 vols., Paris 1825)

Fain, A. J. F., *Manuscrit de 1814* (Paris 1825)

Fleury de Chaboulon, P. A. E., *Mémoires pour servir à l'histoire de la vie privée, du retour et du règne de Napoléon en 1815* (2 vols., London 1820)

Friedrich Gentz. Gesammelte Schriften, ed. G. Kronenbitter (12 vols., Hildesheim, Zurich, New York, Olms 1997–2004)

General Wilson's Journal, ed. A Brett-James (London 1964)

Gotteri, M. (ed.), *La police secrète du premier empire. Bulletins quotidiens adressés par Savary à l'empereur, 1810–1814* (7 vols., Paris 1997–2004)

Gouvion Saint-Cyr, L., *Mémoires pour servir à l'histoire militaire sous le directoire, le consulat et l'empire* (4 vols., Paris 1831)

Hauterive, E. d', and Grassion, J. (eds.), *La police secrète du premier empire. Bulletins quotidiens adressés par Fouché à l'empereur, 1804–1810* (5 vols., Paris 1908–64)

Histoire de mon temps. Mémoires du chancelier Pasquier, ed. duc d'Audiffret-Pasquier (6 vols., Paris 1893–5)

Journal du maréchal de Castellane, 1804–1862 (5 vols., Paris 1895–7)

Les relations diplomatiques de la Russie et la France, 1808–1812, d'après les rapports des ambassadeurs d'Alexandre et de Napoléon (7 vols., St Petersburg 1905–14)

Lettres et papiers du chancelier comte de Nesselrode ed. A. von Nesselrode (11 vols., Paris 1904–11)

Lettres inédites de Napoléon 1er, ed. L. Lecestre (2 vols., Paris 1897)

Lieutenant-general C. W. Vane (Stewart), marquess of Londonderry, *Narrative of the War in Germany and France in 1813 and 1814* (London 1830)

Mémoires de Barras, membre du directoire, ed. G. Duruy (4 vols., Paris 1895–6)

Mémoires de Mme la duchesse d'Abrantès, ou souvenirs historiques sur Napoléon, la Révolution, le directoire, le consulat, l'empire et la restauration (18 vols., Paris, 1831–2), vol. I

Mémoires du duc de Raguse (9 vols., Paris 1857)

Mémoires du duc de Rovigo, pour servir à l'histoire de l'empereur Napoléon (8 vols., Paris 1828)

Mémoires du général de Caulaincourt, duc de Vicence, grand écuyer de l'empereur, ed. J. Hanoteau (3 vols., Paris 1933)

Mémoires du général Lejeune, ed. G. Bapst (2 vols., Paris 1895)

Mémoires du prince de Talleyrand, ed. Duc de Broglie (5 vols., Paris 1891–92)

Napoléon Bonaparte. Correspondance générale (12 vols., Paris 2004–)

Napoléon. De la guerre, ed. B. Colson (Paris 2011)

Österreichs Theilnahme an den Befreiungskriegen, ed. R. von Metternich-Winneburg and A. von Klinckowström (Vienna 1887)

Récits de la captivité de l'empereur Napoléon à Ste-Hélène, par M le comte Montholon (2 vols., Paris 1847)

Ségur, Général comte P. de, *Histoire de Napoléon et de la grande armée pendant l'année 1812* (Brussels 1825)

Souvenirs du maréchal Macdonald, duc de Tarente (Paris 1892)

Waldburg-Truchsess, F. L. von, Nouvelle relation de l'itinéraire de Napoléon de Fontainebleau à l'Ile d'Elbe (Paris 1815)

Wilson, Sir Robert, Narrative of events during the invasion of Russia (London 1860)

BIBLIOGRAPHY

Agulhon, M., La vie sociale en Provence intérieure au lendemain de la Révolution (Paris 1970)

Alexander, R. A., Napoleon (London 2001)

Allen, R., Threshold of Terror: The Last Hours of the Monarchy in the French Revolution (Stroud 1999)

Aretin, K. O. von, Heiliges Römisches Reich, 1776–1806. Reichsverfassung und Staatssouveränität (2 vols., Wiesbaden 1967)

d'Arjuzon, A., Caulaincourt, le confident de Napoléon (Paris 2012)

Aymes, J. R., La guerre d'indépendance espagnole, 1808–1814 (Paris 1973)

Baker, K. M., Inventing the French Revolution: Essays on French Political Culture in the 18th Century (Cambridge 1990)

Balzac, H. de, Oeuvres complètes (24 vols., Paris 1869–76)

Blanning, T. C. W., The Origins of the French Revolutionary Wars (London 1986)

Barbero, A., The Battle: A New History of Waterloo (New York 2005)

Bartlett, C. J., Castlereagh (London 1966)

Barton, D. P., Bernadotte, Prince and King, 1810–1844 (London 1925)

Bastid, P., Sieyès et sa pensée (Paris 1939)

Bastid, P., Benjamin Constant et sa doctrine (Paris 1966)

Berdahl, R., The Politics of the Prussian nobility: The Development of a Conservative Ideology, 1770–1848 (Princeton, NJ, 1988)

Berding, H., Napoleonische Herrschafts-und Gesellschaftspolitik im Königreich Westfalen, 1807–1813 (Gottingen 1973)

Bergeron, L., L'épisode napoléonien. Aspects intérieurs, 1799–1815 (Paris 1972)

Bergès, L., Résister à la conscription, 1798–1814. Le cas des départements aquitains (Paris 2002)

Bernhardi, T. von, Denkwürdigkeiten aus dem Leben von kaiserl russ. Generals der Infanterie Carl Friedrich Grafen von Toll (4 vols., Leipzig 1856–8)

Bertaud, J.-P., La presse et le pouvoir de Louis XIII à Napoléon 1er (Paris 2000)

Bertaud, J.-P., Quand les enfants parlaient de gloire. L'armée au coeur de la France de Napoléon (Paris 2006)

Bertier de Sauvigny, G. de, Le comte Ferdinand de Bertier (1782–1864) et l'énigme de la Congrégation (Paris 1948)

Bertier de Sauvigny, G de., Metternich et son temps (Paris 1959)

Bertier de Sauvigny, G. de, Metternich (Paris 1986)

Bew, P., Castlereagh: A Life (Oxford 2012)

Billard, M., La conspiration de Malet (Paris 1907)

Billard, M., *Les maris de Marie-Louise* (Paris 1908)

Blanning, T. C. W., *The French Revolution and Germany: Occupation and Resistance in the Rhineland, 1795–1802* (Oxford 1983)

Bornarel, F., *Cambon et la Révolution française* (Paris 1905)

Boudon, J.-O., *Histoire du consulat et de l'empire* (Paris 2000)

Boudon, J.-O., Napoléon et les cultes. Les religions à l'aube du 19ème siècle, 1800–1815 (Paris 2002)

Bredin, J. D., *Sieyès. La clé de la Révolution française* (Paris 1988)

Broers, M., *Europe under Napoleon, 1799–1815* (London 1996)

Broers, M., *Napoleonic Imperialism and the Savoyard Monarchy, 1776–1821: State-Building in Piedmont* (Lampeter 1997)

Broers, M., *The Politics of Religion in Napoleonic Italy: The War against God, 1801–1814* (London and New York 2002)

Broers, M., *The Napoleonic Empire in Italy, 1796–1814: Cultural Imperialism in a European Context?* (London and Basingstoke 2005)

Cabanis, A., *La presse sous le consulat et l'empire, 1799–1814* (Paris 1975)

Chamberlain, M. E., *Lord Aberdeen: A Political Biography* (London 1983)

Chandler, D. G., *The Campaigns of Napoleon* (London 1966; 1978 edn)

Chandler, D. G. (ed.), *Napoleon's Marshals* (London 1987)

Chartier, R., *Les origines culturelles de la Révolution française* (Paris 1990)

Chatel de Brancion, L., *Cambacérès. Maître d'oeuvre de Napoléon* (Paris 2001)

Chuquet, A., *Les cent jours. Le départ de l'Ile d'Elbe* (Paris 1920)

Clark, C., *Iron Kingdom: The Rise and Downfall of Prussia, 1600–1947* (London 2006)

Collins, I., *Napoleon and his Parliaments, 1800–1815* (London 1979)

Connelly, O., *Napoleon's Satellite Kingdoms* (New York 1965)

Connelly, O., *Blundering to Glory: Napoleon's Military Campaigns* (Wilmington, DE, 1987)

Cooper, D., *Talleyrand* (London 1932)

Courville, X. de, *Jomini, ou le devin de Napoléon* (Paris 1935; 1981 edn, Lausanne)

Crépin, A., *La conscription en débats ou le triple apprentissage de la nation, de la citoyenneté, de la république, 1798–1889* (Arras 1998)

Cronin, V., *Napoleon* (London 1971)

Crouzet, F., *L'économie britannique et le blocus continental, 1806–1813* (2 vols., Paris 1958)

Daudet, E., *L'exil et la mort du general Moreau* (Paris 1909)

Davis, J. A., *Naples and Napoleon: Southern Italy and the European Revolutions, 1780–1860* (Oxford 2006)

Derrécagaix, Général V. B., *Le maréchal Berthier, prince de Wagram et de Neuchâtel* (2 vols., Paris 1905)

Derrécagaix, Général V. B., *Les états-majors de Napoléon. Le lieutenant-général comte Belliard, chef d'état-major de Murat* (Paris 1908)

Derry, J. W., *Castlereagh* (London 1976)

Dhombres, J., and N. Dhombres, *Carnot* (Paris 1997)

Duchhardt, H., and K, Teppe (eds.), *Karl vom und zum Stein: der Akteur, der Autor, seine Wirkungs-und-Rezeptionsgeschichte* (Mainz 2003)

Duffy, C., *Borodino and the War of 1812* (London 1972)

Dwyer, P. G., *Napoleon: The Path to Power, 1769–1799* (London 2007)

Dwyer, P. G., *Citizen Emperor: Napoleon in Power* (London 2013)

Ellis, G., *Napoleon's Continental Blockade: The Case of Alsace* (Oxford 1981)

Ellis, G., *The Napoleonic Empire* (London 1991)

Englund, S., *Napoleon: A Political Life* (Cambridge, MA, 2004)

Ernouf, A., *Maret, duc de Bassano* (Paris 1878)

Esdaile, C., *The Spanish Army In The Peninsular War: The Causes, Experiences and Consequences of Military Humiliation* (Manchester 1988)

Esdaile, C., *The Peninsular War: A New History* (London 2002)

Esdaile, C., *Fighting Napoleon: Guerrillas, Bandits and Adventurers in Spain, 1808–1814* (New Haven and London 2004)

Esdaile, C. (ed.), *Popular Resistance in the French Wars: Patriots, Partisans and Land Pirates* (London and Basingstoke 2005)

Esdaile, C., *Napoleon's Wars: An International History, 1803–1815* (London 2007)

Farge, A., *Dire et mal dire. L'opinion publique au 18ème siècle* (Paris 1992)

Forrest, A., *Conscripts and Deserters: The Army and French Society during the Revolution and Empire* (Oxford 1989)

Forrest, A., *Napoleon's Men: The Soldiers of the Revolution and Empire* (London and New York 2002)

Forrest, A. (ed., with P. Wilson), *The Bee and the Eagle: Napoleonic France and the End of the Holy Roman Empire, 1806* (London and Basingstoke 2009)

Forsyth, M., *Reason and Revolution: The Political Thought of the Abbé Sieyès* (Leicester 1987)

Fournier, A., *Napoleon I. Eine Biographie* (Vienna and Leipzig 1886–9), Eng. version, *Napoleon I: A Biography*, trans. A. E. Adams (London 1911)

Fournier, A., *Der Congress von Châtillon* (Vienna 1900)

Fraser, F., *Pauline Bonaparte. Venus of empire* (New York 2009)

Friederich, R. von, *Die Befreiungskriege, 1813–1815* (2 vols., Berlin 1911–12)

Gaffarel, P., *Les complots de Toulon et de Marseille, 1812–1813* (Aix-en-Provence 1907)

Gagliardo, J., *Reich and Nation: The Holy Roman Empire as Idea and Reality, 1763–1806* (Bloomington, IL, 1980)

Garnier, J. P., *Barras, le roi du directoire* (Paris 1970)

Geschichte der Kämpfe Österreichs. Kriege unter der Regierung des Kaisers Franz, Befreiungskriege 1813 und 1814 (5 vols., Vienna 1913), vol. 3, E Glaise von Horstenau, *Feldzug von Dresden*

Gillet, J.-C., *Murat* (Paris 2008)

Godechot, J., *La contre-révolution, doctrine et action, 1789–1804* (Paris 1961)

Godsey, W. D., *Nobles and Nation in Central Europe: Free Imperial Knights in the Age of Revolution* (Cambridge 2004)

Grab, A., *Napoleon and the Transformation of Europe* (London and Basingstoke 2003)

Gray, M., *Prussia in Transition: Society and Politics under the Stein Reform Ministry of 1808* (Philadelphia, PN, 1986)

Gusdorf, G., *La conscience révolutionnaire. Les Idéologues* (Paris 1978)

Hamel, E., *Histoire des deux conspirations du général Malet* (Paris 1873)

Handelsman, M., *Napoleon et la Pologne, 1806–1807* (Paris 1909)

Hartley, J., *Alexander 1* (London 1994)

Heckscher, E., *The Continental System: An Economic Interpretation* (Oxford 1922)

Hermon-Belot, R., *L'abbé Grégoire. La politique et la vérité* (Paris 2000)

Herold, J. C., *The Mind of Napoleon: Selection from his Written and Spoken Words* (New York 1955)

Hillemand, P., *Pathologie de Napoléon* (Paris and Geneva 1970)

Hinde, W., *Castlereagh* (London 1981)

Hofschroer, P., *1815: The Waterloo Campaign* (2 vols., London 2006)

Holland Rose, J., *The Life of Napoleon I* (London 1901)

Holmes, S., *Benjamin Constant and the Making of Modern Liberalism* (New Haven and London 1984)

Houssaye, H., *1814* (Paris 1888, 1911 edn)

Houssaye, H., *1815* (3 vols., Paris 1893–1905)

Hulot, F., *Le maréchal Ney* (Paris 2000)

Hulot, F., *Le général Moreau, adversaire et victime de Napoléon* (Paris 2001)

Iremonger, L., *Lord Aberdeen* (London 1978)

Jones, C., *The Longman Companion to the French Revolution* (London and Harlow 1988; 1990 edn)

Jones, P. M., *Reform and Revolution in France: The Politics of Transition, 1774–1791* (Cambridge 1995)

Josselson, M., and D. Josselson, *The Commander: A Life of Barclay de Tolly* (Oxford 1980)

Kauffmann, J.-P., *The Black Room at Longwood: Napoleon's Exile on St Helena* (New York 1999)

Kelly, G. A., *The Humane Comedy: Constant, Tocqueville, and French liberalism* (Cambridge 1992)

Kemble, J., *Napoleon Immortal: The Medical History and Private Life of Napoleon Bonaparte* (London 1959)

Kemble, J., *St Helena during Napoleon's Exile* (London 1969)

Kerchnawe, H., and A. Veltzé, *Feldmarschall Karl Fürst zu Schwarzenberg* (Vienna and Leipzig 1913)

Kieswetter, J. K., *Etienne-Denis Pasquier: The Last Chancellor of France* (Philadelphia, PA, 1977)

Kissinger, H., *A World Restored: Metternich, Castlereagh and the Problems of Peace, 1812–1822* (London 1957; 1973 edn)

Klier, J. D., *Russia Gathers her Jews: The Origins of the 'Jewish Question' in Russia, 1772–1825* (Dekalb, IL, 1986)

Kraehe, E., *Metternich's German Policy* (2 vols., Princeton, NJ, 1963–83), vol. 1, *The contest with Napoleon, 1799–1814*

Kronenbitter, G., *Wort und Macht. Friedrich Gentz als politischer Schriftsteller* (Berlin 1994)

Lachouque, H., *Napoléon à Waterloo* (Paris 1965)

Lacour-Gayet, G., *Talleyrand (1754–1838)* (4 vols., Paris 1928–34)

Lafond, P., *Garat. 1762–1823* (Paris 1899)

Le Barbier, L., *Le général de La Horie, 1766–1812* (Paris 1904)

Lee, L. E., *The Politics of Harmony. Civil Service, Liberalism and Social Reform in Baden, 1800–1850* (Newark, NJ, 1980)

Lefebvre, G., *Napoléon* (Paris 1935)

Leggiere, M. V., *Napoleon and Berlin: The Napoleonic Wars in Prussia, 1813* (Stroud 2002)

Leggiere, M. V., *The Fall of Napoleon: The Allied Invasion of France, 1813–1814* (Cambridge 2007)

Lentz, T., *Savary. Le séide de Napoléon* (Paris 2001)

Lentz, T., *Nouvelle histoire du premier empire* (4 vols., Paris 2002–10)

Lentz, T., *La conspiration du général Malet. 23 octobre 1812* (Paris 2012)

Lentz, T., *Napoléon diplomate* (Paris 2012)

Lewis, G., *The Second Vendée: The Continuity of Counter-Revolution in the Department of the Gard, 1799–1815* (Oxford 1978)

Ley, F., *Alexandre 1er et sa Sainte-Alliance, 1811–1825* (Paris 1975)

Lieven, D., *Russia against Napoleon: The Battle for Europe, 1807–1814* (London 2009; 2010 edn)

Longford, E., *Wellington: The Years of the Sword* (London 1969)

Lovett, G. H., *Napoleon and the Birth of Modern Spain* (2 vols., New York 1971)

Lovie, J., and A. Palluel-Guillard, *L'épisode napoléonien. Aspects extérieurs, 1799–1815* (Paris 1972)

Luckwaldt, F., *Österreich und die Anfänge des Befreiungskrieges von 1813* (Berlin 1898)

Madelin, L., *Fouché, 1759–1820* (2 vols., Paris 1901)

Mann, G., *Secretary of Europe. The Life of Friedrich Gentz, Enemy of Napoleon* trans. W. H. Woglom (New Haven, CT, 1946)

Mansel, P., *Louis XVIII* (London 1981)

Marzagalli, S., *Les boulevards de la fraude. Le négoce maritime et le blocus continental, 1806–1813* (Paris 1999)

Masson, F., *L'affaire Maubreuil* (Paris 1907)

Masson, F., *La vie et les conspirations du général Malet* (Paris 1921)

Monnier, R., *L'espace publique démocratique. Essai sur l'opinion à Paris, de la Révolution au directoire* (Paris 1994)

Muir, R., *Britain and the Defeat of Napoleon, 1807–1815* (New Haven and London 1996)

Nafziger, G., *Napoleon at Lützen and Bautzen* (Chicago 1992)

Necheles, R. F., *The Abbé Grégoire, 1787–1831: The Odyssey of an Egalitarian* (Westport, CT, 1971)

Oncken, W., *Österreich und Preussen im Befreiungskriege* (2 vols., Berlin 1876–9)

Palmer, A., *Metternich* (London and New York, 1972)

Palmer, A., *Alexander 1* (London 1974)

Paret, P., *Yorck and the Era of Prussian Reform, 1807–1815* (Princeton, NJ, 1966)

Parkinson, R., *Hussar General: The Life of Blücher, Man of Waterloo* (London 1975)

Perceval, E. de, *Un adversaire de Napoléon. Le vicomte Lainé, 1767–1835* (2 vols., Paris 1926)

Perrin, E., *Le maréchal Ney* (Paris 1993)

Petiteau, N., *Les Français et l'empire, 1799–1815* (Paris 2008)

Petre, F. L., *Napoleon's Last Campaign in Germany. 1813* (London 1912)

Pigeard, A., *La conscription au temps de Napoléon, 1798–1814* (Paris 2003)

Pingaud, L., *Bernadotte, Napoléon et les Bourbons, 1797–1844* (Paris 1901)

Plongeron, B., *Des résistances religieuses à Napoléon, 1799–1813* (Paris 2006)

Price, M., *The Fall of the French Monarchy: Louis XVI, Marie Antoinette and the Baron de Breteuil* (London 2002)

Rath, R. J., *The Fall of the Napoleonic Kingdom of Italy, 1814* (New York 1941)

Reinhard, M., *Le grand Carnot* (2 vols., Paris 1950–52)

Rey, M.-P., *Alexandre 1er, Le tsar qui vainquit Napoléon* (Paris 2009)

Reynié, D., *Le triomphe de l'opinion publique. L'espace public français du 16ème au 20ème siècle* (Paris 1998)

Ritter, G., *Stein. Eine politische Biographie* (Stuttgart 1958)

Roberts, A., *Waterloo: Napoleon's Last Gamble* (London 2005)

Roche, D., *France in the Enlightenment* (Cambridge, MA, 1998)

Rothenberg, G., *The Art of Warfare in the Age of Napoleon* (London 1977)

Rothenberg, G., *Napoleon's Great Adversaries: Archduke Charles and the Austrian Army, 1792–1814* (London 1982)

Rouart, J. M., *Napoléon ou la destinée* (Paris 2012)

Rowe, M., *From Reich to State: The Rhineland in the Revolutionary Age, 1780–1830* (Cambridge 2003)

Schom, A., *One Hundred Days: Napoleon's Road to Waterloo* (London 1992)

Schroeder, P. W., *The Transformation of European Politics, 1763–1848* (Oxford, 1994; 1996 edition)

Schwarzenberg, K. zu, *Feldmarschall Fürst Schwarzenberg, der Sieger von Leipzig* (Vienna 1964)

Scott, F. D., *Bernadotte and the Fall of Napoleon* (Cambridge 1934)

Sené, C., *Joseph Cambon (1756–1820). Le financier de la Révolution* (Paris 1987)

Sepinwall, A. G., *The Abbé Grégoire and the French Revolution: The Making of Modern Universalism* (Berkeley, CA, and London 2005)

Serna, P., *La république des girouettes, 1789–1815 et au-delà. Une anomalie politique: la France de l'extrême centre* (Paris 2005)

Shapiro, G., and J. Markoff, *Revolutionary Demands: A Content Analysis of the cahiers de doléances of 1789* (Stanford, CA, 1998)

Sherwig, J. M., *Guineas and Gunpowder: British Foreign Aid in the War with France, 1793–1815* (Cambridge, MA, 1969)

Siemann, W., *Metternich: Staatsmann zwischen Restauration und Moderne* (Munich 2010)

Simms, B., *The Impact of Napoleon: Prussian High Politics, Foreign Policy and Executive Reform, 1797–1806* (Cambridge 1997)

Simms, B., *The Struggle for Mastery in Germany, 1779–1850* (London and Basingstoke 1998)

Sked, A., *Metternich and Austria: A Re-evaluation* (London and Basingstoke 2008)

Sked, A., *Radetzky: Imperial Victor and Military Genius* (London 2011)

Smith, D., *1813. Leipzig: Napoleon and the Battle of the Nations* (London 2001)

Sorel, A., *L'Europe et la Révolution française* (8 vols., Paris 1885–1904)

Srbik, H. von, *Metternich, der Staatsmann und der Mensch* (3 vols., Munich, 1925–54)

Stamm-Kuhlmann, T., *König in Preussens grosser Zeit. Friedrich Wilhelm III, der Melancholiker auf dem Thron* (Berlin 1992)

Sweet, P. R., *Wilhelm von Humboldt: A Biography* (2 vols., Columbus, OH, 1978)

Thiry, J., *Le sénat de Napoléon* (Paris 1932)

Thiry, J., *La campagne de 1812* (Paris 1969)

Thiry, J., *La chute de Napoléon 1er. Lützen et Bautzen* (Paris 1971)

Thiry, J., *La chute de Napoléon 1er. Leipzig* (Paris 1972)

Thompson, J. M., *Napoleon Bonaparte: His Rise and Fall* (Oxford 1952)

Tulard, J., *Napoléon, ou le mythe du sauveur* (Paris 1977)

Tulard, J., *Le grand empire, 1804–1815* (Paris 1982)

Tulard, J., *Murat, ou l'éveil des nations* (Paris 1983)

Tulard, J. (ed.), *La contre-révolution. Origines, histoire, postérité* (Paris 1990)

Tulard, J., *Napoléon II* (Paris 1992)

Tulard, J., *Joseph Fouché* (Paris 1998)

Unger, W. von, *Blücher* (2 vols., Berlin 1907–8)

Unwin, B., *Terrible Exile: The Last Days of Napoleon on St Helena* (London 2010)

Villefosse, L. de, and J. Bouissounouse, *L'opposition à Napoléon* (Paris 1969)

Villepin, D. de, *Les cent jours, ou l'esprit de sacrifice* (Paris 2001)

Wandycz, P., *The Lands of Partitioned Poland, 1795–1918* (Seattle, WA, 1974)

Waresquiel, E. de, *Talleyrand. Le prince immobile* (Paris 2003)

Waresquiel, E. de, *Cent jours. La tentation de l'impossible, mars-juillet 1815* (Paris 2008)

Webster, C. K. (ed.), *British Diplomacy, 1813–1815* (London 1921)

Webster, C. K., *The Foreign Policy of Castlereagh: Britain and the Reconstruction of Europe, 1812–1815* (London 1931)

Welch, C. B., *Liberty and Utility: The French Ideologues and the Transformation of Liberalism* (New York 1984)

Wood, D., *Benjamin Constant: A Biography* (London 1993)

Woolf, S. J., *A History of Italy, 1700–1860: The Social Constraints of Political Change* (London 1979)

Woolf, S. J., *Napoleon's Integration of Europe* (London 1991)

Young, P., *Napoleon's Marshals* (London 1973)

Zamoyski, A., *1812: Napoleon's Fatal March on Moscow* (London 2004; 2005 edn)

Zamoyski, A., *Rites of Peace: The Fall of Napoleon and the Congress of Vienna* (London 2007)

Zawadski, W. H., *A Man of Honour: Adam Czartoryski as a Statesman of Russia and Poland, 1795–1831* (Oxford 1993)

Zorgbibe, C., *Metternich, le séducteur diplomate* (Paris 2009)

ARTICLES

Anderson, R. C., 'State-Building and Bureaucracy in early 19th-Century Nassau', *Central European History*, 24:2–3 (1991)

Barral, G., 'La santé de Napoléon 1er', *La Chronique Médicale*, 7 (1900)

Blanning, T. C. W., 'The French Revolution and the Modernization of Germany', *Central European History*, 22:9 (1989)

Broers, M., 'Napoleon, Charlemagne and Lotharingia: Acculturation and the Limits of Napoleonic Europe', *The Historical Journal*, 44:1 (2001)

Crouzet, F., 'Wars, Blockade and Economic Change in Europe, 1792–1815', *Journal of Economic History*, 24:4 (1964)

Gray, M. W., '"Modifying the Traditional for the Good of the Whole": Commentary on State-Building and Bureaucracy in Nassau, Baden and Saxony in the Early 19th Century', *Central European History*, 24:2–3 (1991)

Hanoteau, J., 'Une nouvelle relation de l'entrevue de Napoléon et de Metternich à Dresde', *Revue d'histoire diplomatique* (Oct.–Dec. 1933)

Lee, L. E., 'Baden between Revolutions: State-Building and Citizenship, 1800–1848', *Central European History*, 24:2–3 (1991)

Price, M., 'Napoleon and Metternich in 1813: Some New and Some Neglected Evidence', *French History*, 26:4 (2012)

Sahlins, P., 'Natural Frontiers Revisited: France's Boundaries since the Seventeenth Century', *The American Historical Review*, 5:5 (Dec. 1990)

Schmitt, H. A., 'Germany without Prussia: A Closer Look at the Confederation of the Rhine', *German Studies Review*, 6:1 (1983)

Smets, J., 'Le Rhin, frontière naturelle de la France', *Annales historiques de la Révolution française*, 314 (1998)

Wertheimer, E., 'Clam-Martinitz, Graf Karl Joseph Nepomuk', *Allgemeine Deutsche Biographie* (vol. 47, Leipzig, 1903)

Woloch, I., 'Napoleonic Conscription: State Power and Civil Society', *Past and Present*, 111 (May 1986)

Zeller, G., 'La monarchie d'ancien régime et les frontières naturelles', *Revue d'histoire moderne*, 8 (1933)

Picture Acknowledgements

Index

Illustrations are indicated in **bold** type